CLAMP SCHOOL DETECTIVES

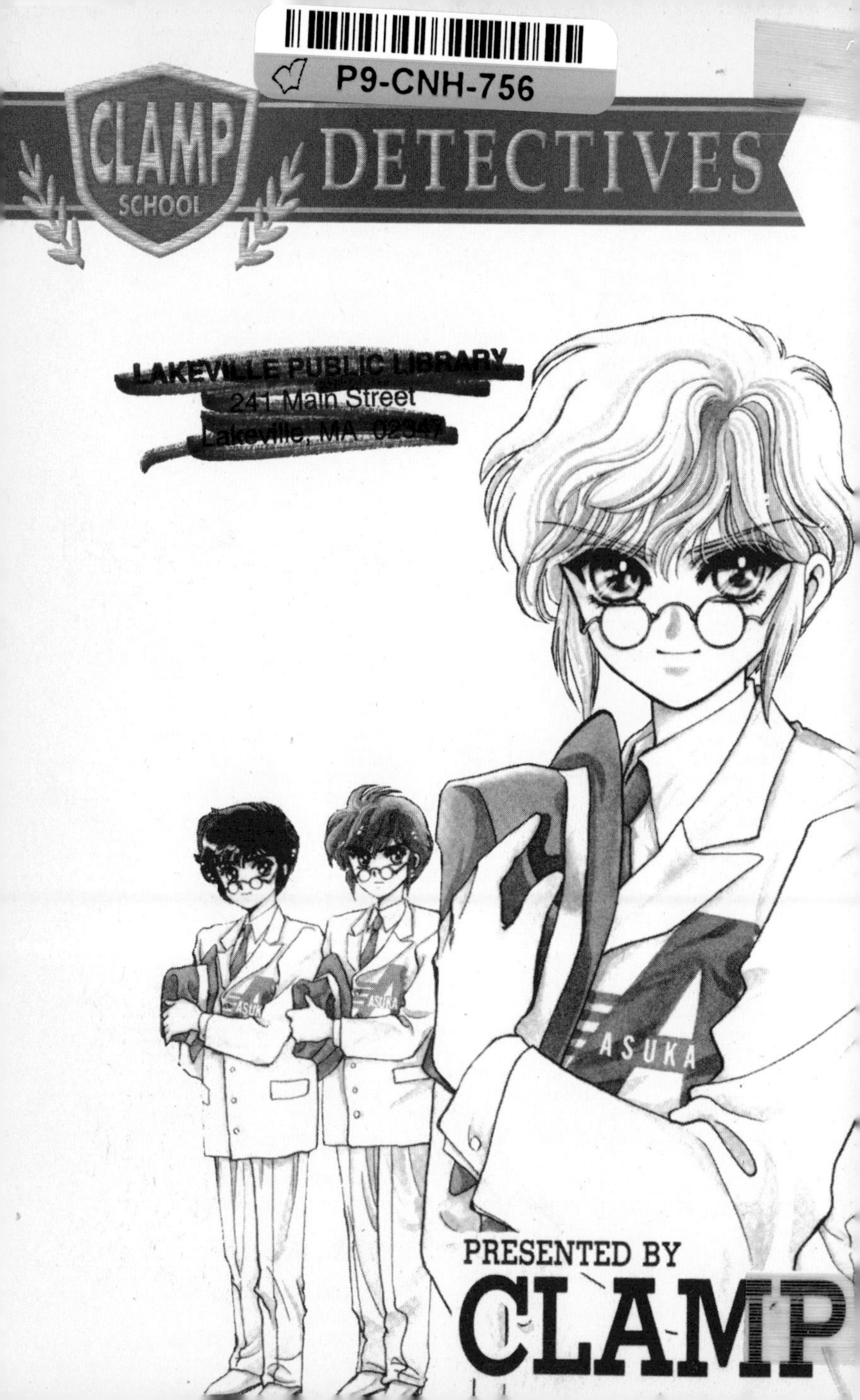
ASUKA
ASUKA
ASUKA

PRESENTED BY

CLAMP

ALSO AVAILABLE FROM 🐱 TOKYOPOP®

MANGA

ANGELIC LAYER*
BABY BIRTH* (September 2003)
BATTLE ROYALE*
BRAIN POWERED* (June 2003)
BRIGADOON* (August 2003)
CARDCAPTOR SAKURA
CARDCAPTOR SAKURA: MASTER OF THE CLOW*
CLAMP SCHOOL DETECTIVES*
CHOBITS*
CHRONICLES OF THE CURSED SWORD (July 2003)
CLOVER
CONFIDENTIAL CONFESSIONS* (July 2003)
CORRECTOR YUI
COWBOY BEBOP*
COWBOY BEBOP: SHOOTING STAR* (June 2003)
DEMON DIARY (May 2003)
DIGIMON
DRAGON HUNTER (June 2003)
DRAGON KNIGHTS*
DUKLYON: CLAMP SCHOOL DEFENDERS* (September 2003)
ERICA SAKURAZAWA* (May 2003)
ESCAFLOWNE* (July 2003)
FAKE*(May 2003)
FLCL* (September 2003)
FORBIDDEN DANCE* (August 2003)
GATEKEEPERS*
G-GUNDAM* (June 2003)
GRAVITATION* (June 2003)
GTO*
GUNDAM WING
GUNDAM WING: ENDLESS WALTZ*
GUNDAM: THE LAST OUTPOST*
HAPPY MANIA*
HARLEM BEAT
INITIAL D*
I.N.V.U.
ISLAND
JING: KING OF BANDITS* (June 2003)
JULINE
KARE KANO*
KINDAICHI CASE FILES* (June 2003)
KING OF HELL (June 2003)

KODOCHA*
LOVE HINA*
LUPIN III*
MAGIC KNIGHT RAYEARTH* (August 2003)
MAN OF MANY FACES* (May 2003)
MARMALADE BOY*
MARS*
MIRACLE GIRLS
MIYUKI-CHAN IN WONDERLAND* (October 2003)
MONSTERS, INC.
NIEA_7* (August 2003)
PARADISE KISS*
PARASYTE
PEACH GIRL
PEACH GIRL: CHANGE OF HEART*
PET SHOP OF HORRORS* (June 2003)
PLANET LADDER
PLANETS* (October 2003)
PRIEST
RAGNAROK
RAVE*
REAL BOUT HIGH SCHOOL*
REALITY CHECK
REBIRTH
REBOUND*
SABER MARIONETTE J* (July 2003)
SAILOR MOON
SAINT TAIL
SAMURAI DEEPER KYO* (June 2003)
SCRYED*
SHAOLIN SISTERS*
SHIRAHIME-SYO* (December 2003)
THE SKULL MAN*
SORCERER HUNTERS
TOKYO MEW MEW*
UNDER THE GLASS MOON (June 2003)
VAMPIRE GAME* (June 2003)
WILD ACT* (July 2003)
WISH*
X-DAY* (August 2003)
ZODIAC P.I.* (July 2003)

CINE-MANGA™

AKIRA*
CARDCAPTORS
JIMMY NEUTRON (COMING SOON)
KIM POSSIBLE
LIZZIE McGUIRE
SPONGEBOB SQUAREPANTS (COMING SOON)
SPY KIDS 2

NOVELS

SAILOR MOON
KARMA CLUB

TOKYOPOP KIDS

STRAY SHEEP (September 2003)

ART BOOKS

CARDCAPTOR SAKURA*
MAGIC KNIGHT RAYEARTH*

ANIME GUIDES

GUNDAM TECHNICAL MANUALS
COWBOY BEBOP
SAILOR MOON SCOUT GUIDES

CLAMP SCHOOL DETECTIVES

By
CLAMP

Los Angeles • Tokyo

Translator - Ray Yoshimoto
English Adaption - Jamie S. Rich
Copy Editor - Carol Fox
Associate Editor - Silke Niehusmann
Retouch and Lettering - Rob Steen
Cover Layout - Raymond Makowski

Editor - Jake Forbes
Managing Editor - Jill Freshney
Production Coordinator - Antonio DePietro
Production Manager - Jennifer Miller
Art Director - Matthew Alford
Director of Editorial - Jeremy Ross
VP of Production & Manufacturing - Ron Klamert
President & C.O.O. - John Parker
C.E.O. & Publisher - Stuart Levy

Email: editor@TOKYOPOP.com
Come visit us online at www.TOKYOPOP.com

A **TOKYOPOP** Manga
TOKYOPOP® is an imprint of Mixx Entertainment, Inc.,
5900 Wilshire Blvd. Suite 2000, Los Angeles, CA 90036

CLAMP SCHOOL DETECTIVES volume 1 ©1992 by CLAMP.
First published in Japan in 1992 by KADOKAWA SHOTEN PUBLISHING CO., LTD., Tokyo.
English translation rights arranged with KADOKAWA SHOTEN PUBLISHING. CO., LTD., Tokyo
through TUTTLE-MORI AGENCY, INC., Tokyo.

English text © 2003 by Mixx Entertainment, Inc.
TOKYOPOP® is a registered trademark of Mixx Entertainment, Inc.

ISBN: 1-59182-294-7

3 3577 00044 1756

First TOKYOPOP printing: April 2003

10 9 8 7 6 5 4 3 2 1
Printed in the USA

CONTENTS

Introduction 6

File 1: Forever on Earth 7

File 2: Sleuths 71

File 3: Lost in a Maze 113

File 4: My Fair Lady 155

Omake 198

Appendix 202

Editor's Note

CLAMP School Detectives is a series steeped in formality by its very nature. From the aristocratic Chairman Nokoru, to the overly-polite Akira, how characters address each other is an important part of what gives this series its charm. For that reason, the original name suffixes have been retained.

"Name suffixes?" you ask? In the Japanese language there are a number of suffixes (also called *honorifics*) which come after the name which indicate a level or respect between two people. Whether a character is called Nokoru-sama or Nokoru-kun means a great deal in how that character is perceived. Here's a brief listing of name suffixes and when they are used.

-kun—Indicates friendly familiarity with someone on the same level or younger. It also indicates cuteness, as when girls call Akira "Akira-kun." It is only used for boys.

-chan—The female equivalent of –kun.

-san—Indicates respect. –san is the most common suffix and is used among peers who are not on an intimate level. It's the equivalent of Mr. and Mrs.

-sama—Indicates a great level or respect or admiration and is used towards someone much older or of high standing. Most people use –sama with Nokoru because he comes from an aristocratic family.

-senpai—The term for upperclassman. It can also be used for someone in an organization who has more experience.

-sensei—The term for teacher. It can also apply to someone who is a mentor figure or a master of a trade.

If two people are good friends, they might agree not to use honorifics with each other, as is the case when Nokoru addresses Suoh and Akira. If a person wishes to show respect, he or she might address someone by their family name, as the humble Akira does when speaking about Nokoru and Suoh.

Also, while reading *CLAMP School Detectives* you might notice little numbers in some of the bubbles next to unusual terms. At the end of the book you'll find an appendix with longer explanations of these Japanese concepts. You can look them up while you read, see them all at the end or skip them all together as you see fit.

I hope you find that retaining the name suffixes adds to your enjoyment of *CLAMP School Detectives*. If you like reading your manga this way and would like to see suffixes in other TOKYOPOP® series, or if you find it distracting or confusing, let us know! Send your comments to editor@tokyopop.com.

Ja mata!
Jake Forbes

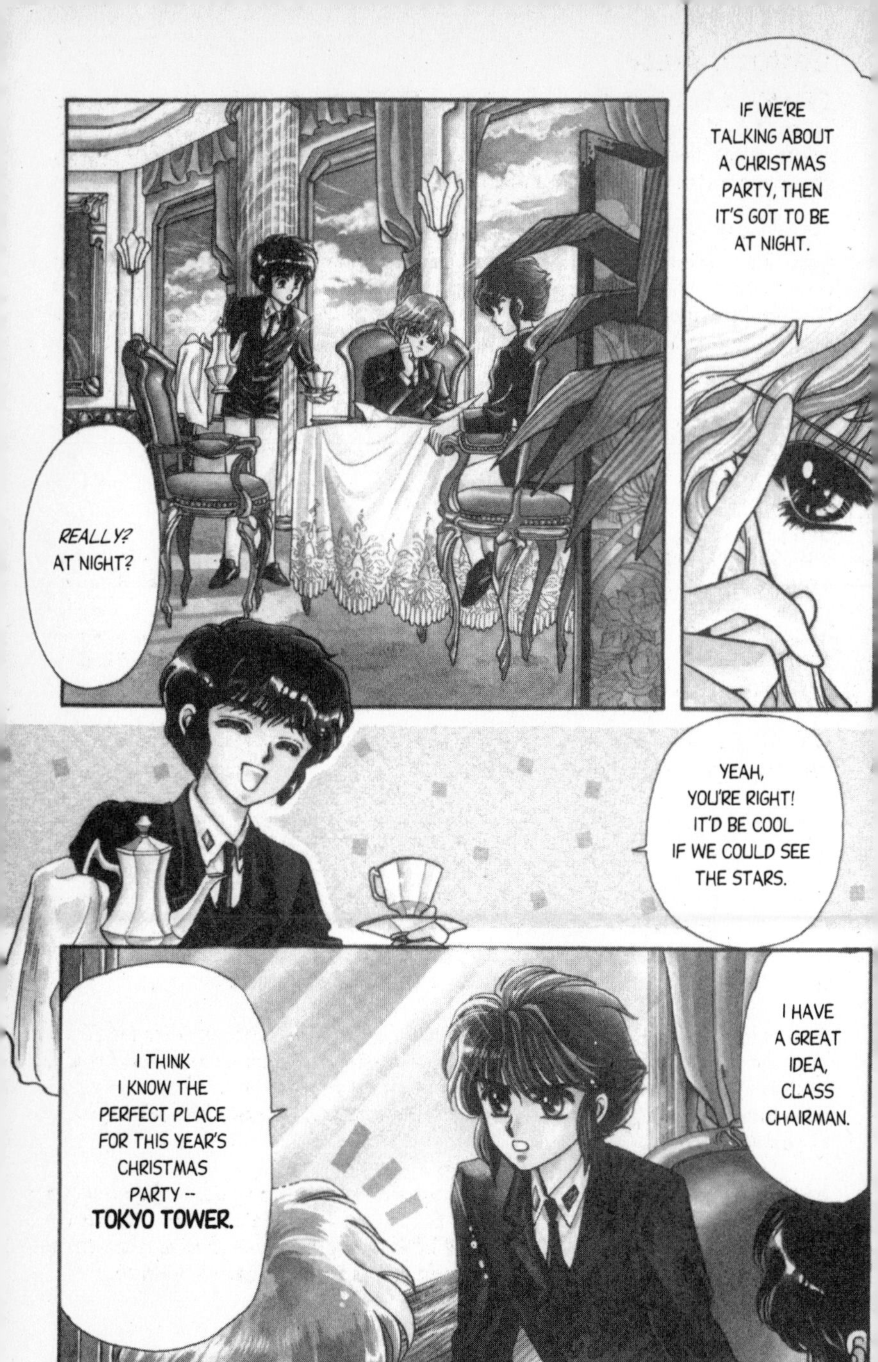
IF WE'RE TALKING ABOUT A CHRISTMAS PARTY, THEN IT'S GOT TO BE AT NIGHT.
REALLY? AT NIGHT?
YEAH, YOU'RE RIGHT! IT'D BE COOL IF WE COULD SEE THE STARS.
I HAVE A GREAT IDEA, CLASS CHAIRMAN.
I THINK I KNOW THE PERFECT PLACE FOR THIS YEAR'S CHRISTMAS PARTY -- **TOKYO TOWER.**

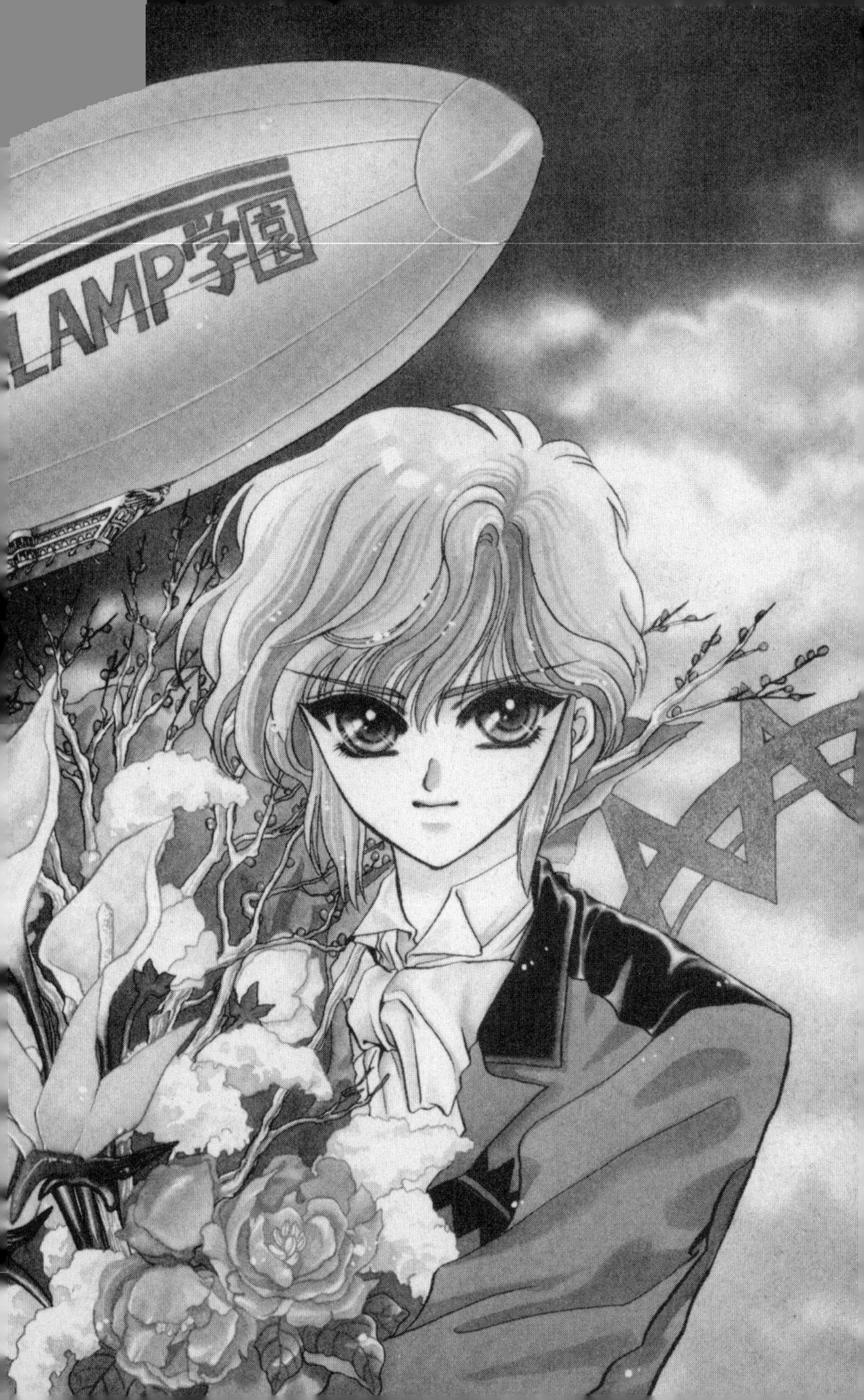
LAMP学園

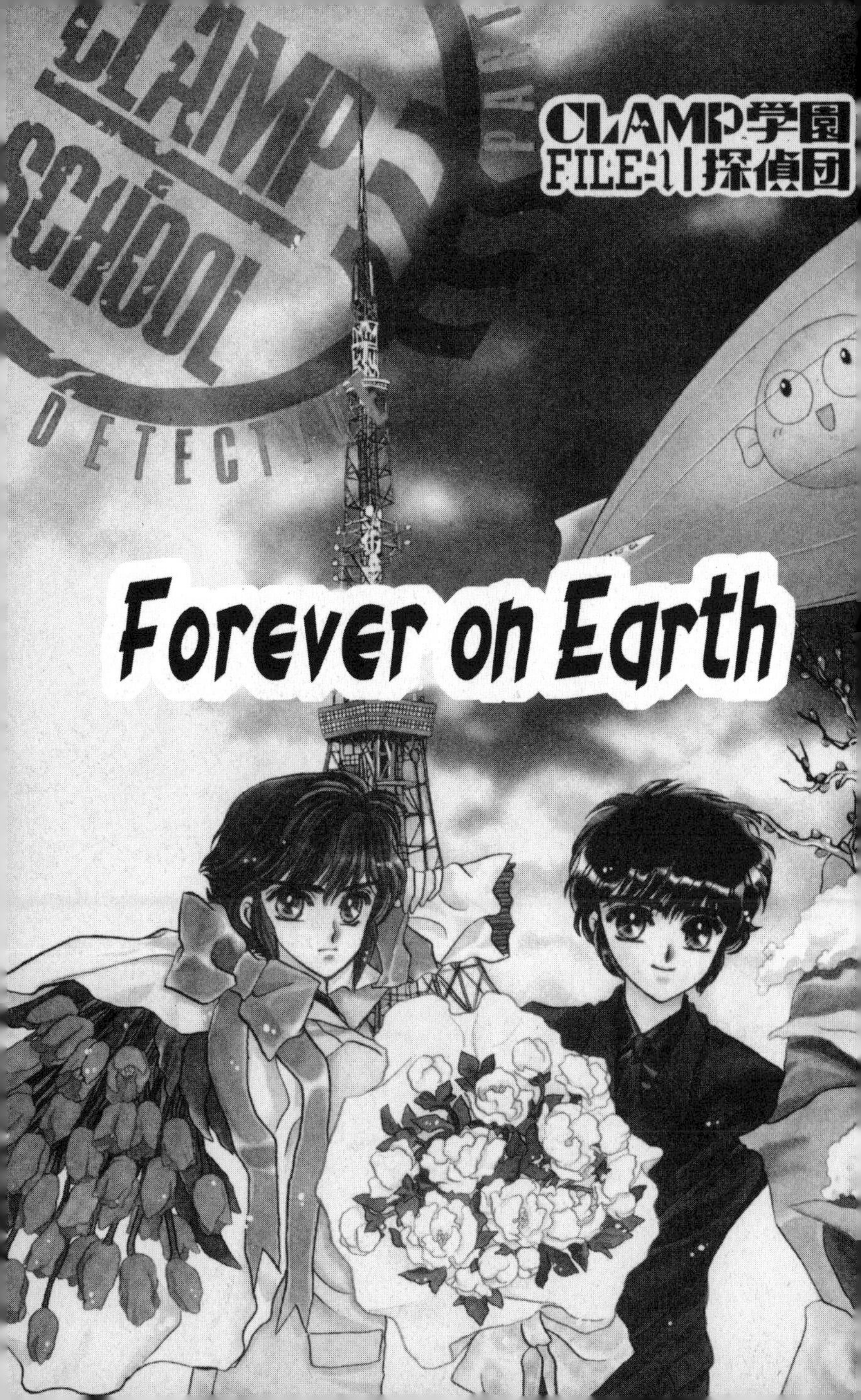
CLAMP SCHOOL
DETECT
CLAMP学園
FILE:11 探偵団
Forever on Earth

CLAMP学園
探偵団

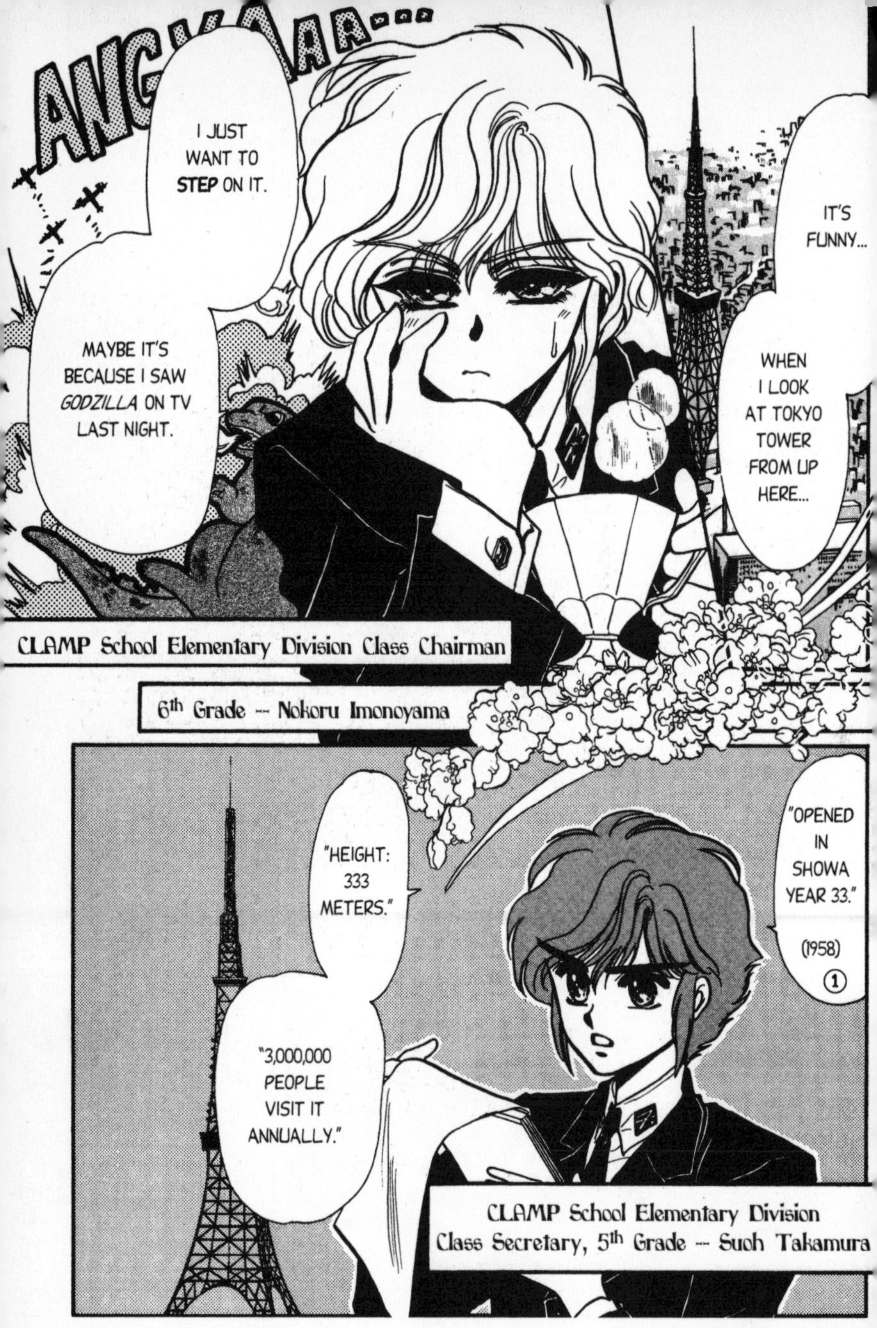
IT'S FUNNY...
WHEN I LOOK AT TOKYO TOWER FROM UP HERE...
I JUST WANT TO STEP ON IT.
ANG... AAR...
MAYBE IT'S BECAUSE I SAW GODZILLA ON TV LAST NIGHT.
CLAMP School Elementary Division Class Chairman
6th Grade -- Nokoru Imonoyama
"OPENED IN SHOWA YEAR 33."
(1958)
①
"HEIGHT: 333 METERS."
"3,000,000 PEOPLE VISIT IT ANNUALLY."
CLAMP School Elementary Division
Class Secretary, 5th Grade -- Suoh Takamura

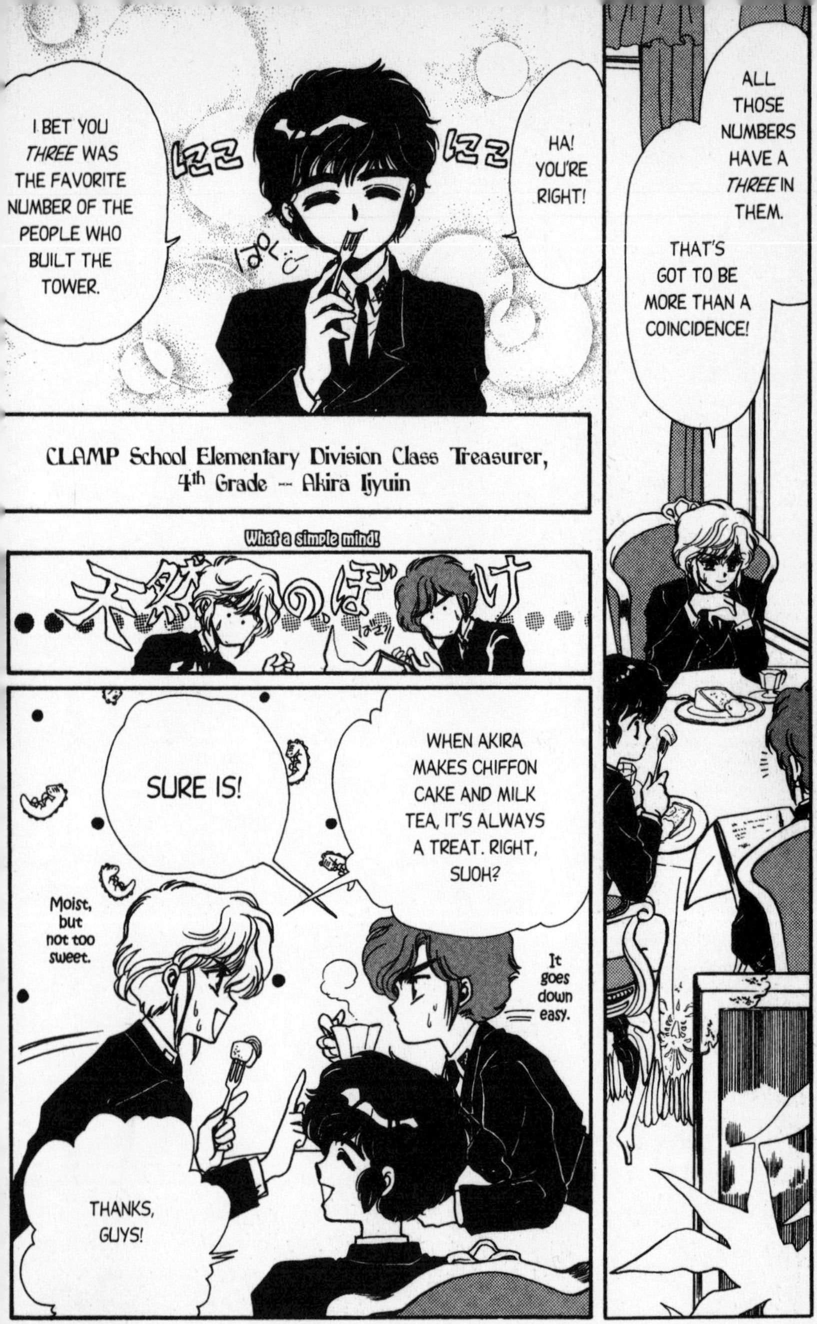
ALL THOSE NUMBERS HAVE A *THREE* IN THEM.
THAT'S GOT TO BE MORE THAN A COINCIDENCE!
にこ
HA! YOU'RE RIGHT!
にこ
I BET YOU *THREE* WAS THE FAVORITE NUMBER OF THE PEOPLE WHO BUILT THE TOWER.
ぱく
CLAMP School Elementary Division Class Treasurer, 4th Grade -- Akira Ijyuin
What a simple mind!
天然のぼけ
WHEN AKIRA MAKES CHIFFON CAKE AND MILK TEA, IT'S ALWAYS A TREAT. RIGHT, SUOH?
SURE IS!
It goes down easy.
Moist, but not too sweet.
THANKS, GUYS!

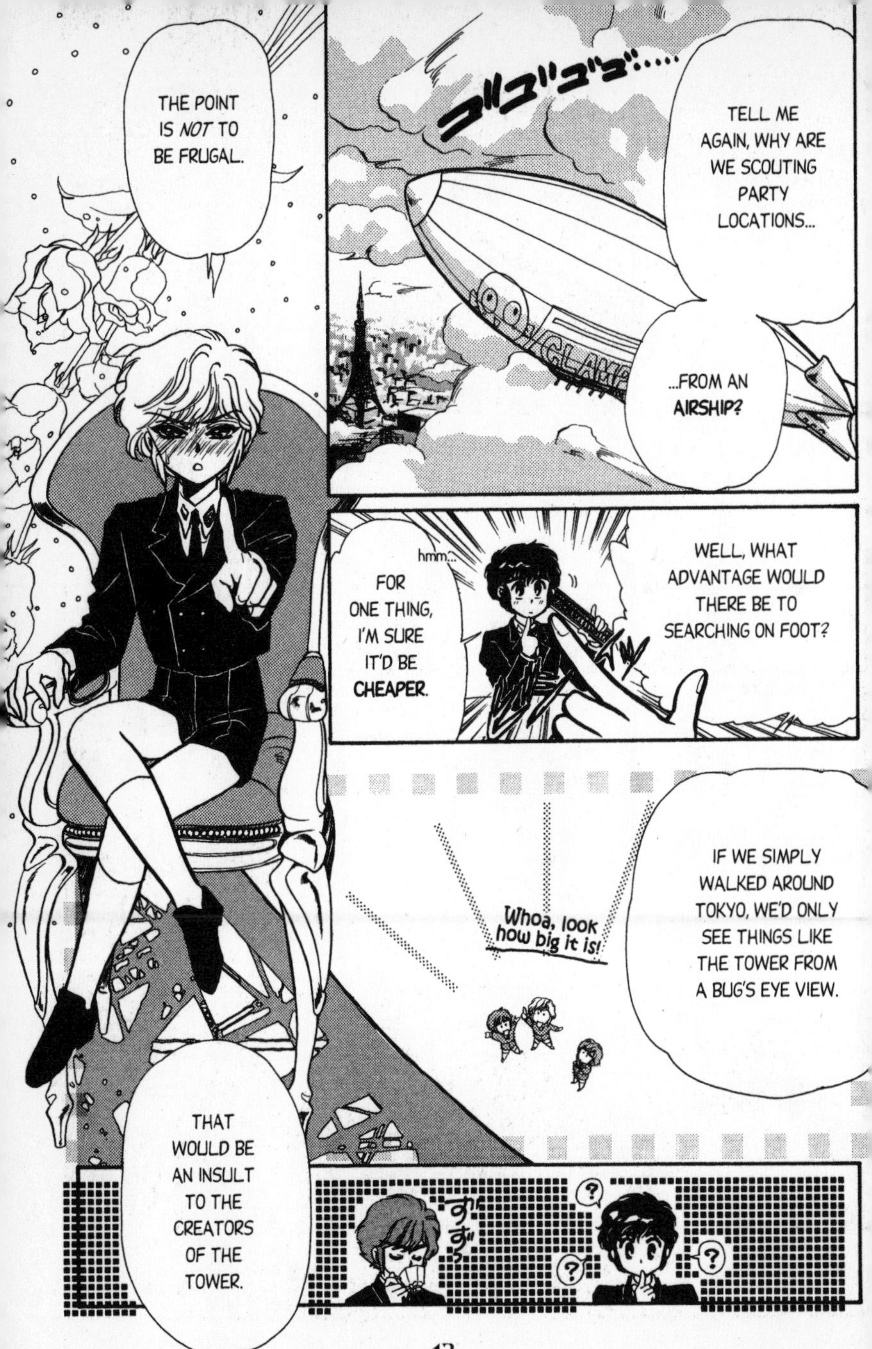
ゴゴゴ....
TELL ME AGAIN, WHY ARE WE SCOUTING PARTY LOCATIONS...
...FROM AN AIRSHIP?
WELL, WHAT ADVANTAGE WOULD THERE BE TO SEARCHING ON FOOT?
hmm...
FOR ONE THING, I'M SURE IT'D BE CHEAPER.
THE POINT IS NOT TO BE FRUGAL.
IF WE SIMPLY WALKED AROUND TOKYO, WE'D ONLY SEE THINGS LIKE THE TOWER FROM A BUG'S EYE VIEW.
Whoa, look how big it is!
THAT WOULD BE AN INSULT TO THE CREATORS OF THE TOWER.
ずず
?
?
?

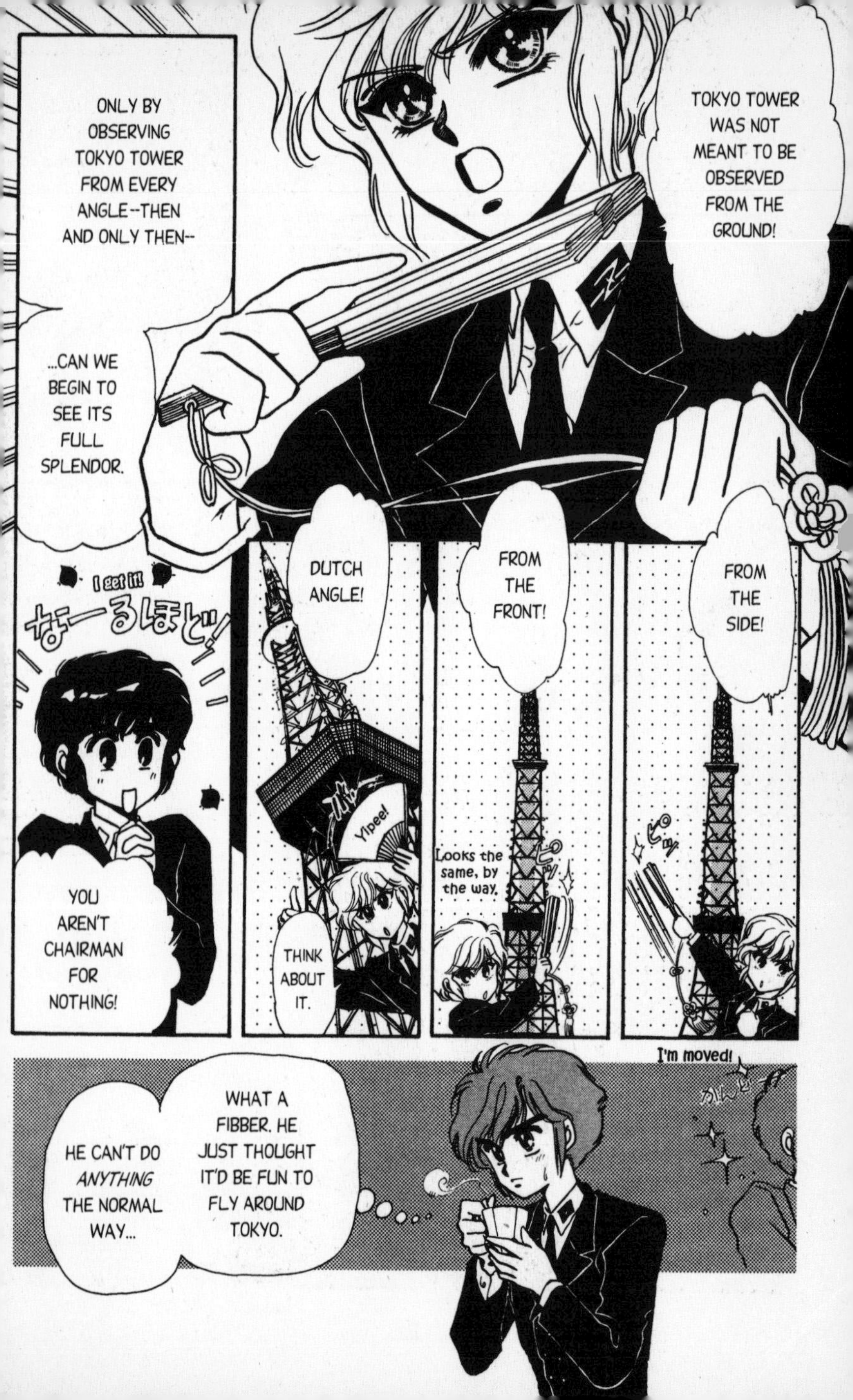
TOKYO TOWER WAS NOT MEANT TO BE OBSERVED FROM THE GROUND!
ONLY BY OBSERVING TOKYO TOWER FROM EVERY ANGLE--THEN AND ONLY THEN--
...CAN WE BEGIN TO SEE ITS FULL SPLENDOR.
FROM THE SIDE!
FROM THE FRONT!
Looks the same, by the way.
DUTCH ANGLE!
Yipee!
THINK ABOUT IT.
I get it!
なーるほど!
YOU AREN'T CHAIRMAN FOR NOTHING!
I'm moved!
WHAT A FIBBER. HE JUST THOUGHT IT'D BE FUN TO FLY AROUND TOKYO.
HE CAN'T DO *ANYTHING* THE NORMAL WAY...

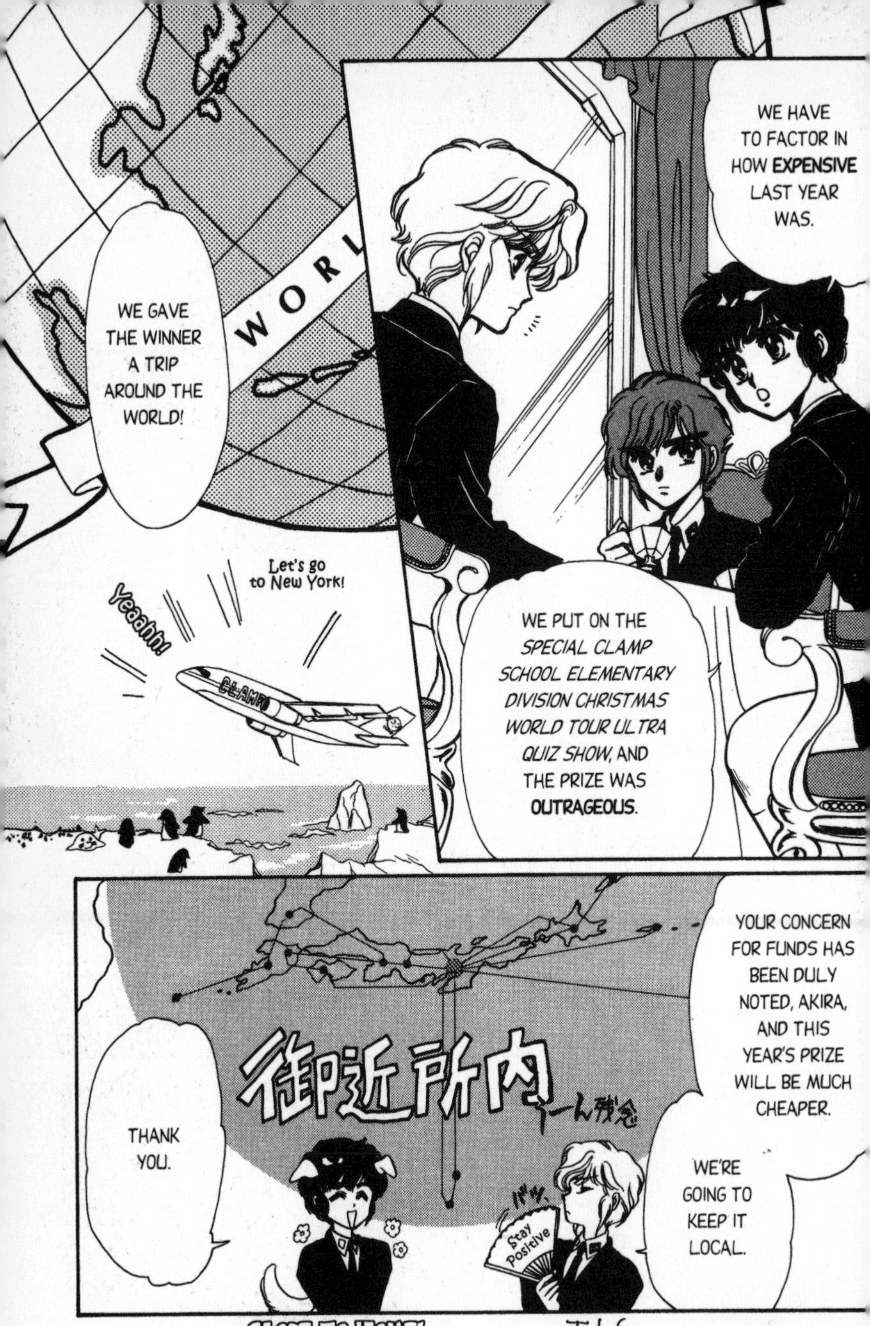
WE HAVE TO FACTOR IN HOW **EXPENSIVE** LAST YEAR WAS.
WE PUT ON THE *SPECIAL CLAMP SCHOOL ELEMENTARY DIVISION CHRISTMAS WORLD TOUR ULTRA QUIZ SHOW*, AND THE PRIZE WAS **OUTRAGEOUS**.
WE GAVE THE WINNER A TRIP AROUND THE WORLD!
WORL
Let's go to New York!
Yeoohh!
CLAMP
YOUR CONCERN FOR FUNDS HAS BEEN DULY NOTED, AKIRA, AND THIS YEAR'S PRIZE WILL BE MUCH CHEAPER.
WE'RE GOING TO KEEP IT LOCAL.
THANK YOU.
御近所内
ーん残念
Stay Positive

CLOSE TO HOME!

Too bad.

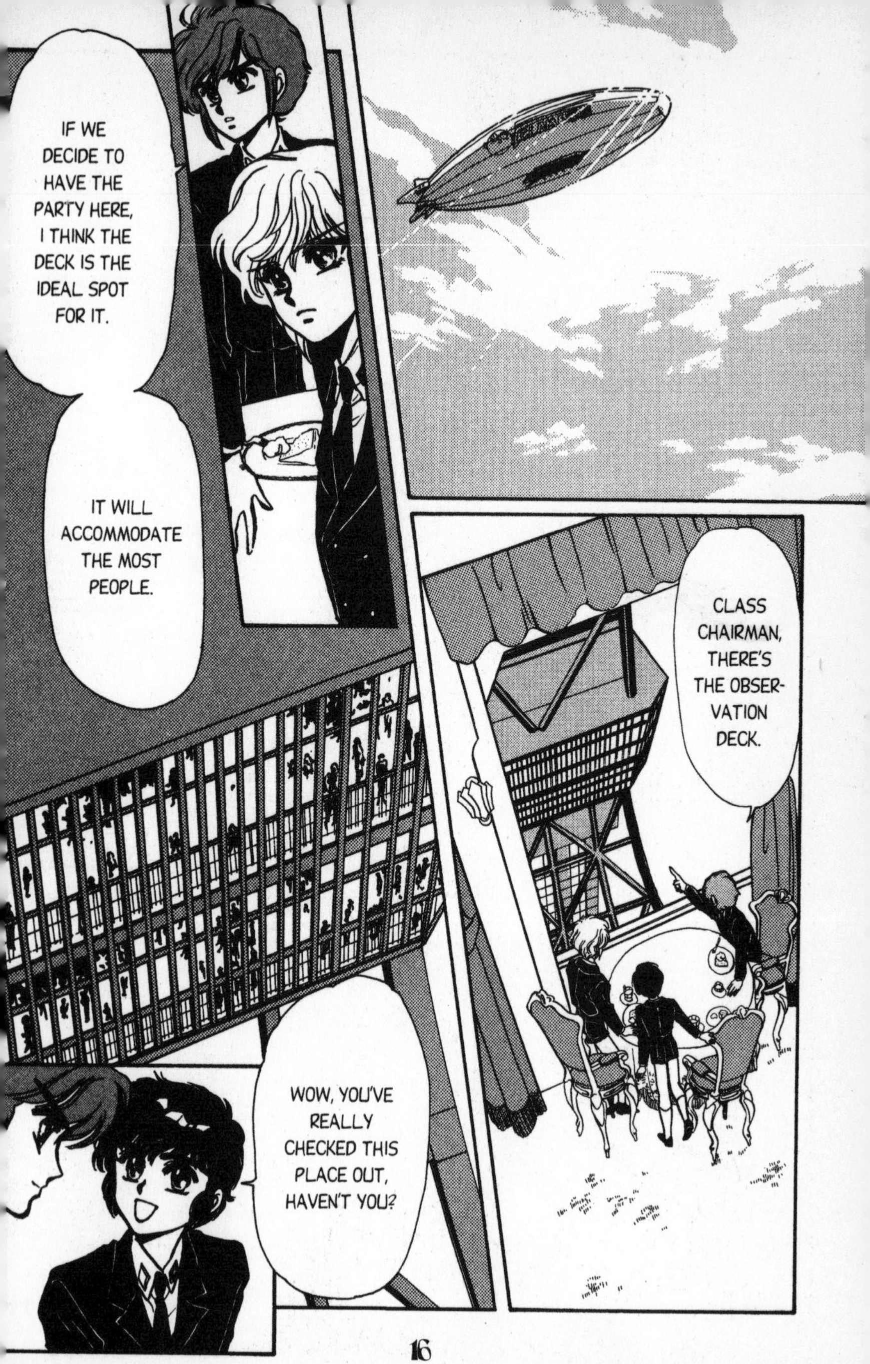
CLASS CHAIRMAN, THERE'S THE OBSERVATION DECK.
IF WE DECIDE TO HAVE THE PARTY HERE, I THINK THE DECK IS THE IDEAL SPOT FOR IT.
IT WILL ACCOMMODATE THE MOST PEOPLE.
WOW, YOU'VE REALLY CHECKED THIS PLACE OUT, HAVEN'T YOU?

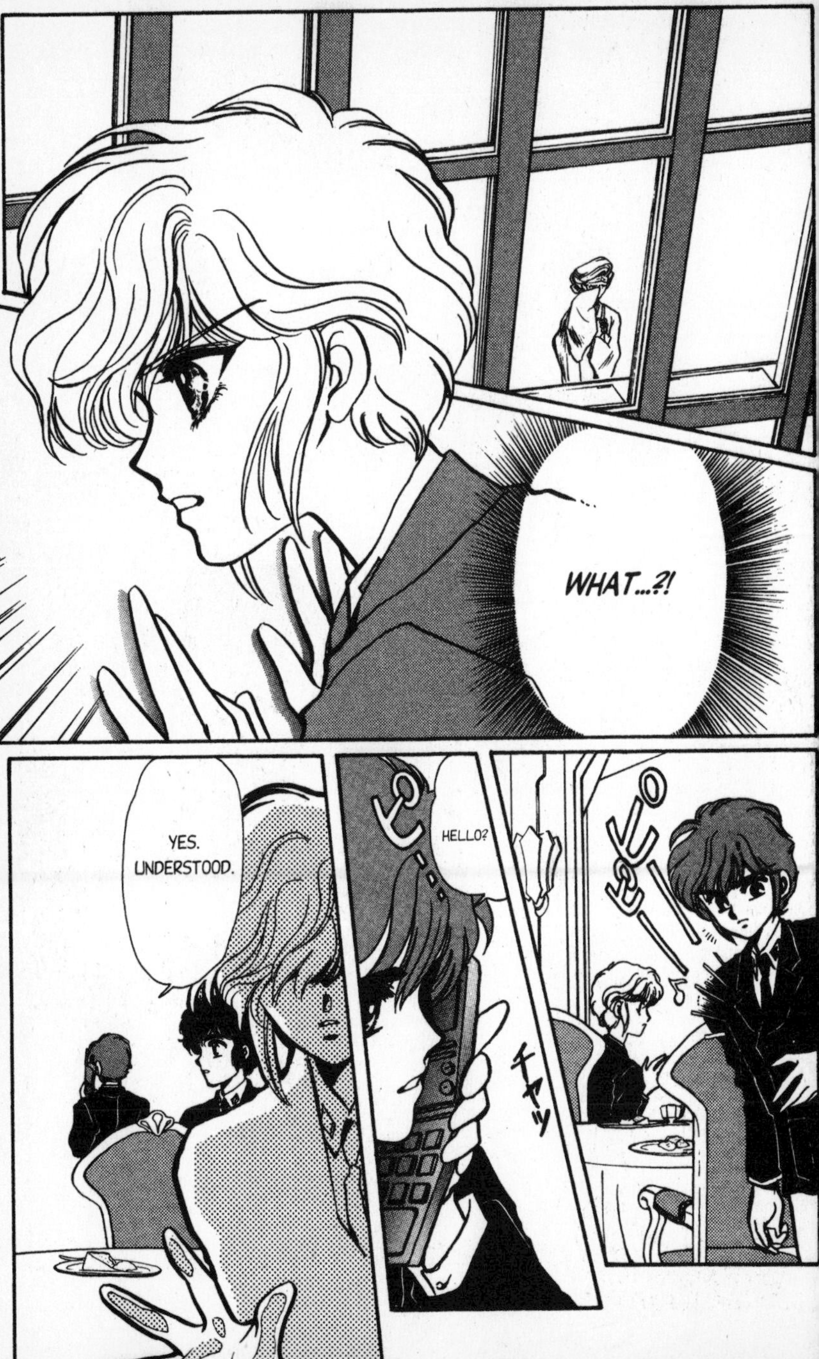
WHAT...?!
HELLO?
チャッ
YES. UNDERSTOOD.

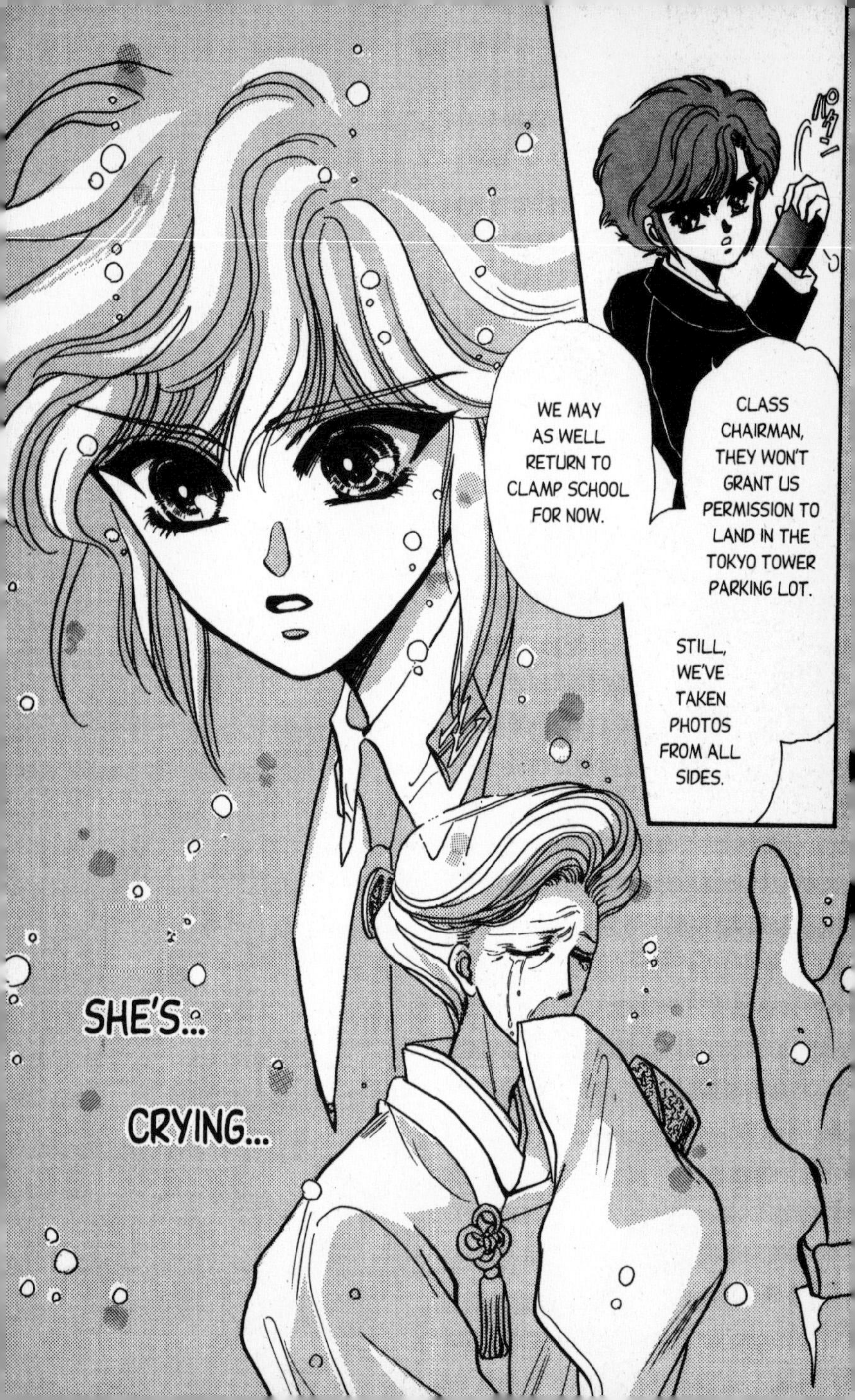
CLASS CHAIRMAN, THEY WON'T GRANT US PERMISSION TO LAND IN THE TOKYO TOWER PARKING LOT.
WE MAY AS WELL RETURN TO CLAMP SCHOOL FOR NOW.
STILL, WE'VE TAKEN PHOTOS FROM ALL SIDES.
SHE'S...
CRYING...

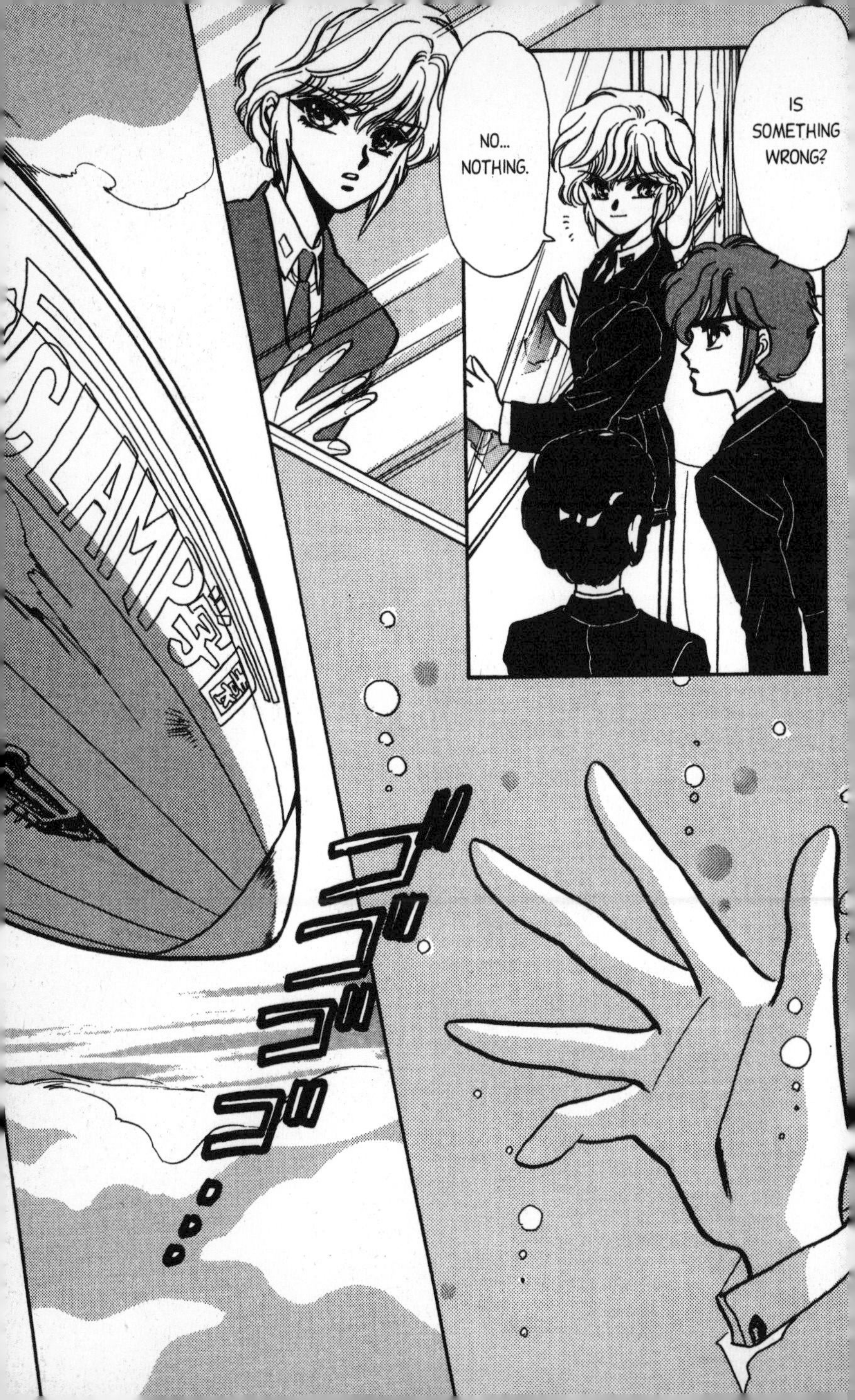
IS SOMETHING WRONG?
NO... NOTHING.
CLAMP
ゴゴゴゴ…

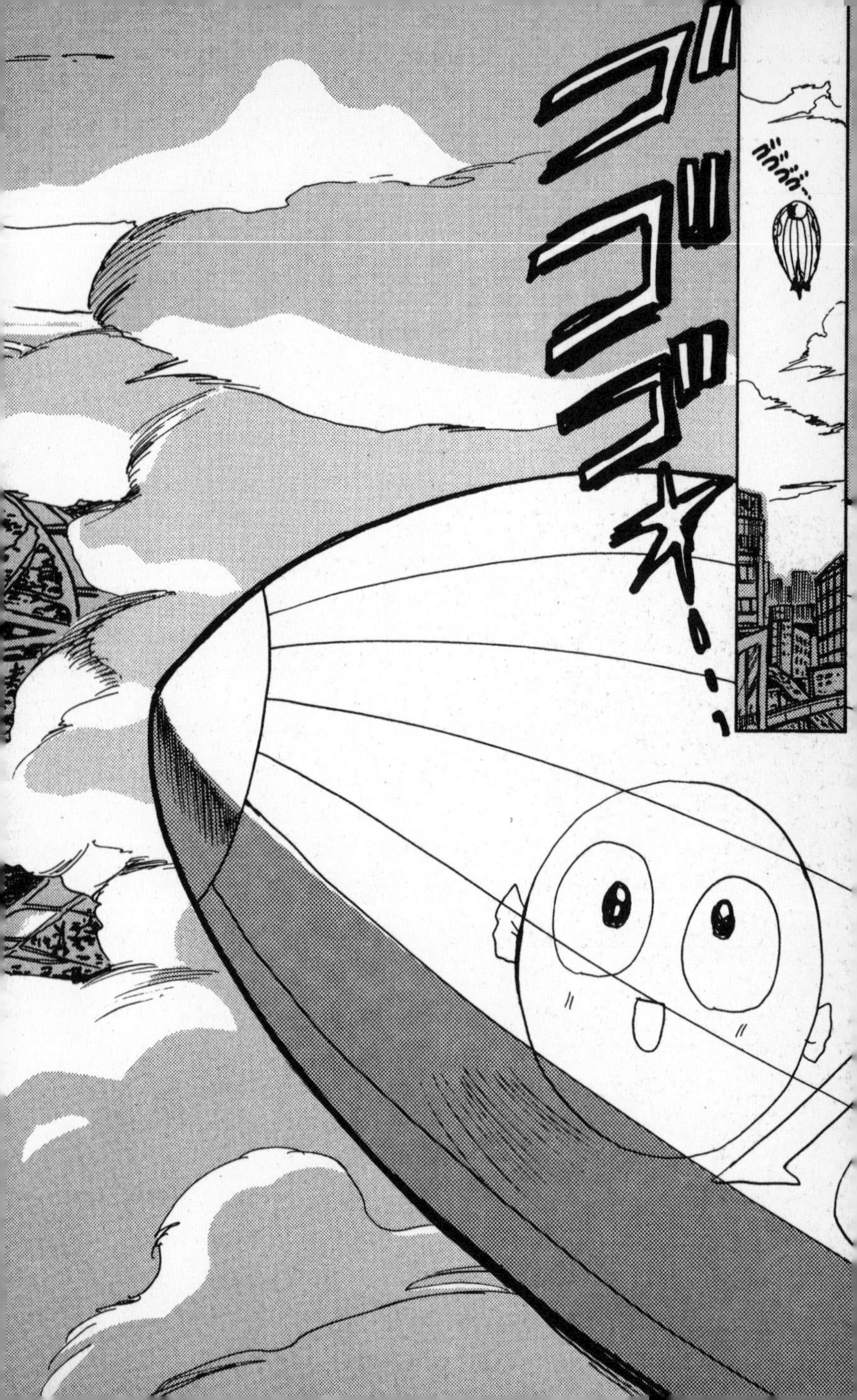
ゴゴゴゴ…
ゴゴゴォ☆…

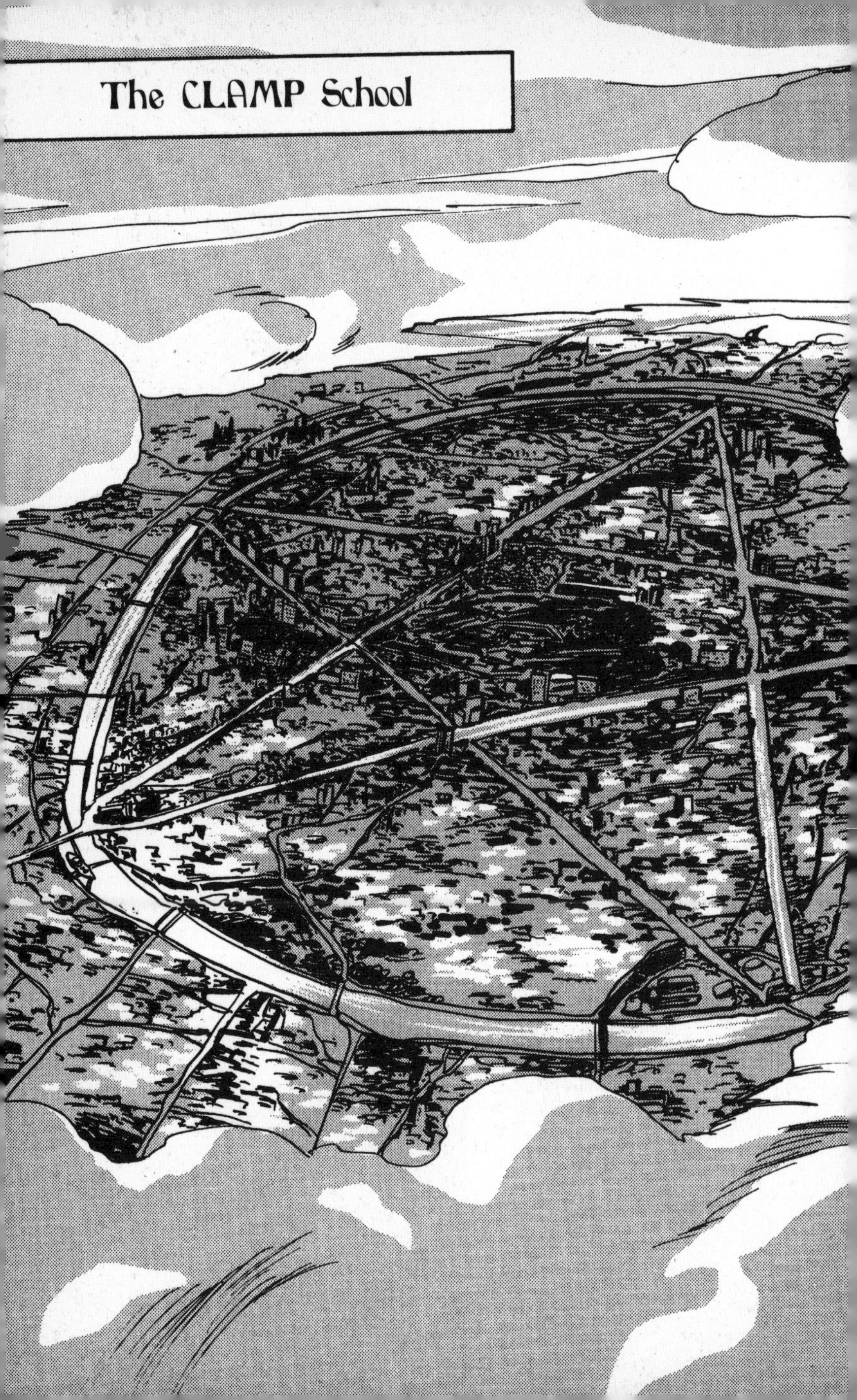
The CLAMP School

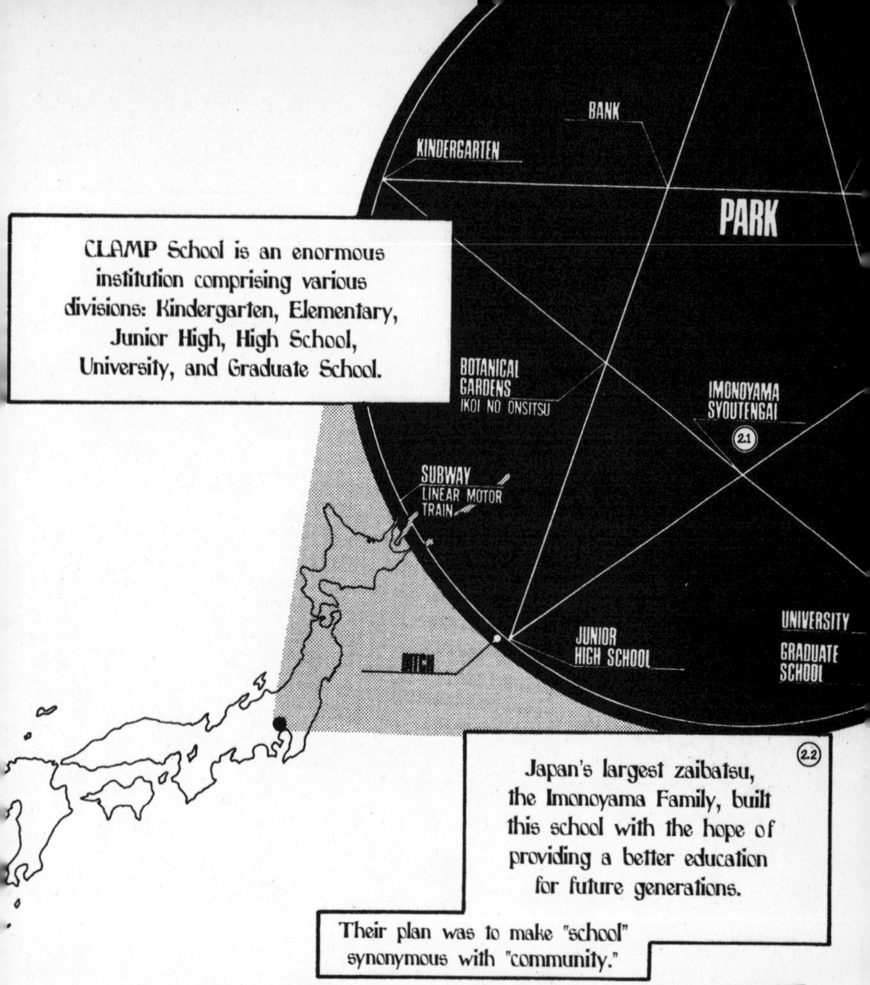
BANK
KINDERGARTEN
PARK
CLAMP School is an enormous institution comprising various divisions: Kindergarten, Elementary, Junior High, High School, University, and Graduate School.
BOTANICAL GARDENS
IKOI NO ONSITSU
IMONOYAMA SYOUTENGAI
21
SUBWAY
LINEAR MOTOR TRAIN
UNIVERSITY
GRADUATE SCHOOL
JUNIOR HIGH SCHOOL
22
Japan's largest zaibatsu, the Imonoyama Family, built this school with the hope of providing a better education for future generations.
Their plan was to make "school" synonymous with "community."

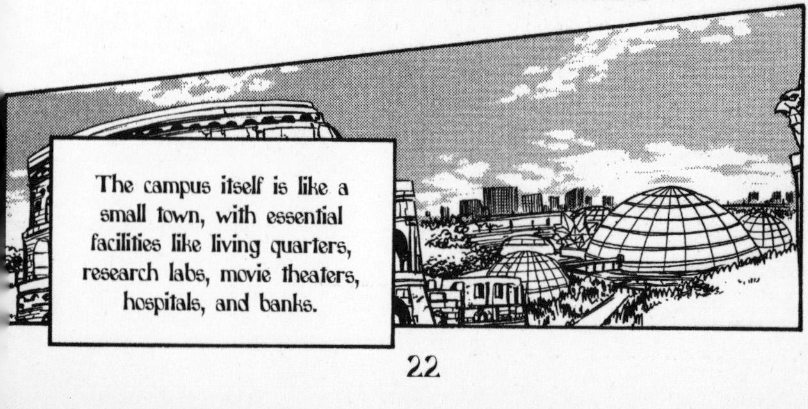
The campus itself is like a small town, with essential facilities like living quarters, research labs, movie theaters, hospitals, and banks.

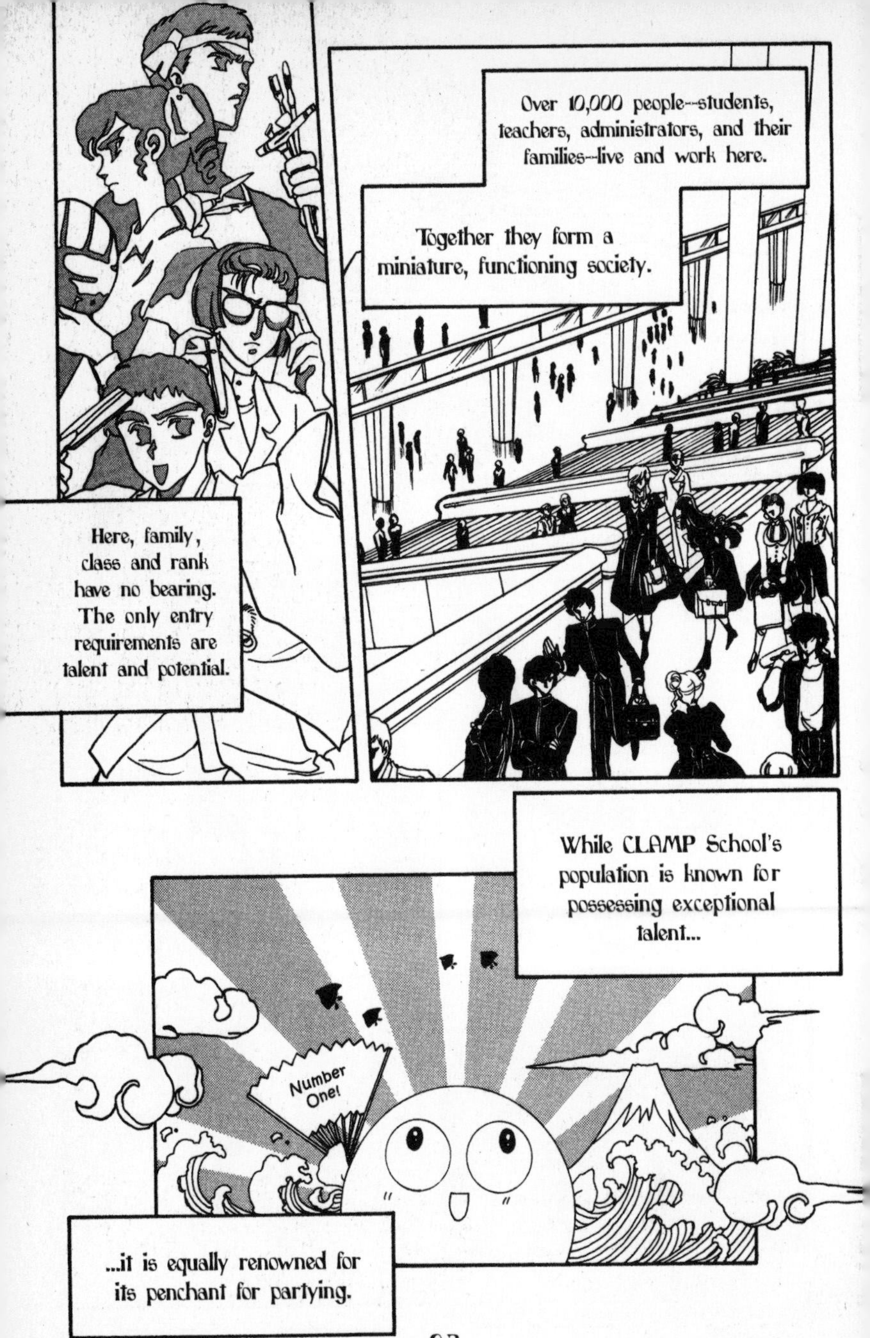
Over 10,000 people--students, teachers, administrators, and their families--live and work here.
Together they form a miniature, functioning society.
Here, family, class and rank have no bearing. The only entry requirements are talent and potential.
While CLAMP School's population is known for possessing exceptional talent...
Number One!
...it is equally renowned for its penchant for partying.

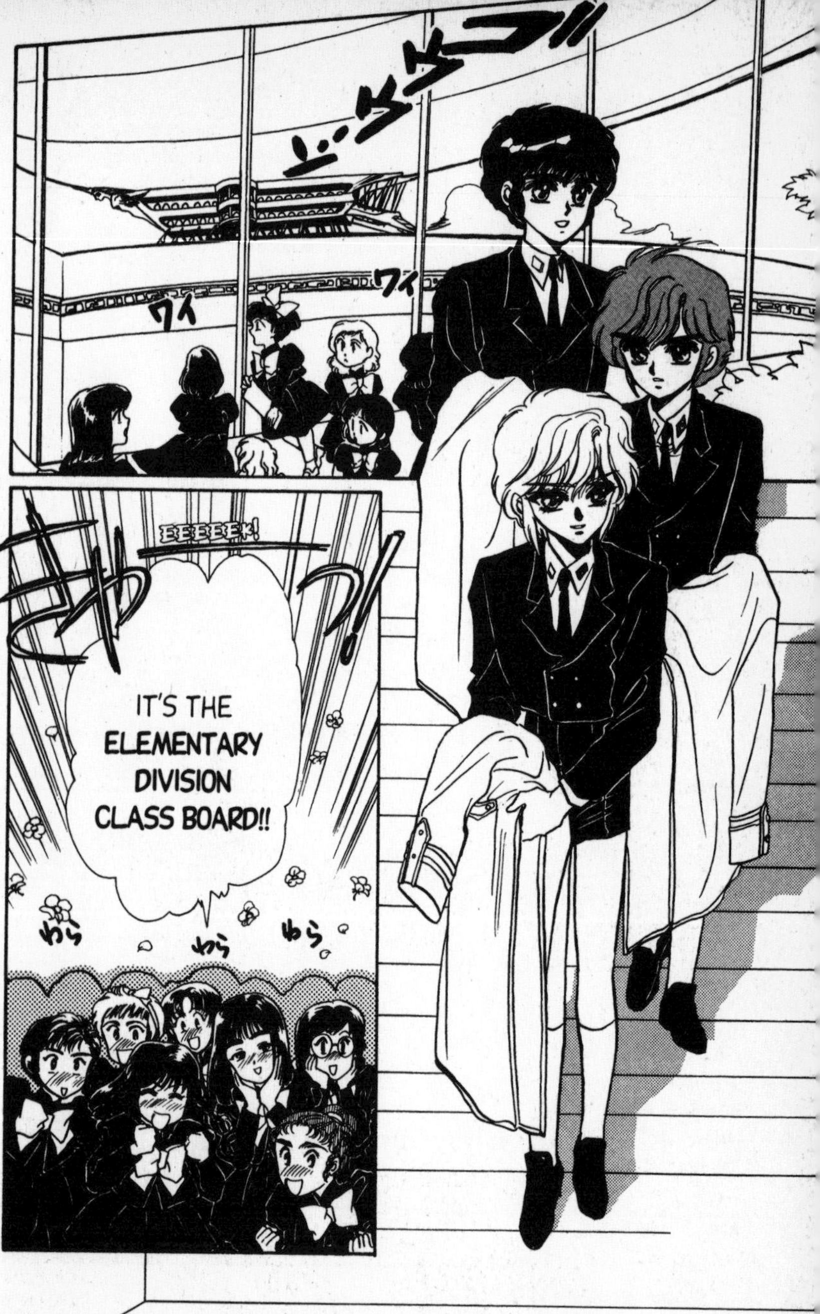
ワイ
ワイ
きゃーっ!
EEEEEEK!
IT'S THE ELEMENTARY DIVISION CLASS BOARD!!
わら
わら
わら

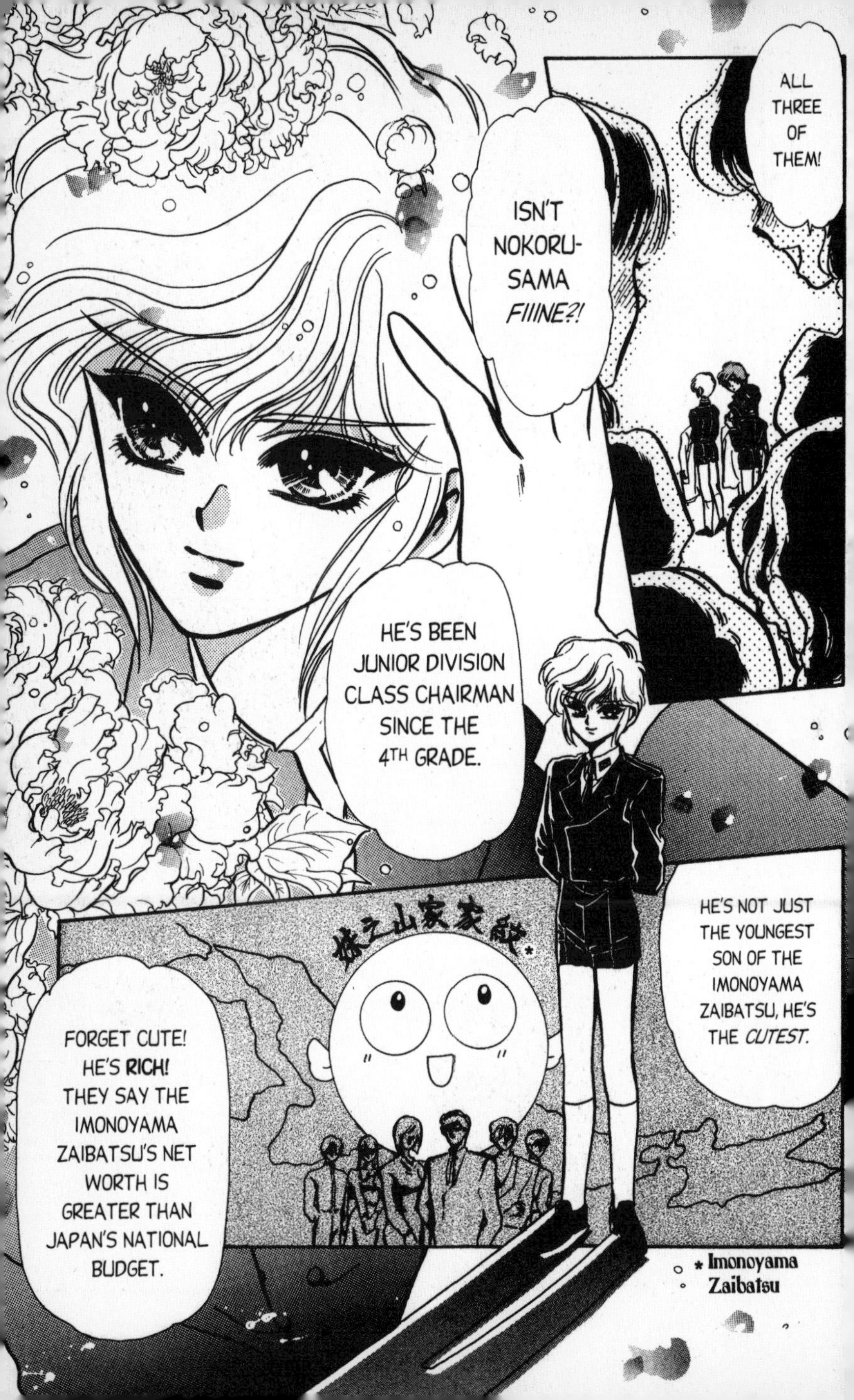
ALL THREE OF THEM!
ISN'T NOKORU-SAMA *FIIINE?!*
HE'S BEEN JUNIOR DIVISION CLASS CHAIRMAN SINCE THE 4TH GRADE.
HE'S NOT JUST THE YOUNGEST SON OF THE IMONOYAMA ZAIBATSU, HE'S THE *CUTEST*.
妹之山家家紋*
FORGET CUTE! HE'S **RICH!** THEY SAY THE IMONOYAMA ZAIBATSU'S NET WORTH IS GREATER THAN JAPAN'S NATIONAL BUDGET.
* Imonoyama Zaibatsu

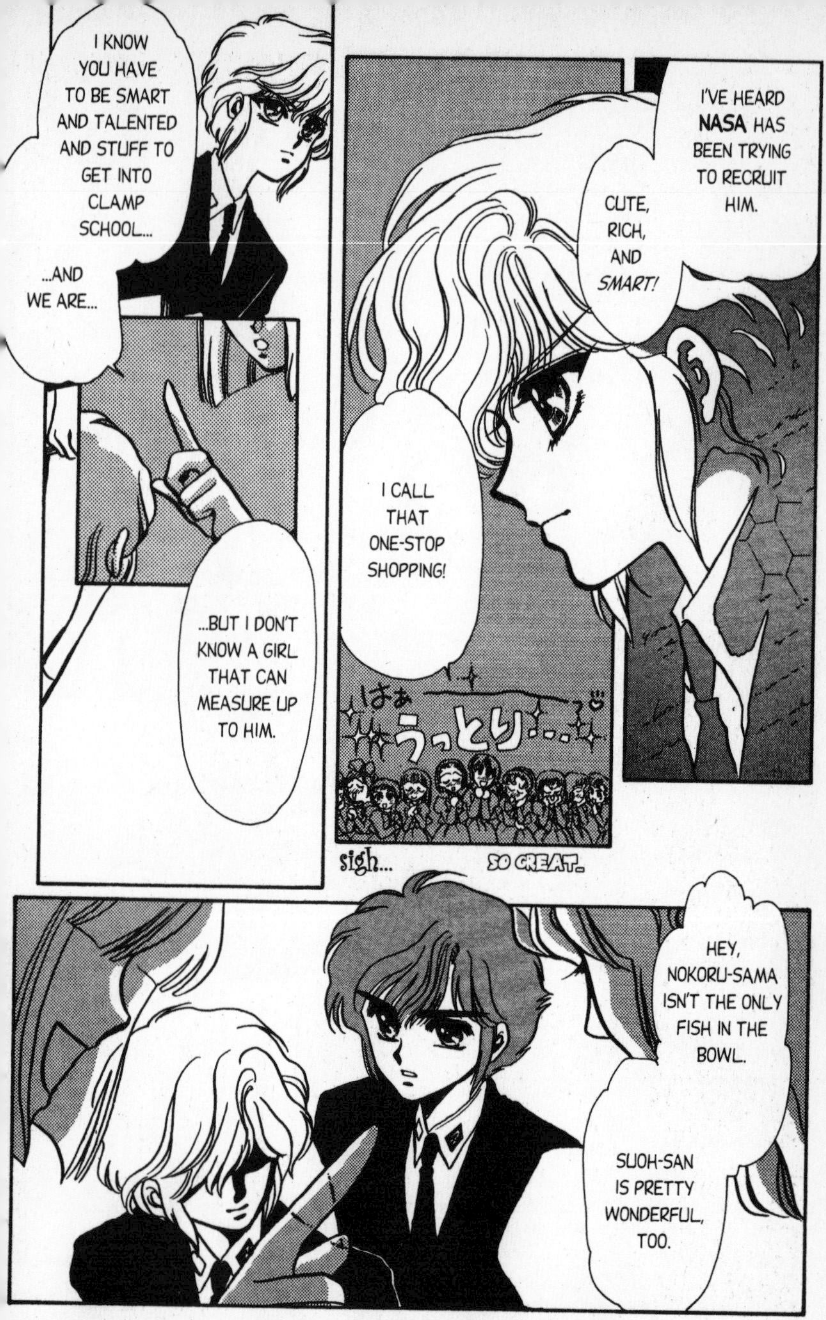
I'VE HEARD NASA HAS BEEN TRYING TO RECRUIT HIM.
CUTE, RICH, AND SMART!
I CALL THAT ONE-STOP SHOPPING!
はぁ
うっとり…
sigh...
SO GREAT...
I KNOW YOU HAVE TO BE SMART AND TALENTED AND STUFF TO GET INTO CLAMP SCHOOL...
...AND WE ARE...
...BUT I DON'T KNOW A GIRL THAT CAN MEASURE UP TO HIM.
HEY, NOKORU-SAMA ISN'T THE ONLY FISH IN THE BOWL.
SUOH-SAN IS PRETTY WONDERFUL, TOO.

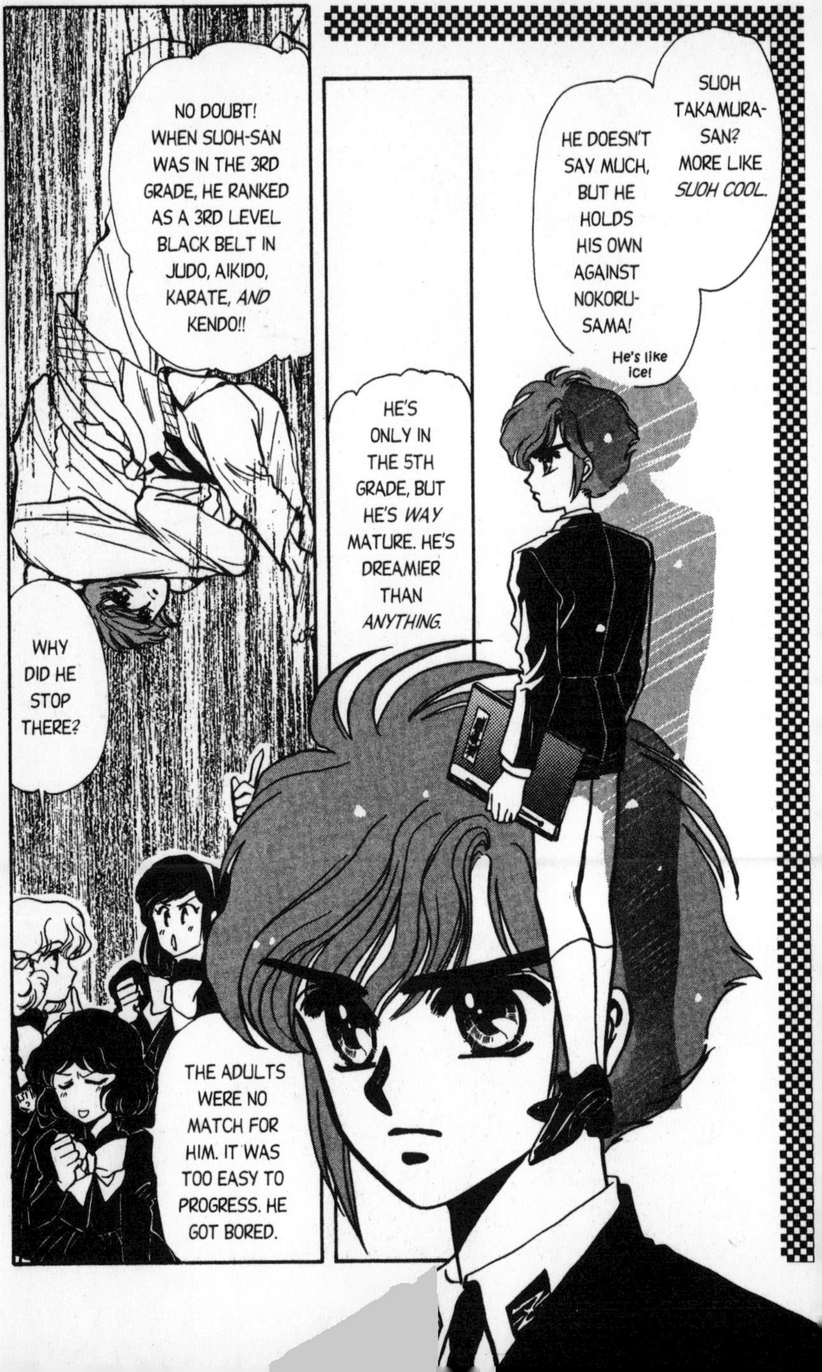
SUOH TAKAMURA-SAN? MORE LIKE *SUOH COOL.*
HE DOESN'T SAY MUCH, BUT HE HOLDS HIS OWN AGAINST NOKORU-SAMA!
He's like ice!
HE'S ONLY IN THE 5TH GRADE, BUT HE'S *WAY* MATURE. HE'S DREAMIER THAN *ANYTHING.*
NO DOUBT! WHEN SUOH-SAN WAS IN THE 3RD GRADE, HE RANKED AS A 3RD LEVEL BLACK BELT IN JUDO, AIKIDO, KARATE, *AND* KENDO!!
WHY DID HE STOP THERE?
THE ADULTS WERE NO MATCH FOR HIM. IT WAS TOO EASY TO PROGRESS. HE GOT BORED.

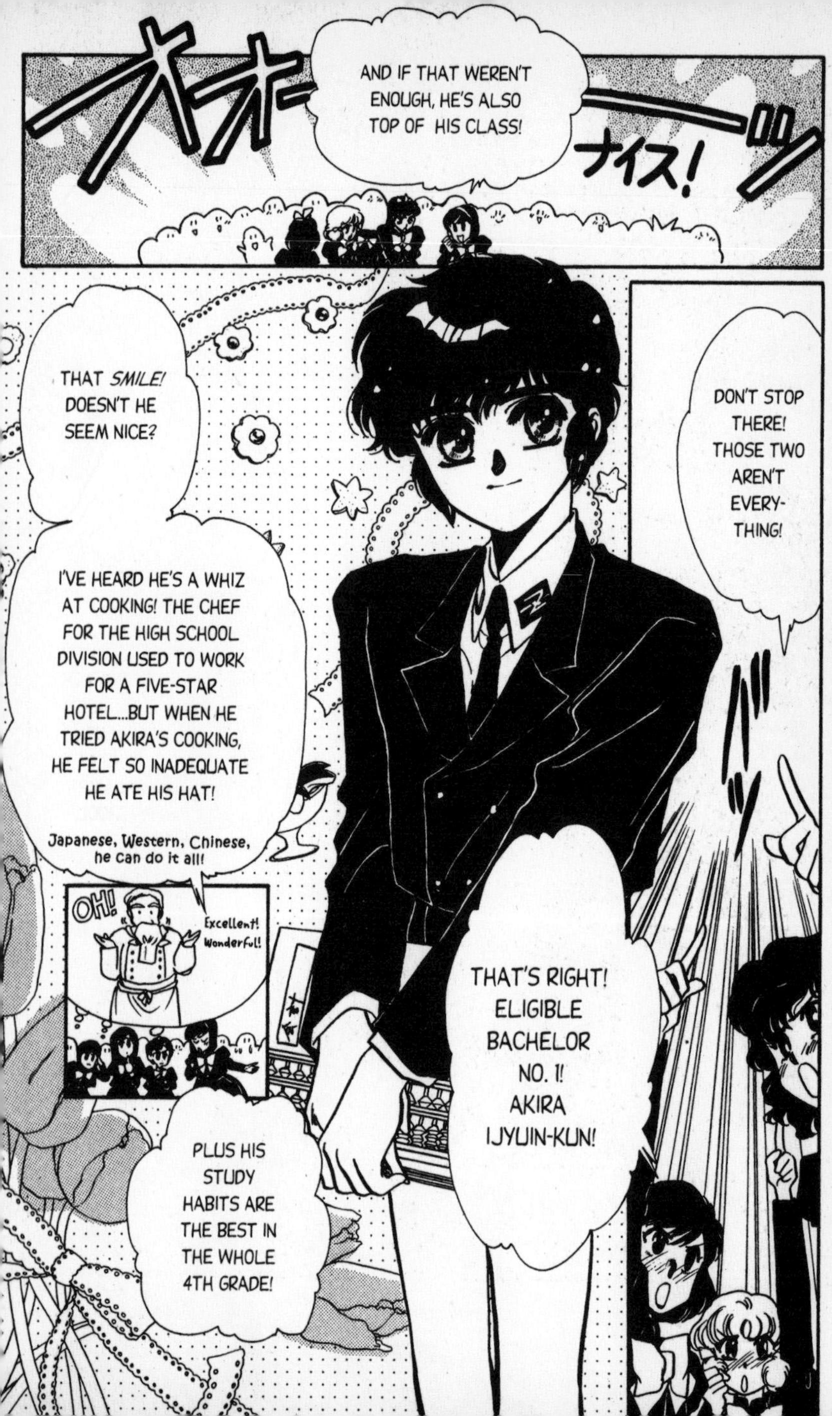
オオーーーッ
ナイス!
AND IF THAT WEREN'T ENOUGH, HE'S ALSO TOP OF HIS CLASS!
DON'T STOP THERE! THOSE TWO AREN'T EVERY-THING!
THAT *SMILE!* DOESN'T HE SEEM NICE?
I'VE HEARD HE'S A WHIZ AT COOKING! THE CHEF FOR THE HIGH SCHOOL DIVISION USED TO WORK FOR A FIVE-STAR HOTEL...BUT WHEN HE TRIED AKIRA'S COOKING, HE FELT SO INADEQUATE HE ATE HIS HAT!
Japanese, Western, Chinese, he can do it all!
OH!
Excellent! Wonderful!
PLUS HIS STUDY HABITS ARE THE BEST IN THE WHOLE 4TH GRADE!
THAT'S RIGHT! ELIGIBLE BACHELOR NO. 1! AKIRA IJYUIN-KUN!

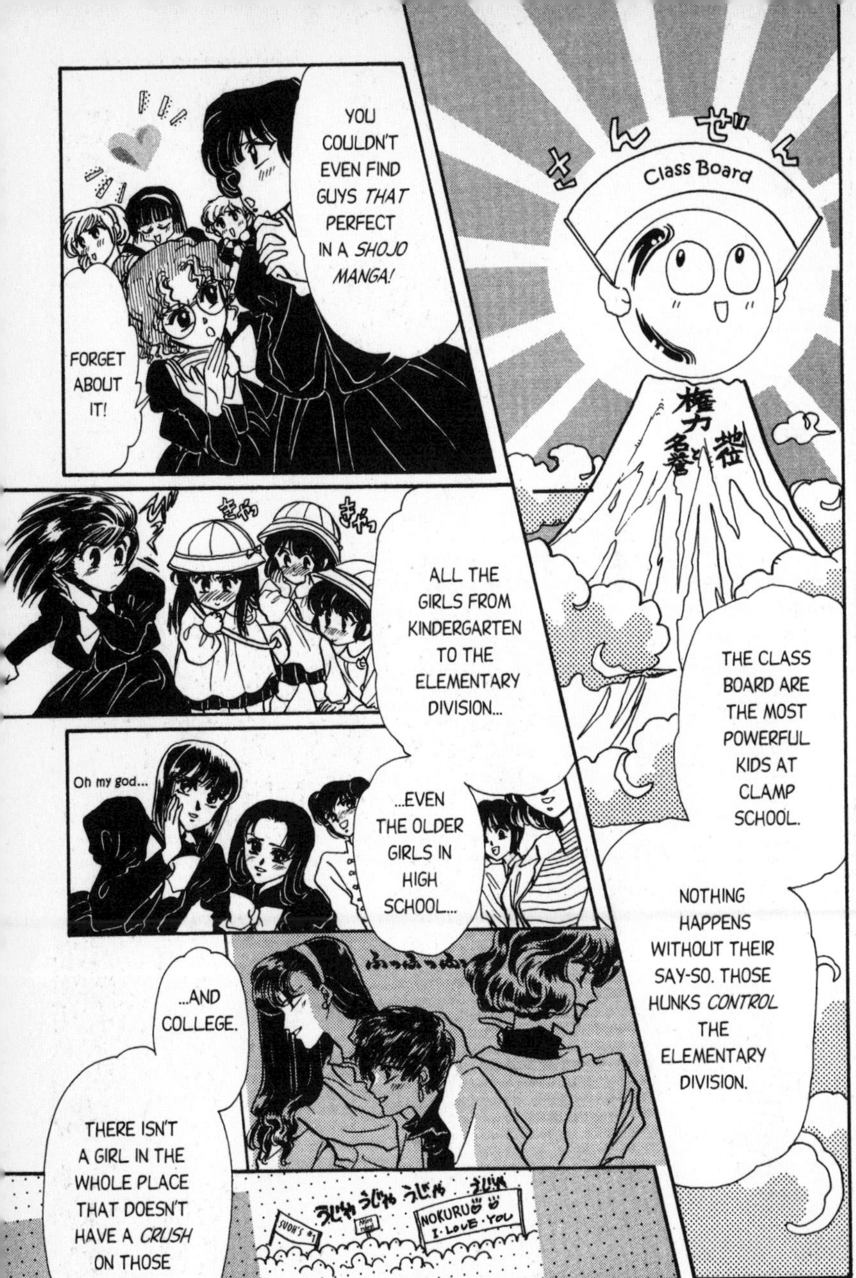
さんぜん
Class Board
権力 名誉と 地位
THE CLASS BOARD ARE THE MOST POWERFUL KIDS AT CLAMP SCHOOL.
NOTHING HAPPENS WITHOUT THEIR SAY-SO. THOSE HUNKS *CONTROL* THE ELEMENTARY DIVISION.
YOU COULDN'T EVEN FIND GUYS *THAT* PERFECT IN A *SHOJO MANGA!*
FORGET ABOUT IT!
ALL THE GIRLS FROM KINDERGARTEN TO THE ELEMENTARY DIVISION...
きゃ
きゃ
...EVEN THE OLDER GIRLS IN HIGH SCHOOL...
Oh my god...
...AND COLLEGE.
THERE ISN'T A GIRL IN THE WHOLE PLACE THAT DOESN'T HAVE A *CRUSH* ON THOSE THREE!
うじゃ うじゃ うじゃ うじゃ
SUOH'S #1
NOKURU I·LOVE·YOU

Text on Mountain:
Power, Rank, Position

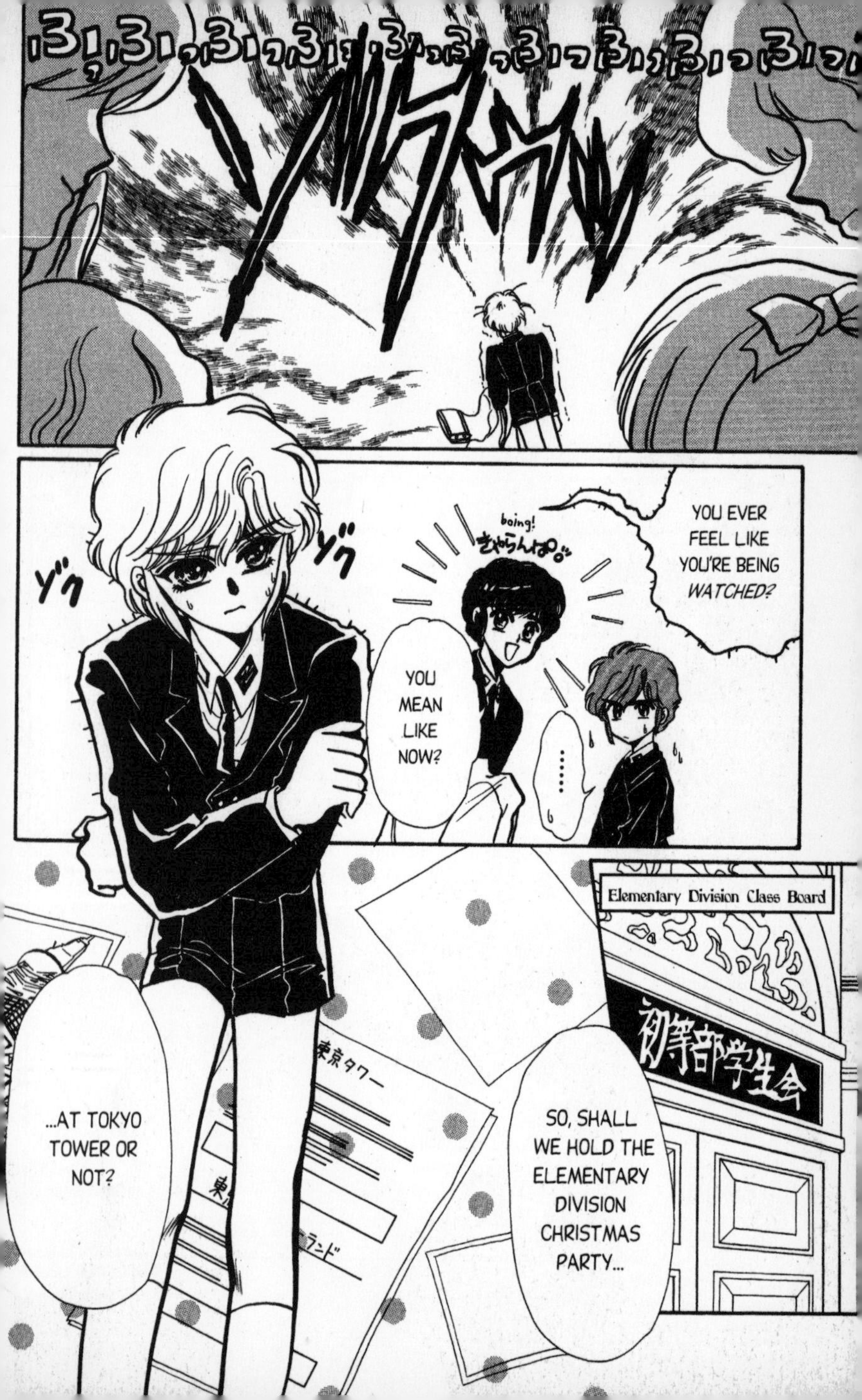
YOU EVER FEEL LIKE YOU'RE BEING WATCHED?
boing!
YOU MEAN LIKE NOW?
......
ゾク
ゾク
Elementary Division Class Board
初等部学生会
SO, SHALL WE HOLD THE ELEMENTARY DIVISION CHRISTMAS PARTY...
...AT TOKYO TOWER OR NOT?
東京タワー

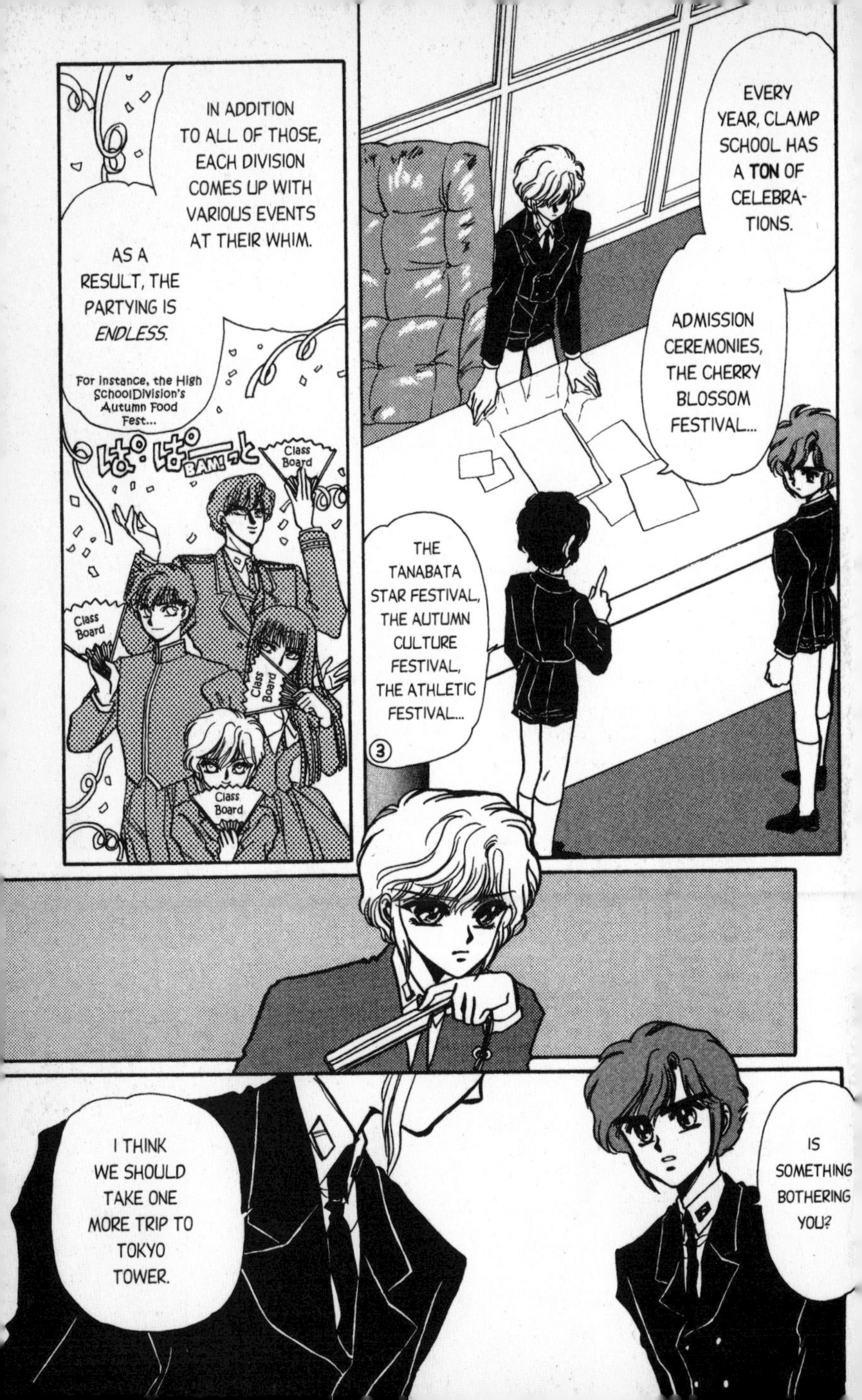
EVERY YEAR, CLAMP SCHOOL HAS A **TON** OF CELEBRA-TIONS.
ADMISSION CEREMONIES, THE CHERRY BLOSSOM FESTIVAL...
THE TANABATA STAR FESTIVAL, THE AUTUMN CULTURE FESTIVAL, THE ATHLETIC FESTIVAL...
IN ADDITION TO ALL OF THOSE, EACH DIVISION COMES UP WITH VARIOUS EVENTS AT THEIR WHIM.
AS A RESULT, THE PARTYING IS *ENDLESS.*
For instance, the High SchoolDivision's Autumn Food Fest...
BAM!
Class Board
Class Board
Class Board
Class Board
IS SOMETHING BOTHERING YOU?
I THINK WE SHOULD TAKE ONE MORE TRIP TO TOKYO TOWER.

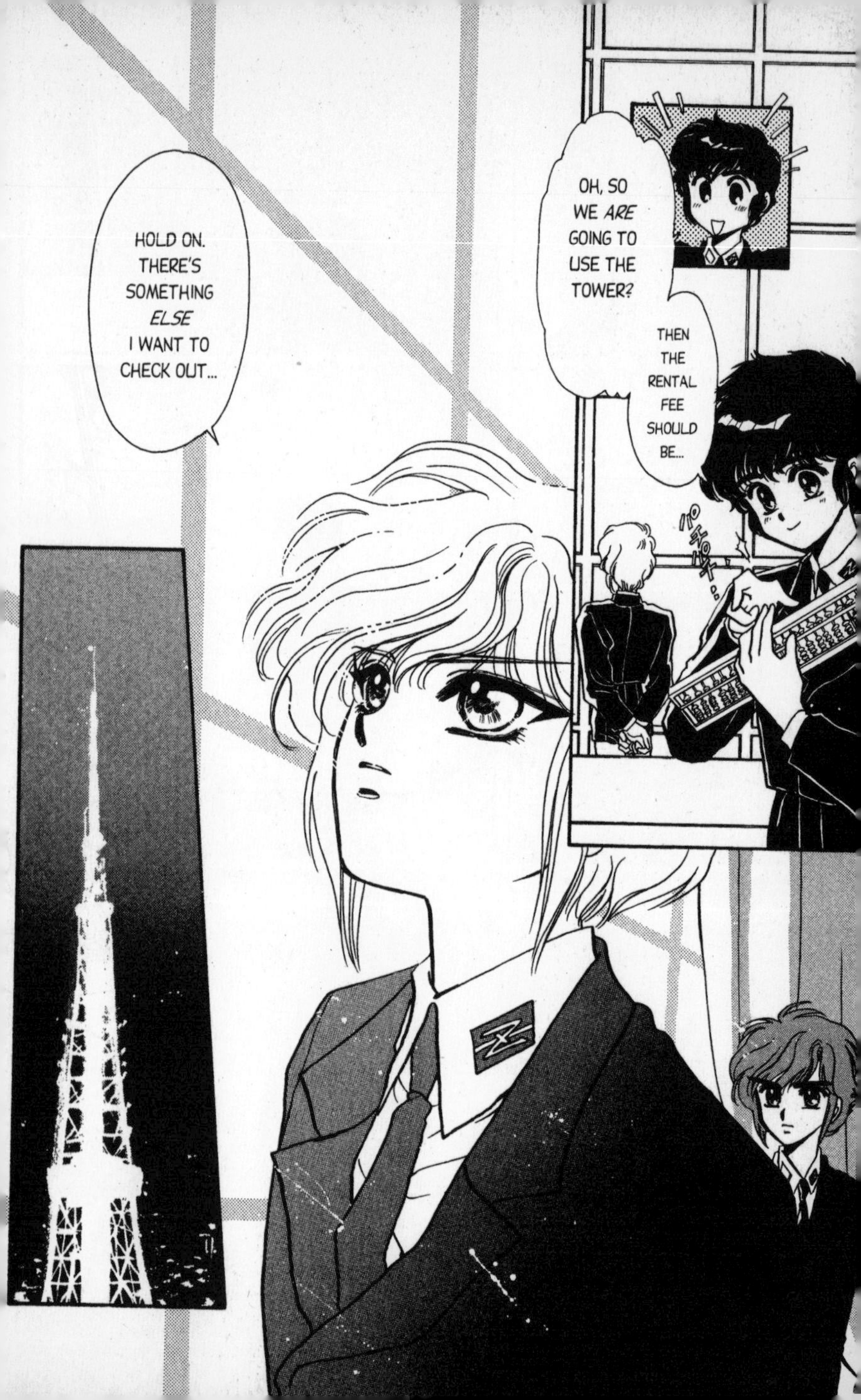
OH, SO WE *ARE* GOING TO USE THE TOWER?
THEN THE RENTAL FEE SHOULD BE...
HOLD ON. THERE'S SOMETHING *ELSE* I WANT TO CHECK OUT...

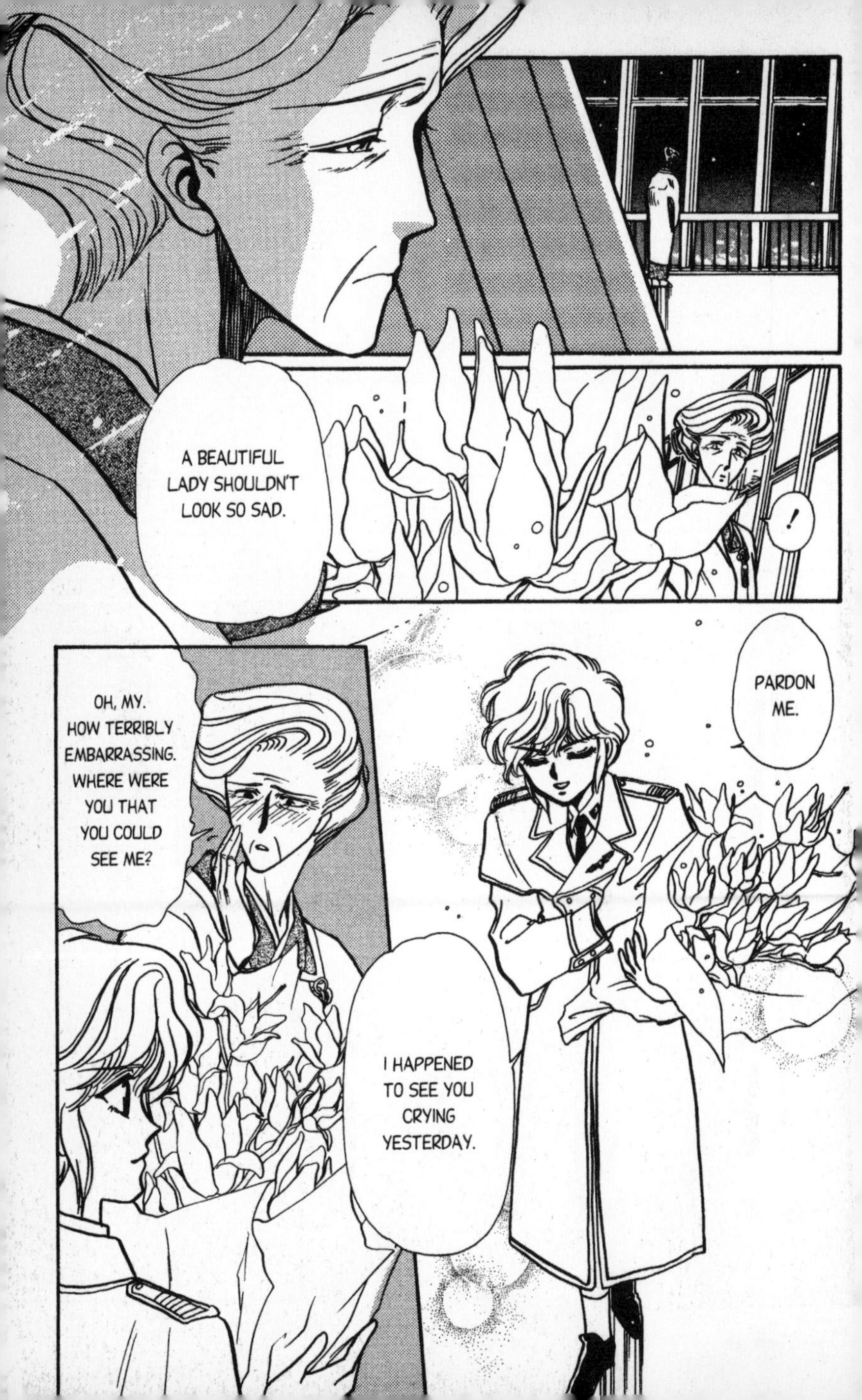
A BEAUTIFUL LADY SHOULDN'T LOOK SO SAD.
!
PARDON ME.
I HAPPENED TO SEE YOU CRYING YESTERDAY.
OH, MY. HOW TERRIBLY EMBARRASSING. WHERE WERE YOU THAT YOU COULD SEE ME?

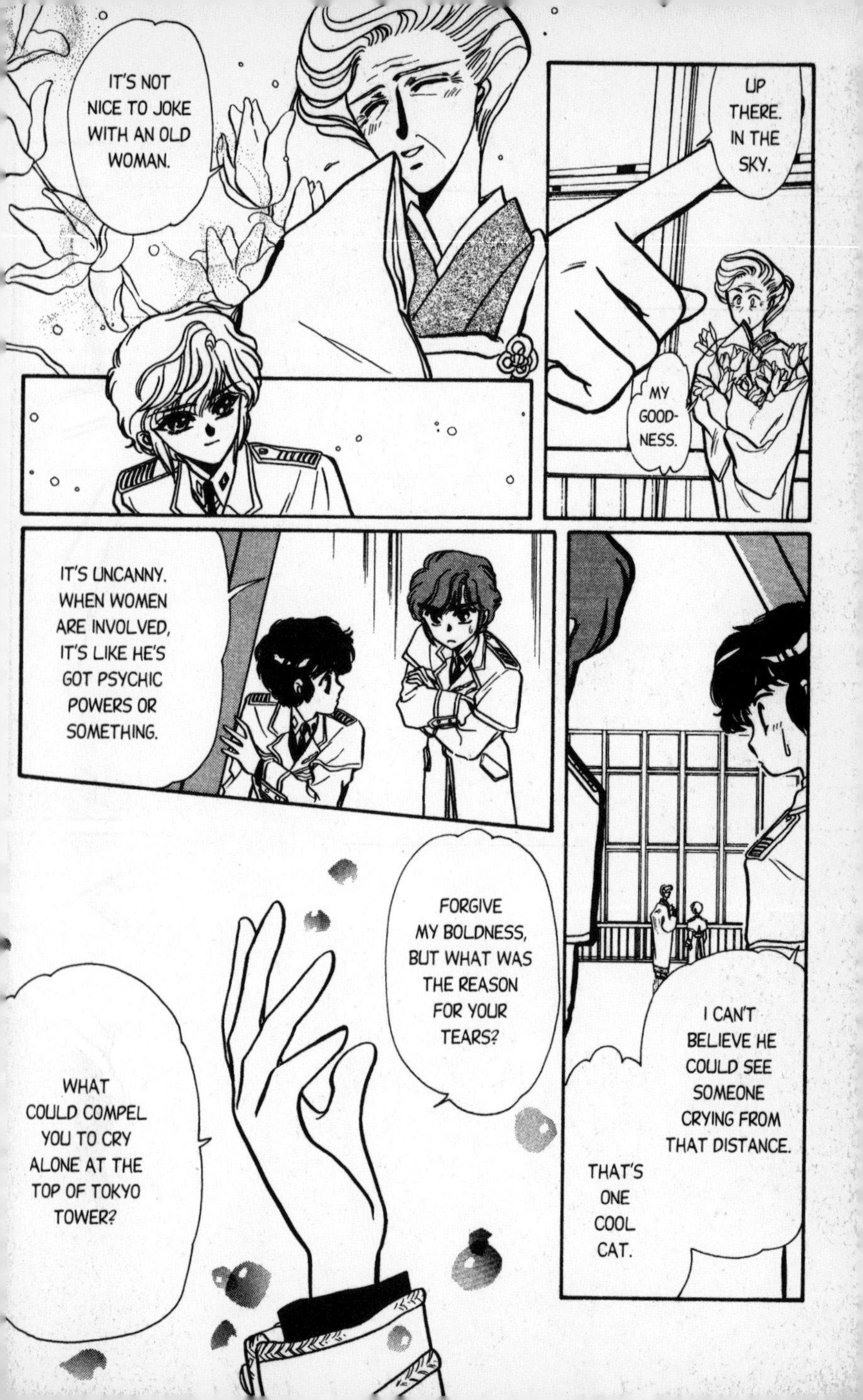
UP THERE. IN THE SKY.
MY GOODNESS.
IT'S NOT NICE TO JOKE WITH AN OLD WOMAN.
I CAN'T BELIEVE HE COULD SEE SOMEONE CRYING FROM THAT DISTANCE.
THAT'S ONE COOL CAT.
IT'S UNCANNY. WHEN WOMEN ARE INVOLVED, IT'S LIKE HE'S GOT PSYCHIC POWERS OR SOMETHING.
FORGIVE MY BOLDNESS, BUT WHAT WAS THE REASON FOR YOUR TEARS?
WHAT COULD COMPEL YOU TO CRY ALONE AT THE TOP OF TOKYO TOWER?

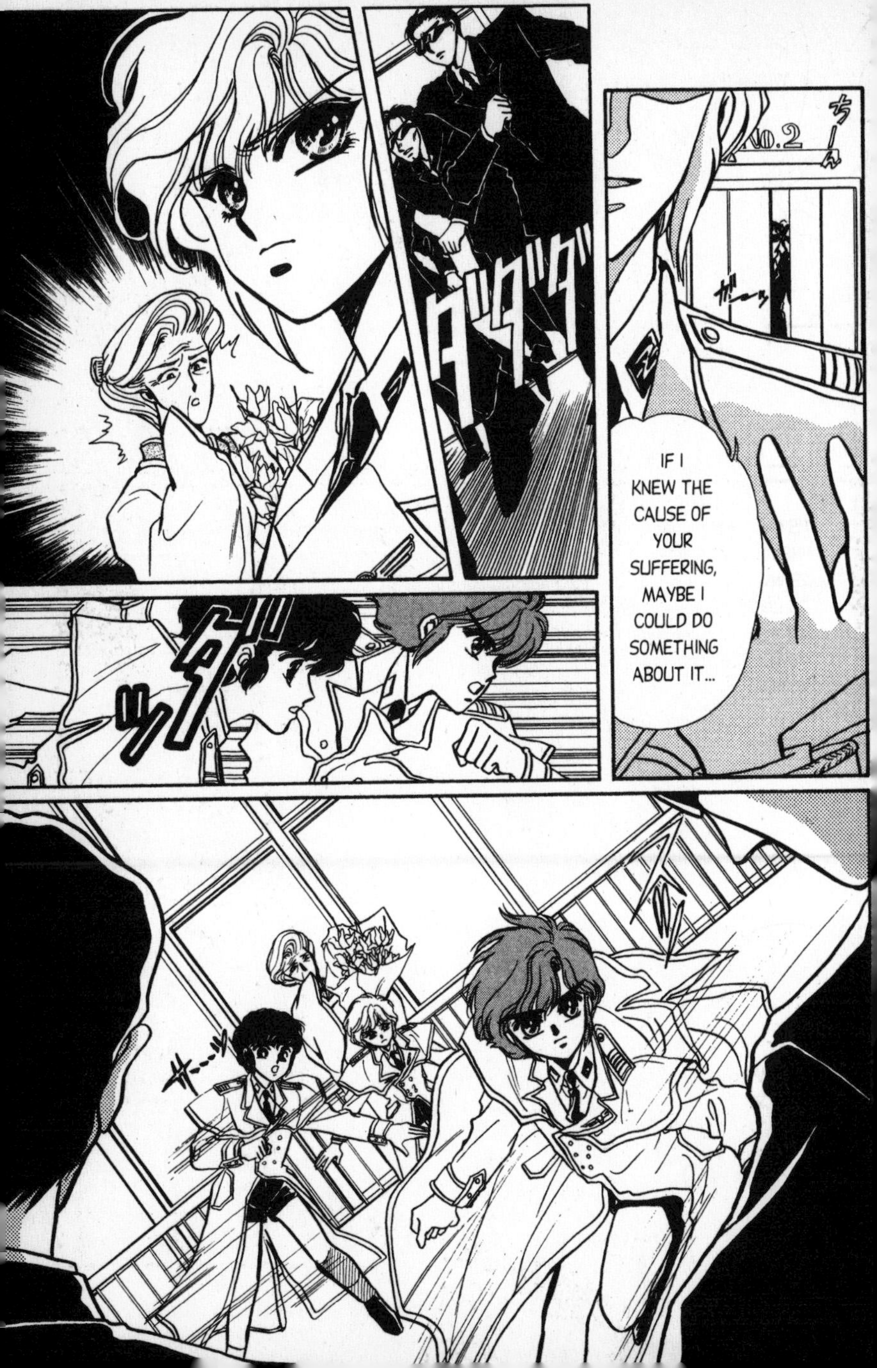
IF I KNEW THE CAUSE OF YOUR SUFFERING, MAYBE I COULD DO SOMETHING ABOUT IT...

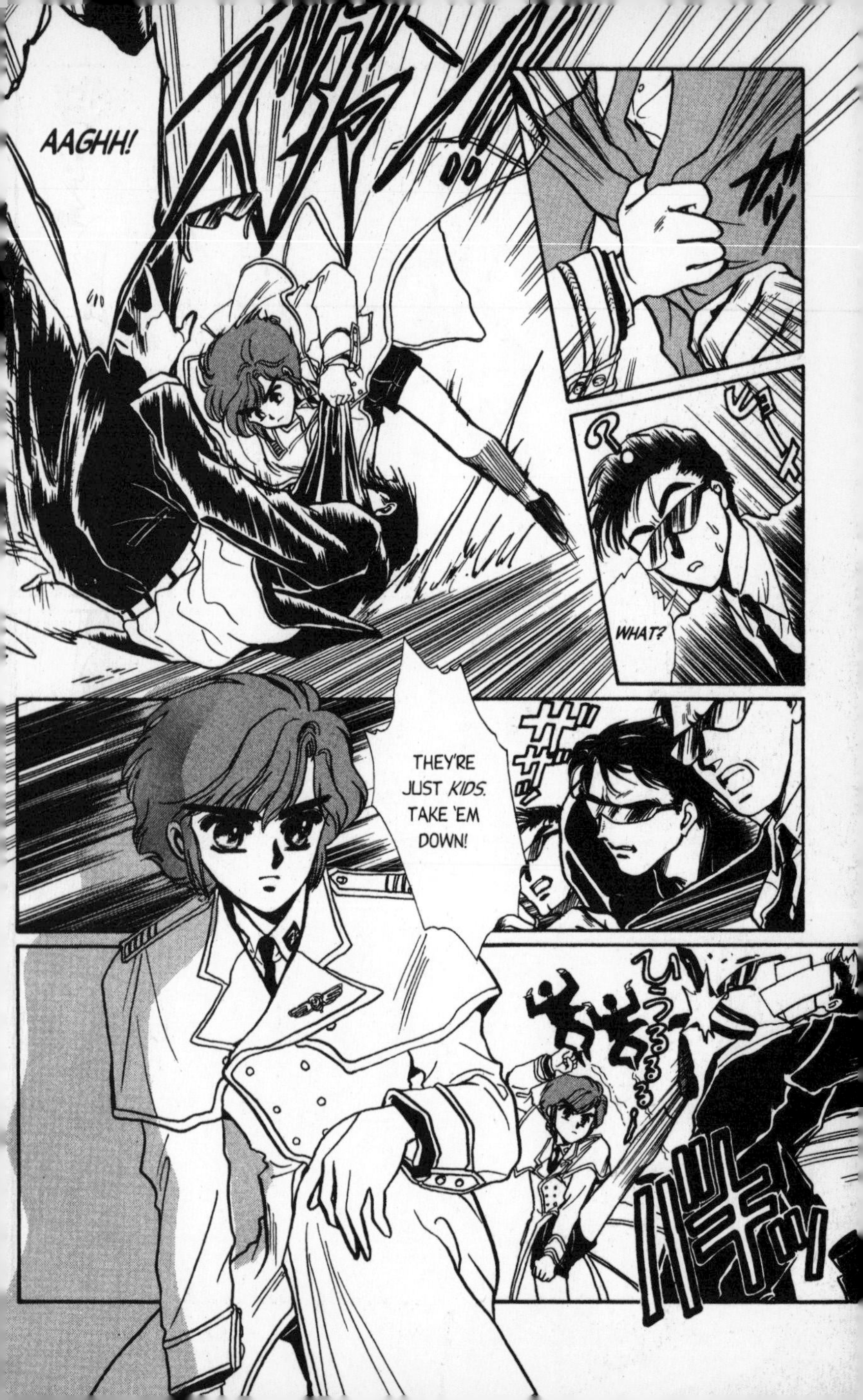
AAGHH!
WHAT?
THEY'RE JUST KIDS. TAKE 'EM DOWN!

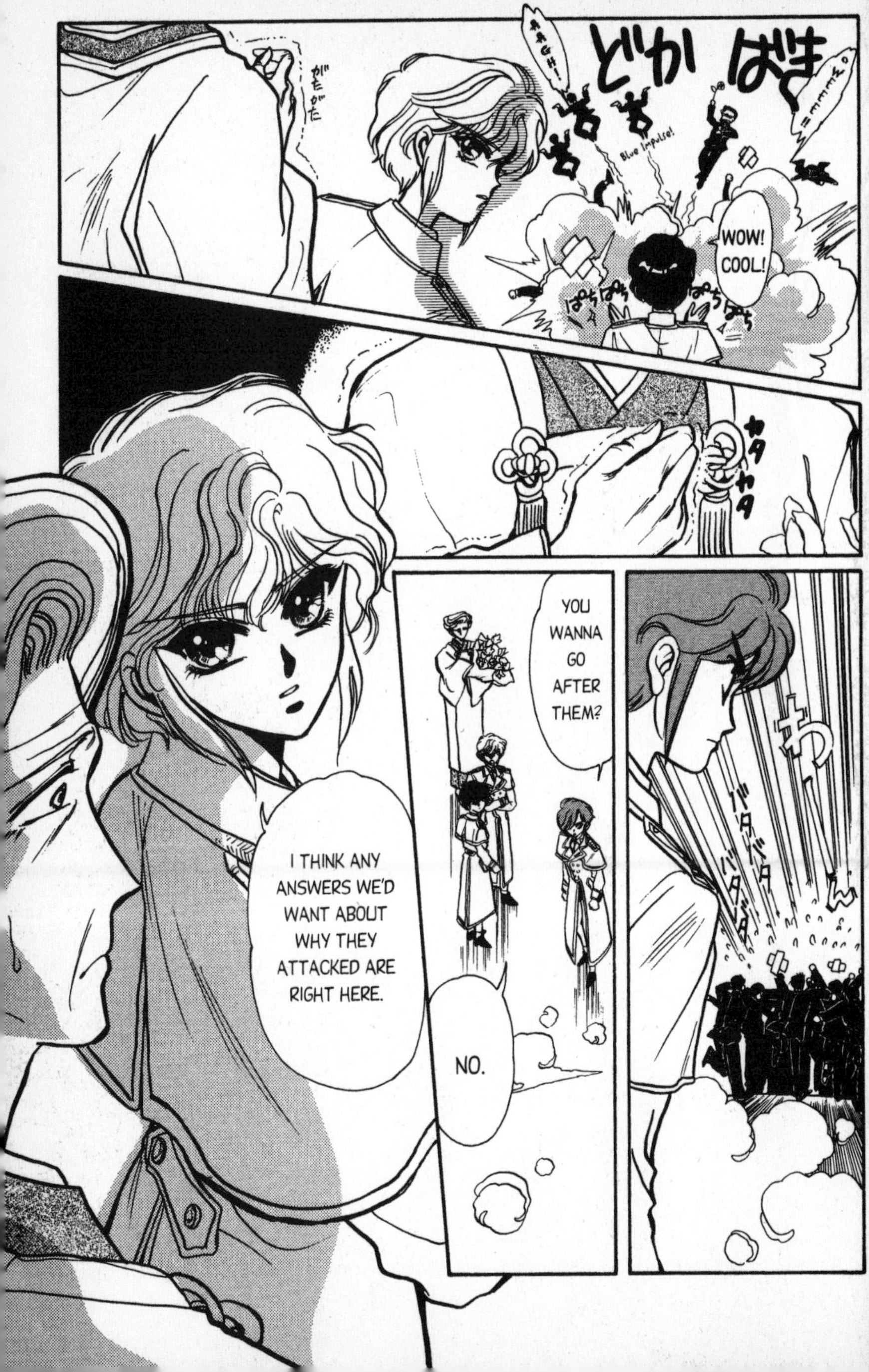

AAAGH!
どかばき
EEEEE!!
Blue Impulse!
WOW! COOL!
ぱちぱち
ぱちぱち
がたがた
カタカタ
わっ
バタバタ
バタバタ
YOU WANNA GO AFTER THEM?
NO.
I THINK ANY ANSWERS WE'D WANT ABOUT WHY THEY ATTACKED ARE RIGHT HERE.

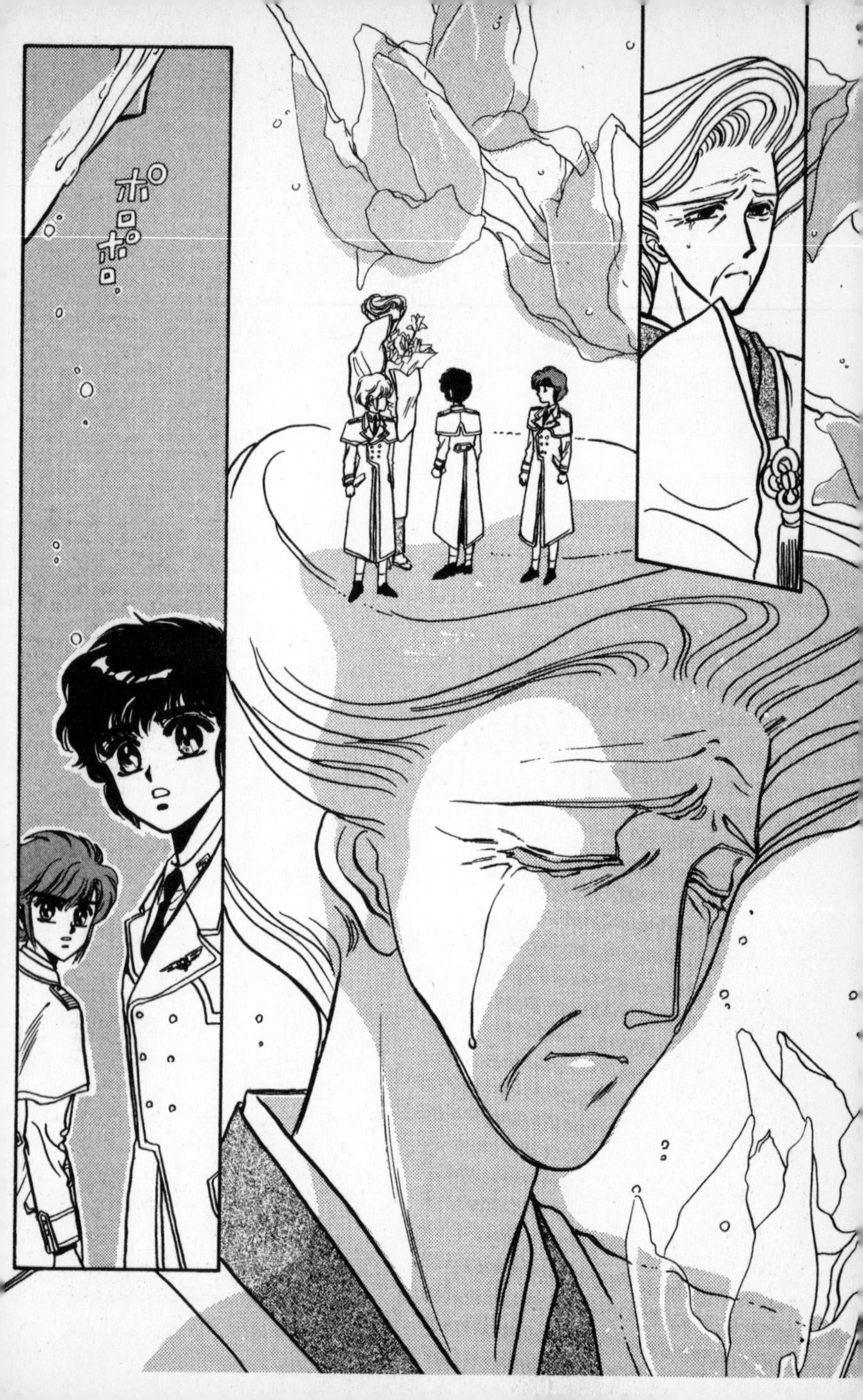
ポロポロ

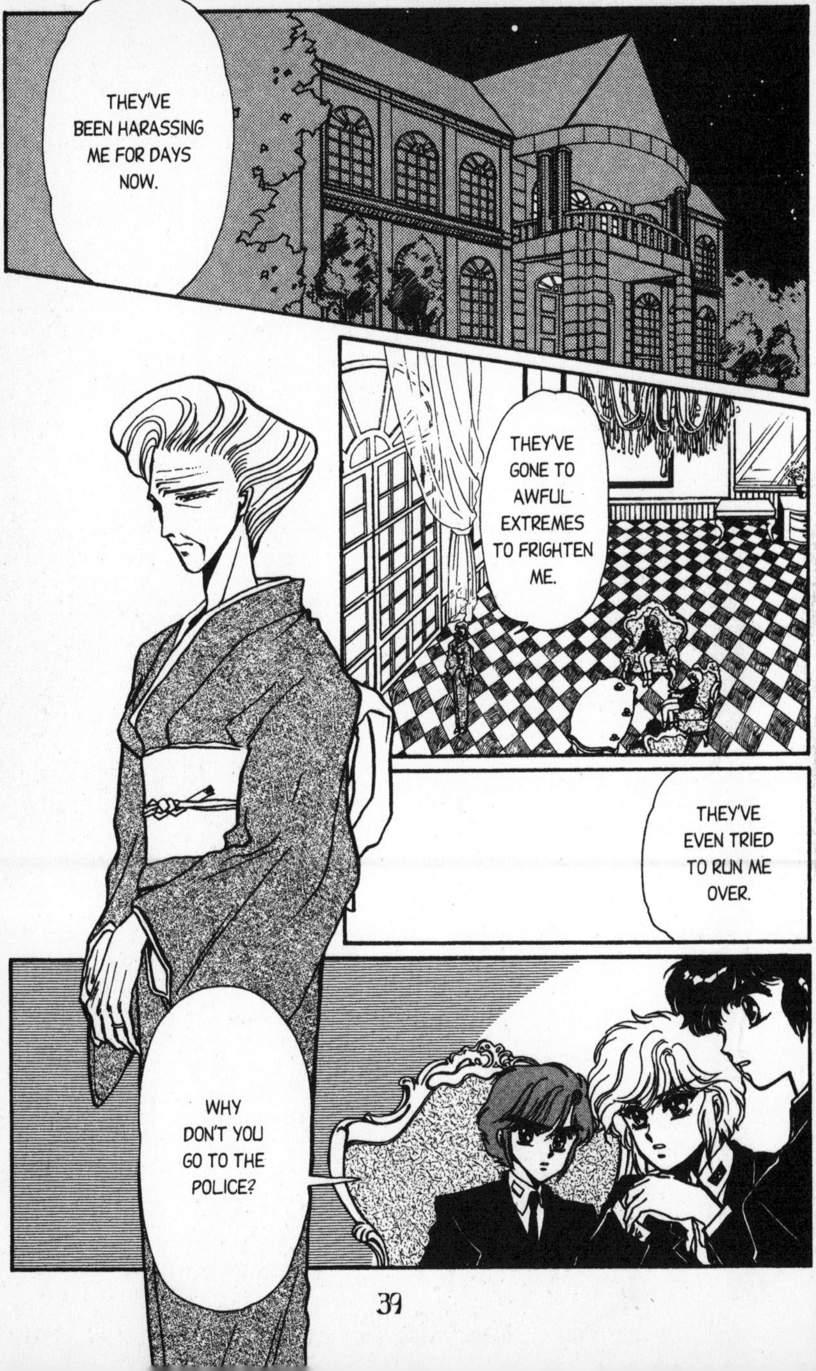
THEY'VE BEEN HARASSING ME FOR DAYS NOW.
THEY'VE GONE TO AWFUL EXTREMES TO FRIGHTEN ME.
THEY'VE EVEN TRIED TO RUN ME OVER.
WHY DON'T YOU GO TO THE POLICE?

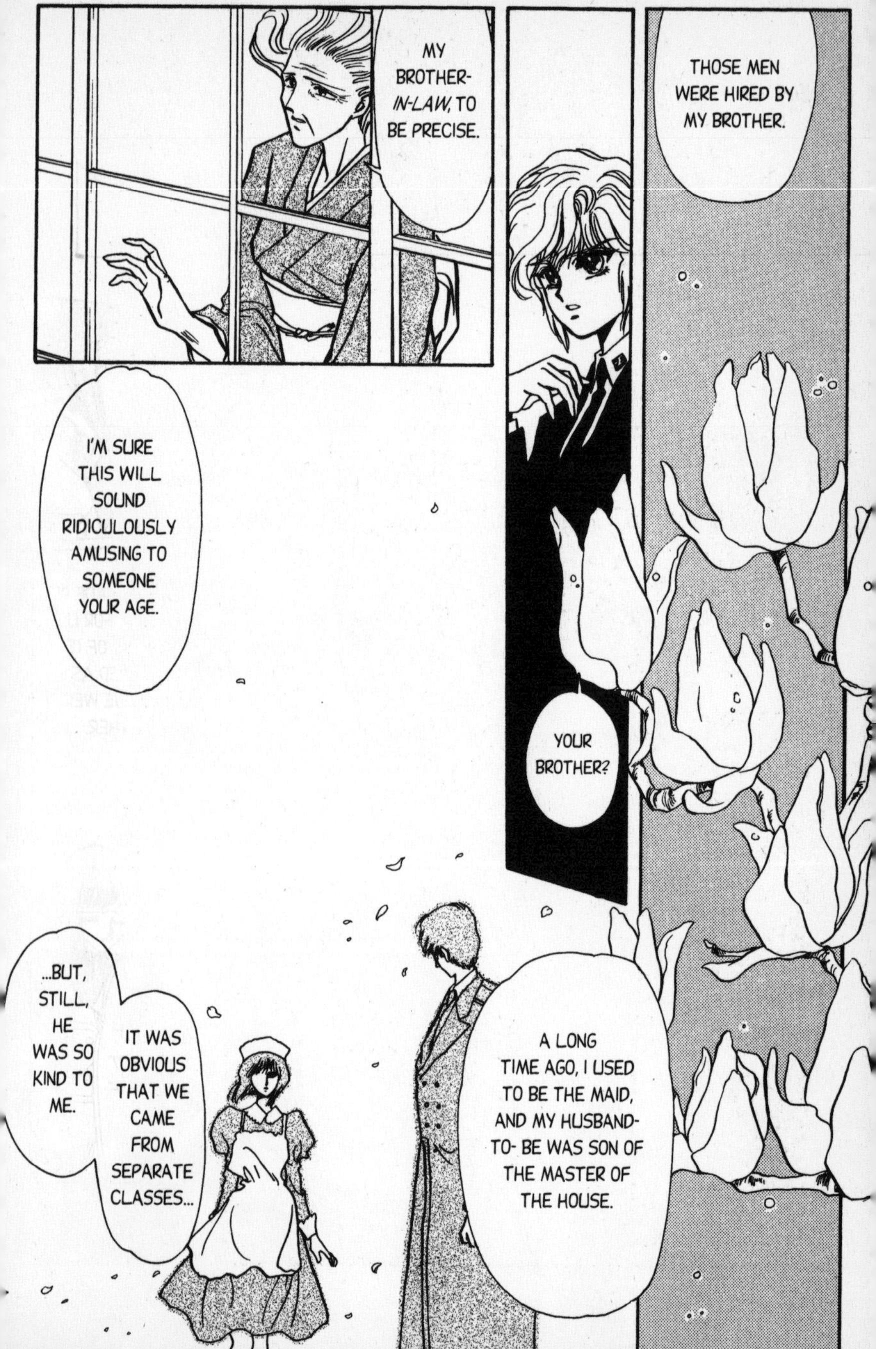

THOSE MEN WERE HIRED BY MY BROTHER.
YOUR BROTHER?
MY BROTHER-*IN-LAW*, TO BE PRECISE.
I'M SURE THIS WILL SOUND RIDICULOUSLY AMUSING TO SOMEONE YOUR AGE.
A LONG TIME AGO, I USED TO BE THE MAID, AND MY HUSBAND-TO- BE WAS SON OF THE MASTER OF THE HOUSE.
IT WAS OBVIOUS THAT WE CAME FROM SEPARATE CLASSES...
...BUT, STILL, HE WAS SO KIND TO ME.

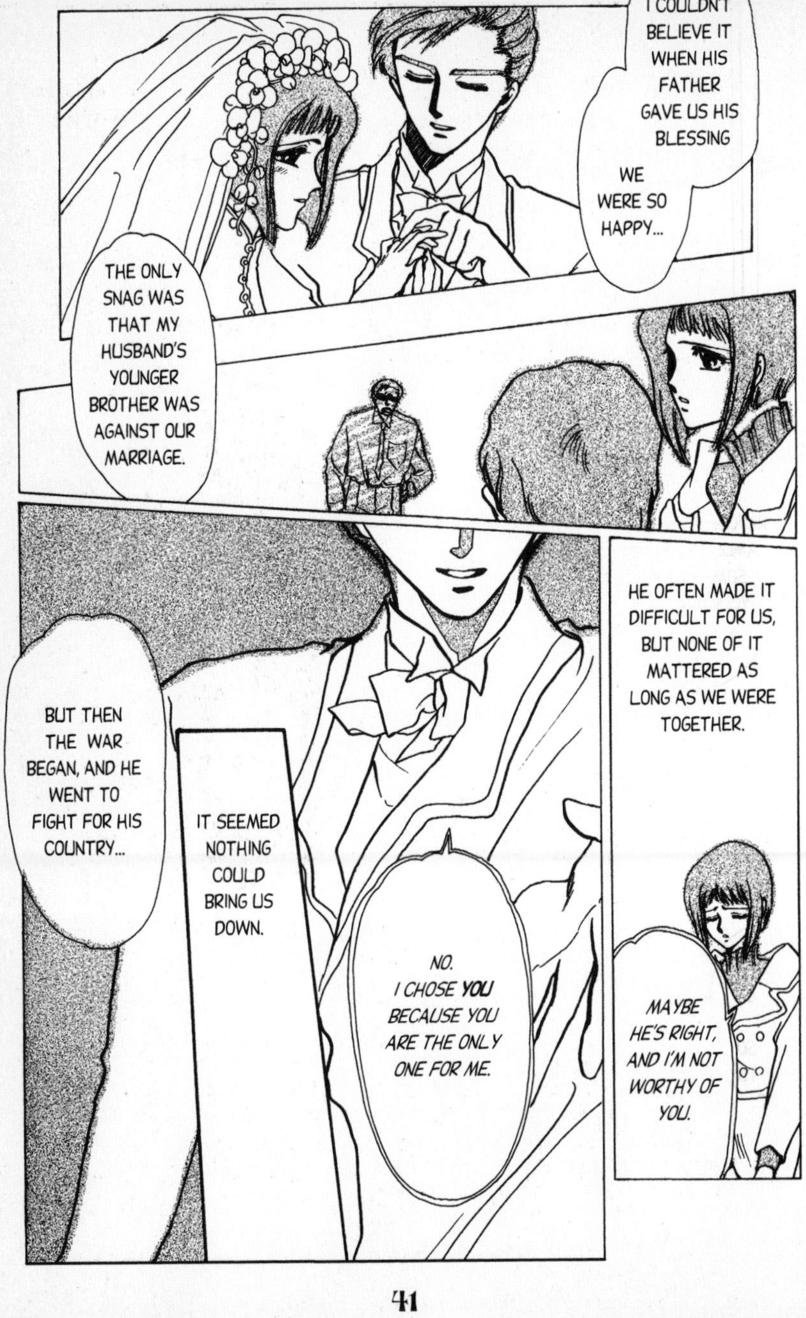
I COULDN'T BELIEVE IT WHEN HIS FATHER GAVE US HIS BLESSING
WE WERE SO HAPPY...
THE ONLY SNAG WAS THAT MY HUSBAND'S YOUNGER BROTHER WAS AGAINST OUR MARRIAGE.
HE OFTEN MADE IT DIFFICULT FOR US, BUT NONE OF IT MATTERED AS LONG AS WE WERE TOGETHER.
MAYBE HE'S RIGHT, AND I'M NOT WORTHY OF YOU.
NO. I CHOSE YOU BECAUSE YOU ARE THE ONLY ONE FOR ME.
IT SEEMED NOTHING COULD BRING US DOWN.
BUT THEN THE WAR BEGAN, AND HE WENT TO FIGHT FOR HIS COUNTRY...

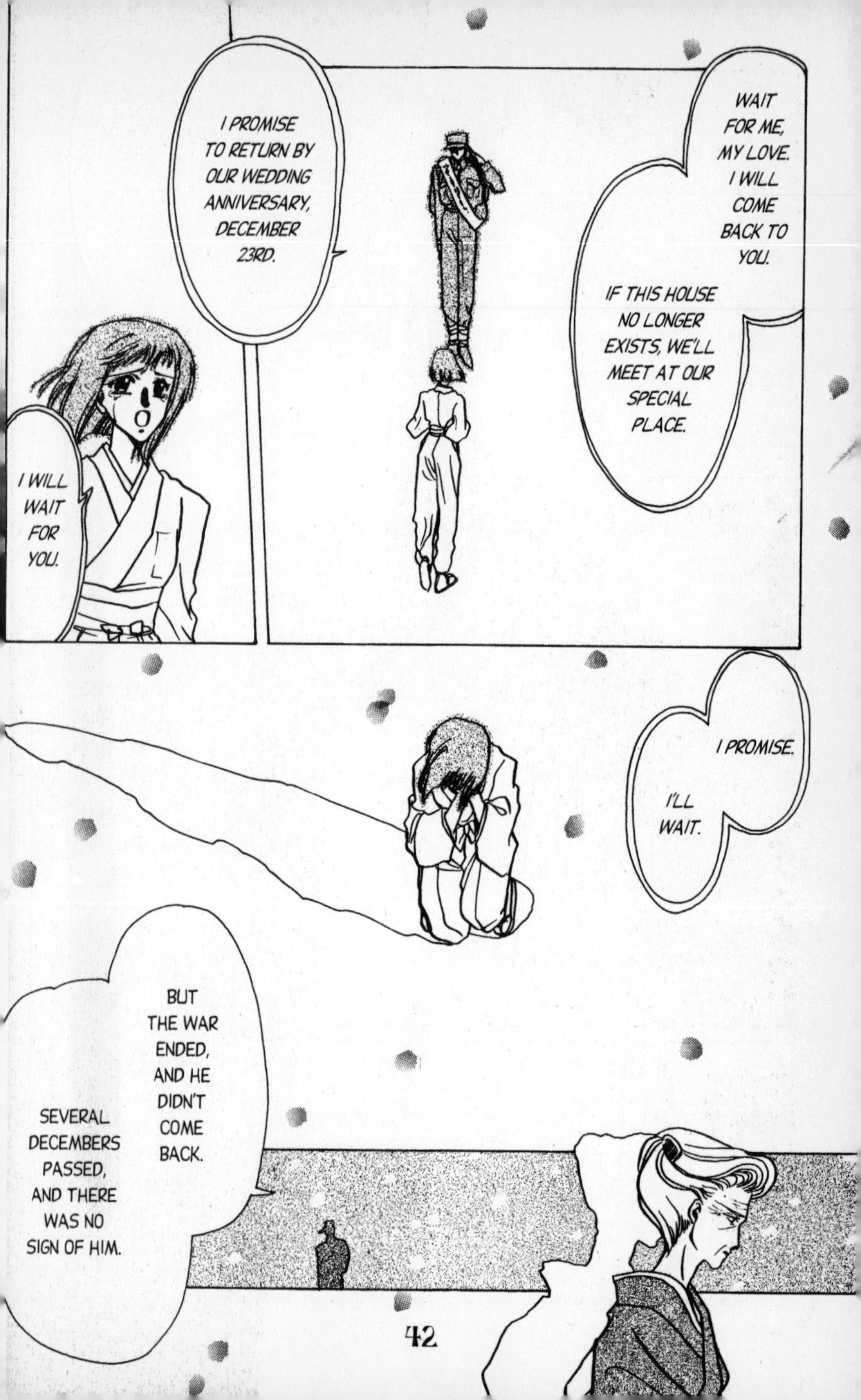
WAIT FOR ME, MY LOVE. I WILL COME BACK TO YOU.
IF THIS HOUSE NO LONGER EXISTS, WE'LL MEET AT OUR SPECIAL PLACE.
I PROMISE TO RETURN BY OUR WEDDING ANNIVERSARY, DECEMBER 23RD.
I WILL WAIT FOR YOU.
I PROMISE.
I'LL WAIT.
BUT THE WAR ENDED, AND HE DIDN'T COME BACK.
SEVERAL DECEMBERS PASSED, AND THERE WAS NO SIGN OF HIM.

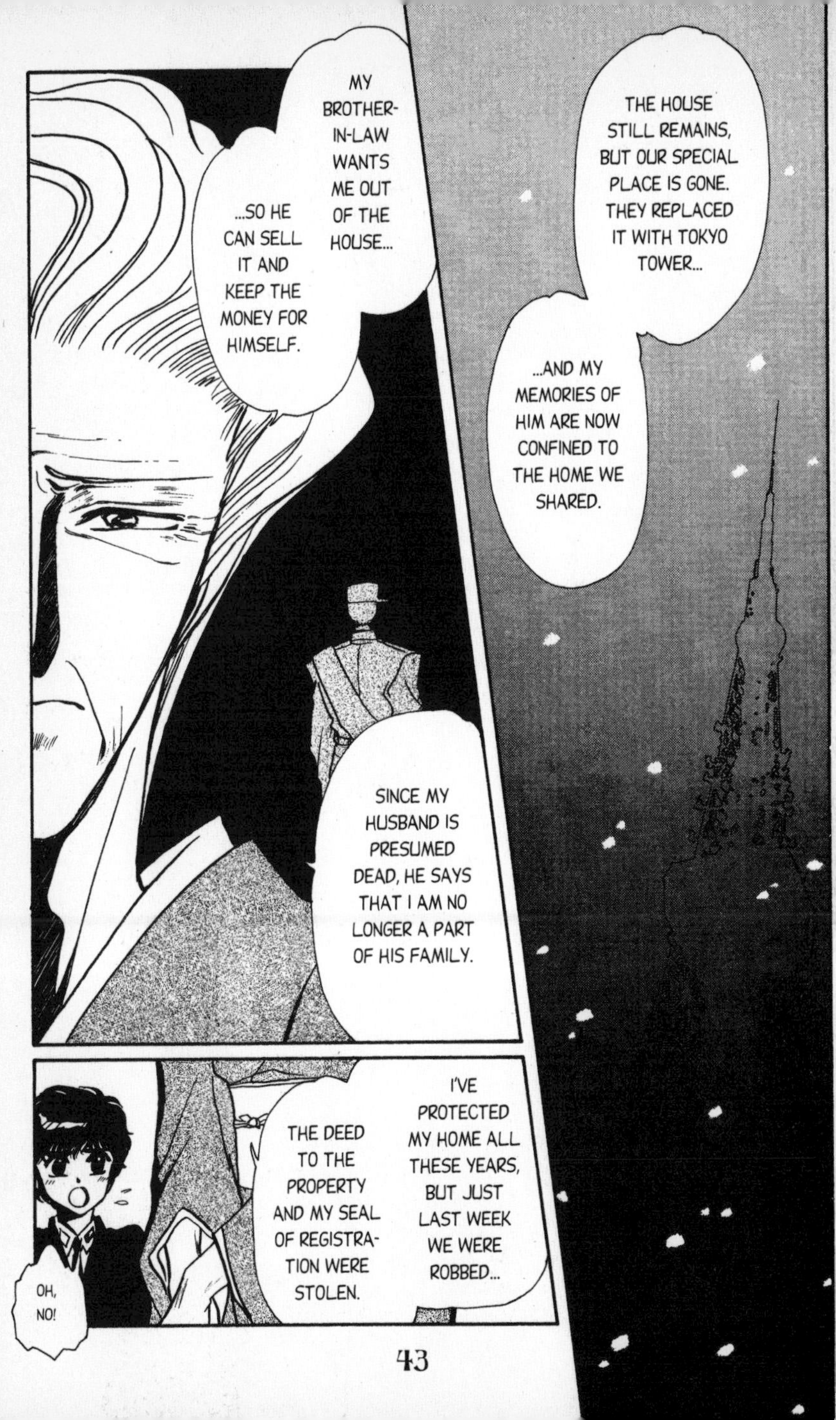
THE HOUSE STILL REMAINS, BUT OUR SPECIAL PLACE IS GONE. THEY REPLACED IT WITH TOKYO TOWER...
...AND MY MEMORIES OF HIM ARE NOW CONFINED TO THE HOME WE SHARED.
MY BROTHER-IN-LAW WANTS ME OUT OF THE HOUSE...
...SO HE CAN SELL IT AND KEEP THE MONEY FOR HIMSELF.
SINCE MY HUSBAND IS PRESUMED DEAD, HE SAYS THAT I AM NO LONGER A PART OF HIS FAMILY.
I'VE PROTECTED MY HOME ALL THESE YEARS, BUT JUST LAST WEEK WE WERE ROBBED...
THE DEED TO THE PROPERTY AND MY SEAL OF REGISTRATION WERE STOLEN.
OH, NO!

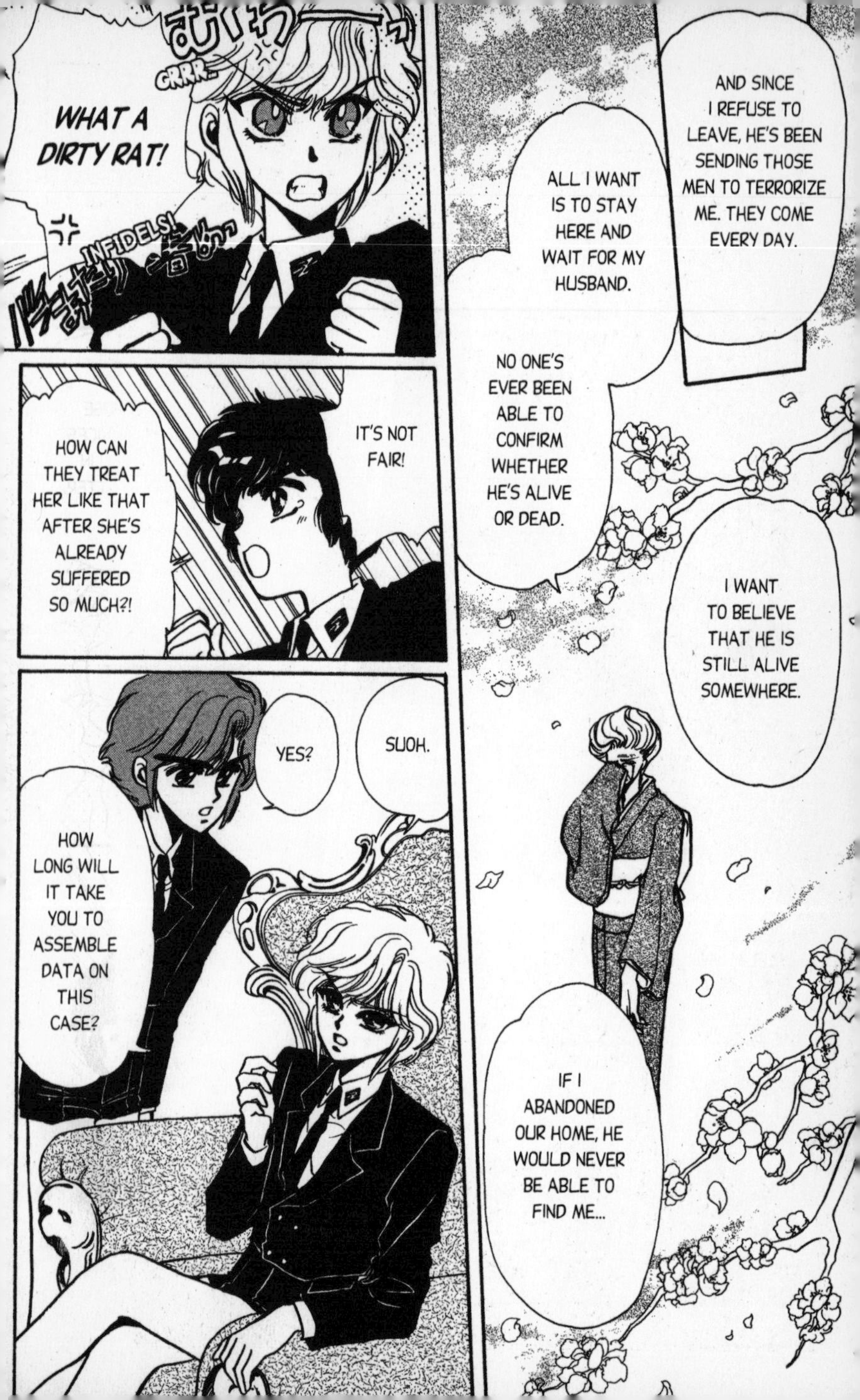
AND SINCE I REFUSE TO LEAVE, HE'S BEEN SENDING THOSE MEN TO TERRORIZE ME. THEY COME EVERY DAY.
ALL I WANT IS TO STAY HERE AND WAIT FOR MY HUSBAND.
NO ONE'S EVER BEEN ABLE TO CONFIRM WHETHER HE'S ALIVE OR DEAD.
I WANT TO BELIEVE THAT HE IS STILL ALIVE SOMEWHERE.
IF I ABANDONED OUR HOME, HE WOULD NEVER BE ABLE TO FIND ME...
GRRR..
WHAT A DIRTY RAT!
INFIDELS!
IT'S NOT FAIR!
HOW CAN THEY TREAT HER LIKE THAT AFTER SHE'S ALREADY SUFFERED SO MUCH?!
SUOH.
YES?
HOW LONG WILL IT TAKE YOU TO ASSEMBLE DATA ON THIS CASE?

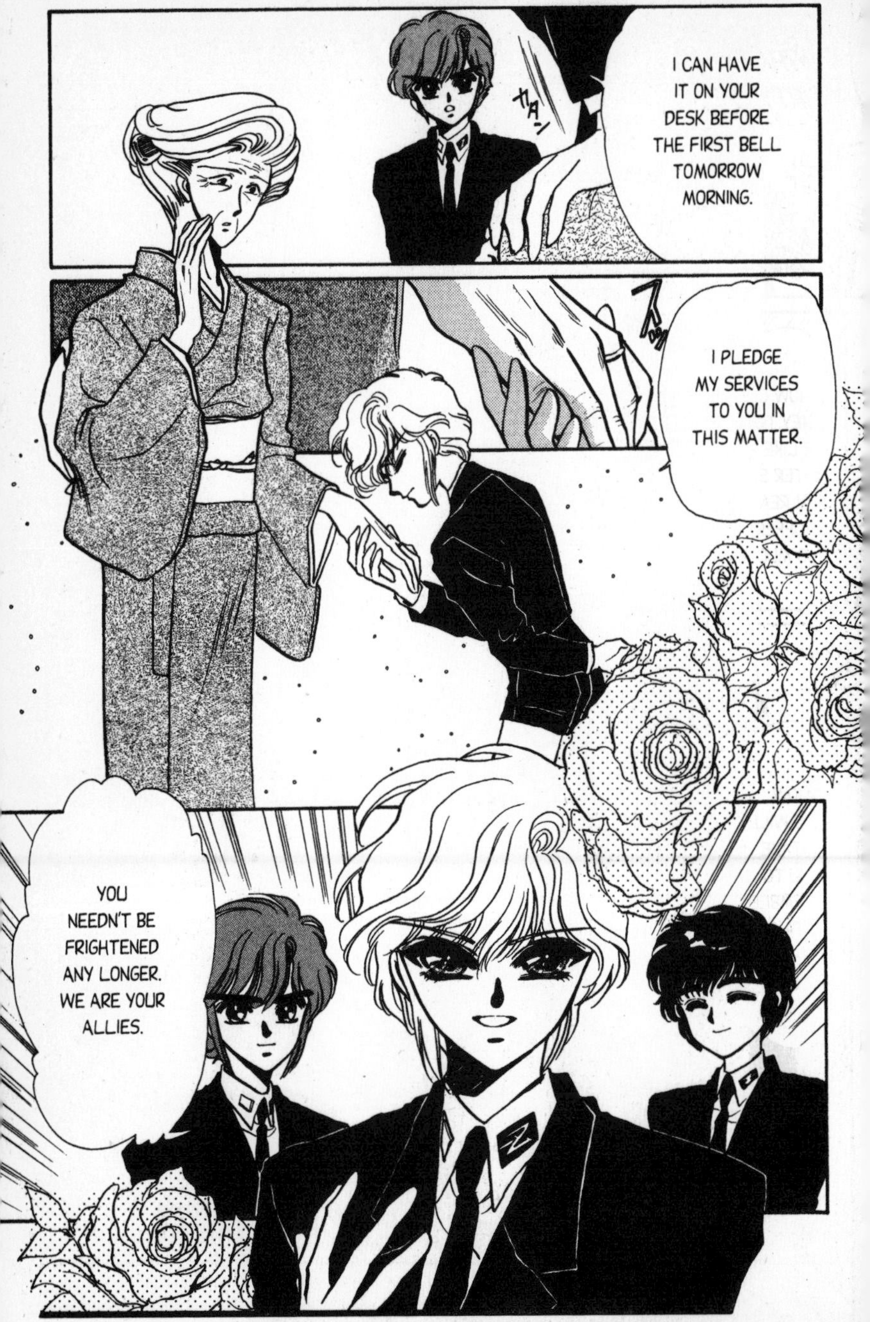
I CAN HAVE IT ON YOUR DESK BEFORE THE FIRST BELL TOMORROW MORNING.
I PLEDGE MY SERVICES TO YOU IN THIS MATTER.
YOU NEEDN'T BE FRIGHTENED ANY LONGER. WE ARE YOUR ALLIES.

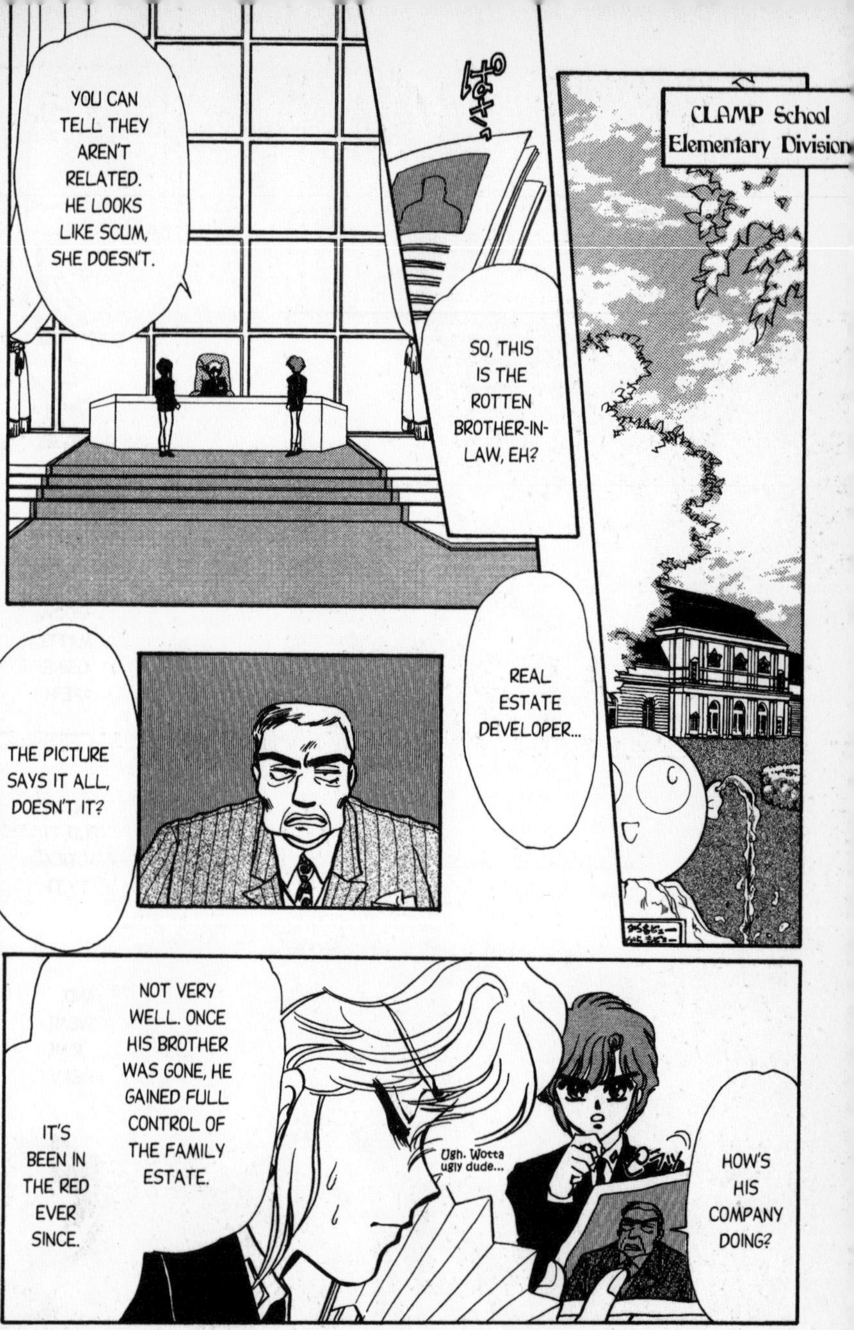
CLAMP School Elementary Division
SO, THIS IS THE ROTTEN BROTHER-IN-LAW, EH?
YOU CAN TELL THEY AREN'T RELATED. HE LOOKS LIKE SCUM, SHE DOESN'T.
REAL ESTATE DEVELOPER...
THE PICTURE SAYS IT ALL, DOESN'T IT?
HOW'S HIS COMPANY DOING?
Ugh. Wotta ugly dude...
NOT VERY WELL. ONCE HIS BROTHER WAS GONE, HE GAINED FULL CONTROL OF THE FAMILY ESTATE.
IT'S BEEN IN THE RED EVER SINCE.

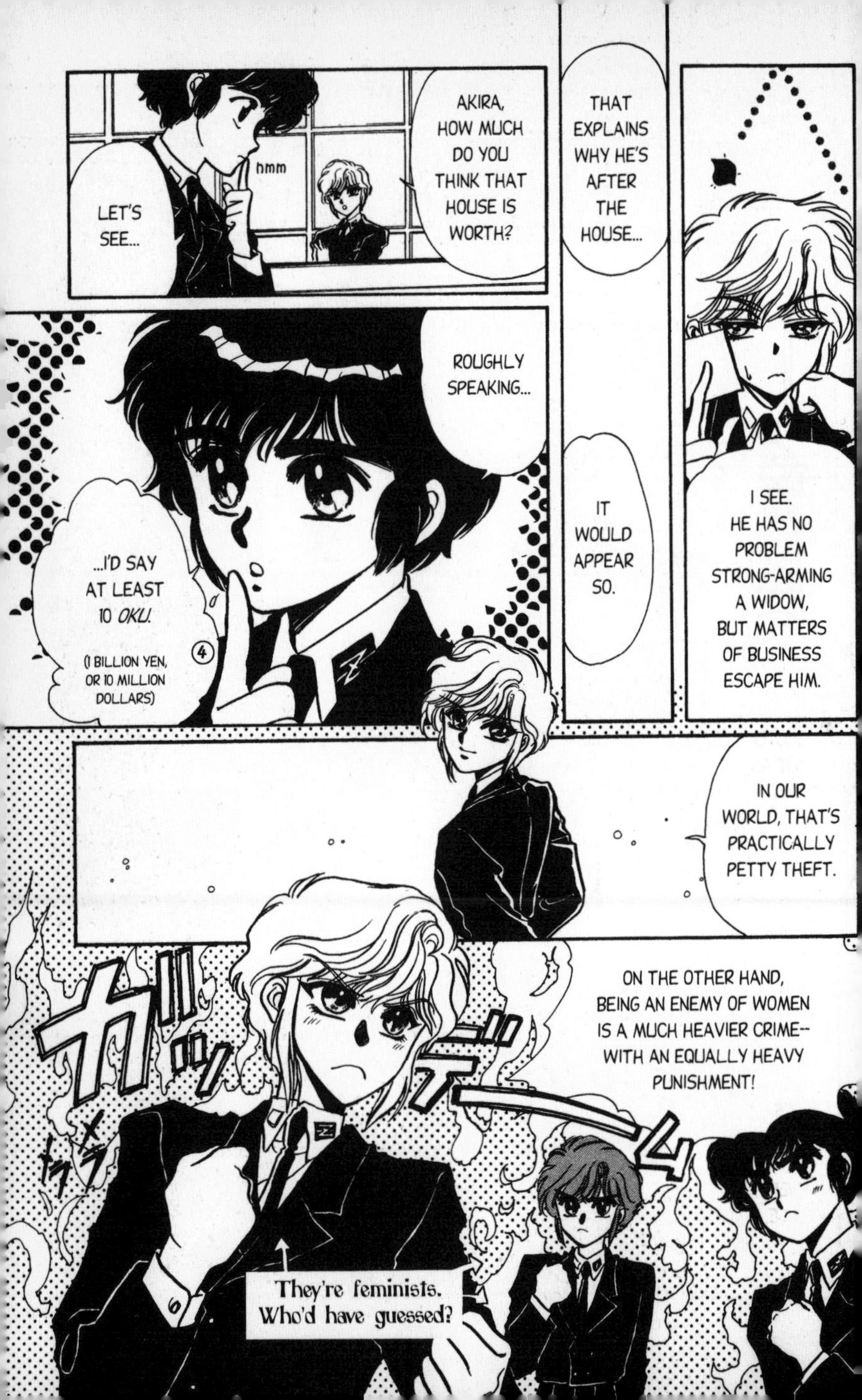

I SEE. HE HAS NO PROBLEM STRONG-ARMING A WIDOW, BUT MATTERS OF BUSINESS ESCAPE HIM.
THAT EXPLAINS WHY HE'S AFTER THE HOUSE...
IT WOULD APPEAR SO.
AKIRA, HOW MUCH DO YOU THINK THAT HOUSE IS WORTH?
hmm
LET'S SEE...
ROUGHLY SPEAKING...
...I'D SAY AT LEAST 10 *OKU*.
④
(1 BILLION YEN, OR 10 MILLION DOLLARS)
IN OUR WORLD, THAT'S PRACTICALLY PETTY THEFT.
ON THE OTHER HAND, BEING AN ENEMY OF WOMEN IS A MUCH HEAVIER CRIME-- WITH AN EQUALLY HEAVY PUNISHMENT!
They're feminists. Who'd have guessed?

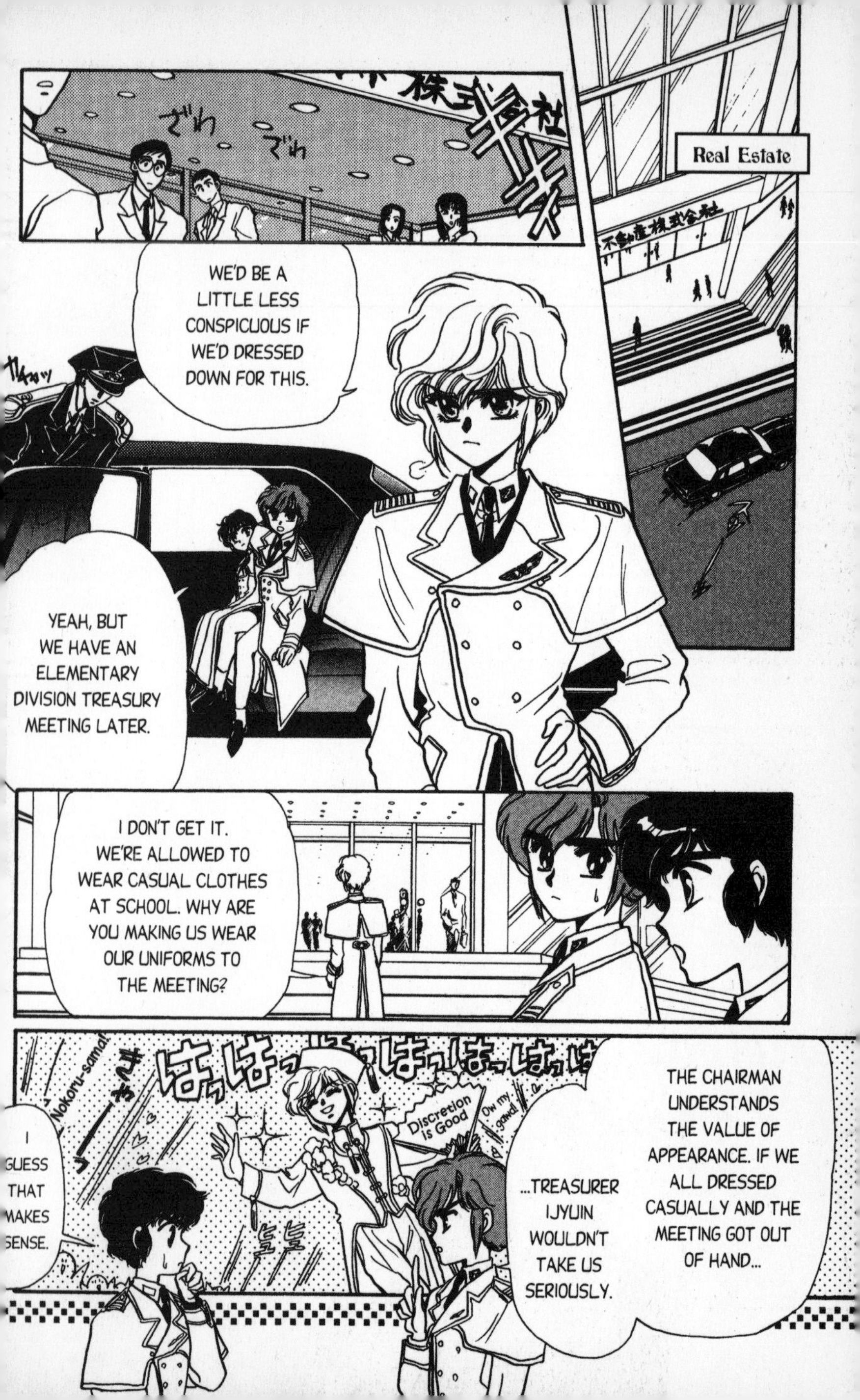
Real Estate
株式会社
ざわ ざわ
WE'D BE A LITTLE LESS CONSPICUOUS IF WE'D DRESSED DOWN FOR THIS.
YEAH, BUT WE HAVE AN ELEMENTARY DIVISION TREASURY MEETING LATER.
I DON'T GET IT. WE'RE ALLOWED TO WEAR CASUAL CLOTHES AT SCHOOL. WHY ARE YOU MAKING US WEAR OUR UNIFORMS TO THE MEETING?
THE CHAIRMAN UNDERSTANDS THE VALUE OF APPEARANCE. IF WE ALL DRESSED CASUALLY AND THE MEETING GOT OUT OF HAND...
...TREASURER IJYUIN WOULDN'T TAKE US SERIOUSLY.
はっはっはっはっはっは
Ow my gawd!
Discretion is Good
Nokoru-sama!
I GUESS THAT MAKES SENSE.

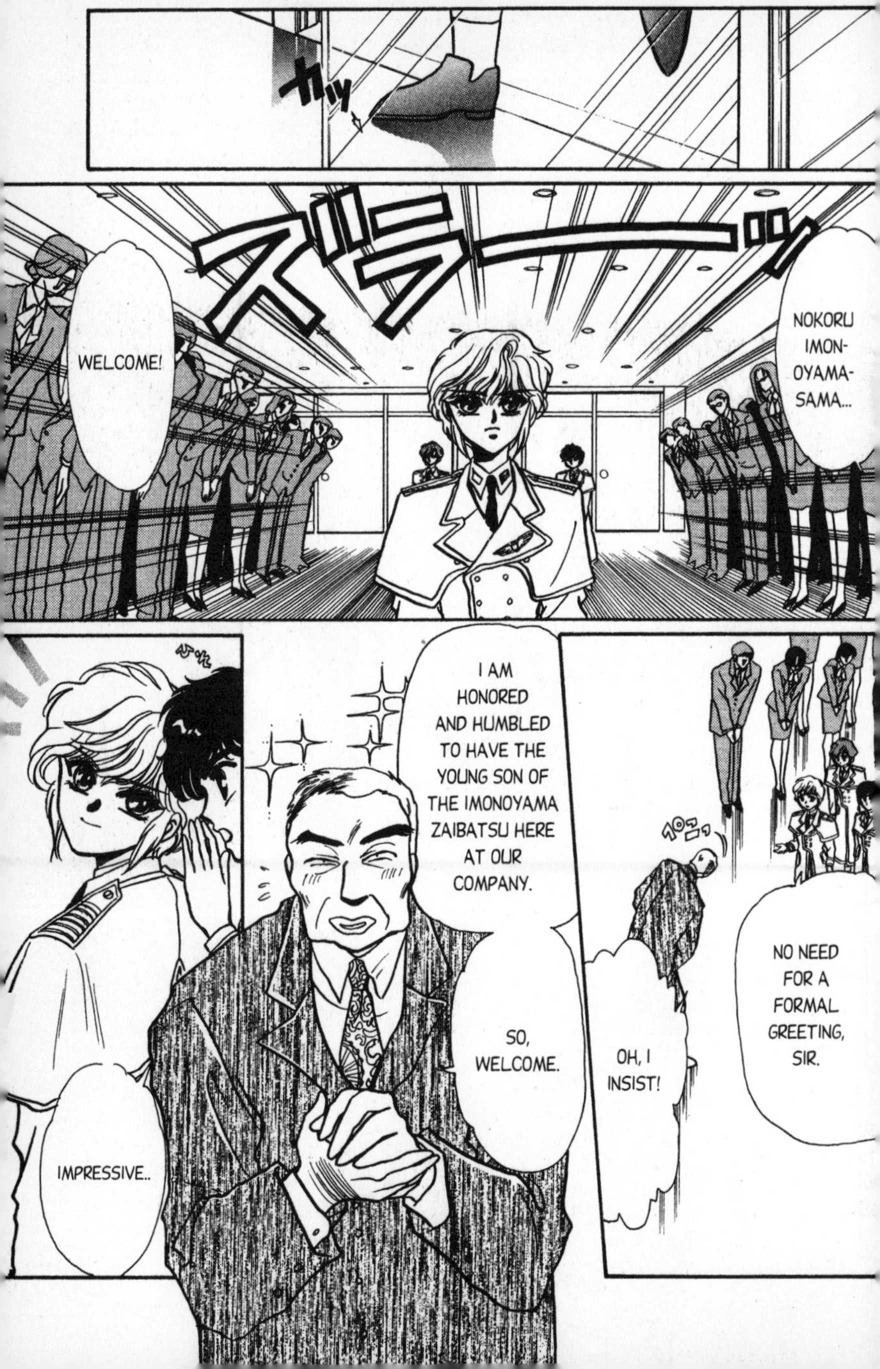
ズラーーッ
NOKORU IMON-OYAMA-SAMA...
WELCOME!
NO NEED FOR A FORMAL GREETING, SIR.
OH, I INSIST!
I AM HONORED AND HUMBLED TO HAVE THE YOUNG SON OF THE IMONOYAMA ZAIBATSU HERE AT OUR COMPANY.
SO, WELCOME.
IMPRESSIVE..

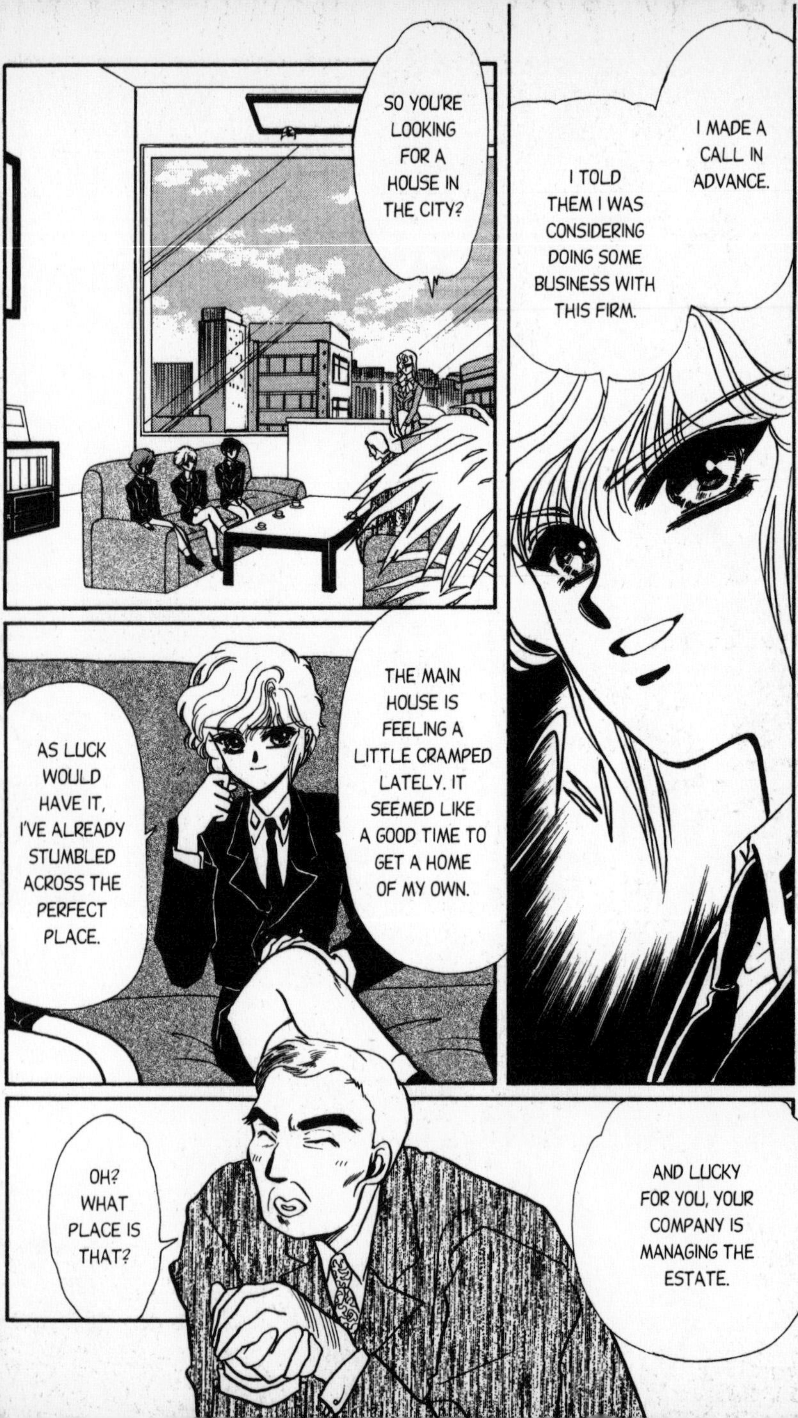
I MADE A CALL IN ADVANCE.
I TOLD THEM I WAS CONSIDERING DOING SOME BUSINESS WITH THIS FIRM.
SO YOU'RE LOOKING FOR A HOUSE IN THE CITY?
THE MAIN HOUSE IS FEELING A LITTLE CRAMPED LATELY. IT SEEMED LIKE A GOOD TIME TO GET A HOME OF MY OWN.
AS LUCK WOULD HAVE IT, I'VE ALREADY STUMBLED ACROSS THE PERFECT PLACE.
AND LUCKY FOR YOU, YOUR COMPANY IS MANAGING THE ESTATE.
OH? WHAT PLACE IS THAT?

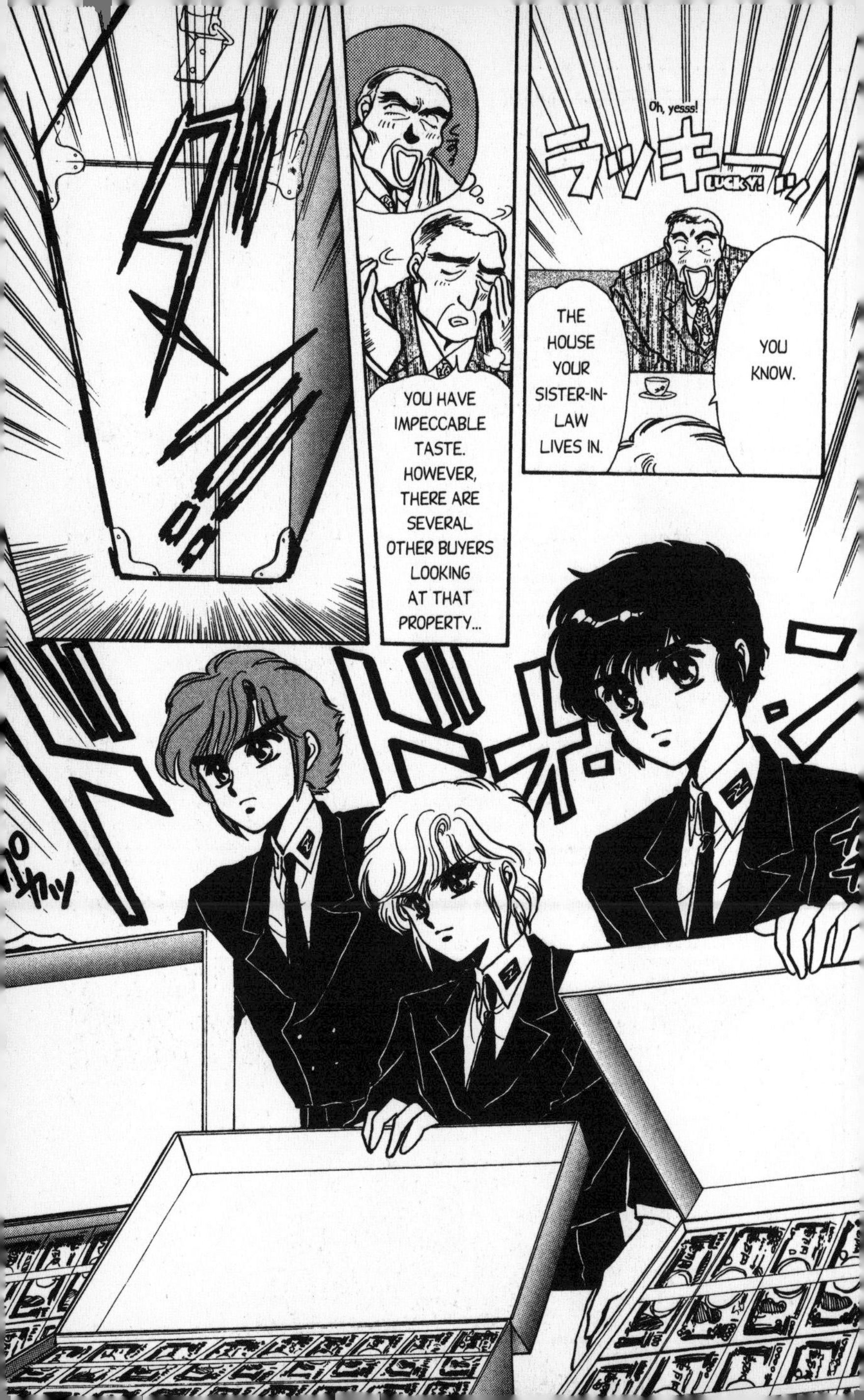

Oh, yesss!
LUCKY!
YOU KNOW.
THE HOUSE YOUR SISTER-IN-LAW LIVES IN.
YOU HAVE IMPECCABLE TASTE. HOWEVER, THERE ARE SEVERAL OTHER BUYERS LOOKING AT THAT PROPERTY...

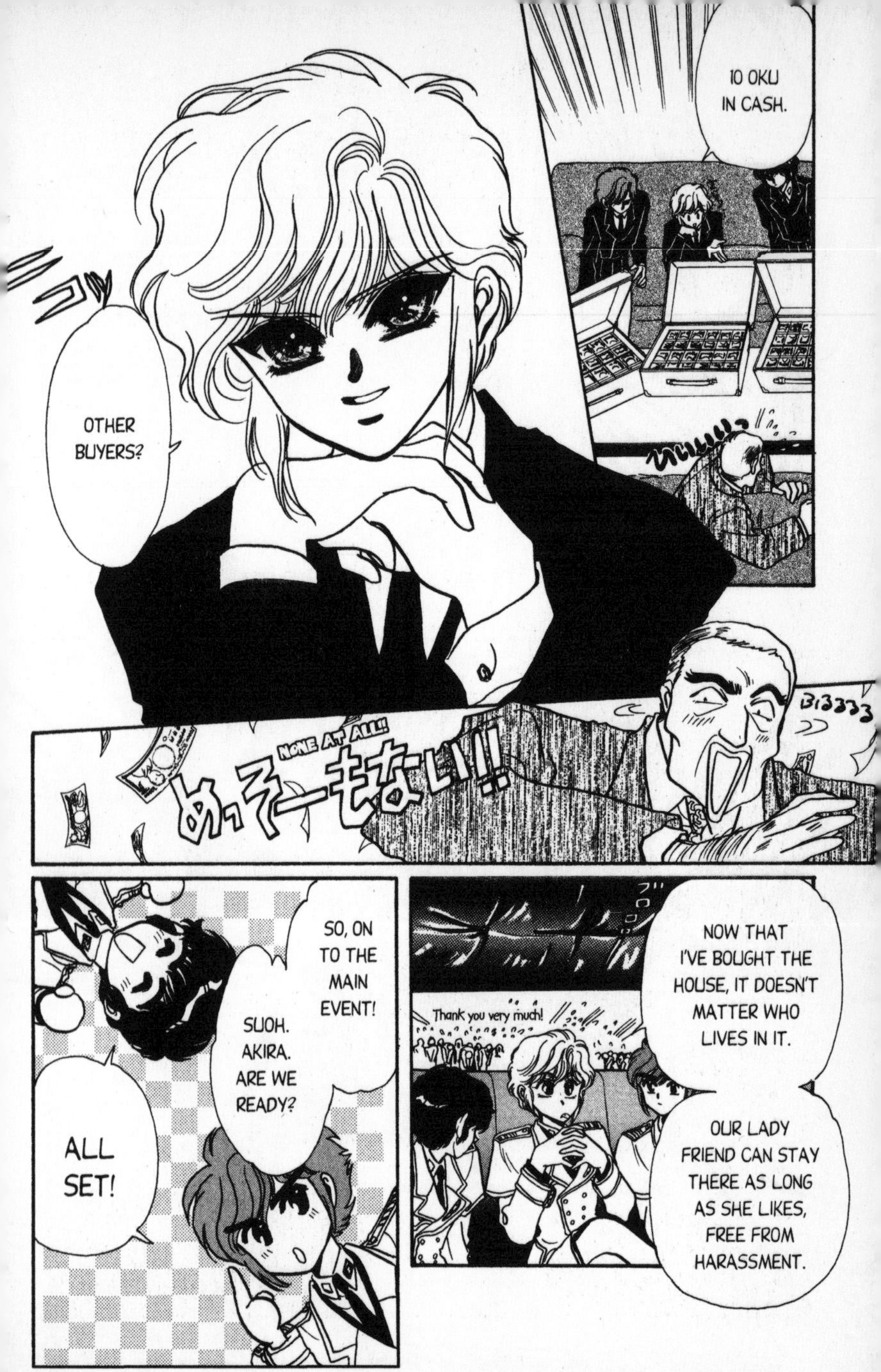
10 OKU IN CASH.
OTHER BUYERS?
NONE AT ALL!
めっそーもない!!
NOW THAT I'VE BOUGHT THE HOUSE, IT DOESN'T MATTER WHO LIVES IN IT.
Thank you very much!
OUR LADY FRIEND CAN STAY THERE AS LONG AS SHE LIKES, FREE FROM HARASSMENT.
SO, ON TO THE MAIN EVENT!
SUOH. AKIRA. ARE WE READY?
ALL SET!

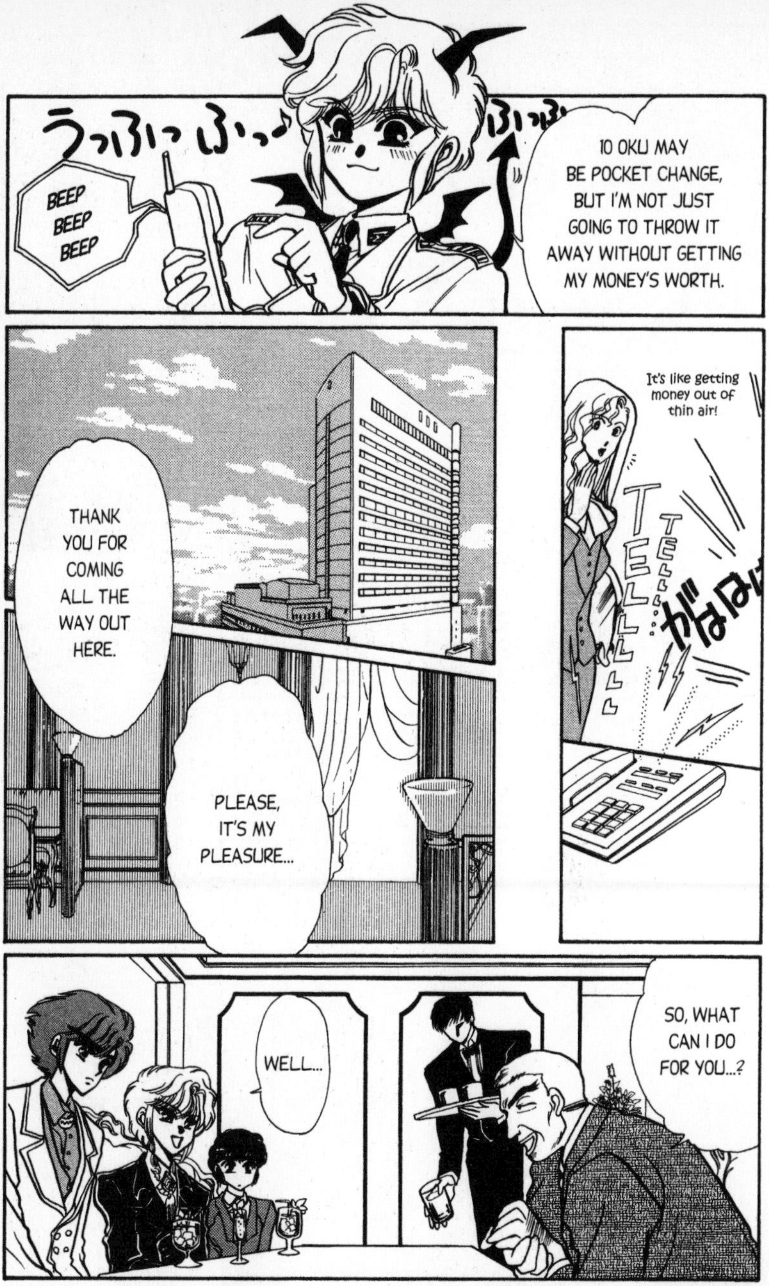
ふっふ
10 OKU MAY BE POCKET CHANGE, BUT I'M NOT JUST GOING TO THROW IT AWAY WITHOUT GETTING MY MONEY'S WORTH.
うっふっ ふっ♪
BEEP BEEP BEEP
It's like getting money out of thin air!
TELL
TELL...
がはは
THANK YOU FOR COMING ALL THE WAY OUT HERE.
PLEASE, IT'S MY PLEASURE...
SO, WHAT CAN I DO FOR YOU...?
WELL...

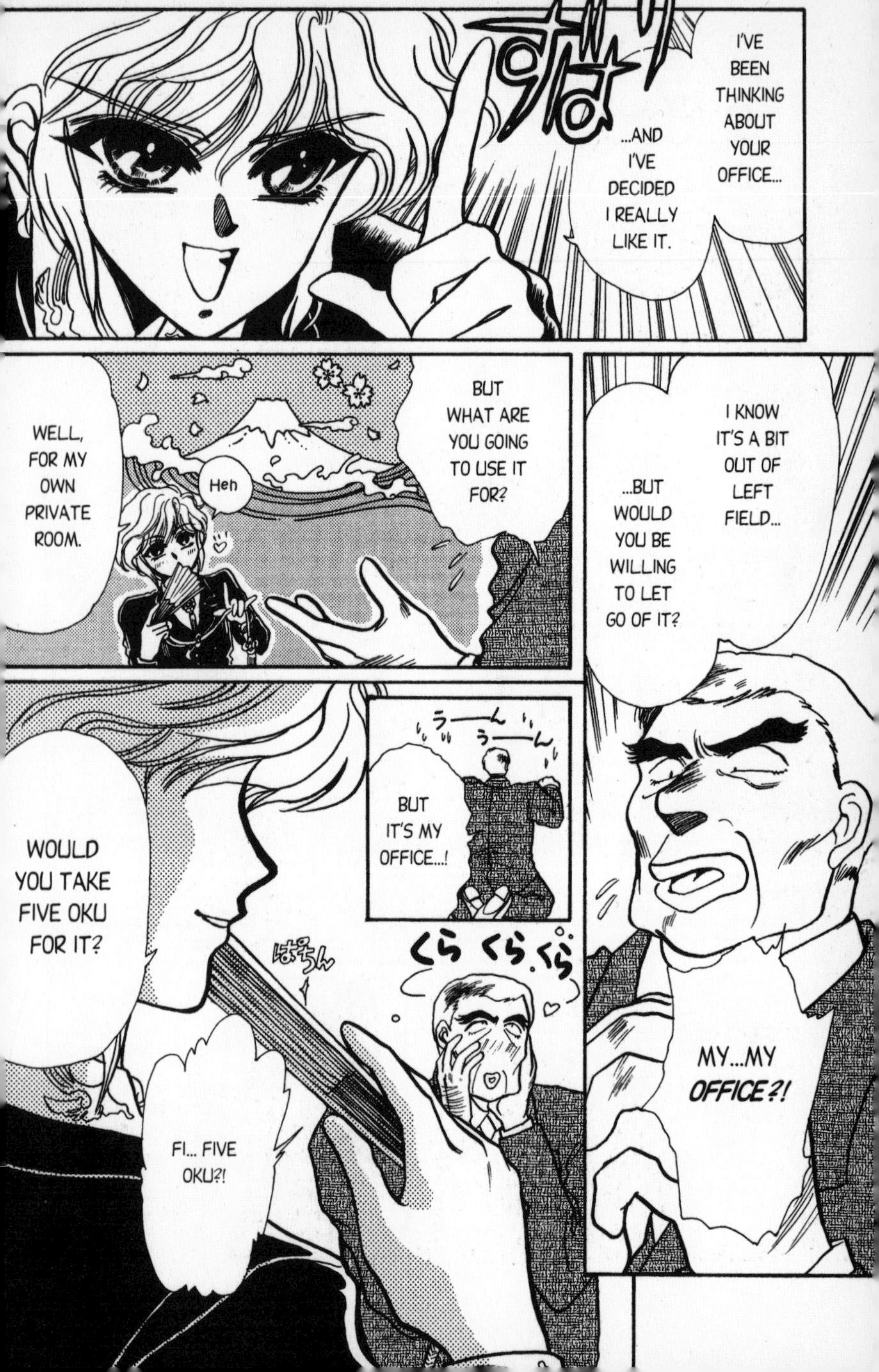
ずばり
I'VE BEEN THINKING ABOUT YOUR OFFICE...
...AND I'VE DECIDED I REALLY LIKE IT.
I KNOW IT'S A BIT OUT OF LEFT FIELD...
...BUT WOULD YOU BE WILLING TO LET GO OF IT?
MY...MY OFFICE?!
BUT WHAT ARE YOU GOING TO USE IT FOR?
Heh
WELL, FOR MY OWN PRIVATE ROOM.
うーん うーん
BUT IT'S MY OFFICE...!
WOULD YOU TAKE FIVE OKU FOR IT?
ぱちん
くら くら くら
FI... FIVE OKU?!

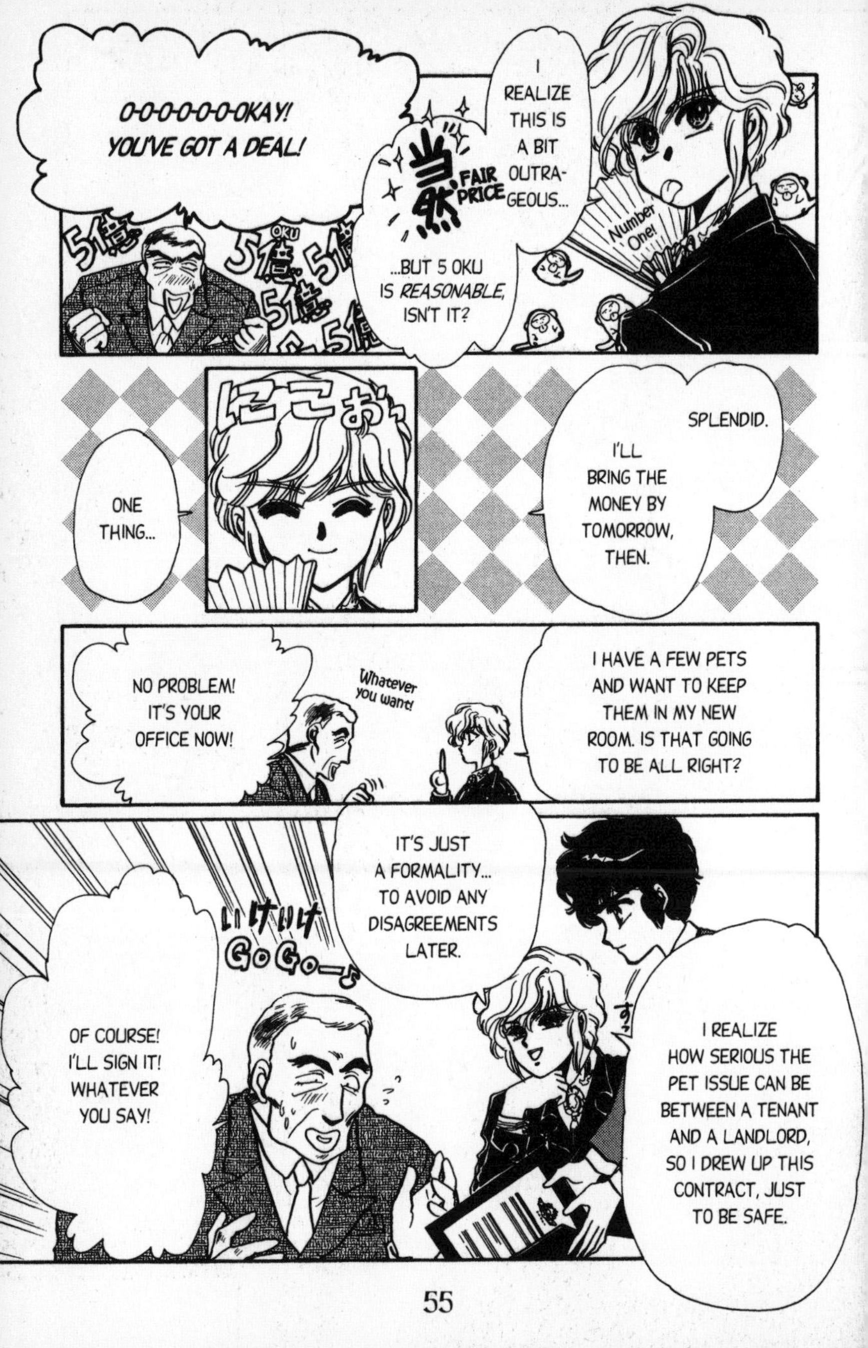
I REALIZE THIS IS A BIT OUTRAGEOUS...
当然 FAIR PRICE
Number One!
...BUT 5 OKU IS *REASONABLE,* ISN'T IT?
5億 OKU
O-O-O-O-O-O-O-OKAY! YOU'VE GOT A DEAL!
SPLENDID.
I'LL BRING THE MONEY BY TOMORROW, THEN.
ONE THING...
I HAVE A FEW PETS AND WANT TO KEEP THEM IN MY NEW ROOM. IS THAT GOING TO BE ALL RIGHT?
Whatever you want!
NO PROBLEM! IT'S YOUR OFFICE NOW!
I REALIZE HOW SERIOUS THE PET ISSUE CAN BE BETWEEN A TENANT AND A LANDLORD, SO I DREW UP THIS CONTRACT, JUST TO BE SAFE.
IT'S JUST A FORMALITY... TO AVOID ANY DISAGREEMENTS LATER.
いけいけ GoGo—♪
OF COURSE! I'LL SIGN IT! WHATEVER YOU SAY!

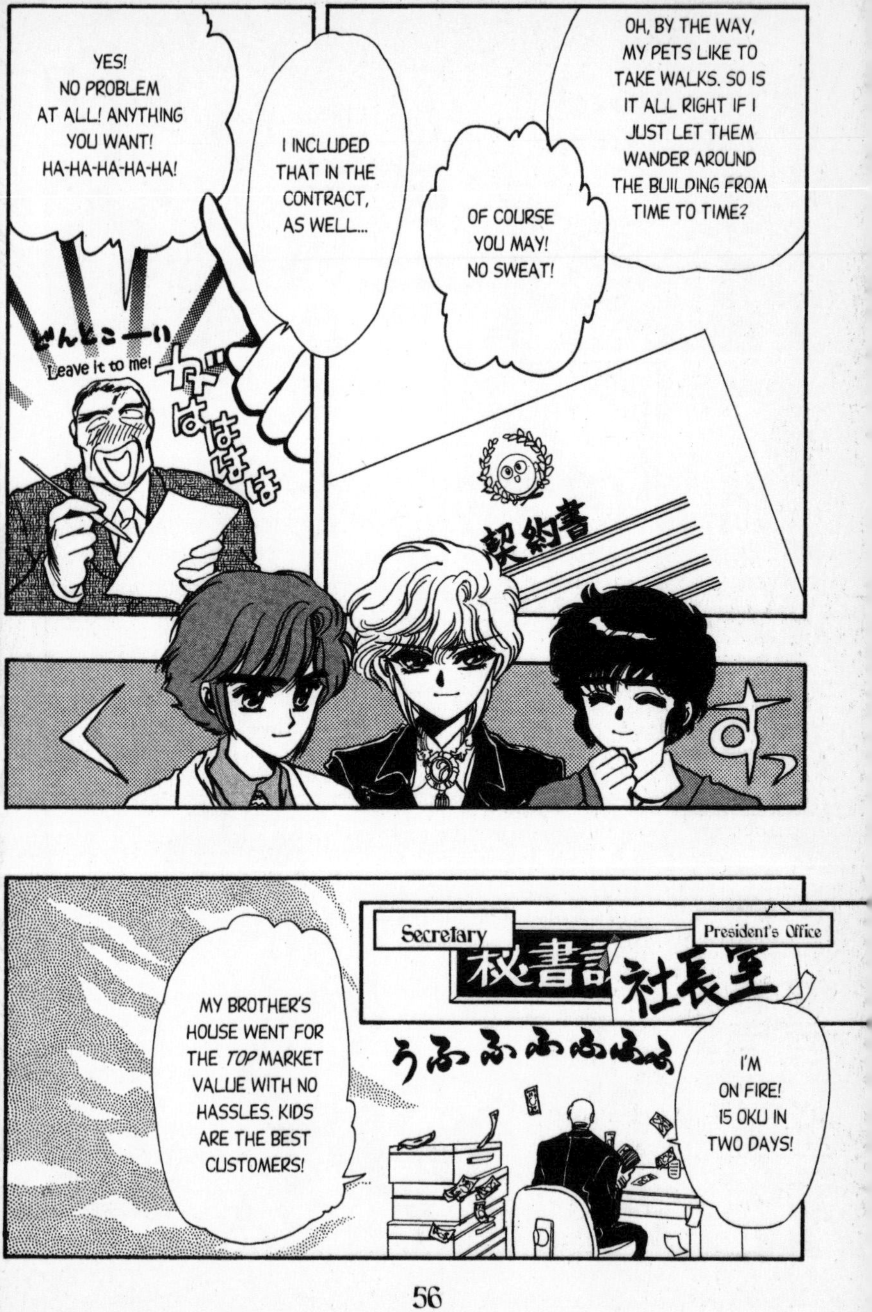
OH, BY THE WAY, MY PETS LIKE TO TAKE WALKS. SO IS IT ALL RIGHT IF I JUST LET THEM WANDER AROUND THE BUILDING FROM TIME TO TIME?
OF COURSE YOU MAY! NO SWEAT!
I INCLUDED THAT IN THE CONTRACT, AS WELL...
契約書
YES! NO PROBLEM AT ALL! ANYTHING YOU WANT! HA-HA-HA-HA-HA!
どんとこーい
Leave it to me!
がはははは
すっ
Secretary
President's Office
社長室
I'M ON FIRE! 15 OKU IN TWO DAYS!
うふふふふふ
MY BROTHER'S HOUSE WENT FOR THE *TOP* MARKET VALUE WITH NO HASSLES. KIDS ARE THE BEST CUSTOMERS!

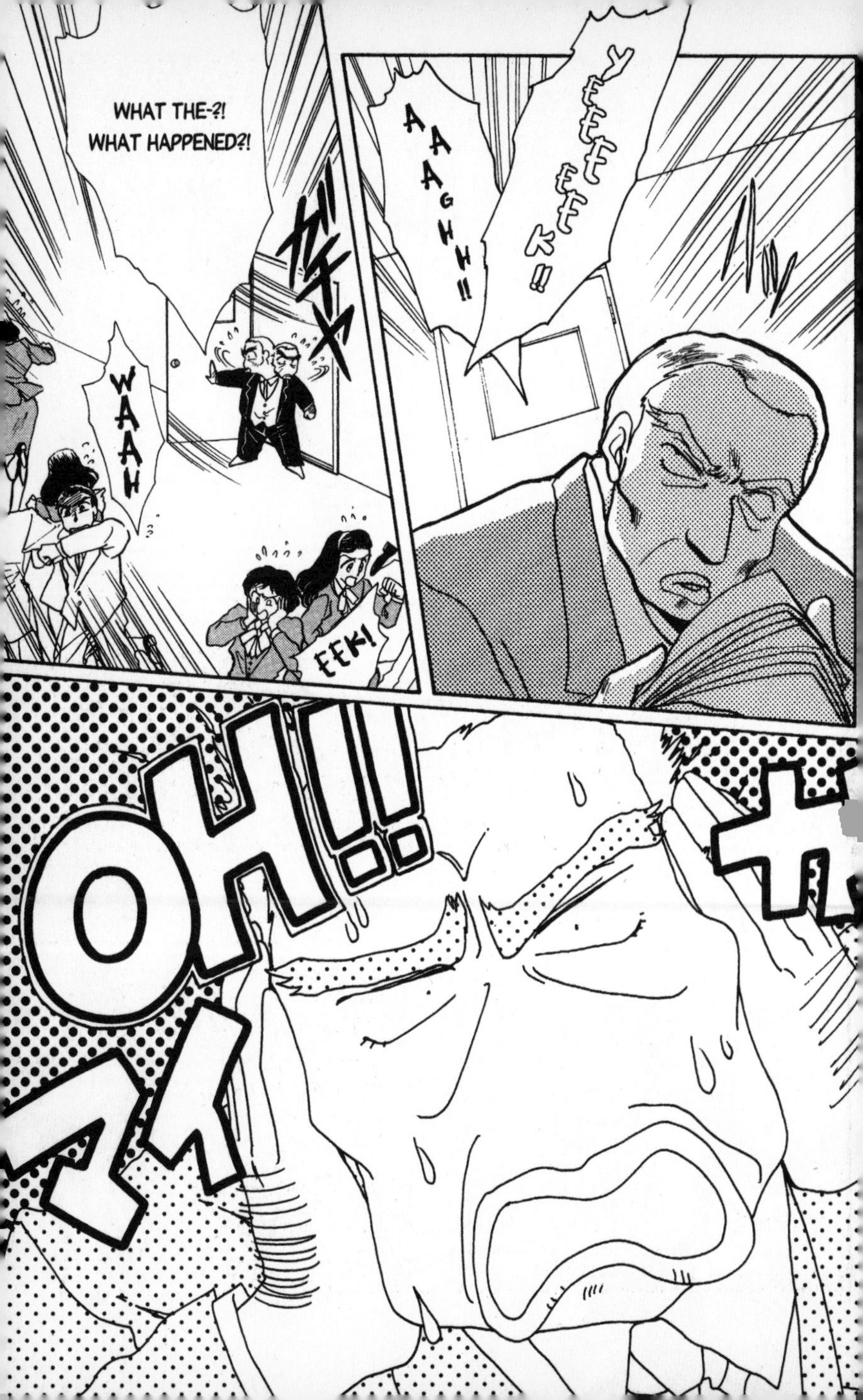
YEEEEEK!!
AAAGHH!!
WHAT THE-?! WHAT HAPPENED?!
WAAAH
EEK!
OH!!

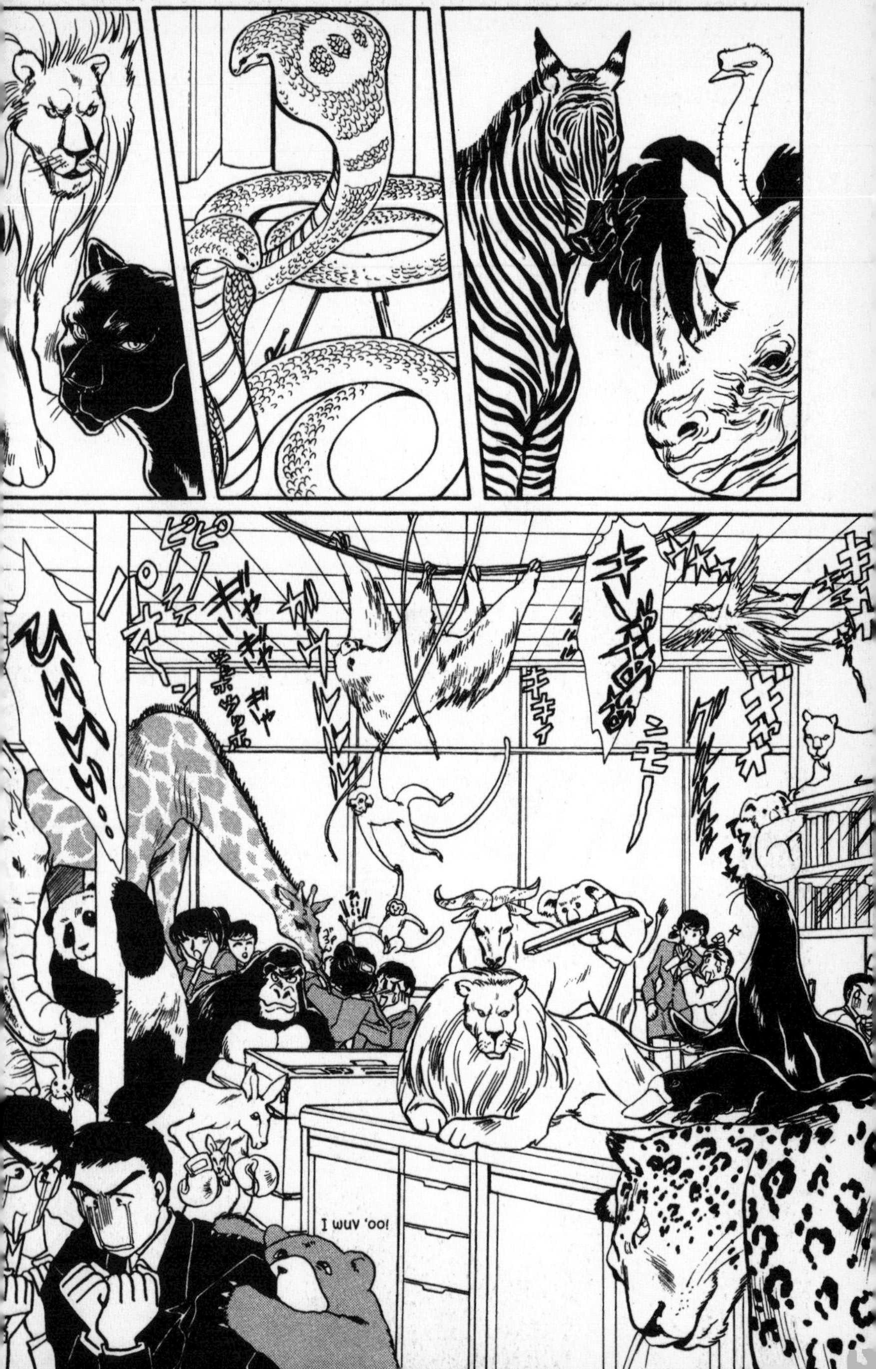
I wuv 'oo!

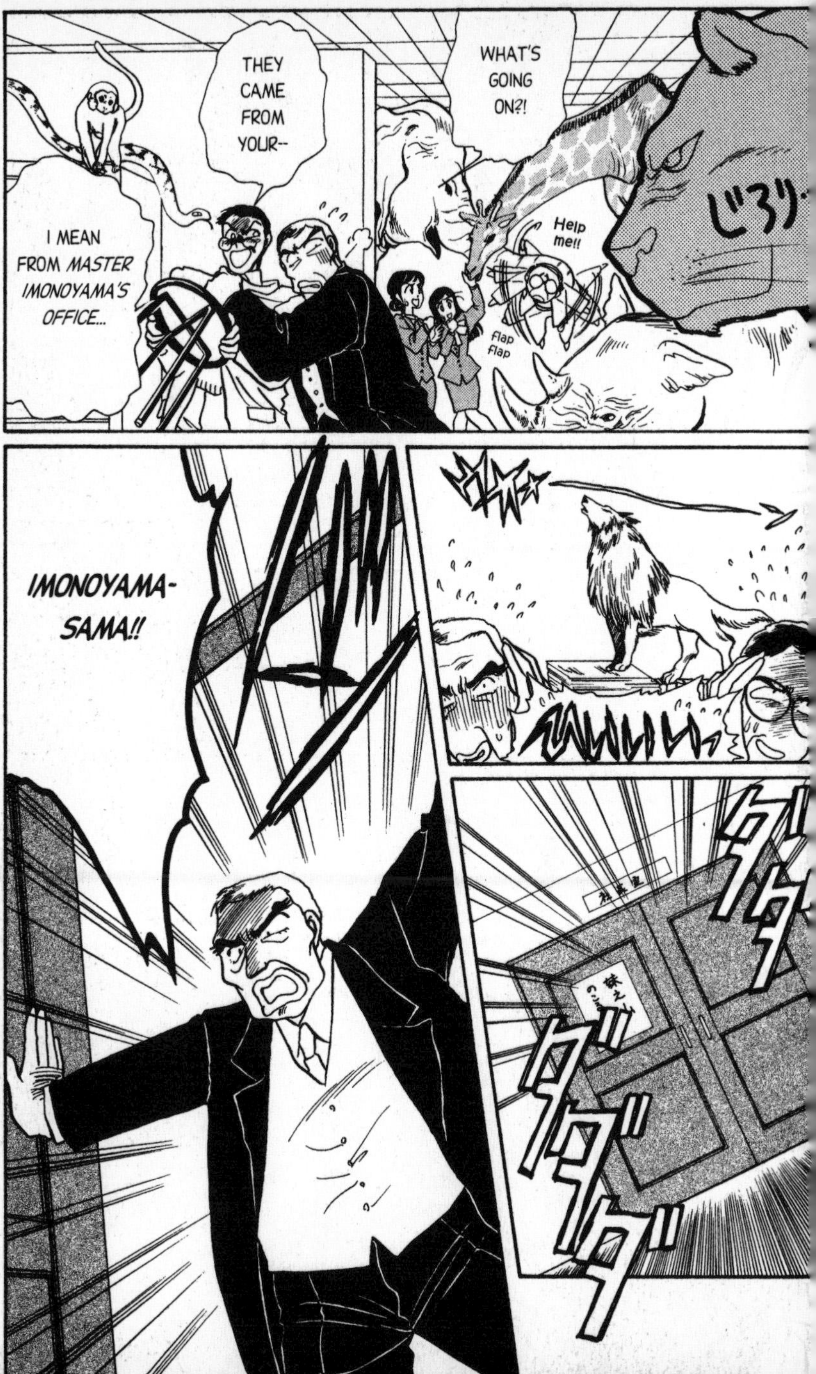
じろり
WHAT'S GOING ON?!
Help me!!
Flap Flap
THEY CAME FROM YOUR--
I MEAN FROM MASTER IMONOYAMA'S OFFICE...
IMONOYAMA-SAMA!!

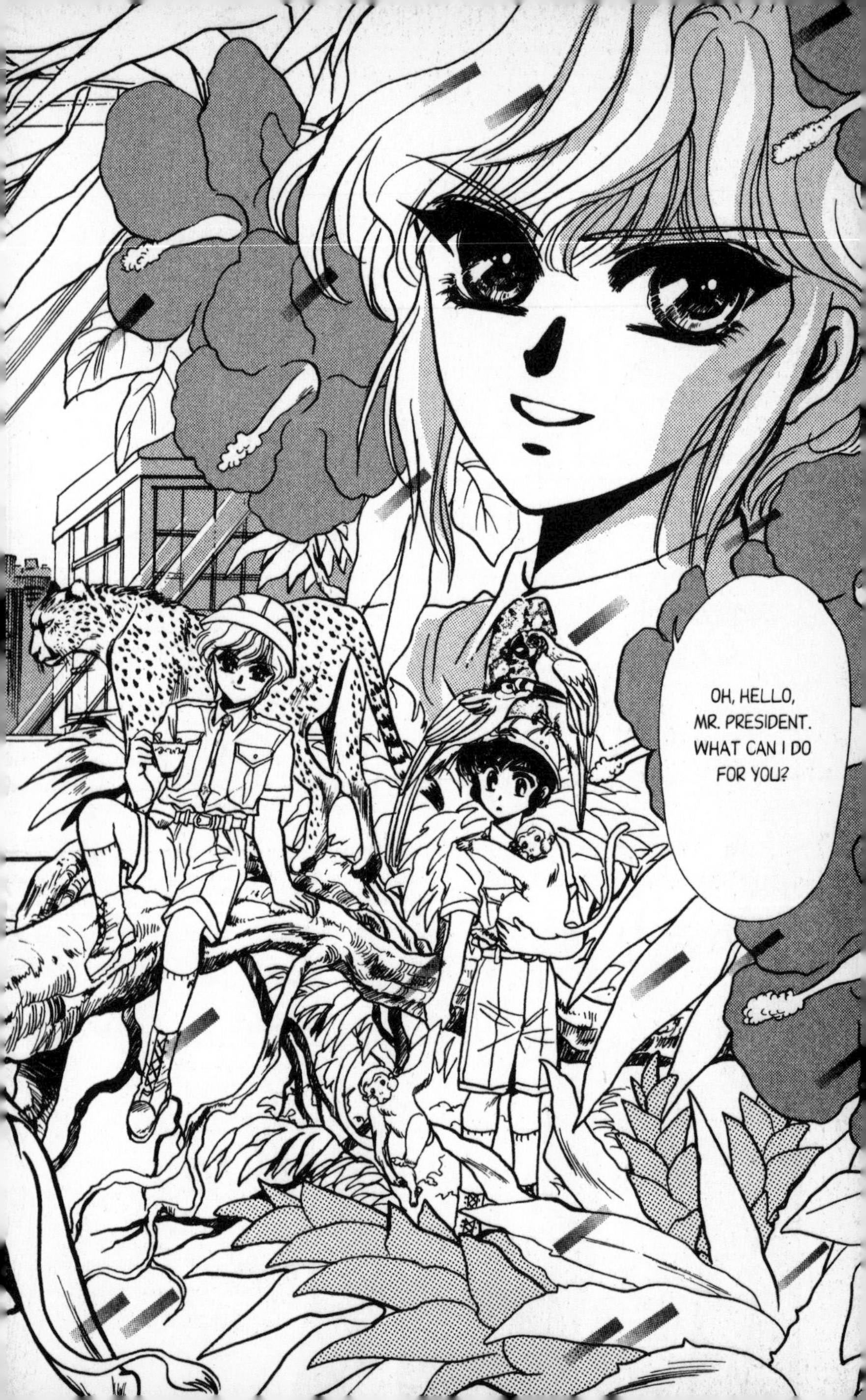
OH, HELLO, MR. PRESIDENT. WHAT CAN I DO FOR YOU?

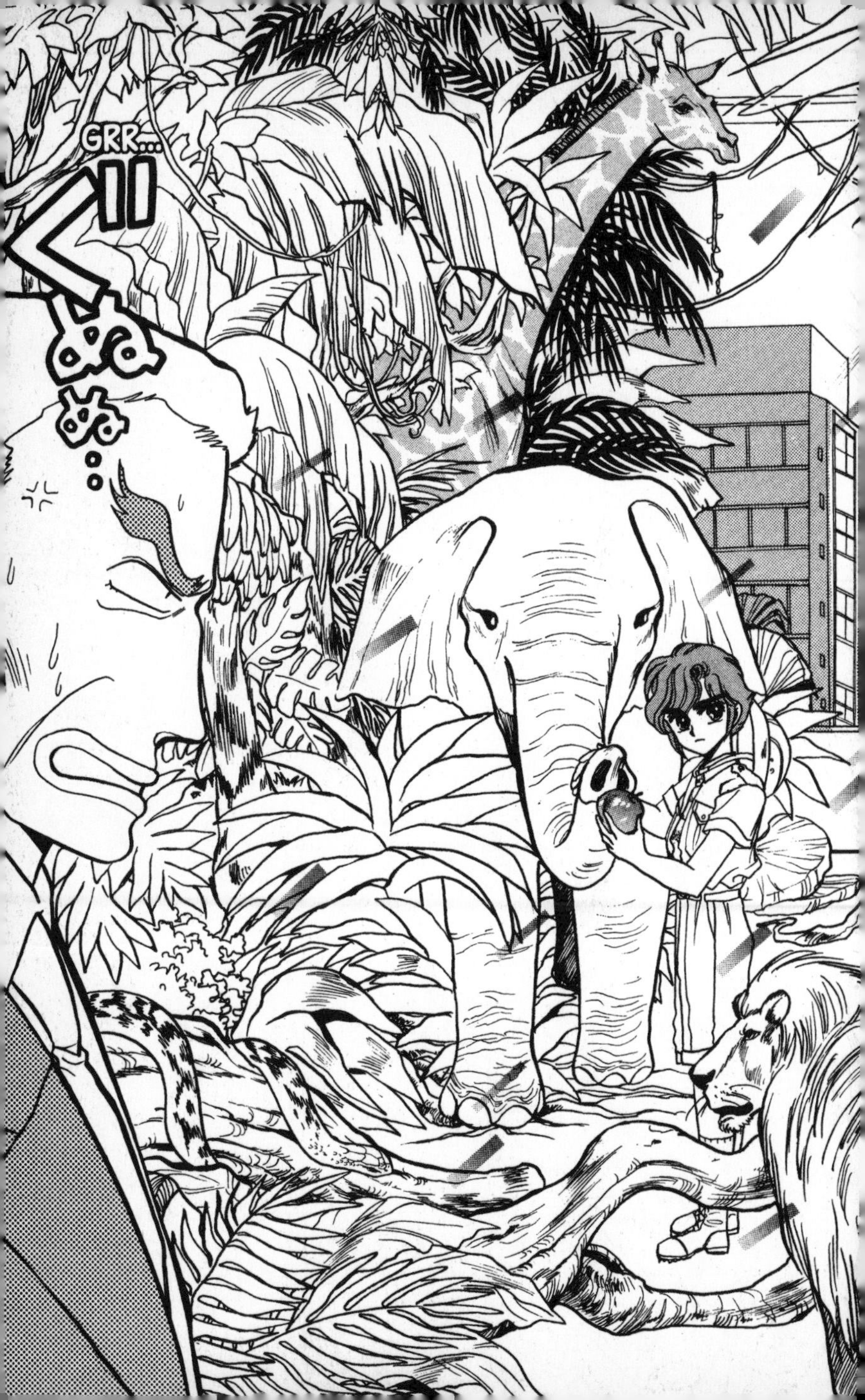
GRR...
くぬぬ…

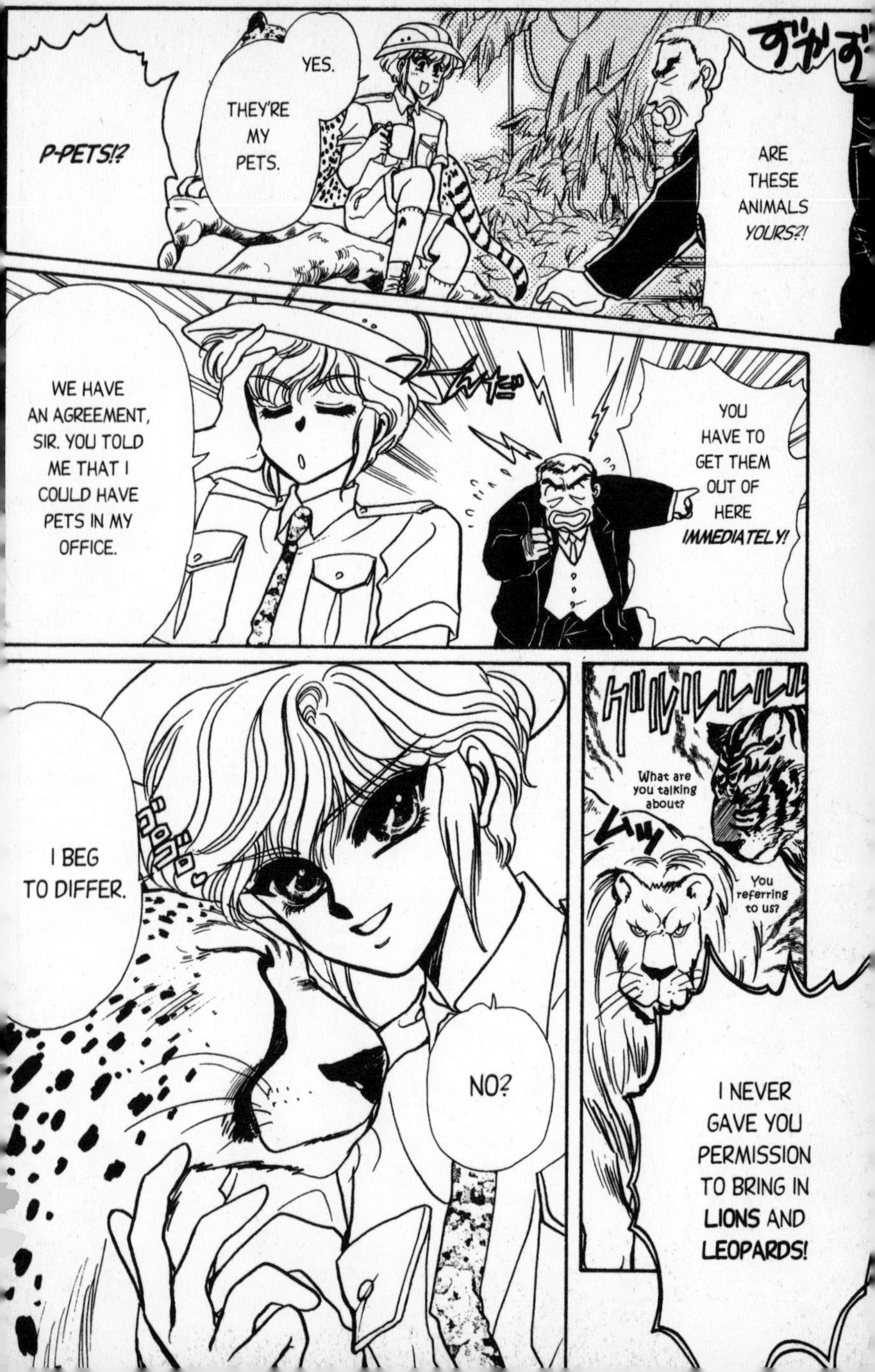
ずかず
ARE THESE ANIMALS YOURS?!
YES.
THEY'RE MY PETS.
P-PETS!?
YOU HAVE TO GET THEM OUT OF HERE IMMEDIATELY!
WE HAVE AN AGREEMENT, SIR. YOU TOLD ME THAT I COULD HAVE PETS IN MY OFFICE.
What are you talking about?
ムッ
You referring to us?
I NEVER GAVE YOU PERMISSION TO BRING IN LIONS AND LEOPARDS!
I BEG TO DIFFER.
NO?

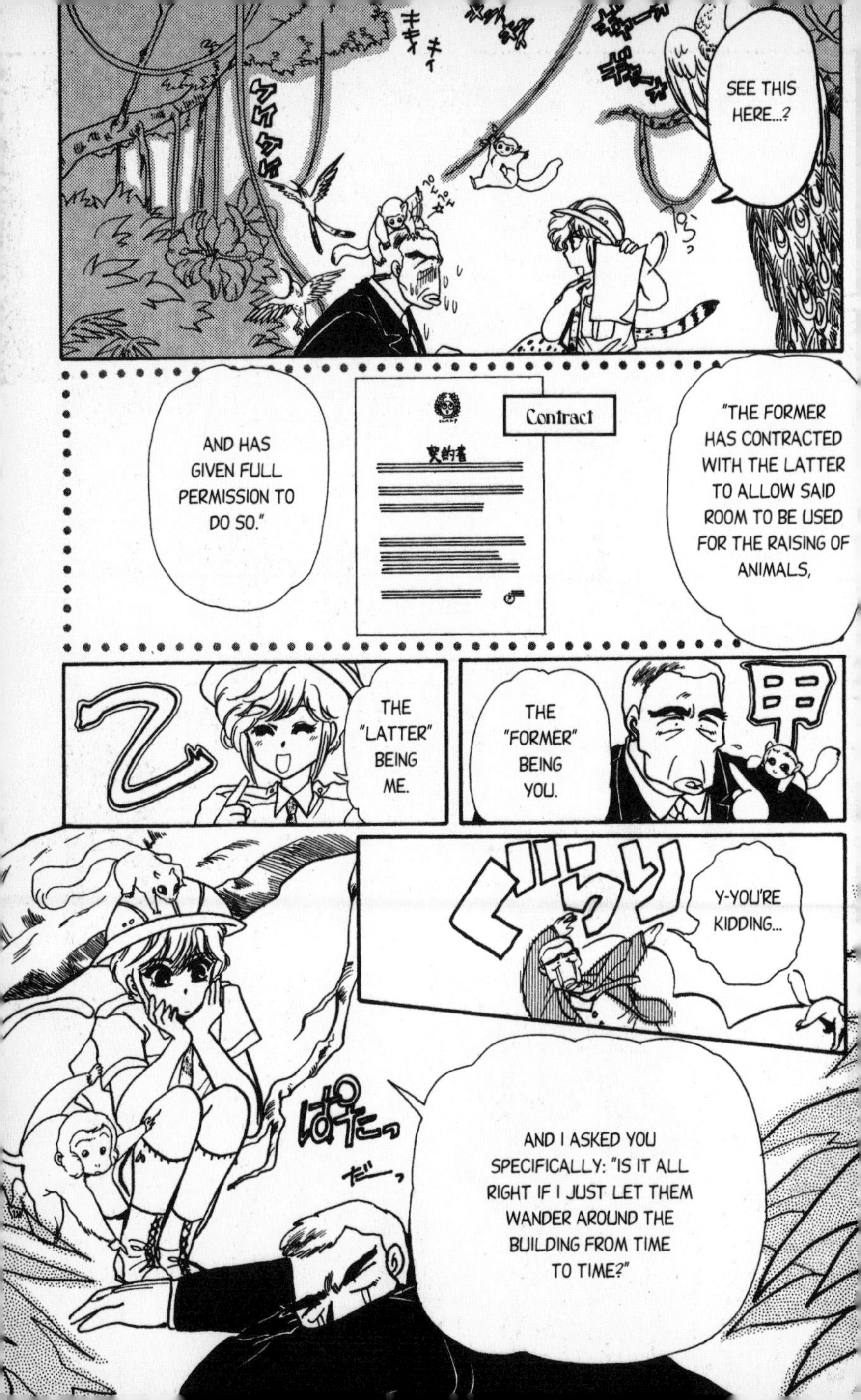
SEE THIS HERE...?
"THE FORMER HAS CONTRACTED WITH THE LATTER TO ALLOW SAID ROOM TO BE USED FOR THE RAISING OF ANIMALS,
Contract
契約書
AND HAS GIVEN FULL PERMISSION TO DO SO."
甲
THE "FORMER" BEING YOU.
乙
THE "LATTER" BEING ME.
ぐらり
Y-YOU'RE KIDDING...
ぱたっ
だっ
AND I ASKED YOU SPECIFICALLY: "IS IT ALL RIGHT IF I JUST LET THEM WANDER AROUND THE BUILDING FROM TIME TO TIME?"

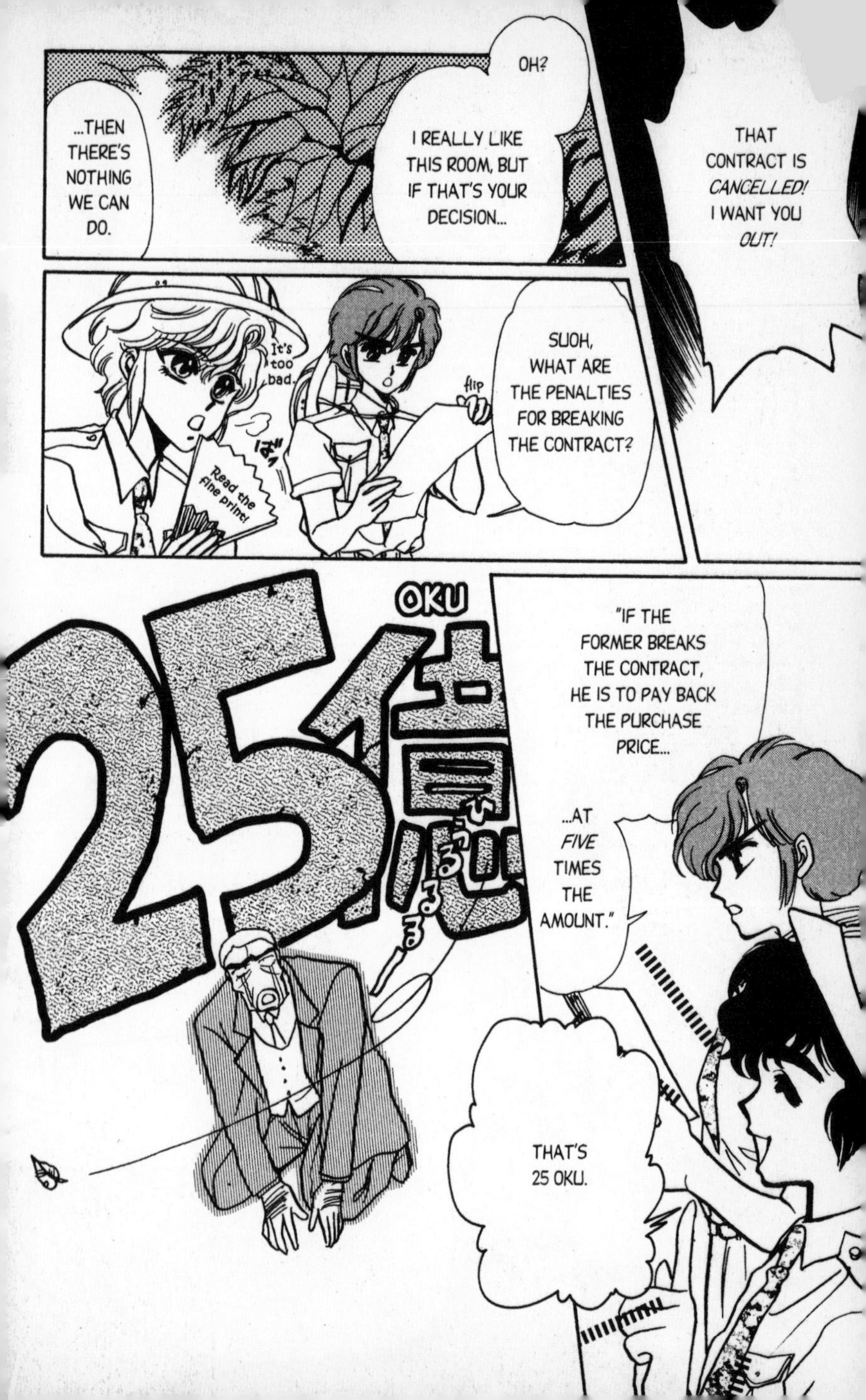
THAT CONTRACT IS *CANCELLED!* I WANT YOU *OUT!*
OH?
I REALLY LIKE THIS ROOM, BUT IF THAT'S YOUR DECISION...
...THEN THERE'S NOTHING WE CAN DO.
SUOH, WHAT ARE THE PENALTIES FOR BREAKING THE CONTRACT?
flip
It's too bad.
Read the fine print!
"IF THE FORMER BREAKS THE CONTRACT, HE IS TO PAY BACK THE PURCHASE PRICE...
...AT *FIVE* TIMES THE AMOUNT."
THAT'S 25 OKU.
OKU
25億

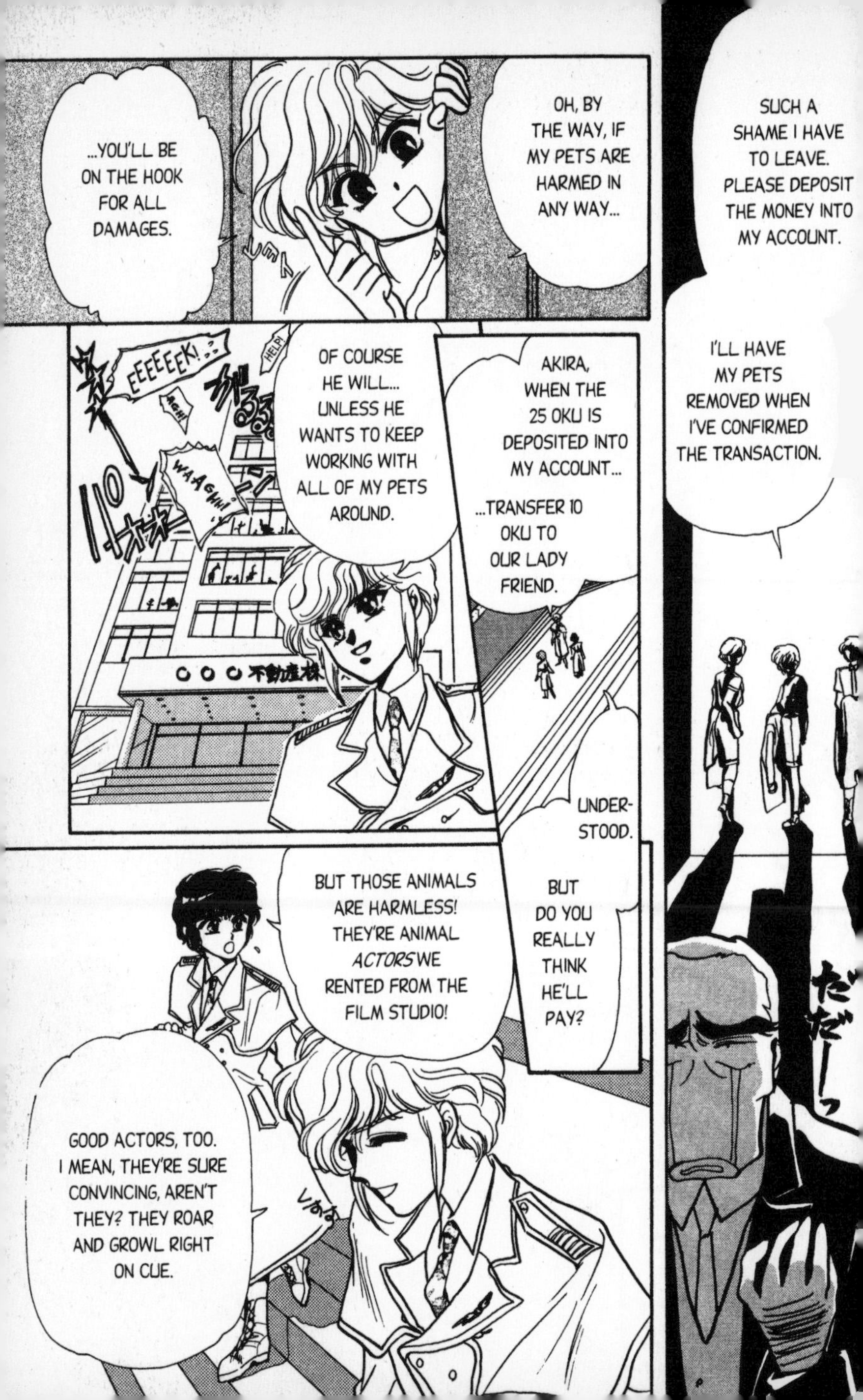
SUCH A SHAME I HAVE TO LEAVE. PLEASE DEPOSIT THE MONEY INTO MY ACCOUNT.
I'LL HAVE MY PETS REMOVED WHEN I'VE CONFIRMED THE TRANSACTION.
OH, BY THE WAY, IF MY PETS ARE HARMED IN ANY WAY...
...YOU'LL BE ON THE HOOK FOR ALL DAMAGES.
AKIRA, WHEN THE 25 OKU IS DEPOSITED INTO MY ACCOUNT...
...TRANSFER 10 OKU TO OUR LADY FRIEND.
UNDER-STOOD.
BUT DO YOU REALLY THINK HE'LL PAY?
OF COURSE HE WILL... UNLESS HE WANTS TO KEEP WORKING WITH ALL OF MY PETS AROUND.
HELP!
EEEEEEK!
WAAGH!
BUT THOSE ANIMALS ARE HARMLESS! THEY'RE ANIMAL *ACTORS* WE RENTED FROM THE FILM STUDIO!
GOOD ACTORS, TOO. I MEAN, THEY'RE SURE CONVINCING, AREN'T THEY? THEY ROAR AND GROWL RIGHT ON CUE.

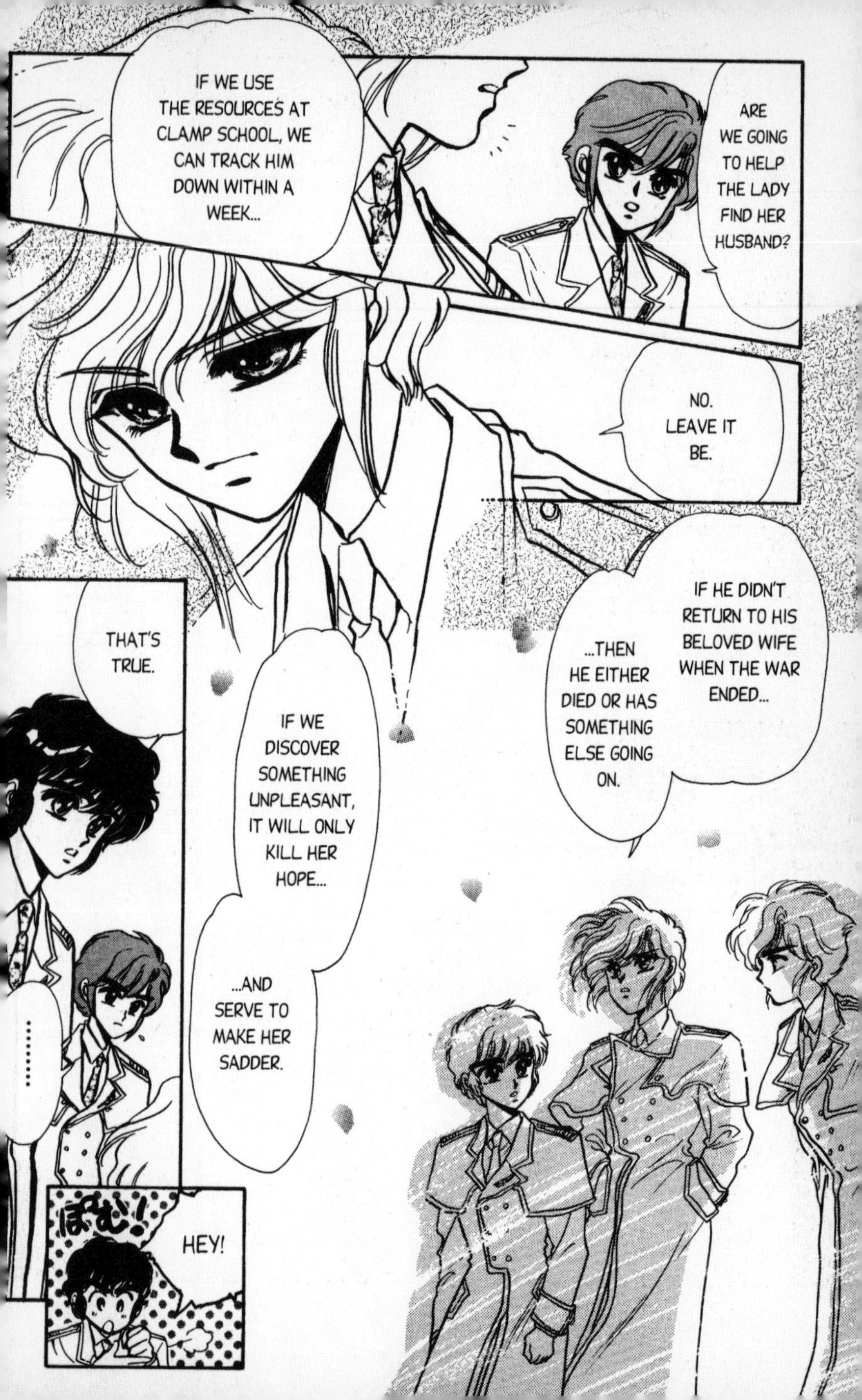

ARE WE GOING TO HELP THE LADY FIND HER HUSBAND?
IF WE USE THE RESOURCES AT CLAMP SCHOOL, WE CAN TRACK HIM DOWN WITHIN A WEEK...
NO. LEAVE IT BE.
IF HE DIDN'T RETURN TO HIS BELOVED WIFE WHEN THE WAR ENDED...
...THEN HE EITHER DIED OR HAS SOMETHING ELSE GOING ON.
IF WE DISCOVER SOMETHING UNPLEASANT, IT WILL ONLY KILL HER HOPE...
...AND SERVE TO MAKE HER SADDER.
THAT'S TRUE.
....
ぽむ!
HEY!

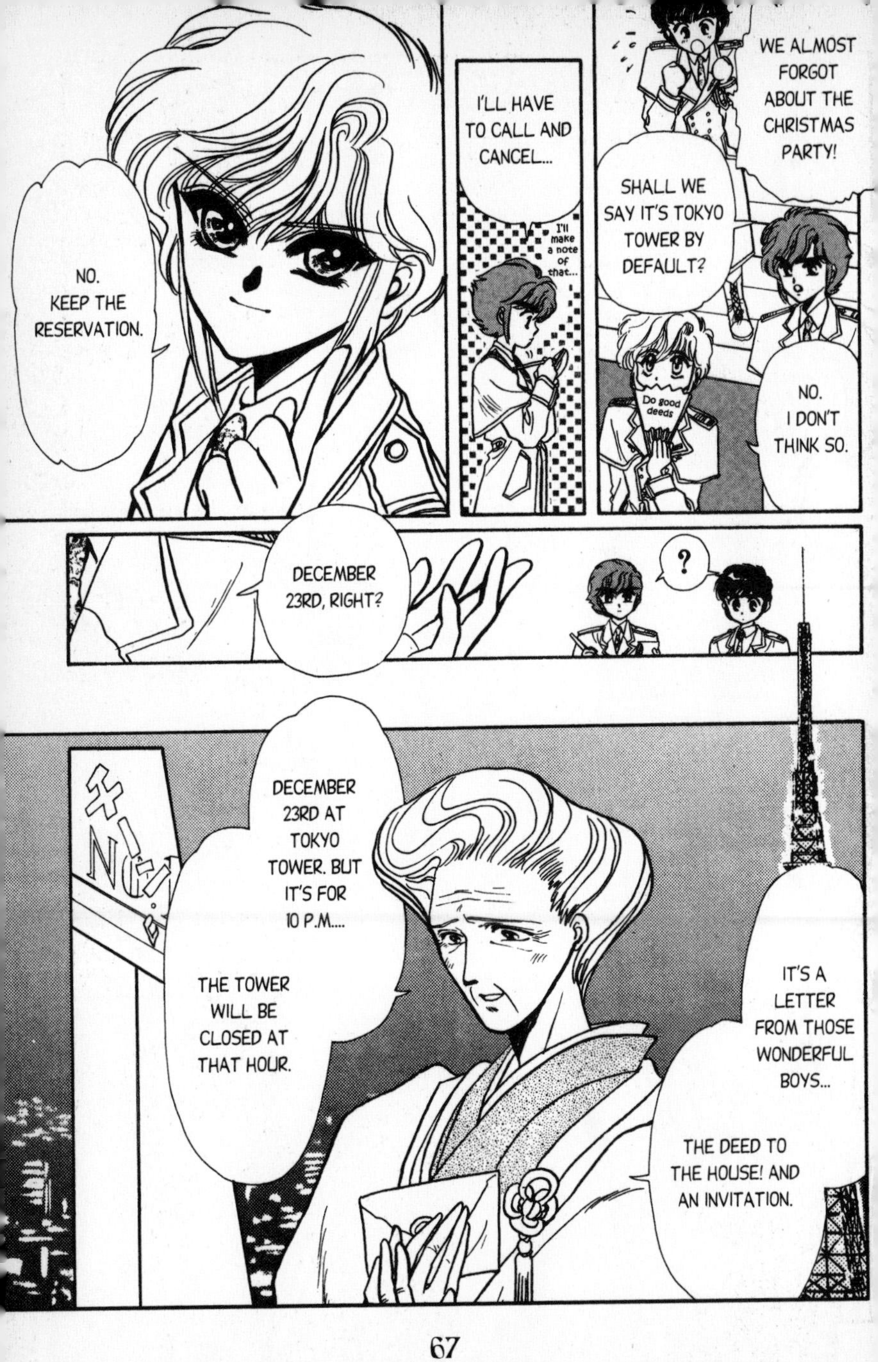
WE ALMOST FORGOT ABOUT THE CHRISTMAS PARTY!
SHALL WE SAY IT'S TOKYO TOWER BY DEFAULT?
Do good deeds
NO. I DON'T THINK SO.
I'LL HAVE TO CALL AND CANCEL...
I'll make a note of that...
NO. KEEP THE RESERVATION.
?
DECEMBER 23RD, RIGHT?
IT'S A LETTER FROM THOSE WONDERFUL BOYS...
THE DEED TO THE HOUSE! AND AN INVITATION.
DECEMBER 23RD AT TOKYO TOWER. BUT IT'S FOR 10 P.M....
THE TOWER WILL BE CLOSED AT THAT HOUR.

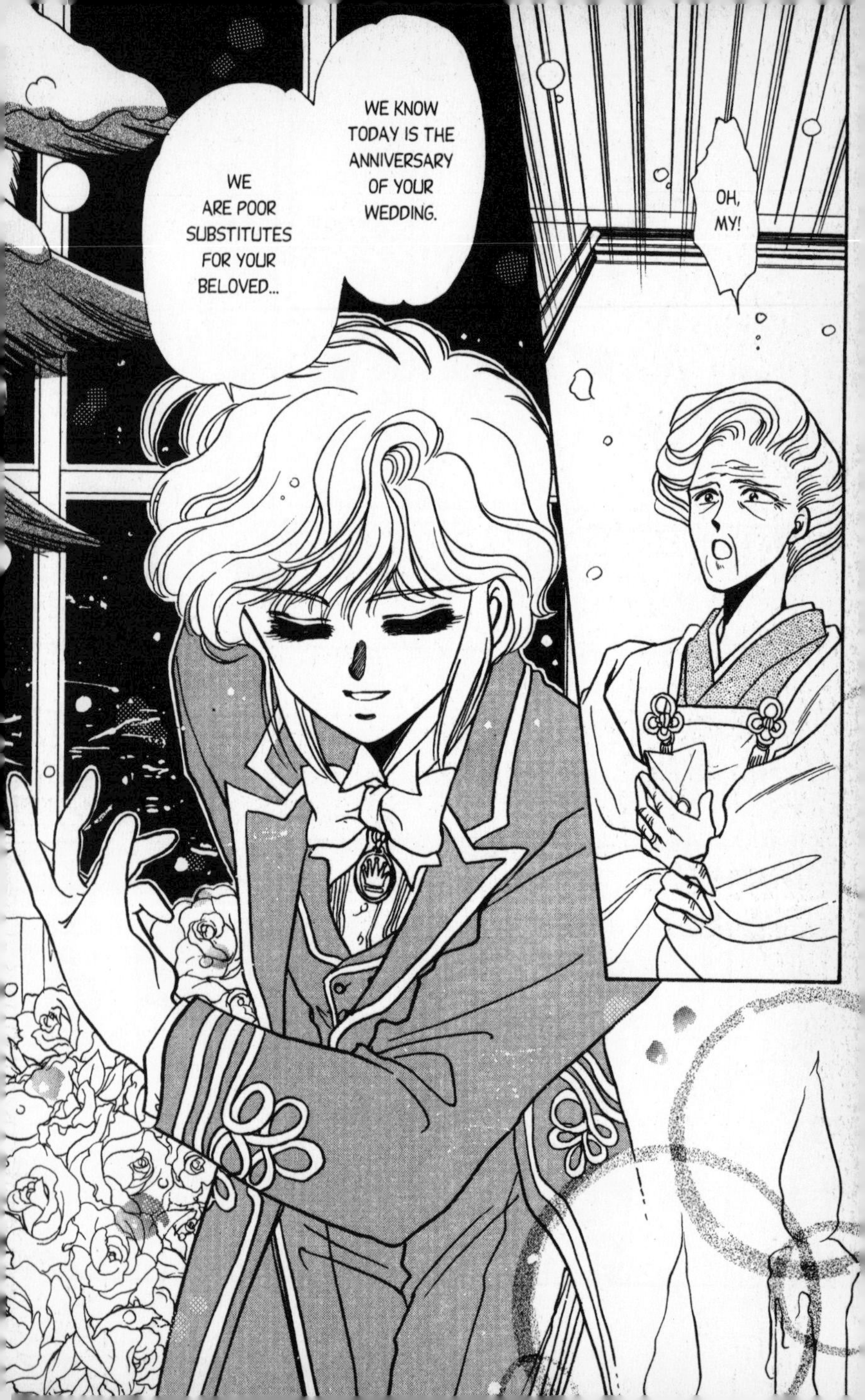
OH, MY!
WE KNOW TODAY IS THE ANNIVERSARY OF YOUR WEDDING.
WE ARE POOR SUBSTITUTES FOR YOUR BELOVED...

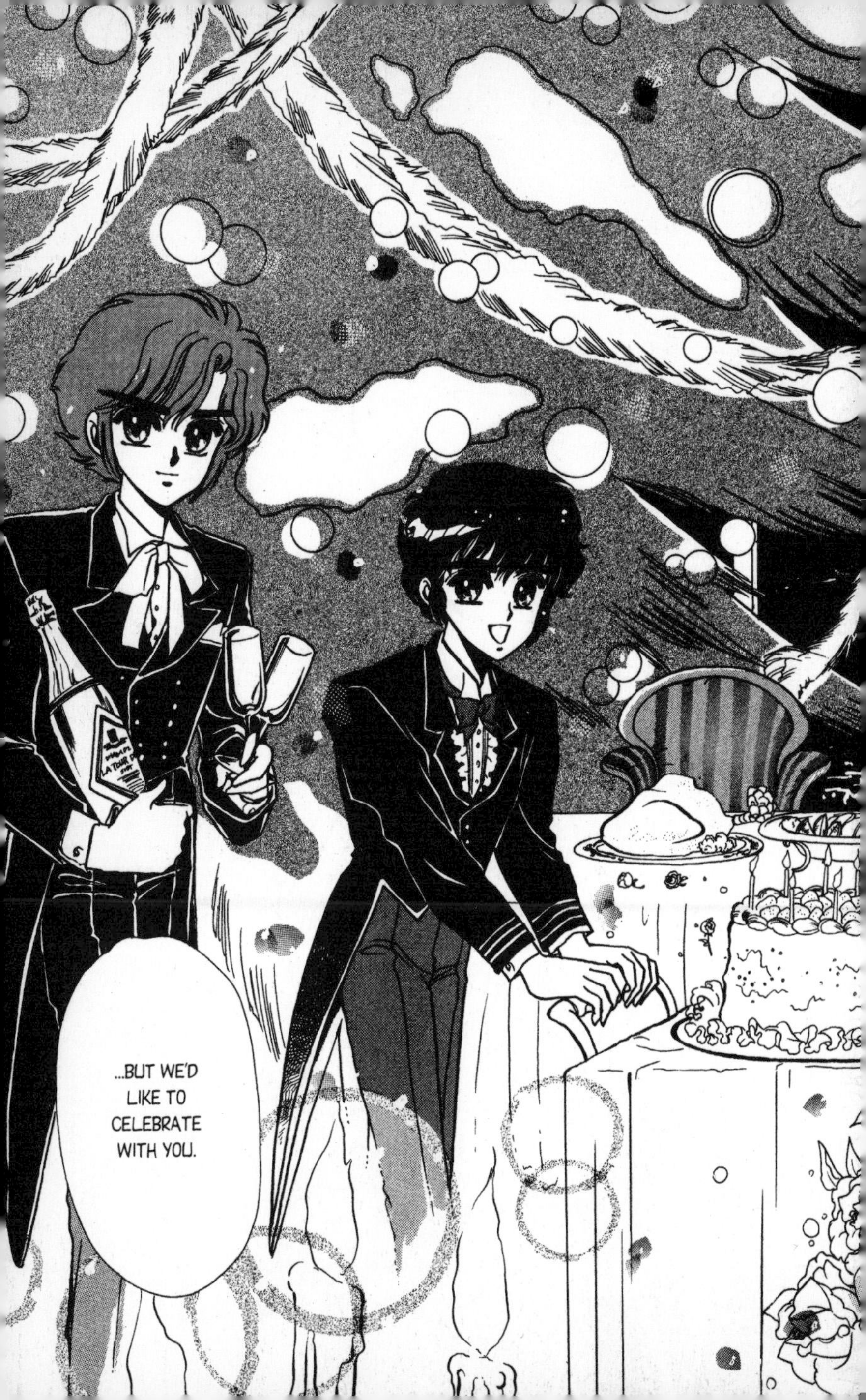
...BUT WE'D LIKE TO CELEBRATE WITH YOU.

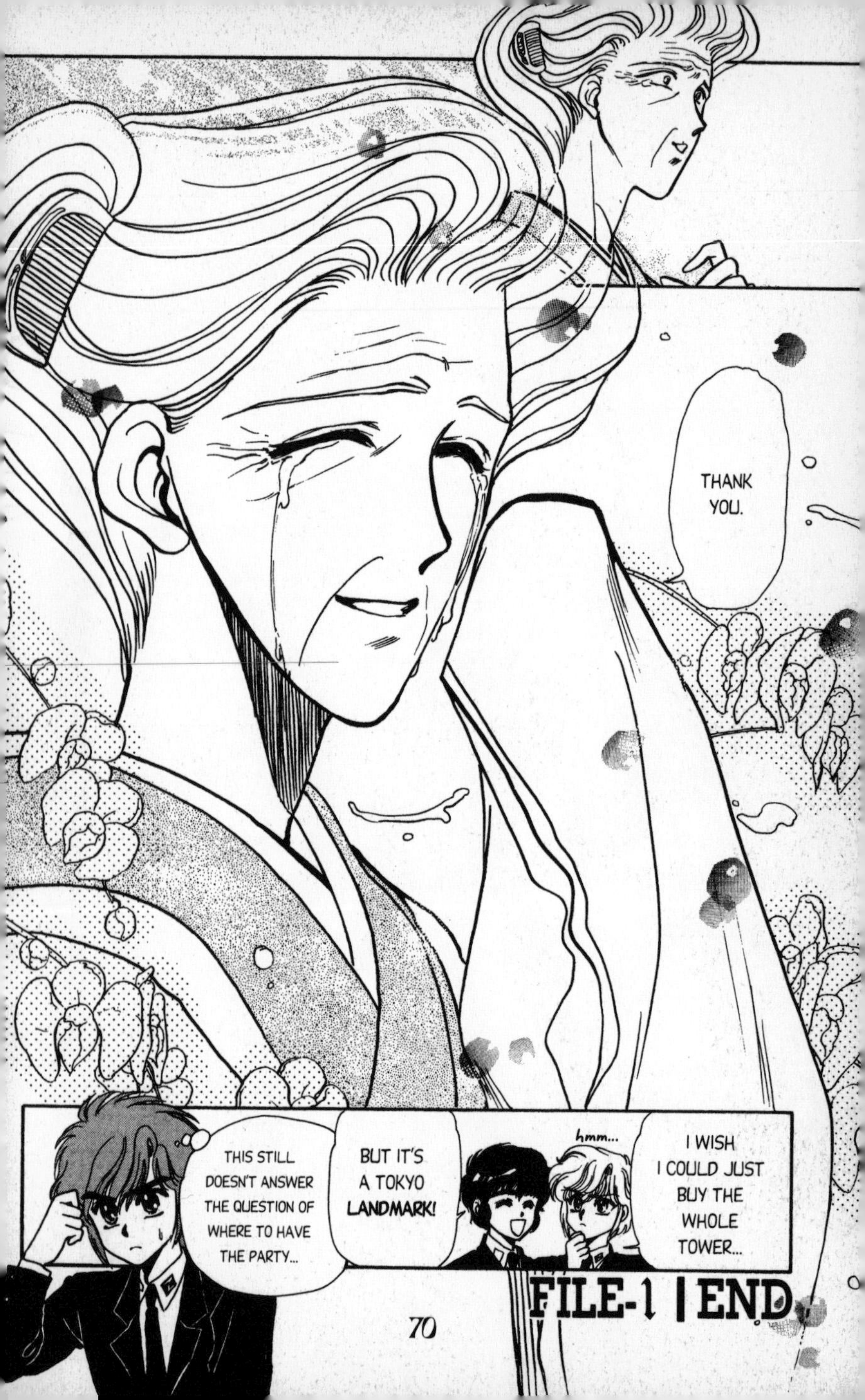
THANK YOU.
I WISH I COULD JUST BUY THE WHOLE TOWER...
hmm...
BUT IT'S A TOKYO LANDMARK!
THIS STILL DOESN'T ANSWER THE QUESTION OF WHERE TO HAVE THE PARTY...
FILE-1 | END

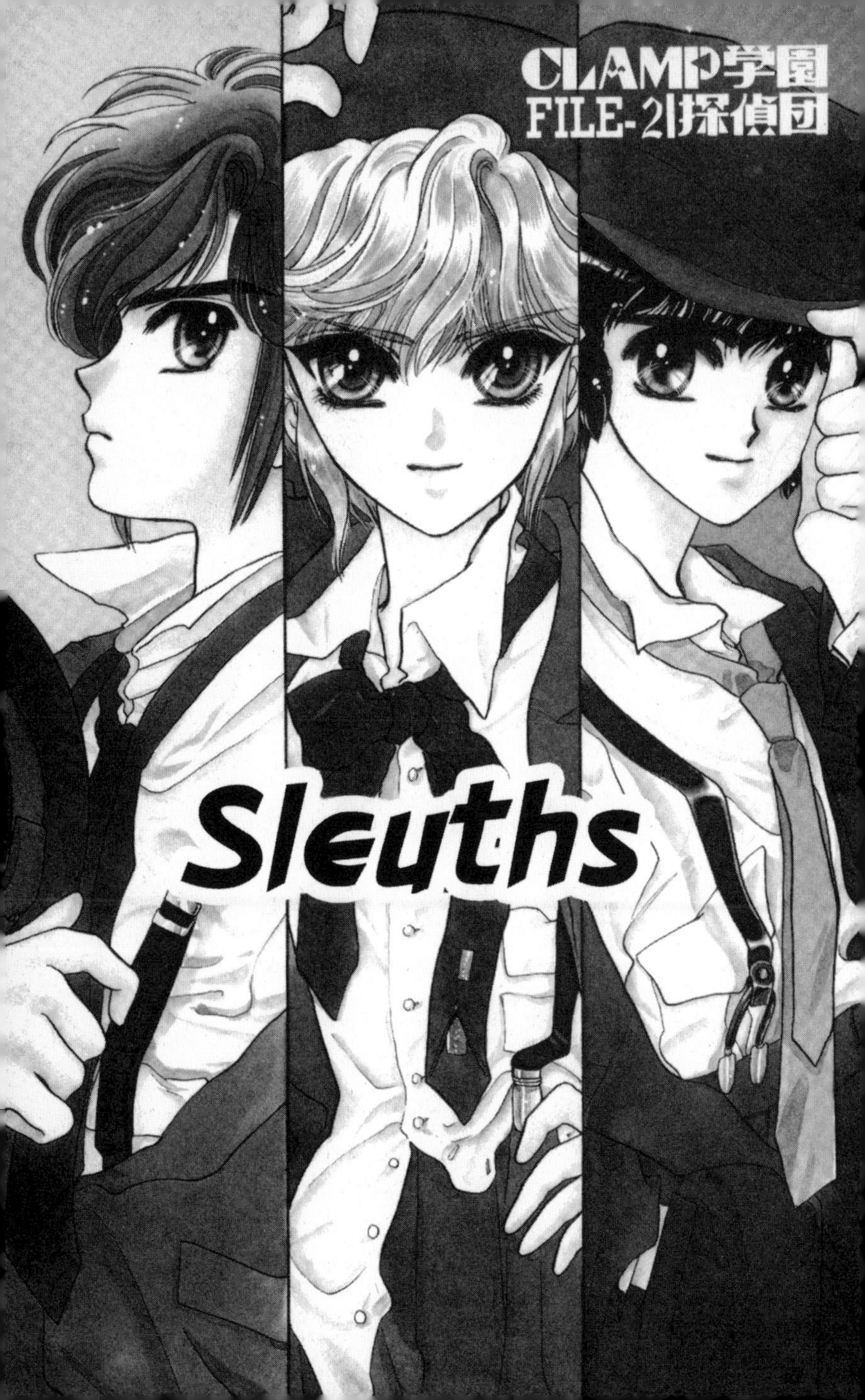
CLAMP學園
FILE-2 探偵団
Sleuths

CLAMP学園
探偵団

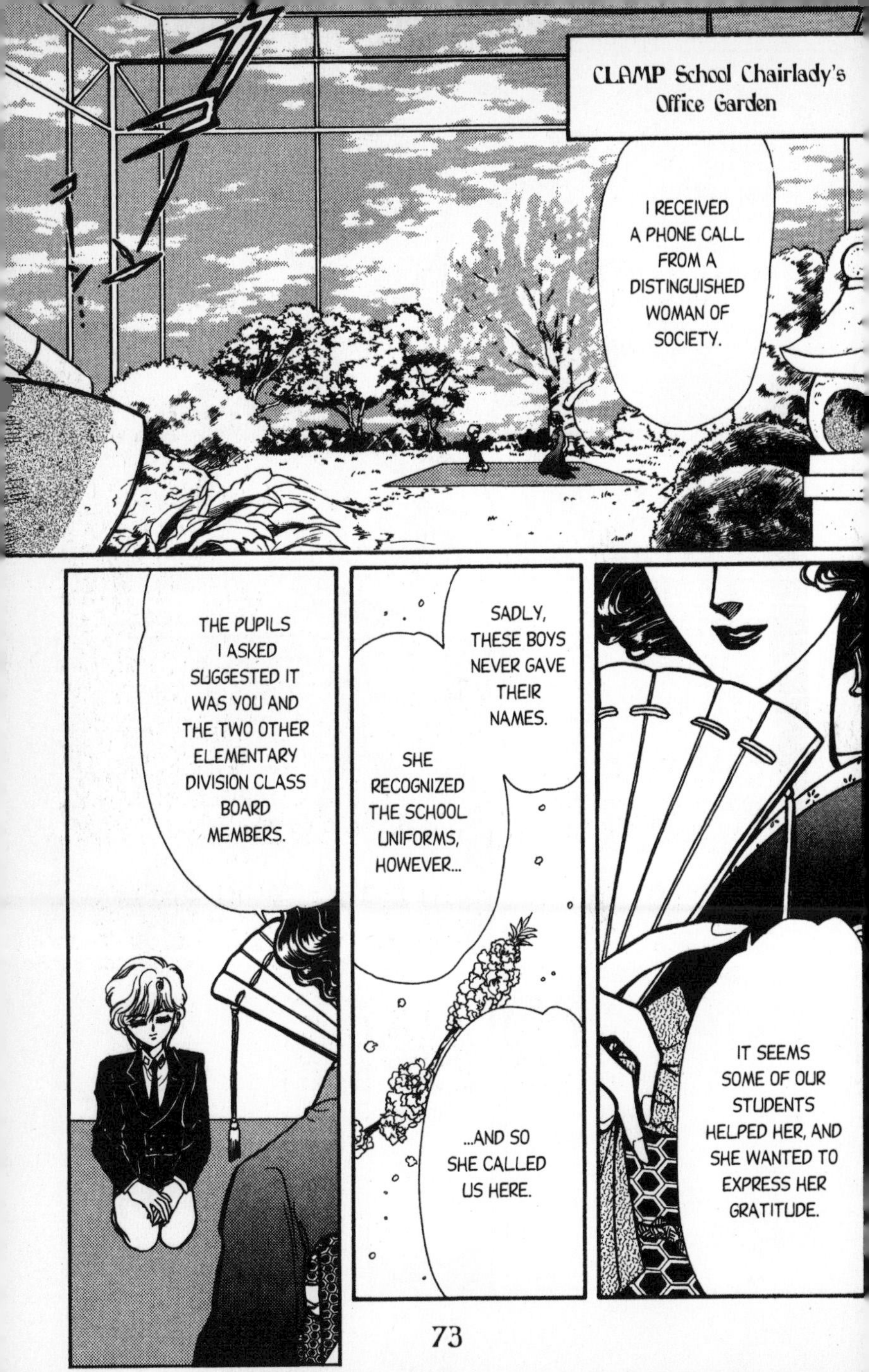
CLAMP School Chairlady's Office Garden
I RECEIVED A PHONE CALL FROM A DISTINGUISHED WOMAN OF SOCIETY.
IT SEEMS SOME OF OUR STUDENTS HELPED HER, AND SHE WANTED TO EXPRESS HER GRATITUDE.
SADLY, THESE BOYS NEVER GAVE THEIR NAMES.
SHE RECOGNIZED THE SCHOOL UNIFORMS, HOWEVER...
...AND SO SHE CALLED US HERE.
THE PUPILS I ASKED SUGGESTED IT WAS YOU AND THE TWO OTHER ELEMENTARY DIVISION CLASS BOARD MEMBERS.

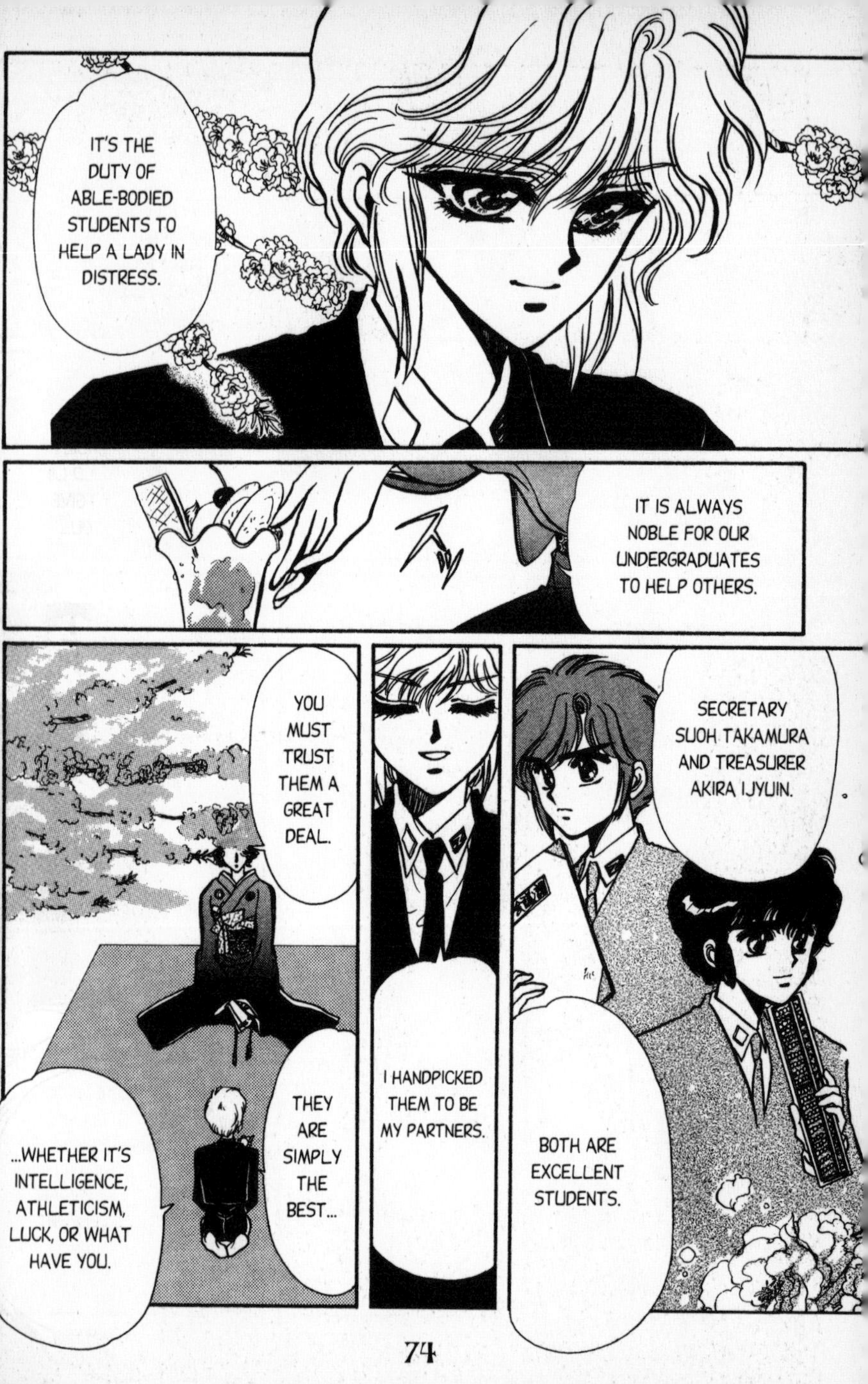
IT'S THE DUTY OF ABLE-BODIED STUDENTS TO HELP A LADY IN DISTRESS.
IT IS ALWAYS NOBLE FOR OUR UNDERGRADUATES TO HELP OTHERS.
SECRETARY SUOH TAKAMURA AND TREASURER AKIRA IJYUIN.
BOTH ARE EXCELLENT STUDENTS.
I HANDPICKED THEM TO BE MY PARTNERS.
YOU MUST TRUST THEM A GREAT DEAL.
THEY ARE SIMPLY THE BEST...
...WHETHER IT'S INTELLIGENCE, ATHLETICISM, LUCK, OR WHAT HAVE YOU.

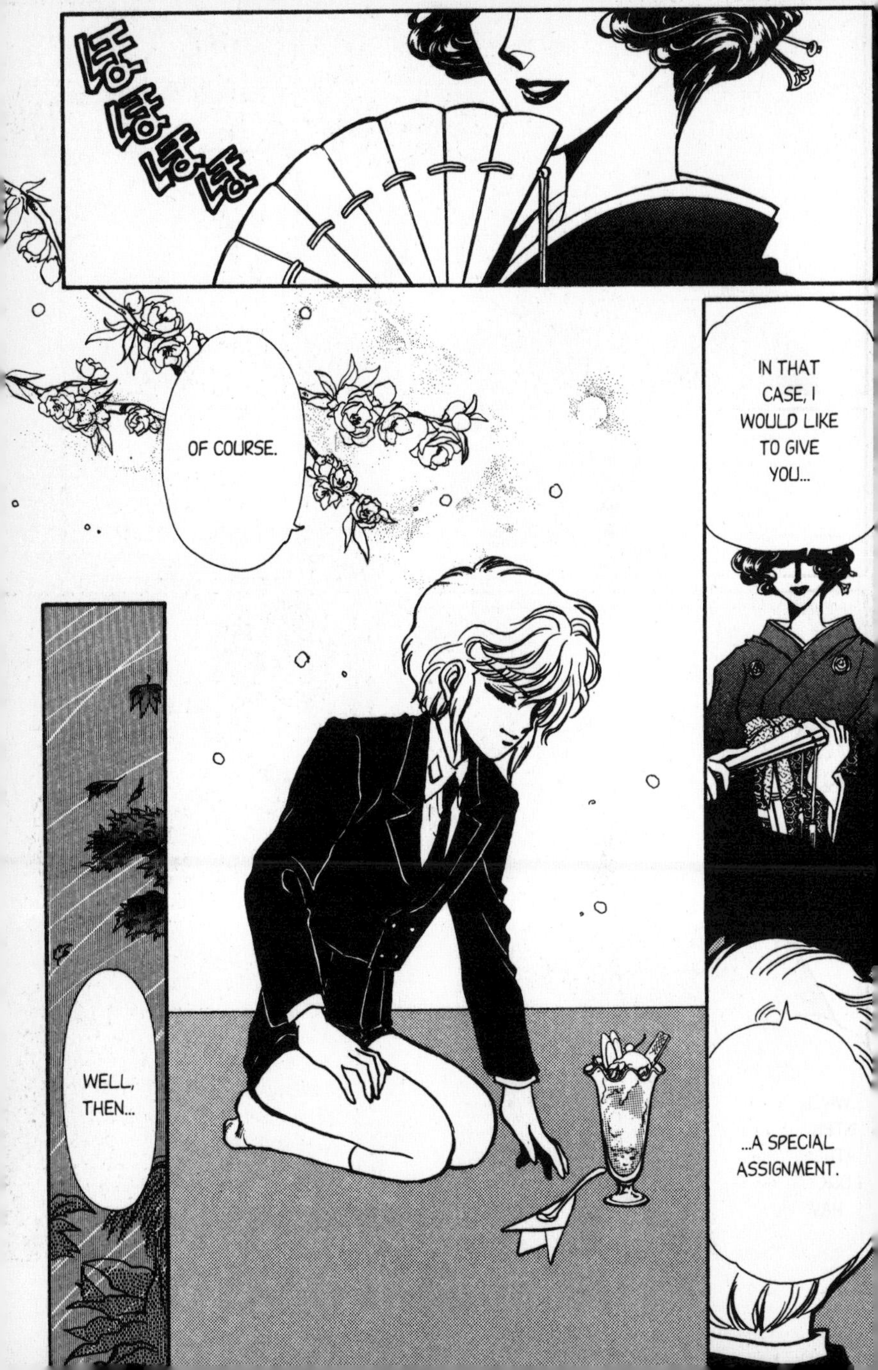
IN THAT CASE, I WOULD LIKE TO GIVE YOU...
...A SPECIAL ASSIGNMENT.
OF COURSE.
WELL, THEN...

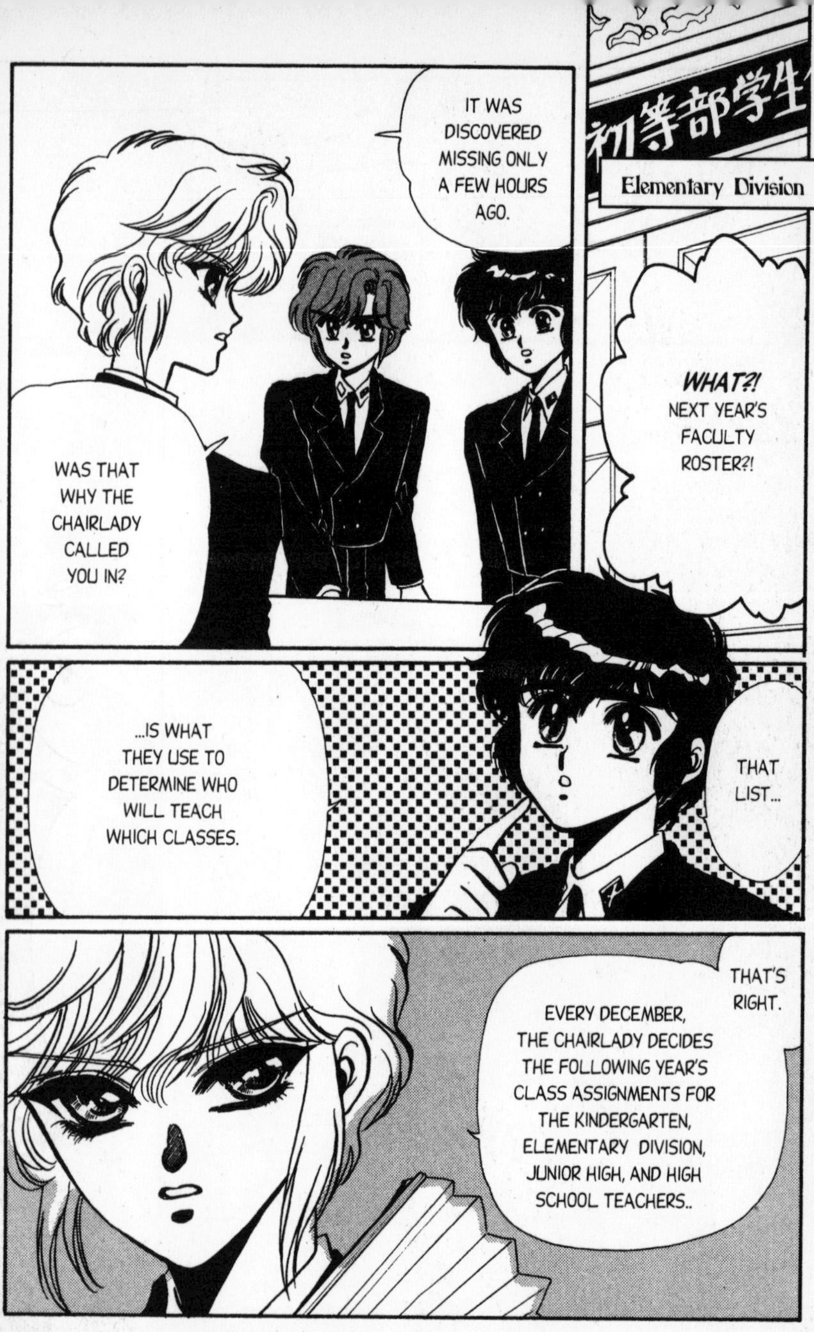
初等部学生
Elementary Division
WHAT?! NEXT YEAR'S FACULTY ROSTER?!
IT WAS DISCOVERED MISSING ONLY A FEW HOURS AGO.
WAS THAT WHY THE CHAIRLADY CALLED YOU IN?
THAT LIST...
...IS WHAT THEY USE TO DETERMINE WHO WILL TEACH WHICH CLASSES.
THAT'S RIGHT.
EVERY DECEMBER, THE CHAIRLADY DECIDES THE FOLLOWING YEAR'S CLASS ASSIGNMENTS FOR THE KINDERGARTEN, ELEMENTARY DIVISION, JUNIOR HIGH, AND HIGH SCHOOL TEACHERS..

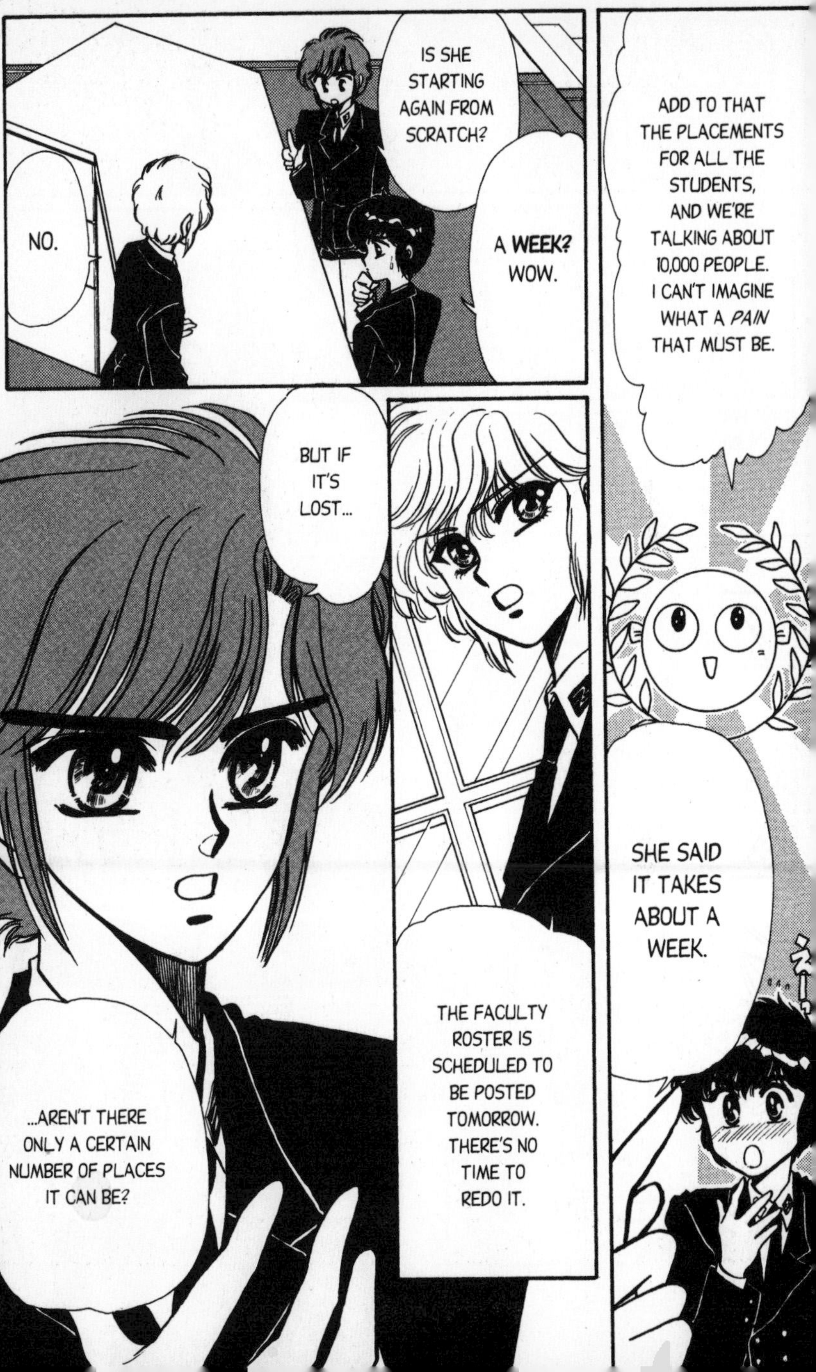
ADD TO THAT THE PLACEMENTS FOR ALL THE STUDENTS, AND WE'RE TALKING ABOUT 10,000 PEOPLE. I CAN'T IMAGINE WHAT A *PAIN* THAT MUST BE.
SHE SAID IT TAKES ABOUT A WEEK.
IS SHE STARTING AGAIN FROM SCRATCH?
A **WEEK?** WOW.
NO.
BUT IF IT'S LOST...
THE FACULTY ROSTER IS SCHEDULED TO BE POSTED TOMORROW. THERE'S NO TIME TO REDO IT.
...AREN'T THERE ONLY A CERTAIN NUMBER OF PLACES IT CAN BE?

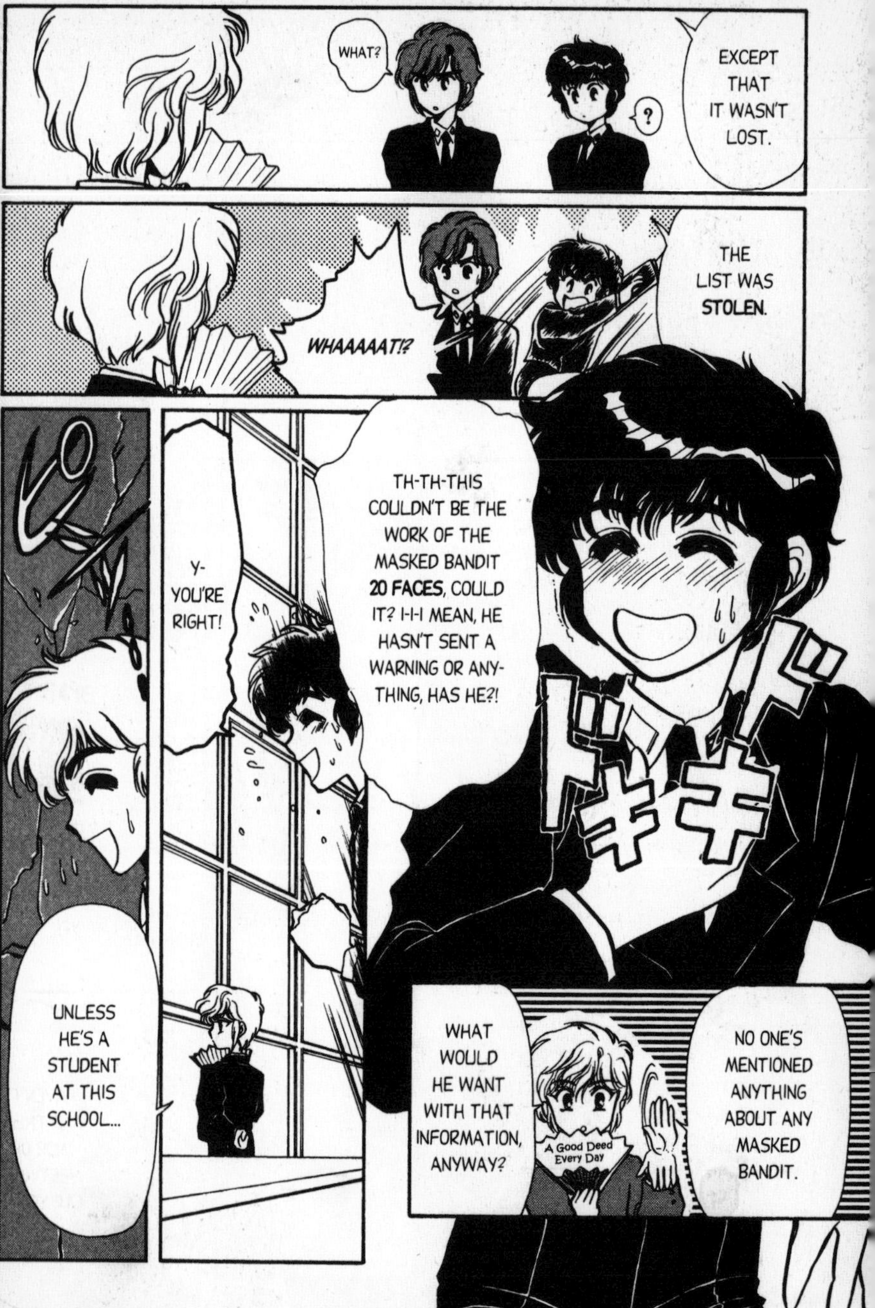
EXCEPT THAT IT WASN'T LOST.
?
WHAT?
THE LIST WAS **STOLEN**.
WHAAAAAT!?
TH-TH-THIS COULDN'T BE THE WORK OF THE MASKED BANDIT **20 FACES**, COULD IT? I-I-I MEAN, HE HASN'T SENT A WARNING OR ANY-THING, HAS HE?!
ドキドキ
NO ONE'S MENTIONED ANYTHING ABOUT ANY MASKED BANDIT.
WHAT WOULD HE WANT WITH THAT INFORMATION, ANYWAY?
A Good Deed Every Day
Y-YOU'RE RIGHT!
UNLESS HE'S A STUDENT AT THIS SCHOOL...

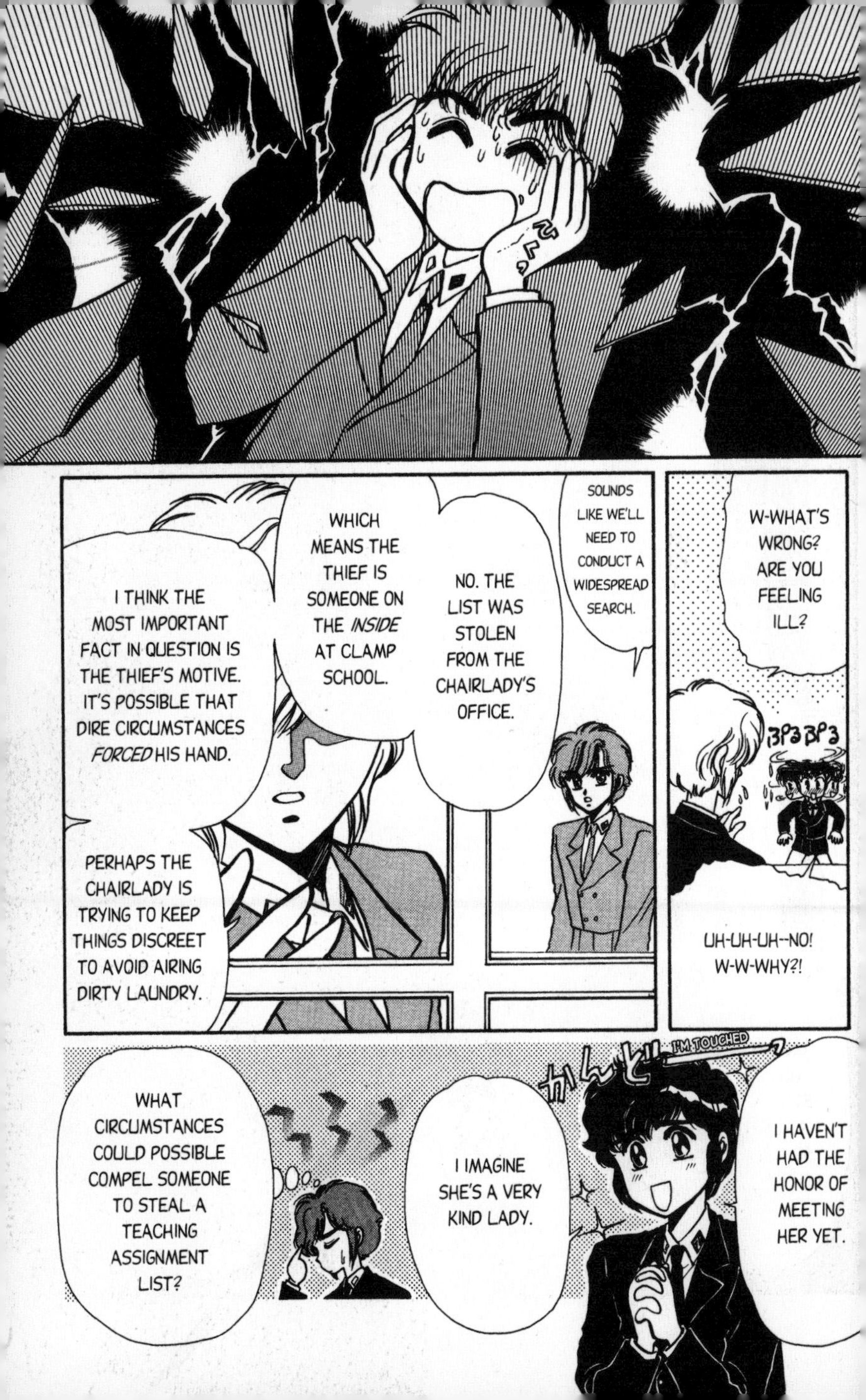
W-WHAT'S WRONG? ARE YOU FEELING ILL?
UH-UH-UH--NO! W-W-WHY?!
SOUNDS LIKE WE'LL NEED TO CONDUCT A WIDESPREAD SEARCH.
NO. THE LIST WAS STOLEN FROM THE CHAIRLADY'S OFFICE.
WHICH MEANS THE THIEF IS SOMEONE ON THE *INSIDE* AT CLAMP SCHOOL.
I THINK THE MOST IMPORTANT FACT IN QUESTION IS THE THIEF'S MOTIVE. IT'S POSSIBLE THAT DIRE CIRCUMSTANCES *FORCED* HIS HAND.
PERHAPS THE CHAIRLADY IS TRYING TO KEEP THINGS DISCREET TO AVOID AIRING DIRTY LAUNDRY.
I'M TOUCHED
I HAVEN'T HAD THE HONOR OF MEETING HER YET.
I IMAGINE SHE'S A VERY KIND LADY.
WHAT CIRCUMSTANCES COULD POSSIBLE COMPEL SOMEONE TO STEAL A TEACHING ASSIGNMENT LIST?

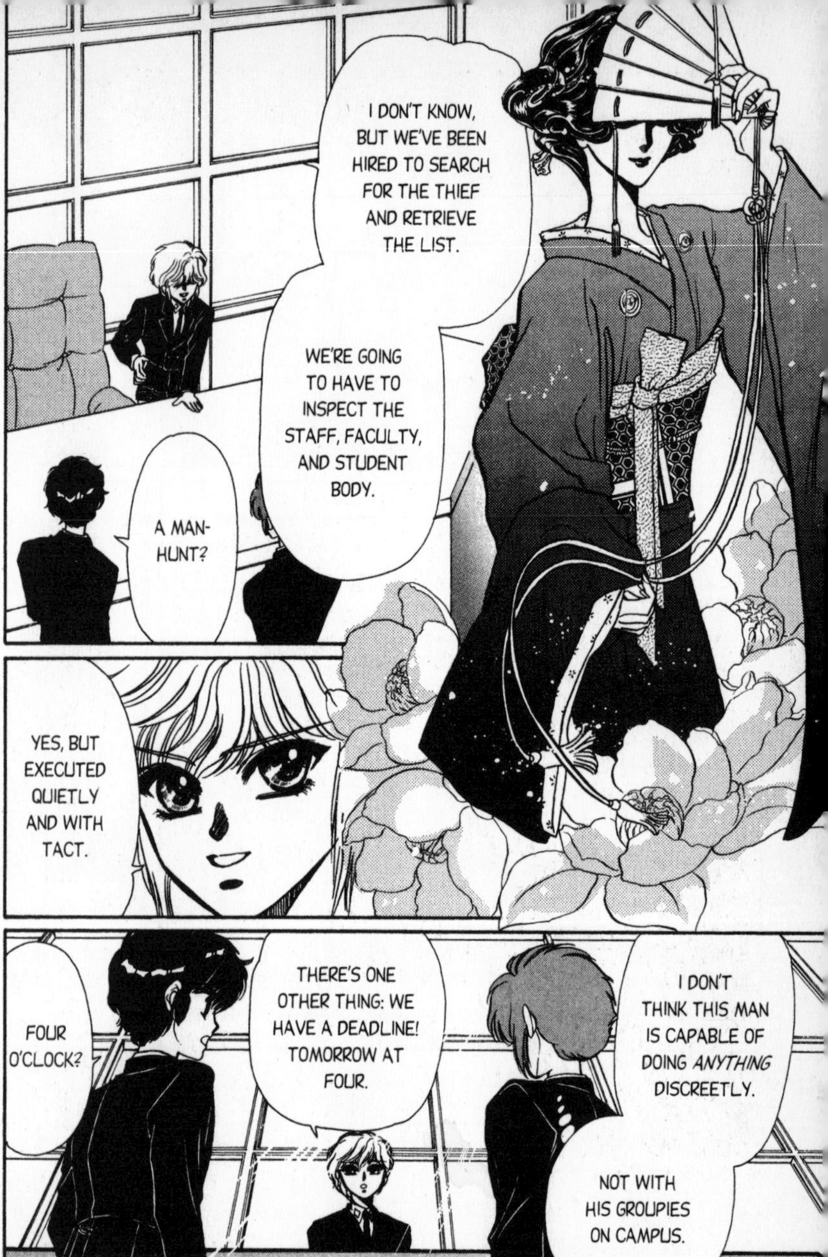
I DON'T KNOW, BUT WE'VE BEEN HIRED TO SEARCH FOR THE THIEF AND RETRIEVE THE LIST.
WE'RE GOING TO HAVE TO INSPECT THE STAFF, FACULTY, AND STUDENT BODY.
A MAN-HUNT?
YES, BUT EXECUTED QUIETLY AND WITH TACT.
I DON'T THINK THIS MAN IS CAPABLE OF DOING *ANYTHING* DISCREETLY.
NOT WITH HIS GROUPIES ON CAMPUS.
THERE'S ONE OTHER THING: WE HAVE A DEADLINE! TOMORROW AT FOUR.
FOUR O'CLOCK?

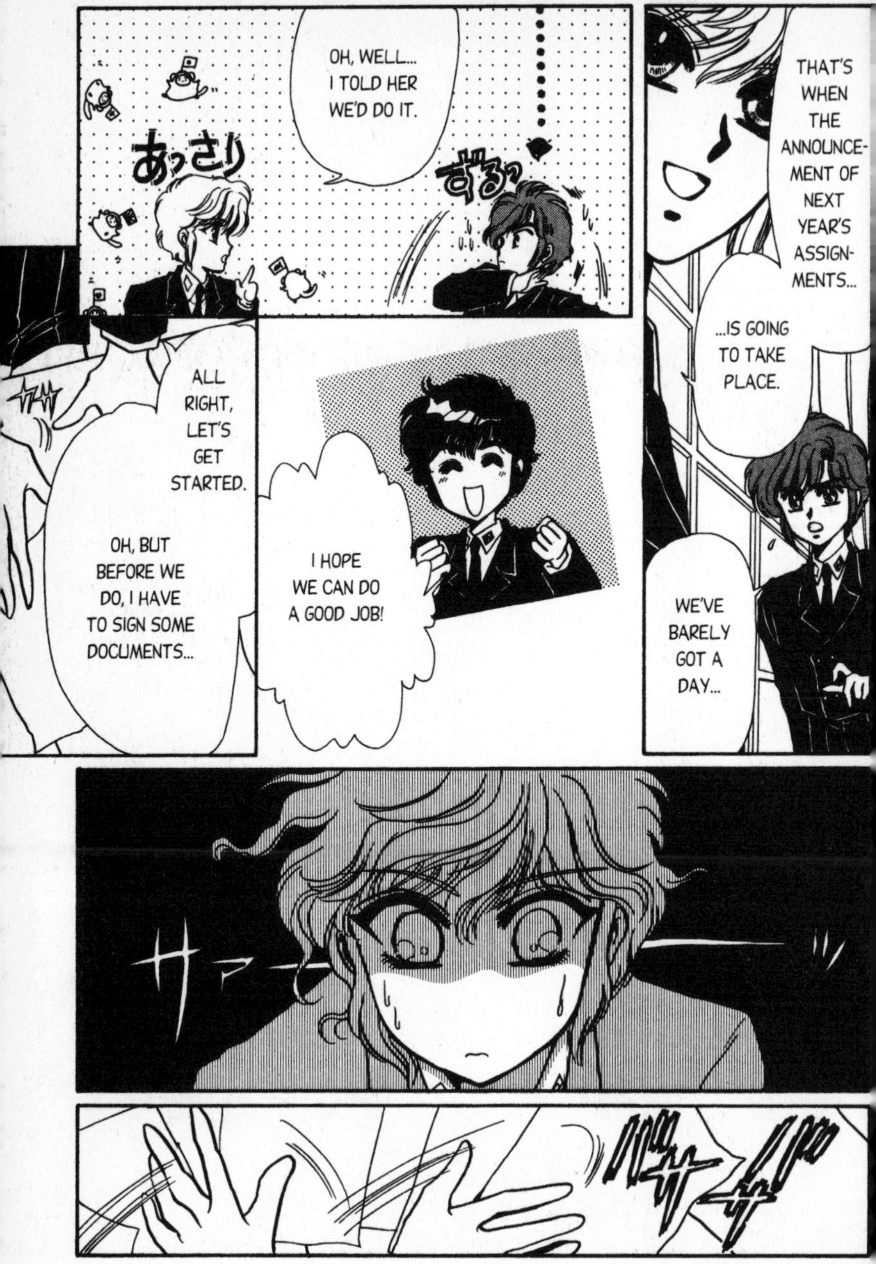
THAT'S WHEN THE ANNOUNCEMENT OF NEXT YEAR'S ASSIGNMENTS...
...IS GOING TO TAKE PLACE.
WE'VE BARELY GOT A DAY...
OH, WELL... I TOLD HER WE'D DO IT.
ずるっ
あっさり
I HOPE WE CAN DO A GOOD JOB!
ALL RIGHT, LET'S GET STARTED.
OH, BUT BEFORE WE DO, I HAVE TO SIGN SOME DOCUMENTS...
サァー

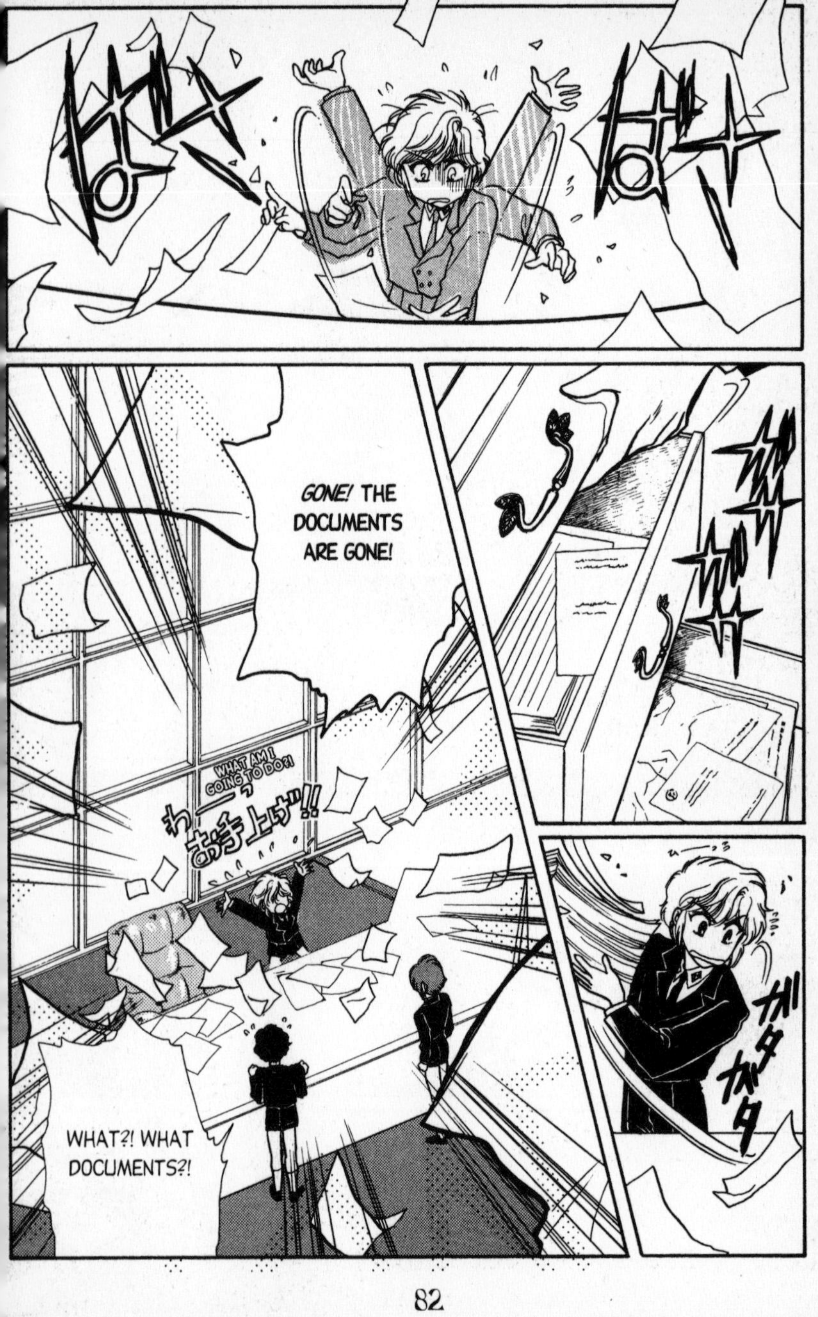
ガタガタ
GONE! THE DOCUMENTS ARE GONE!
WHAT AM I GOING TO DO?!
わーっお手上げ!!
WHAT?! WHAT DOCUMENTS?!

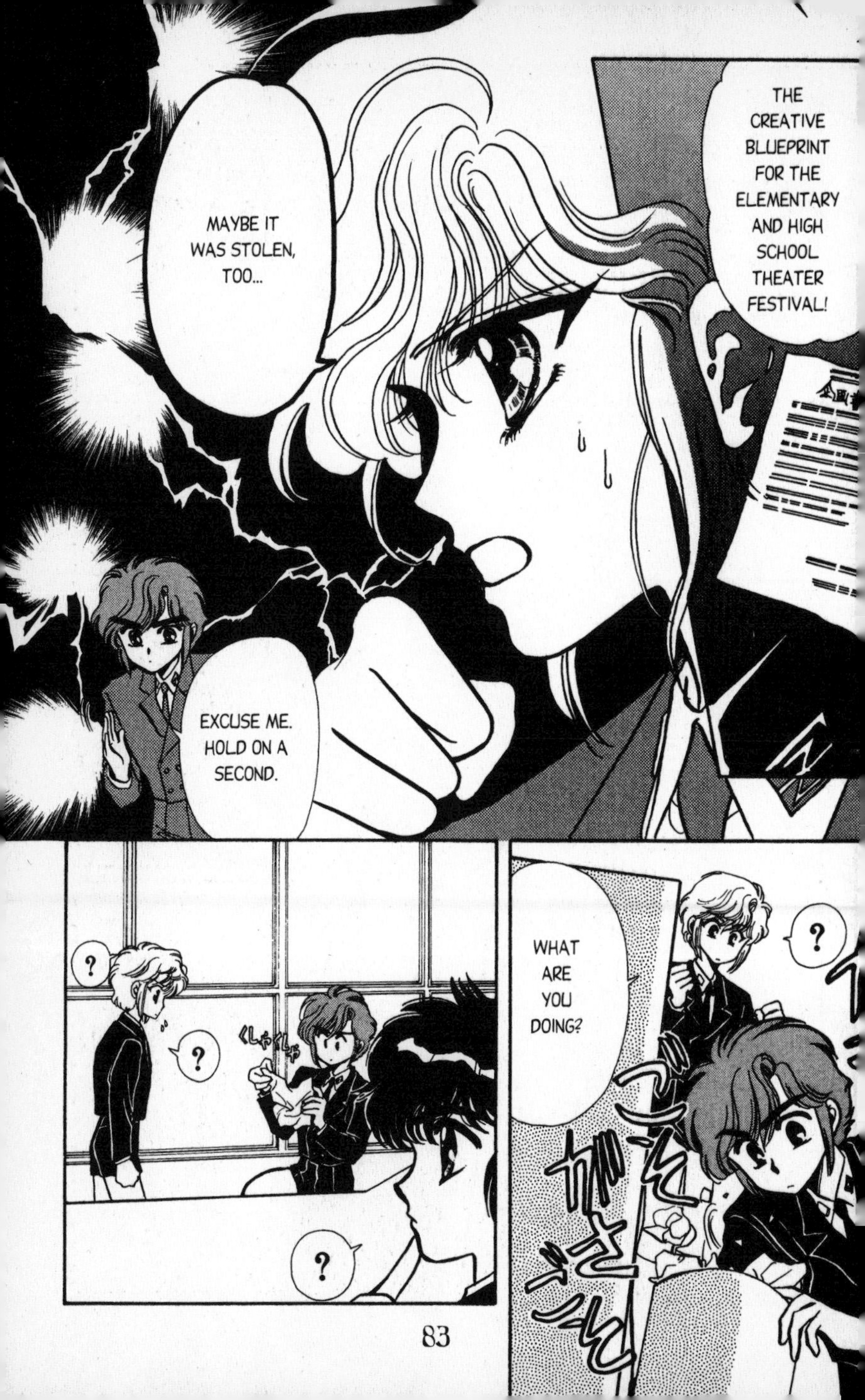
THE CREATIVE BLUEPRINT FOR THE ELEMENTARY AND HIGH SCHOOL THEATER FESTIVAL!
MAYBE IT WAS STOLEN, TOO...
EXCUSE ME. HOLD ON A SECOND.
?
WHAT ARE YOU DOING?
?
?
くしゃくしゃ
?

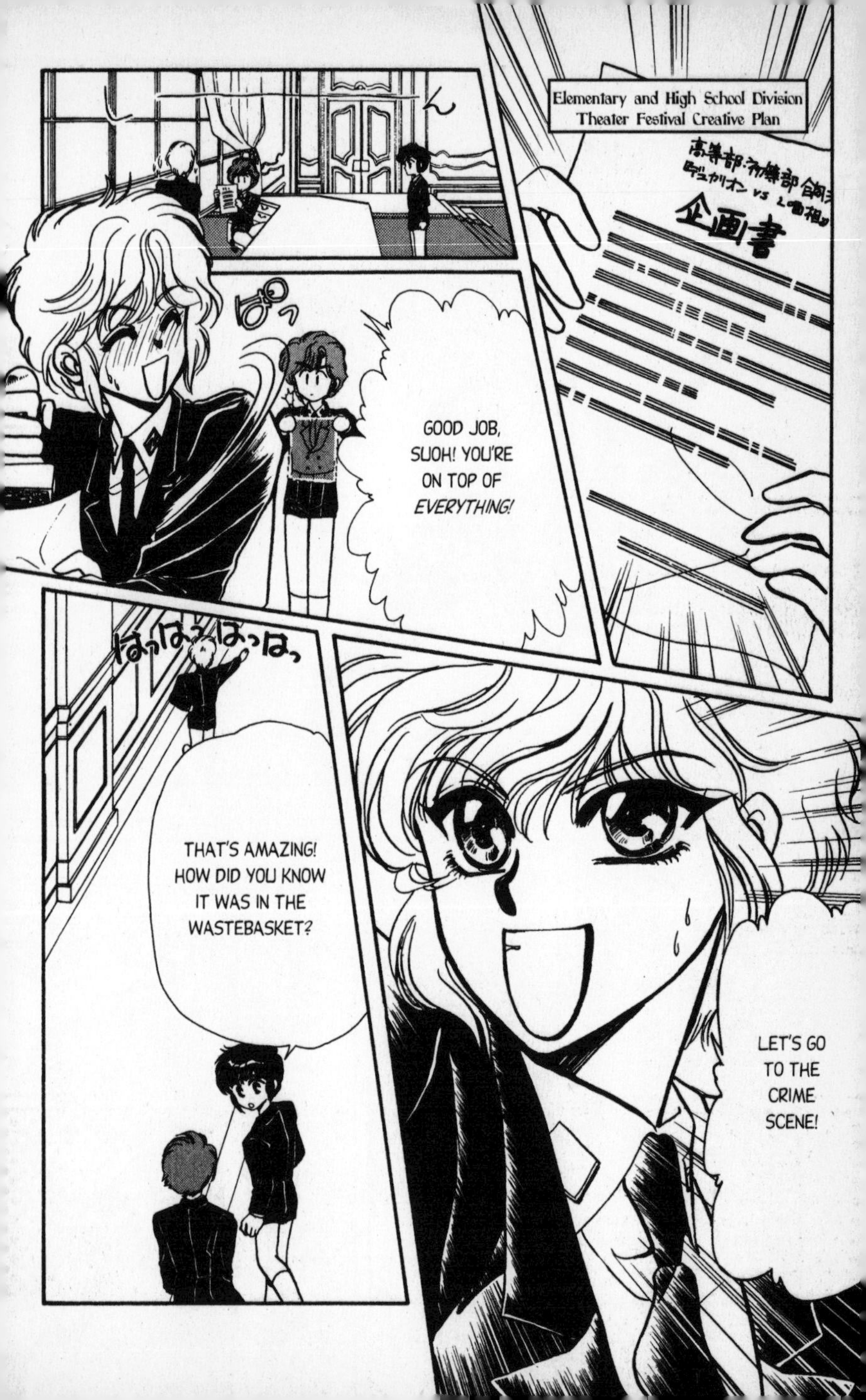
Elementary and High School Division
Theater Festival Creative Plan
企画書
ん
ぱっ
GOOD JOB, SUOH! YOU'RE ON TOP OF *EVERYTHING!*
LET'S GO TO THE CRIME SCENE!
はっはっはっはっ
THAT'S AMAZING! HOW DID YOU KNOW IT WAS IN THE WASTEBASKET?

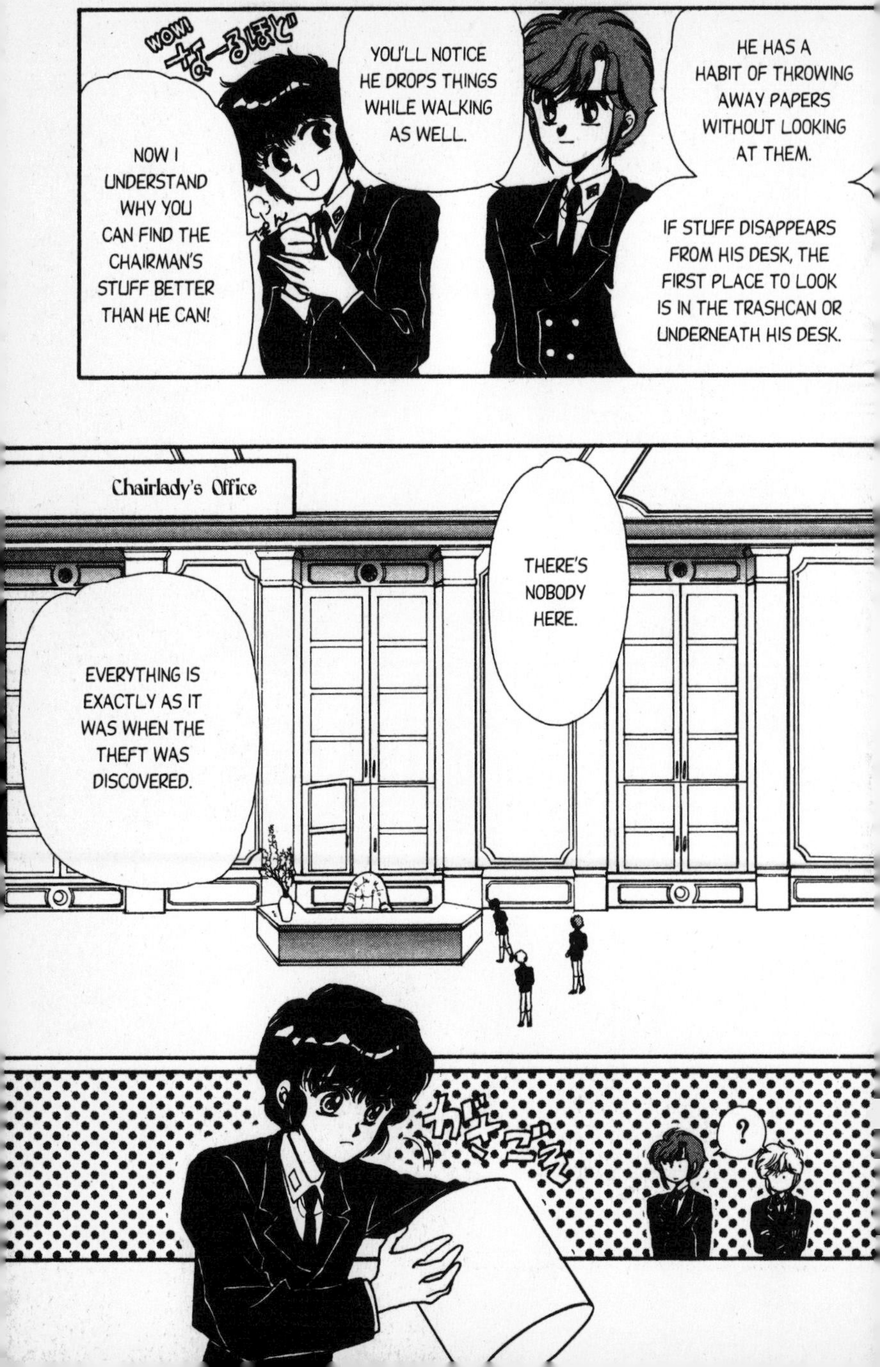
HE HAS A HABIT OF THROWING AWAY PAPERS WITHOUT LOOKING AT THEM.
IF STUFF DISAPPEARS FROM HIS DESK, THE FIRST PLACE TO LOOK IS IN THE TRASHCAN OR UNDERNEATH HIS DESK.
YOU'LL NOTICE HE DROPS THINGS WHILE WALKING AS WELL.
WOW!
なーるほど
NOW I UNDERSTAND WHY YOU CAN FIND THE CHAIRMAN'S STUFF BETTER THAN HE CAN!
Chairlady's Office
THERE'S NOBODY HERE.
EVERYTHING IS EXACTLY AS IT WAS WHEN THE THEFT WAS DISCOVERED.
?

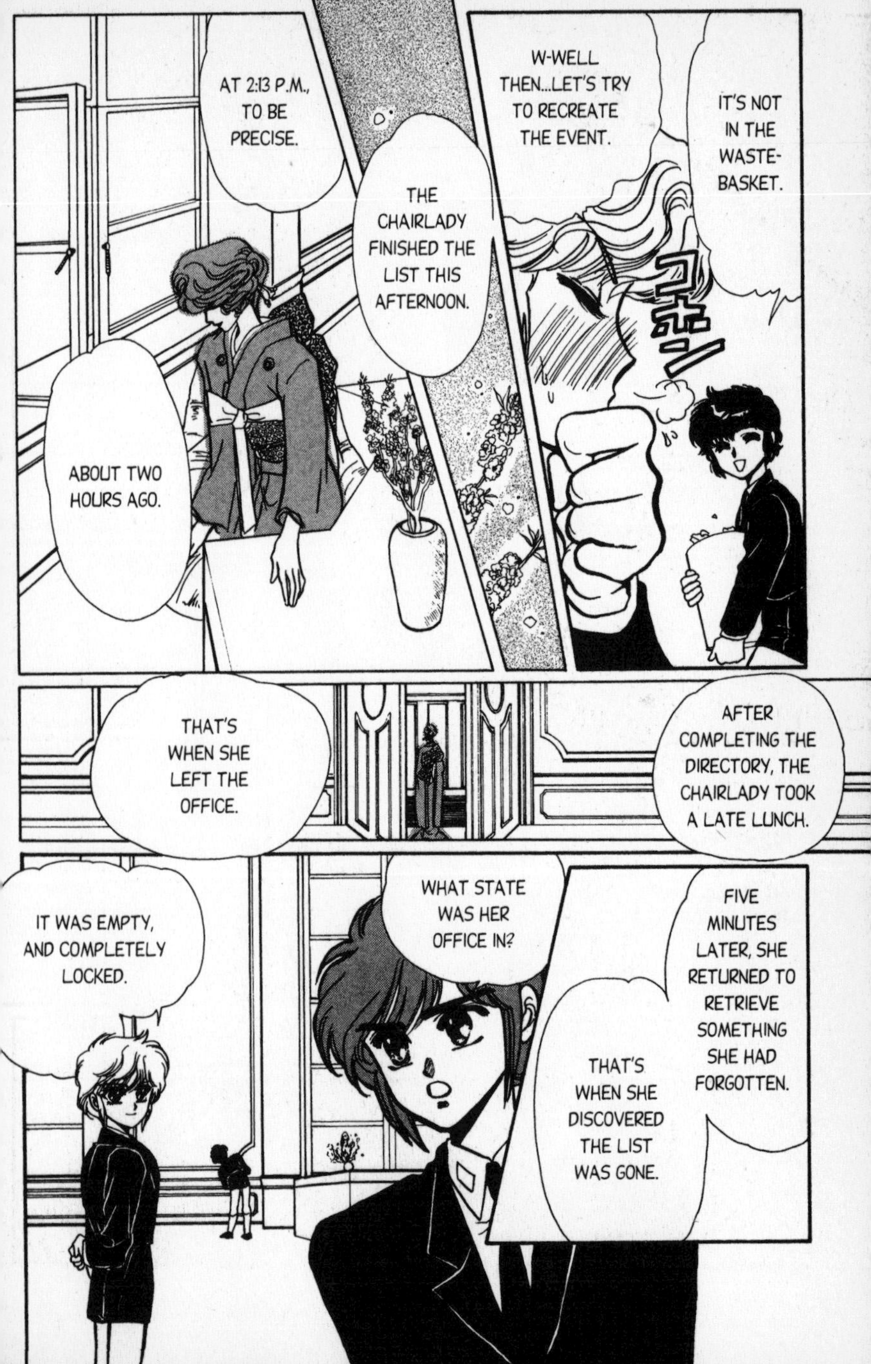
IT'S NOT IN THE WASTE-BASKET.
W-WELL THEN...LET'S TRY TO RECREATE THE EVENT.
THE CHAIRLADY FINISHED THE LIST THIS AFTERNOON.
AT 2:13 P.M., TO BE PRECISE.
ABOUT TWO HOURS AGO.
AFTER COMPLETING THE DIRECTORY, THE CHAIRLADY TOOK A LATE LUNCH.
THAT'S WHEN SHE LEFT THE OFFICE.
FIVE MINUTES LATER, SHE RETURNED TO RETRIEVE SOMETHING SHE HAD FORGOTTEN.
THAT'S WHEN SHE DISCOVERED THE LIST WAS GONE.
WHAT STATE WAS HER OFFICE IN?
IT WAS EMPTY, AND COMPLETELY LOCKED.

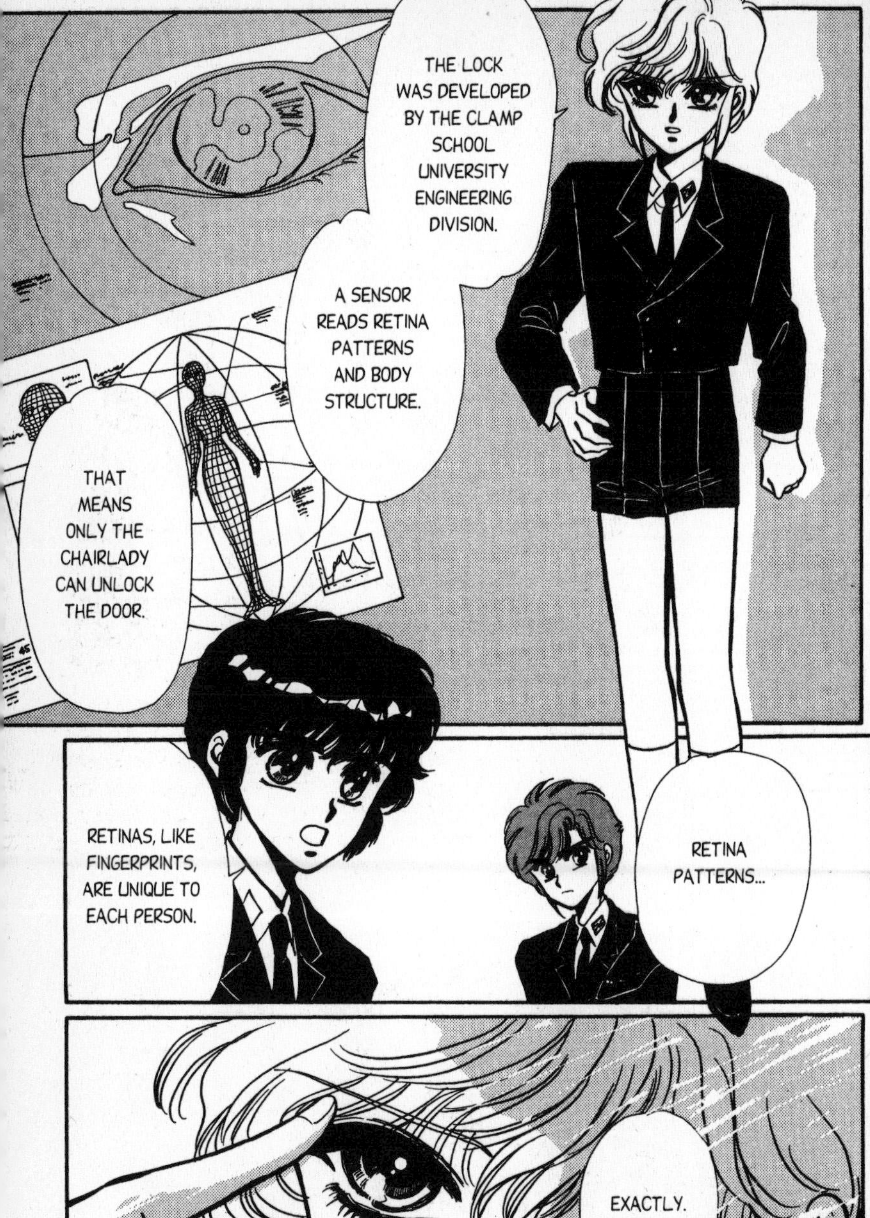
THE LOCK WAS DEVELOPED BY THE CLAMP SCHOOL UNIVERSITY ENGINEERING DIVISION.
A SENSOR READS RETINA PATTERNS AND BODY STRUCTURE.
THAT MEANS ONLY THE CHAIRLADY CAN UNLOCK THE DOOR.
RETINA PATTERNS...
RETINAS, LIKE FINGERPRINTS, ARE UNIQUE TO EACH PERSON.
EXACTLY.

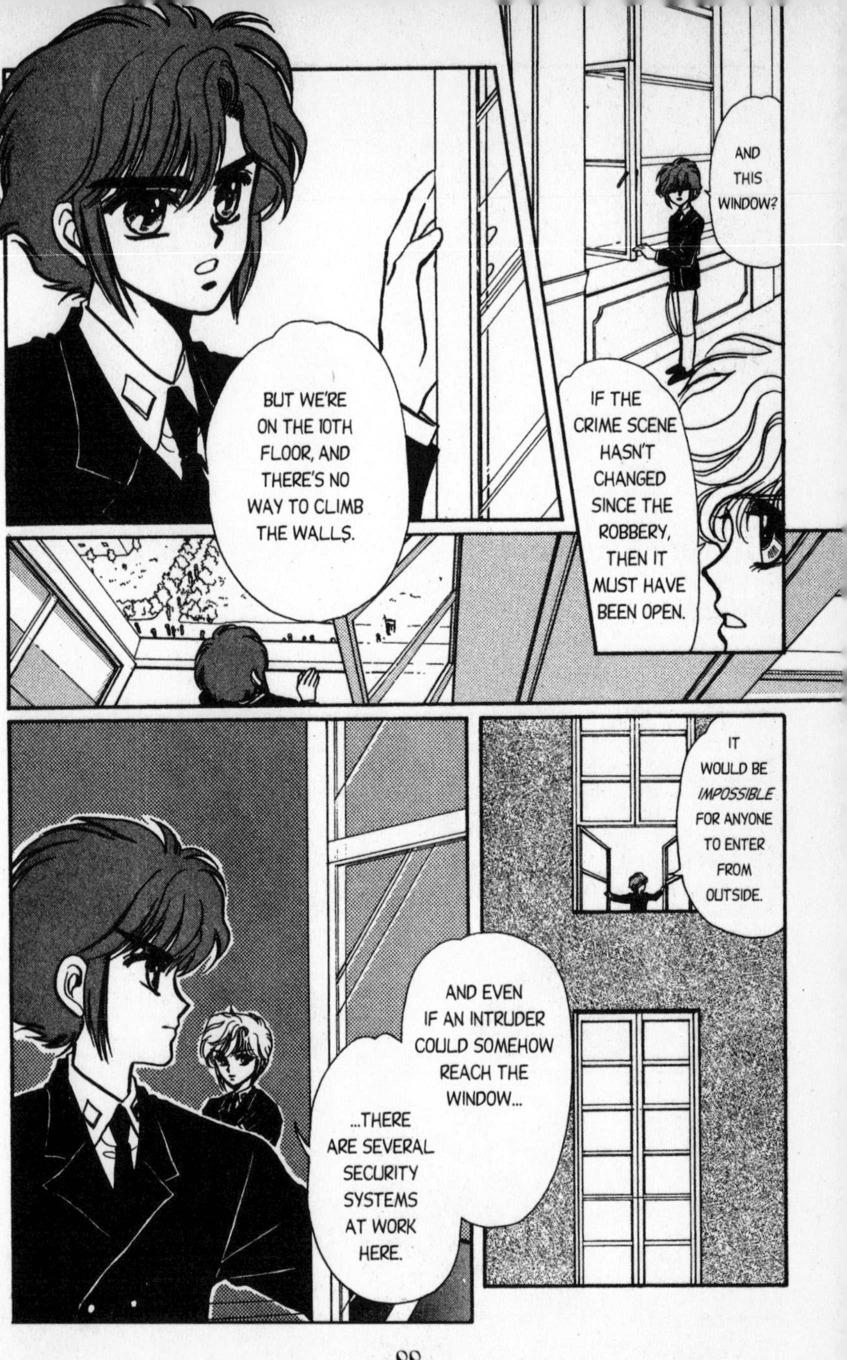
AND THIS WINDOW?
IF THE CRIME SCENE HASN'T CHANGED SINCE THE ROBBERY, THEN IT MUST HAVE BEEN OPEN.
BUT WE'RE ON THE 10TH FLOOR, AND THERE'S NO WAY TO CLIMB THE WALLS.
IT WOULD BE *IMPOSSIBLE* FOR ANYONE TO ENTER FROM OUTSIDE.
AND EVEN IF AN INTRUDER COULD SOMEHOW REACH THE WINDOW...
...THERE ARE SEVERAL SECURITY SYSTEMS AT WORK HERE.

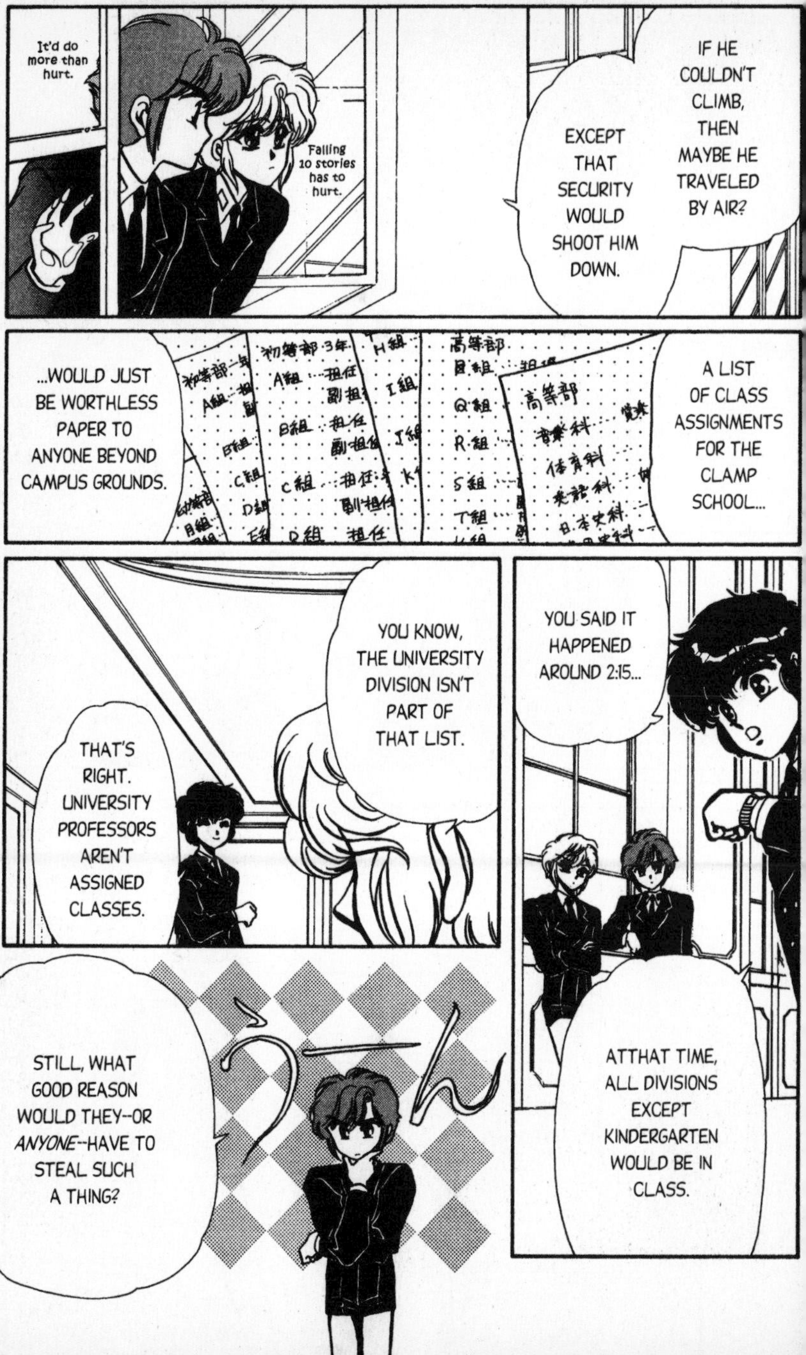
IF HE COULDN'T CLIMB, THEN MAYBE HE TRAVELED BY AIR?
EXCEPT THAT SECURITY WOULD SHOOT HIM DOWN.
Falling 10 stories has to hurt.
It'd do more than hurt.
A LIST OF CLASS ASSIGNMENTS FOR THE CLAMP SCHOOL...
...WOULD JUST BE WORTHLESS PAPER TO ANYONE BEYOND CAMPUS GROUNDS.
YOU SAID IT HAPPENED AROUND 2:15...
AT THAT TIME, ALL DIVISIONS EXCEPT KINDERGARTEN WOULD BE IN CLASS.
YOU KNOW, THE UNIVERSITY DIVISION ISN'T PART OF THAT LIST.
THAT'S RIGHT. UNIVERSITY PROFESSORS AREN'T ASSIGNED CLASSES.
うーん
STILL, WHAT GOOD REASON WOULD THEY--OR *ANYONE*--HAVE TO STEAL SUCH A THING?

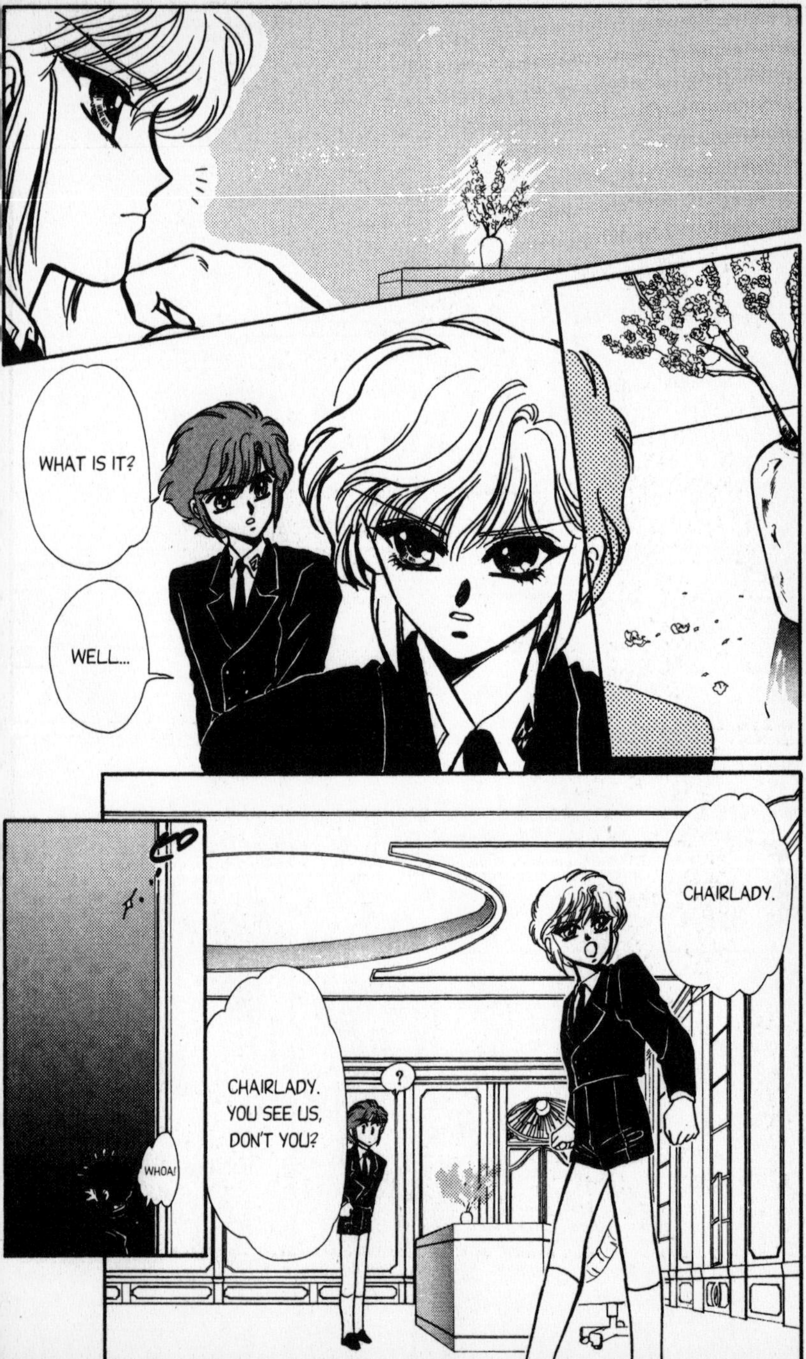
WHAT IS IT?
WELL...
CHAIRLADY.
?
CHAIRLADY. YOU SEE US, DON'T YOU?
WHOA!

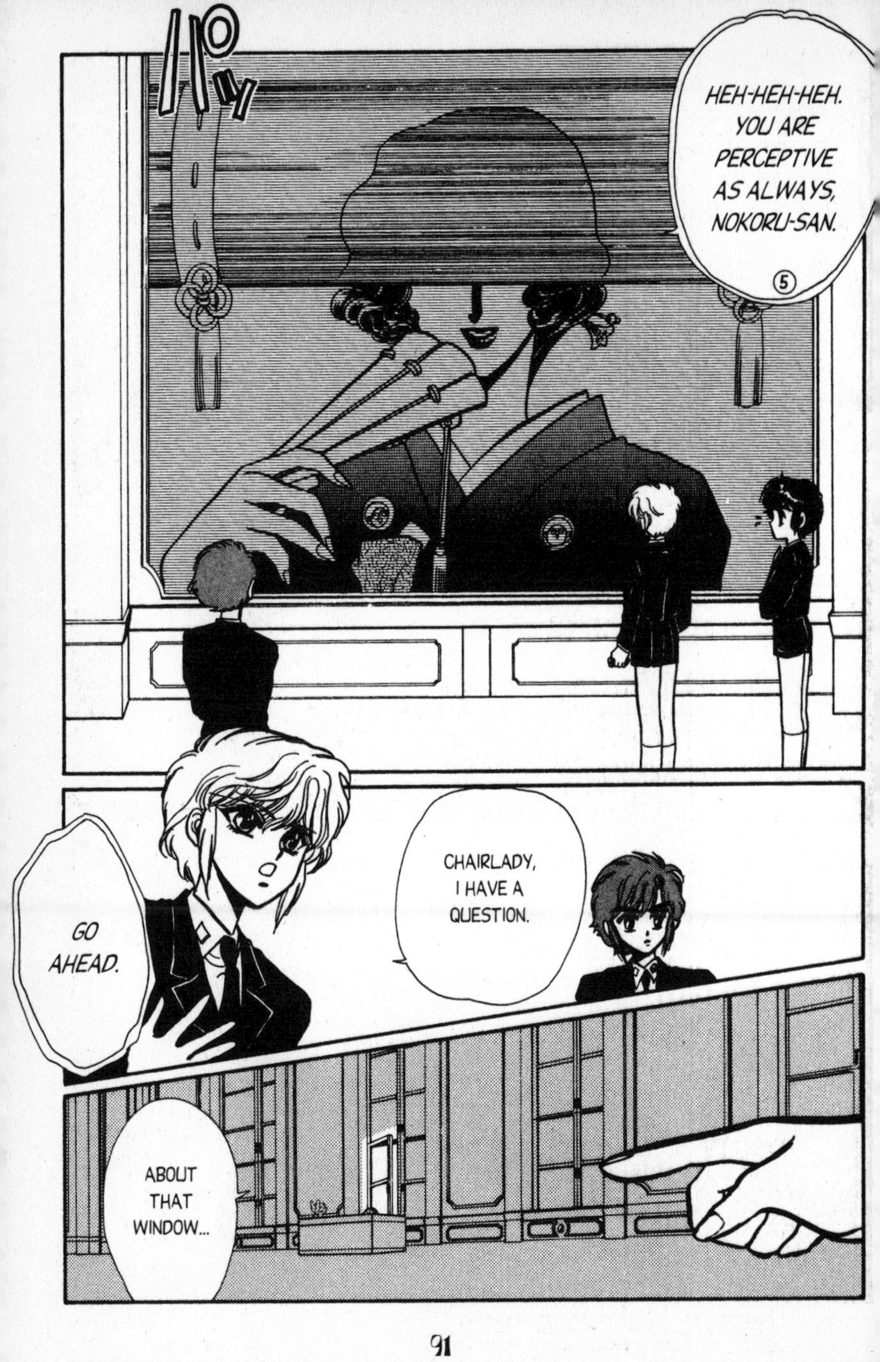
HEH-HEH-HEH. YOU ARE PERCEPTIVE AS ALWAYS, NOKORU-SAN. ⑤
CHAIRLADY, I HAVE A QUESTION.
GO AHEAD.
ABOUT THAT WINDOW...

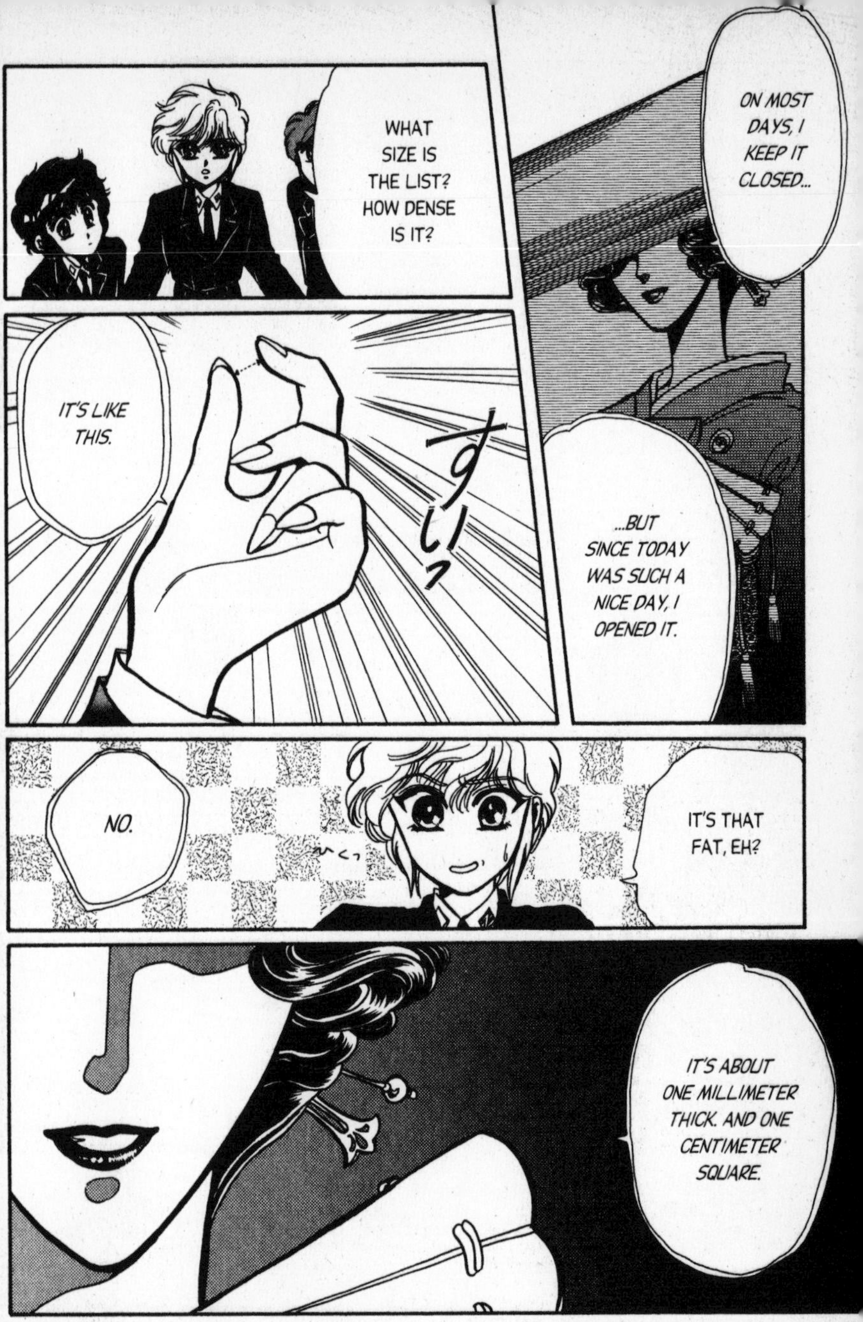
ON MOST DAYS, I KEEP IT CLOSED...
...BUT SINCE TODAY WAS SUCH A NICE DAY, I OPENED IT.
WHAT SIZE IS THE LIST? HOW DENSE IS IT?
IT'S LIKE THIS.
すいっ
IT'S THAT FAT, EH?
NO.
IT'S ABOUT ONE MILLIMETER THICK. AND ONE CENTIMETER SQUARE.

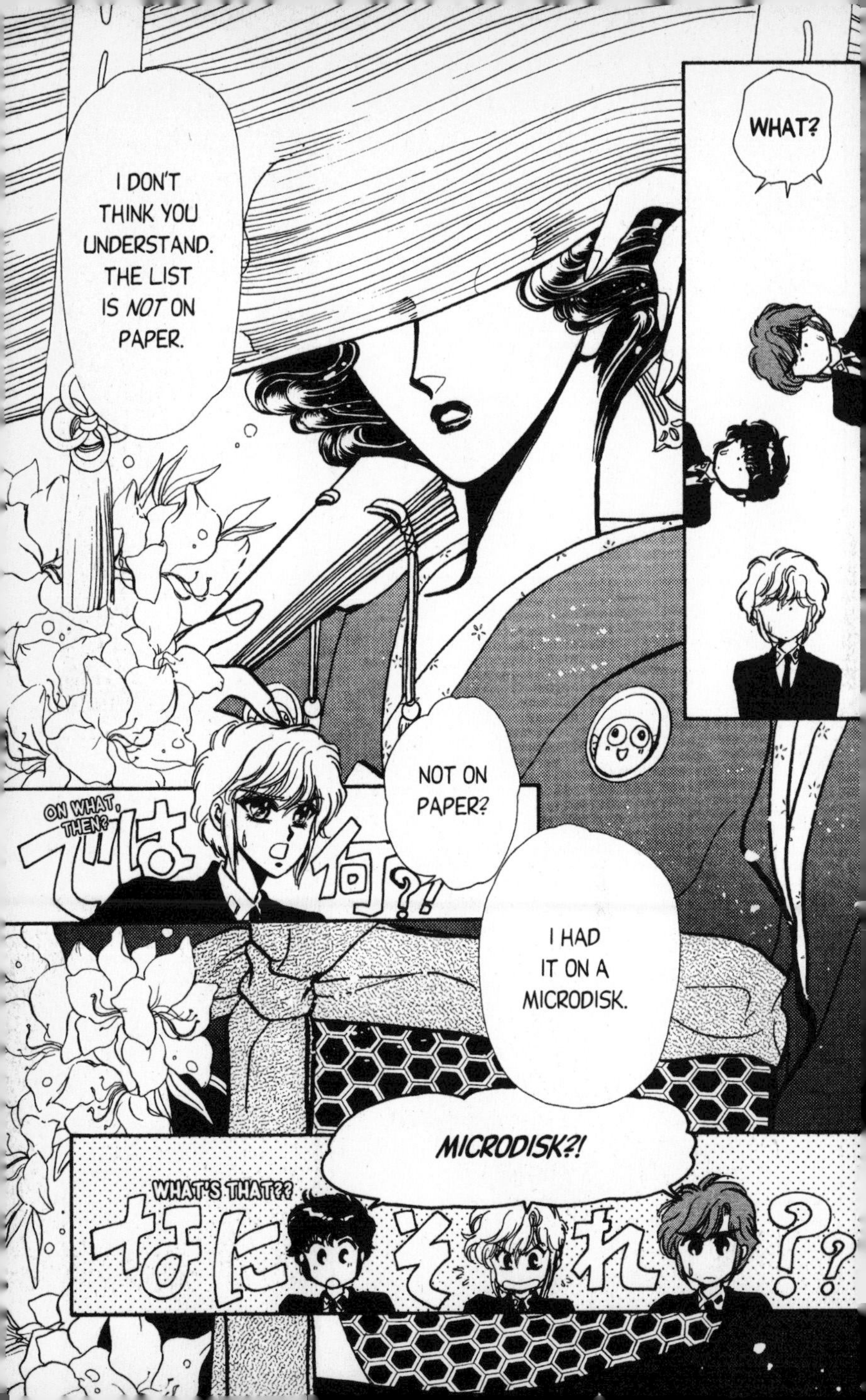
WHAT?
I DON'T THINK YOU UNDERSTAND. THE LIST IS *NOT* ON PAPER.
NOT ON PAPER?
ON WHAT, THEN?
では何?!
I HAD IT ON A MICRODISK.
MICRODISK?!
WHAT'S THAT??
なにそれ??

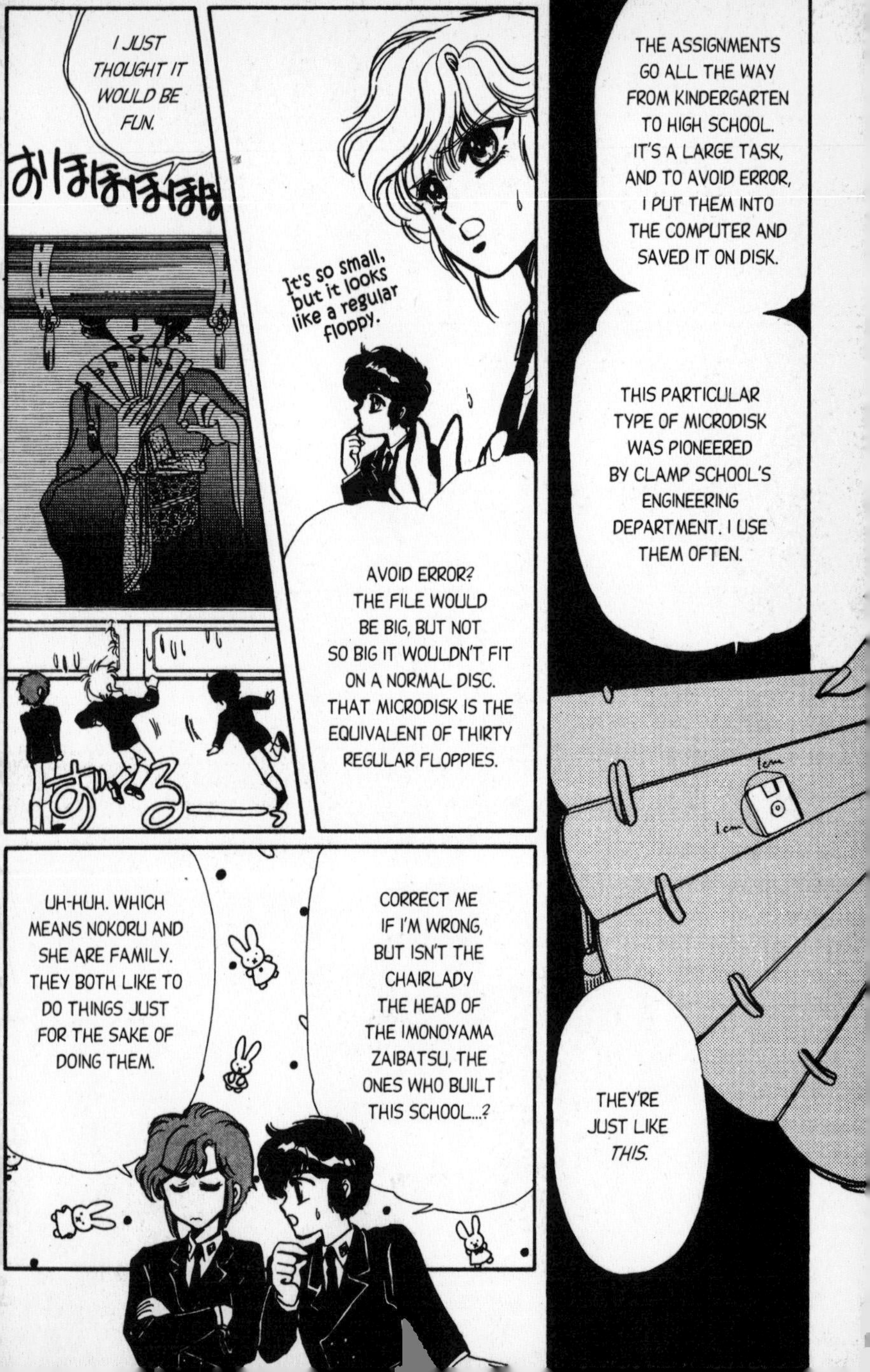
THE ASSIGNMENTS GO ALL THE WAY FROM KINDERGARTEN TO HIGH SCHOOL. IT'S A LARGE TASK, AND TO AVOID ERROR, I PUT THEM INTO THE COMPUTER AND SAVED IT ON DISK.
THIS PARTICULAR TYPE OF MICRODISK WAS PIONEERED BY CLAMP SCHOOL'S ENGINEERING DEPARTMENT. I USE THEM OFTEN.
1cm
1cm
THEY'RE JUST LIKE *THIS.*
It's so small, but it looks like a regular floppy.
AVOID ERROR? THE FILE WOULD BE BIG, BUT NOT SO BIG IT WOULDN'T FIT ON A NORMAL DISC. THAT MICRODISK IS THE EQUIVALENT OF THIRTY REGULAR FLOPPIES.
I JUST THOUGHT IT WOULD BE FUN.
おほほほほほ
CORRECT ME IF I'M WRONG, BUT ISN'T THE CHAIRLADY THE HEAD OF THE IMONOYAMA ZAIBATSU, THE ONES WHO BUILT THIS SCHOOL...?
UH-HUH. WHICH MEANS NOKORU AND SHE ARE FAMILY. THEY BOTH LIKE TO DO THINGS JUST FOR THE SAKE OF DOING THEM.

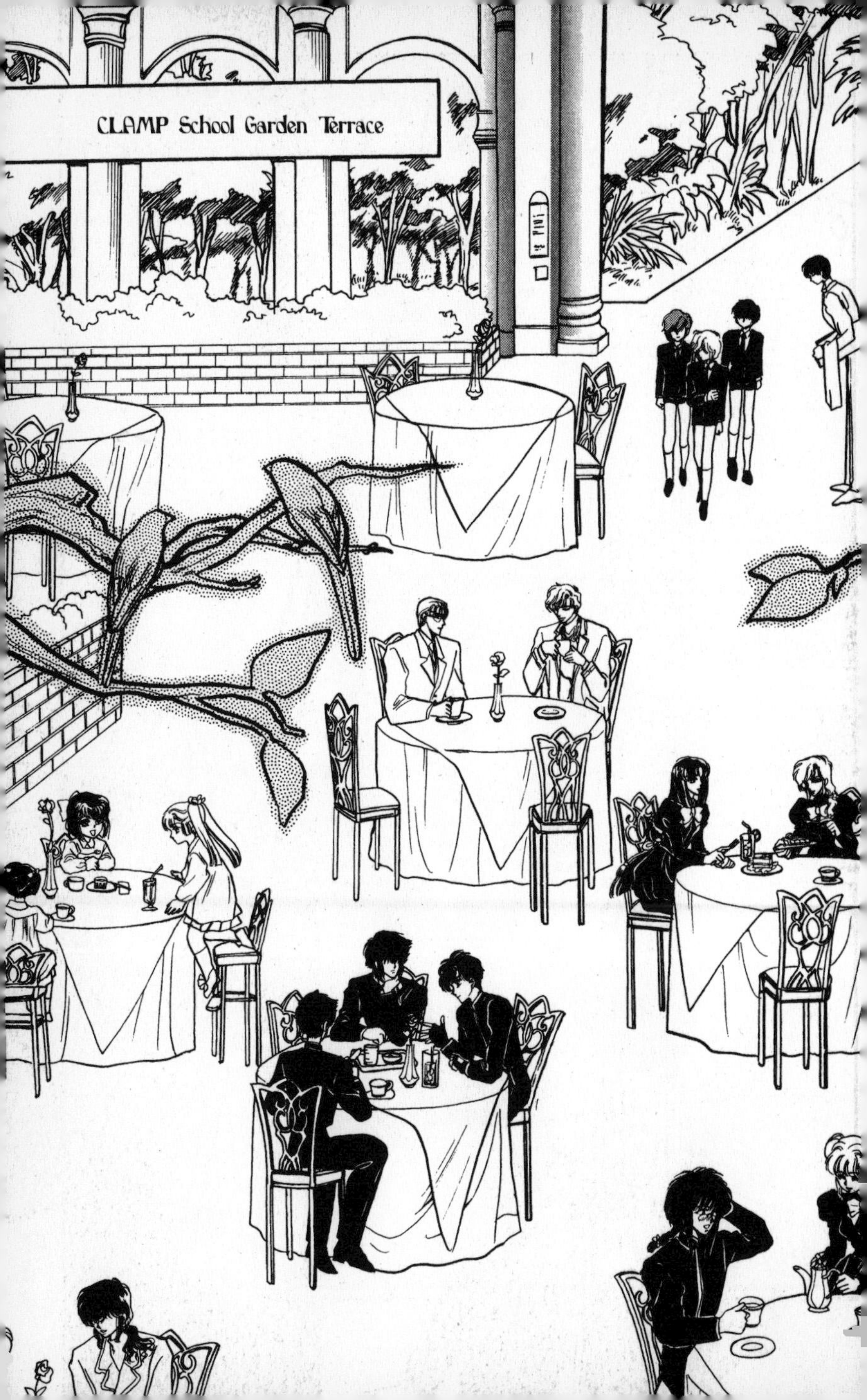
CLAMP School Garden Terrace

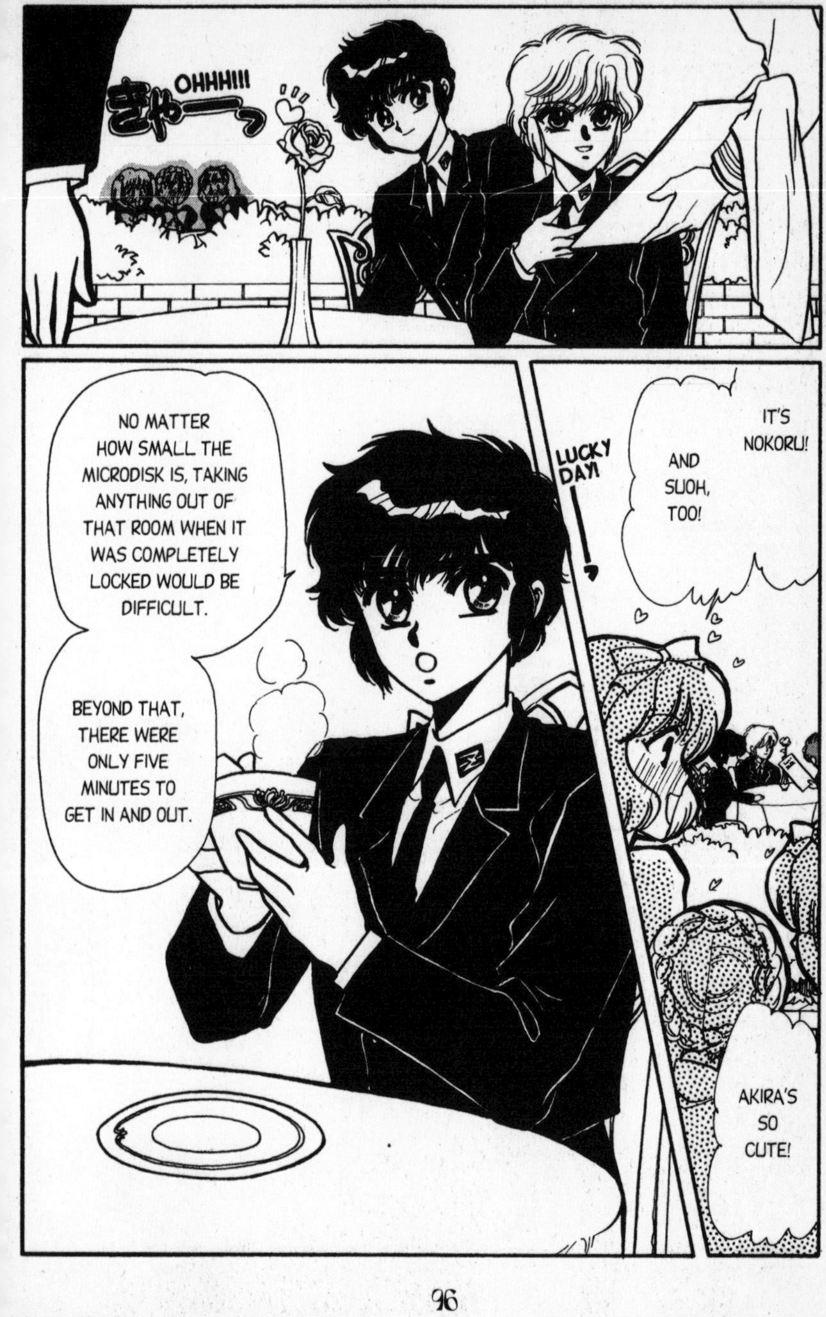
きゃーっ
OHHH!!!
IT'S NOKORU!
AND SUOH, TOO!
LUCKY DAY!
AKIRA'S SO CUTE!
NO MATTER HOW SMALL THE MICRODISK IS, TAKING ANYTHING OUT OF THAT ROOM WHEN IT WAS COMPLETELY LOCKED WOULD BE DIFFICULT.
BEYOND THAT, THERE WERE ONLY FIVE MINUTES TO GET IN AND OUT.

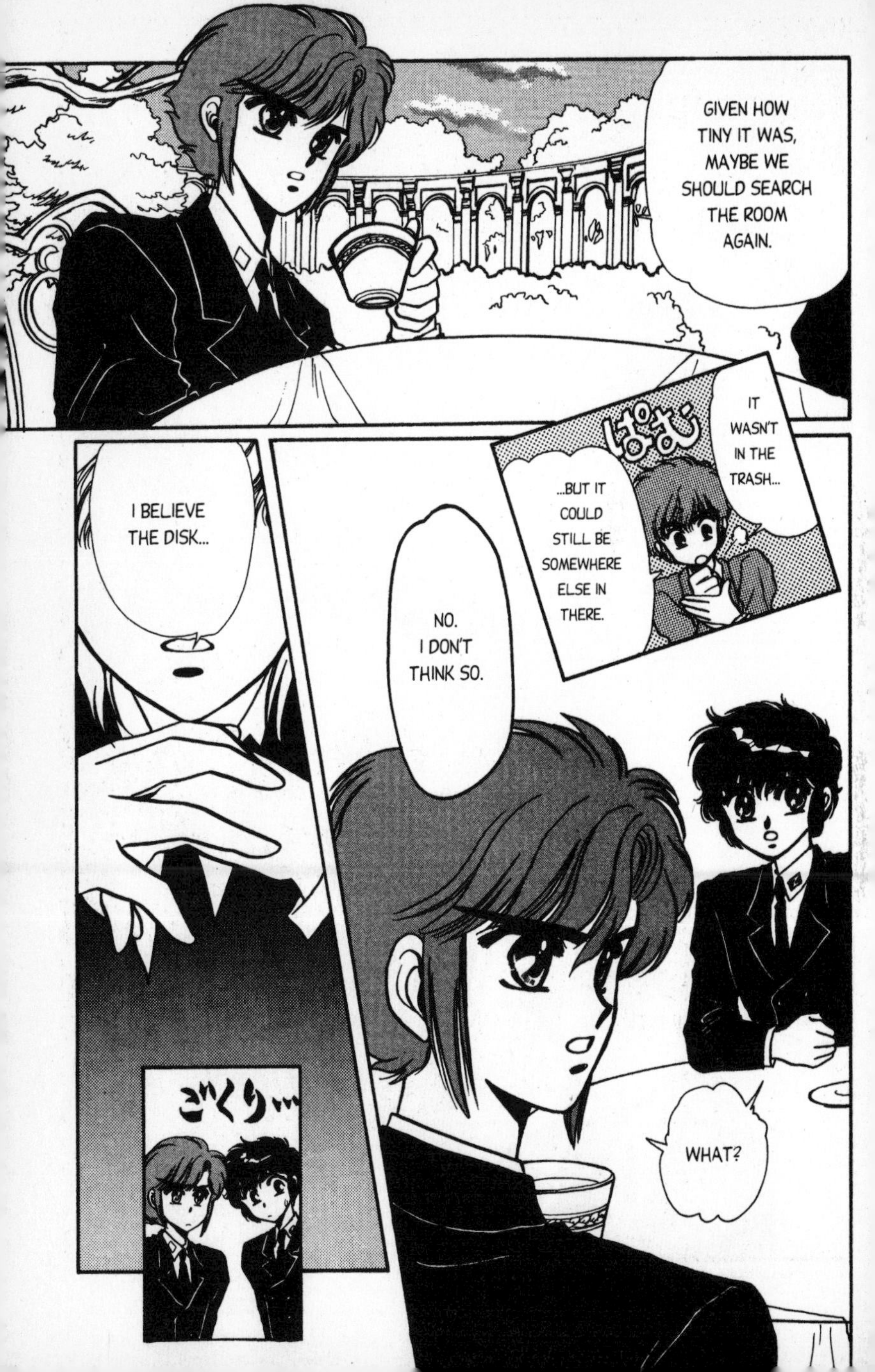
GIVEN HOW TINY IT WAS, MAYBE WE SHOULD SEARCH THE ROOM AGAIN.
IT WASN'T IN THE TRASH...
...BUT IT COULD STILL BE SOMEWHERE ELSE IN THERE.
NO. I DON'T THINK SO.
WHAT?
I BELIEVE THE DISK...
ごくり…

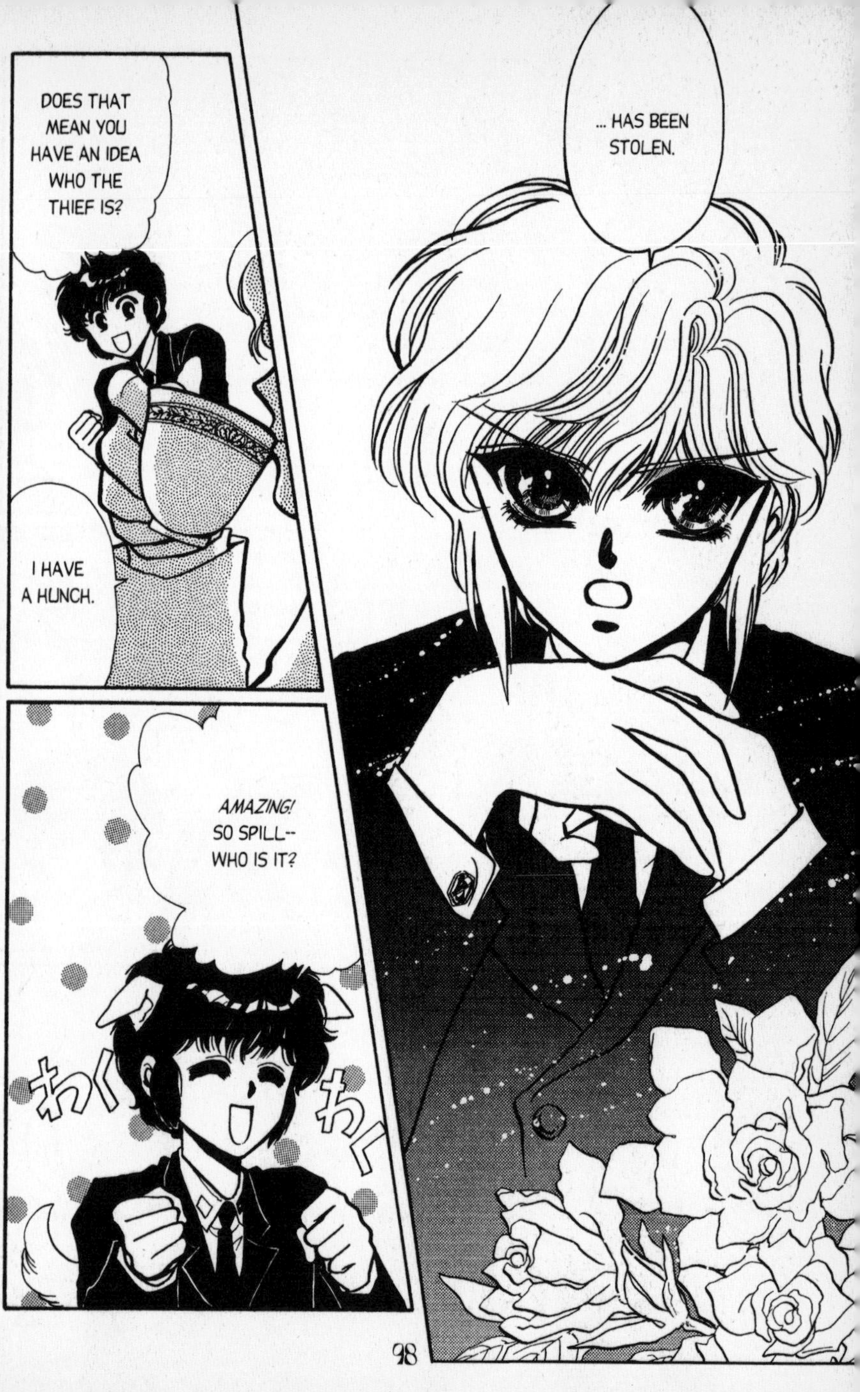
... HAS BEEN STOLEN.
DOES THAT MEAN YOU HAVE AN IDEA WHO THE THIEF IS?
I HAVE A HUNCH.
AMAZING! SO SPILL-- WHO IS IT?
わく
わく

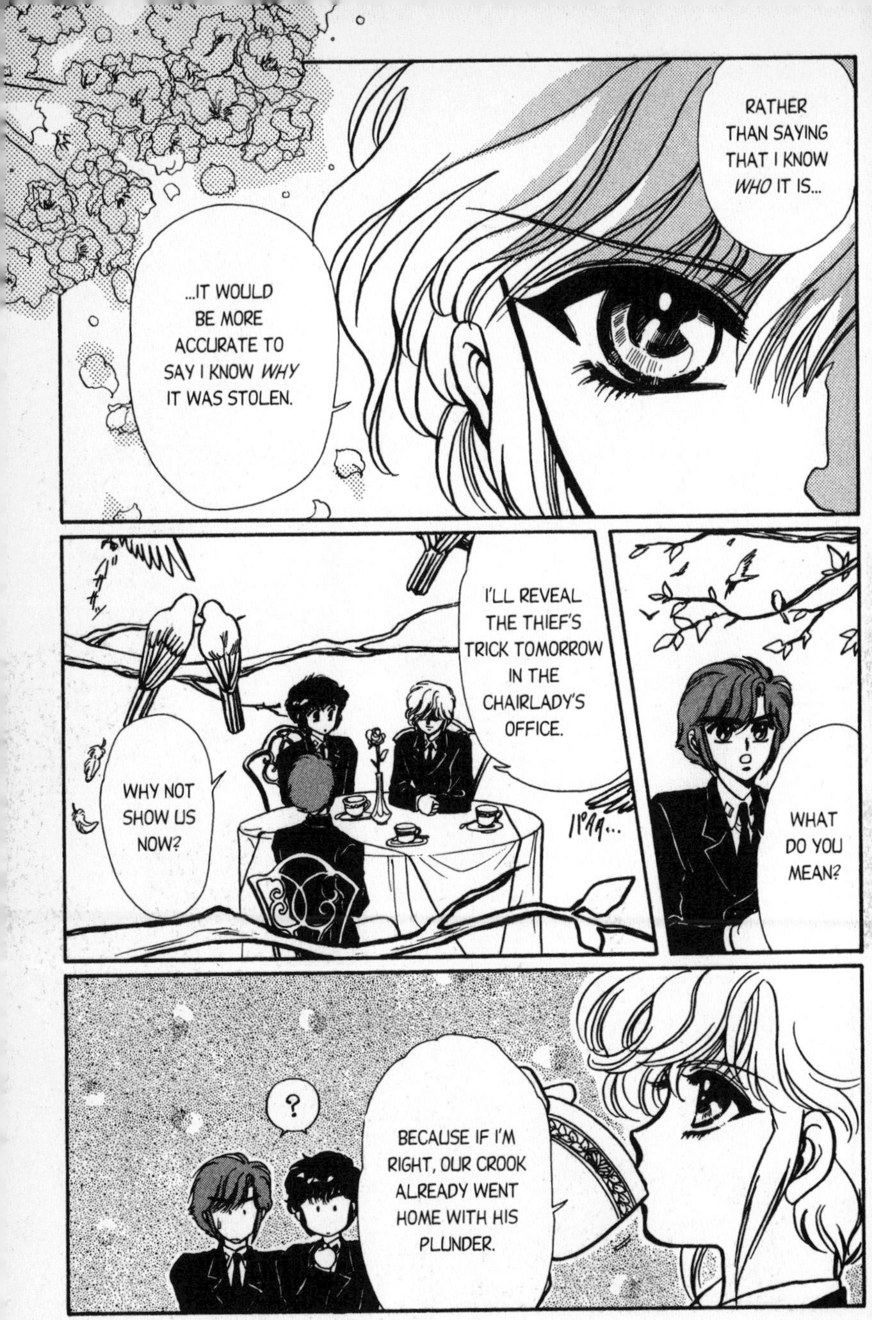
RATHER THAN SAYING THAT I KNOW *WHO* IT IS...
...IT WOULD BE MORE ACCURATE TO SAY I KNOW *WHY* IT WAS STOLEN.
WHAT DO YOU MEAN?
I'LL REVEAL THE THIEF'S TRICK TOMORROW IN THE CHAIRLADY'S OFFICE.
WHY NOT SHOW US NOW?
BECAUSE IF I'M RIGHT, OUR CROOK ALREADY WENT HOME WITH HIS PLUNDER.
?

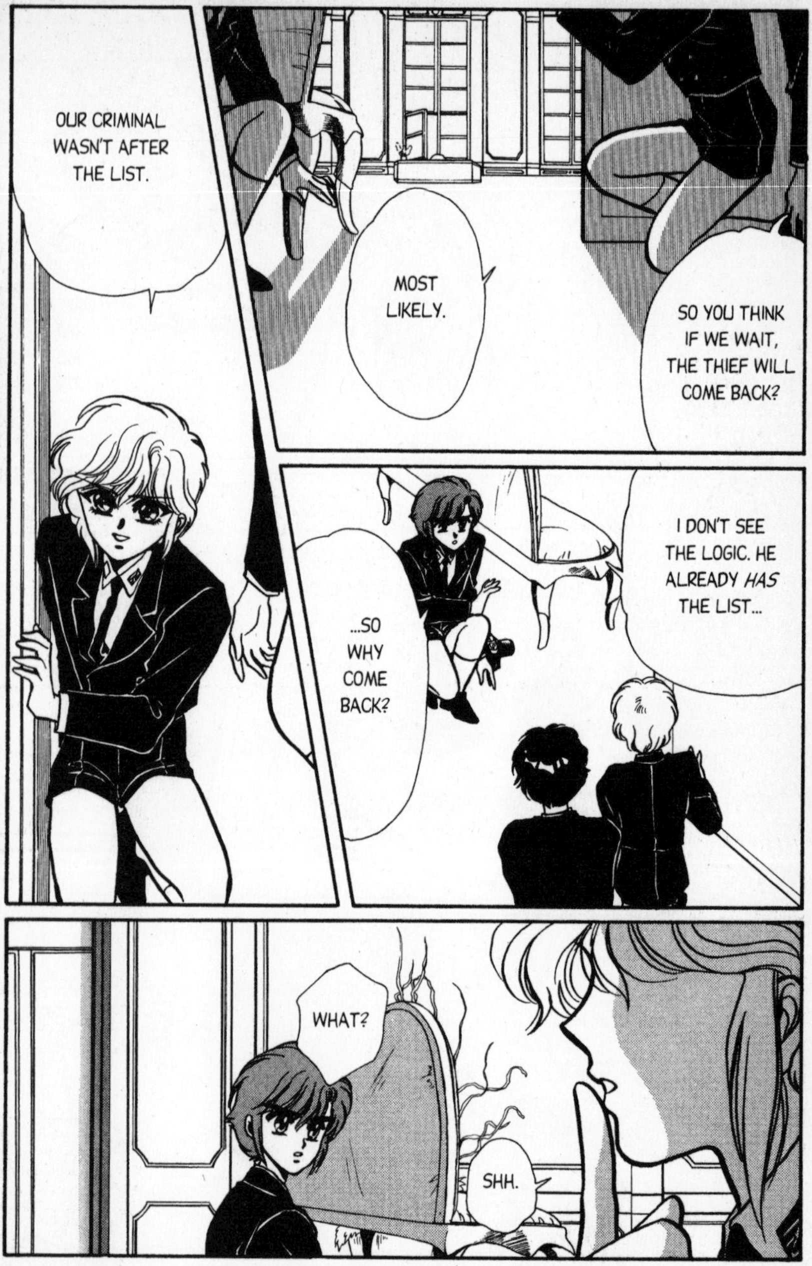
SO YOU THINK IF WE WAIT, THE THIEF WILL COME BACK?
MOST LIKELY.
I DON'T SEE THE LOGIC. HE ALREADY *HAS* THE LIST...
...SO WHY COME BACK?
OUR CRIMINAL WASN'T AFTER THE LIST.
WHAT?
SHH.

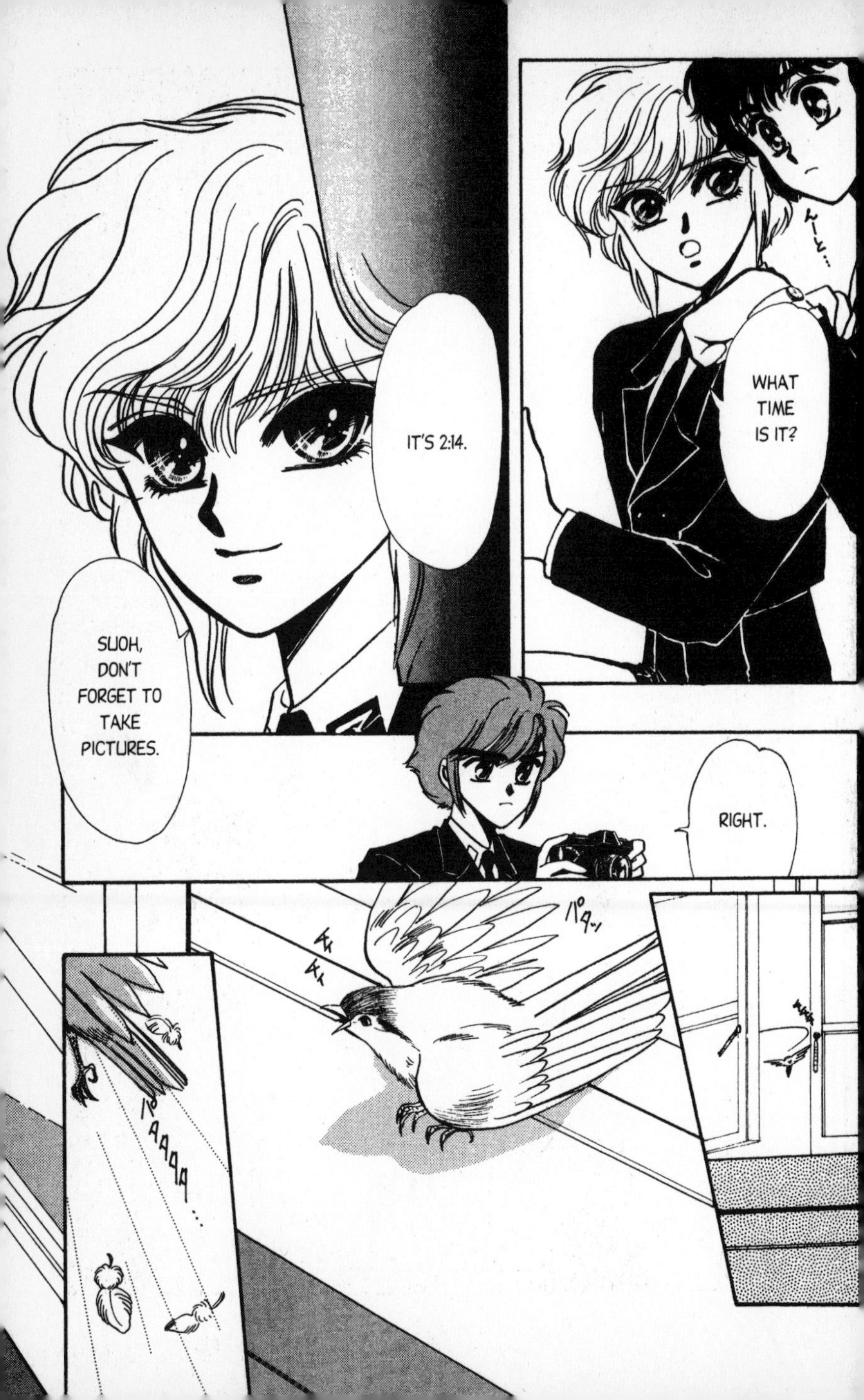
WHAT TIME IS IT?
IT'S 2:14.
SUOH, DON'T FORGET TO TAKE PICTURES.
RIGHT.

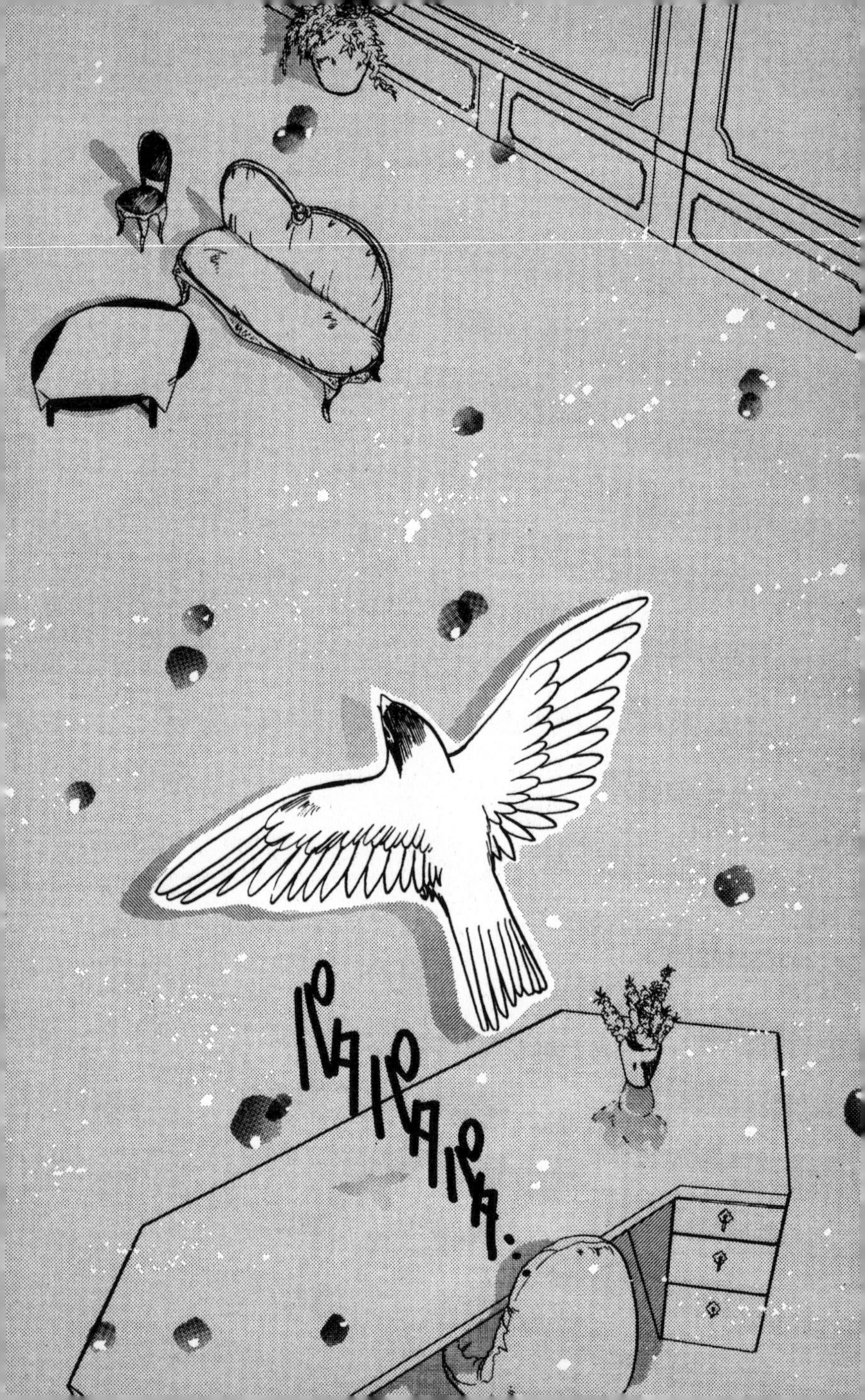
flap flap flap...

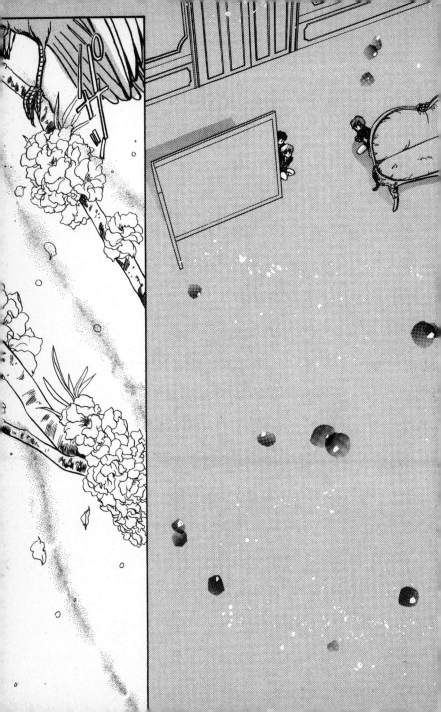

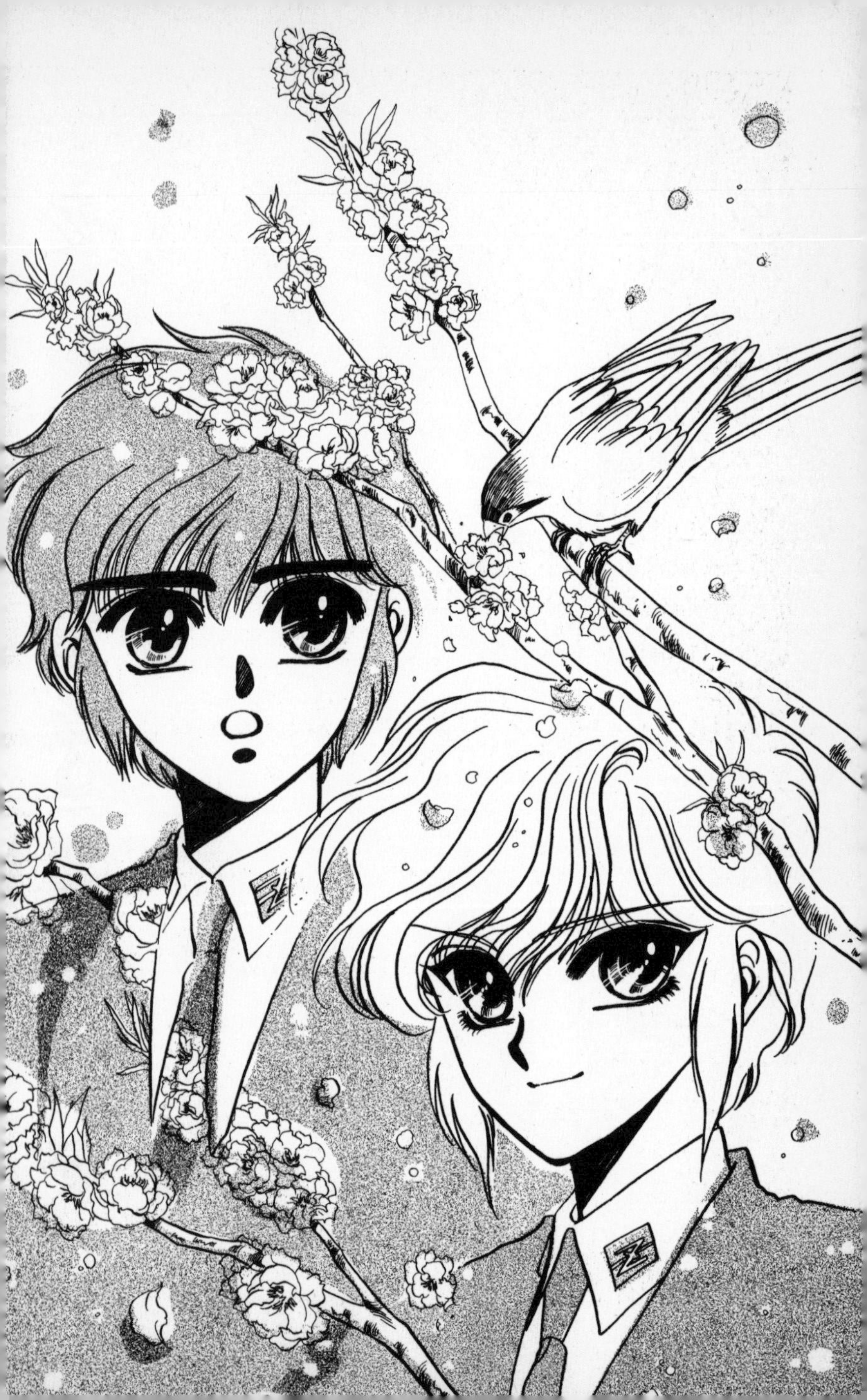

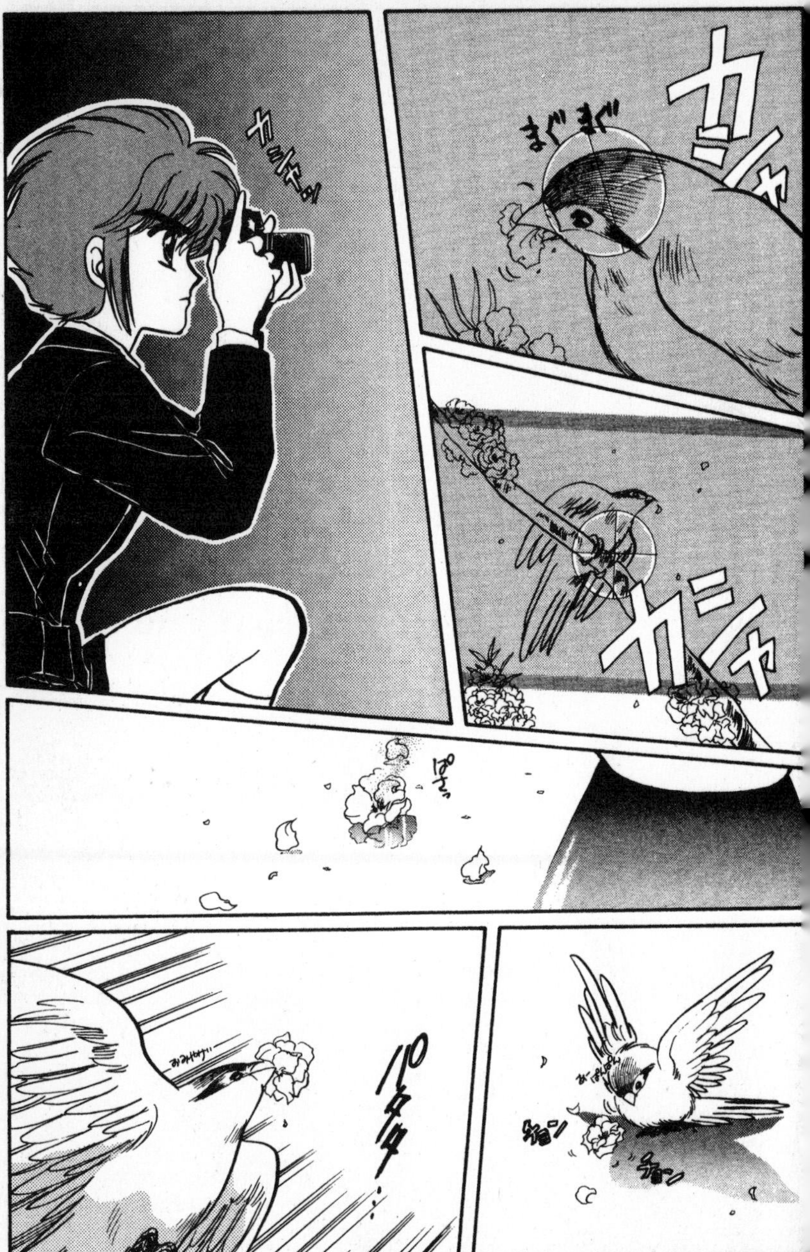
カシャ
まぐまぐ
カシャ
カシャッ
ぱさっ
パタタ…

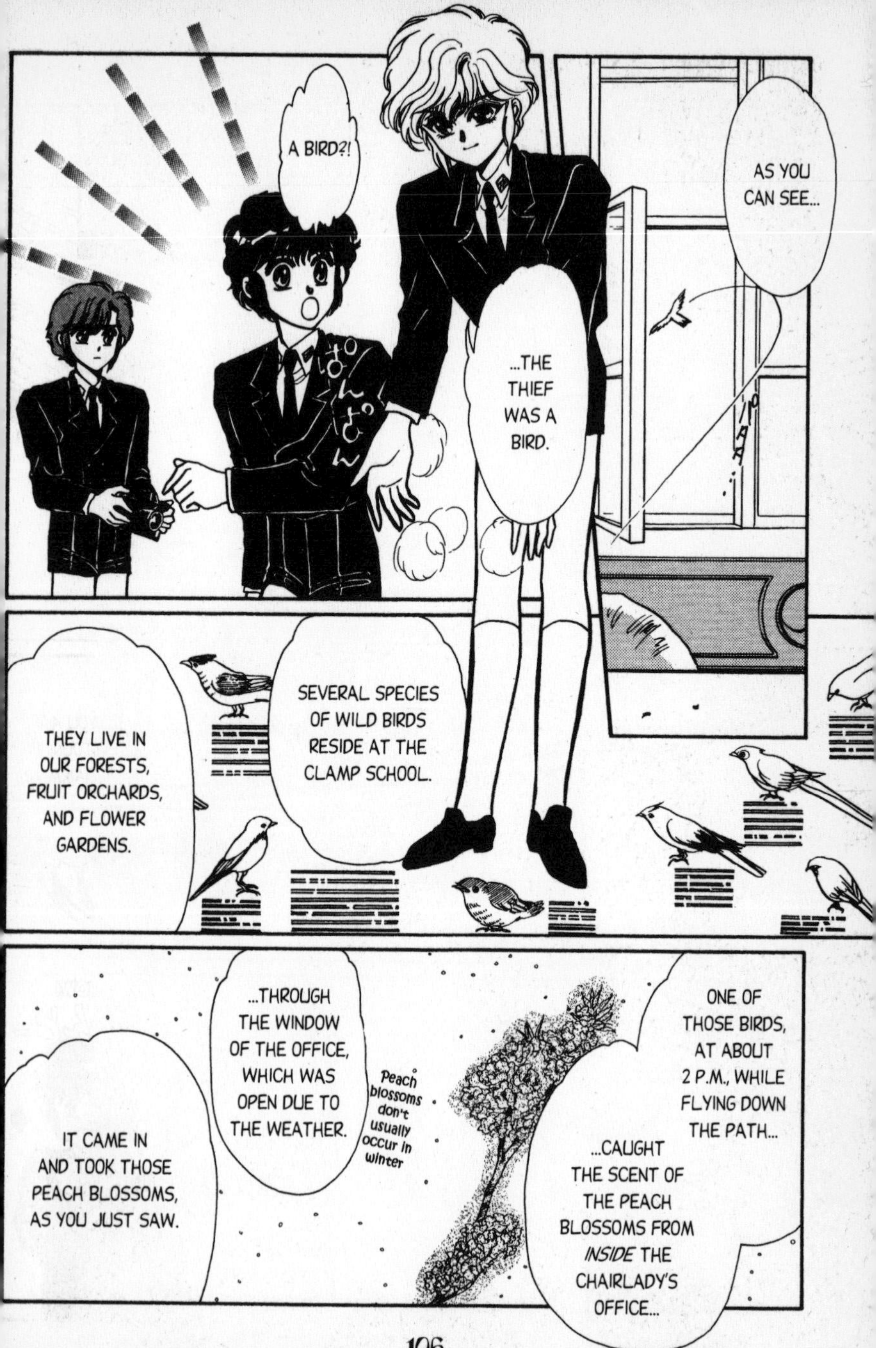
AS YOU CAN SEE...
...THE THIEF WAS A BIRD.
A BIRD?!
SEVERAL SPECIES OF WILD BIRDS RESIDE AT THE CLAMP SCHOOL.
THEY LIVE IN OUR FORESTS, FRUIT ORCHARDS, AND FLOWER GARDENS.
ONE OF THOSE BIRDS, AT ABOUT 2 P.M., WHILE FLYING DOWN THE PATH...
...CAUGHT THE SCENT OF THE PEACH BLOSSOMS FROM *INSIDE* THE CHAIRLADY'S OFFICE...
...THROUGH THE WINDOW OF THE OFFICE, WHICH WAS OPEN DUE TO THE WEATHER.
Peach blossoms don't usually occur in winter
IT CAME IN AND TOOK THOSE PEACH BLOSSOMS, AS YOU JUST SAW.

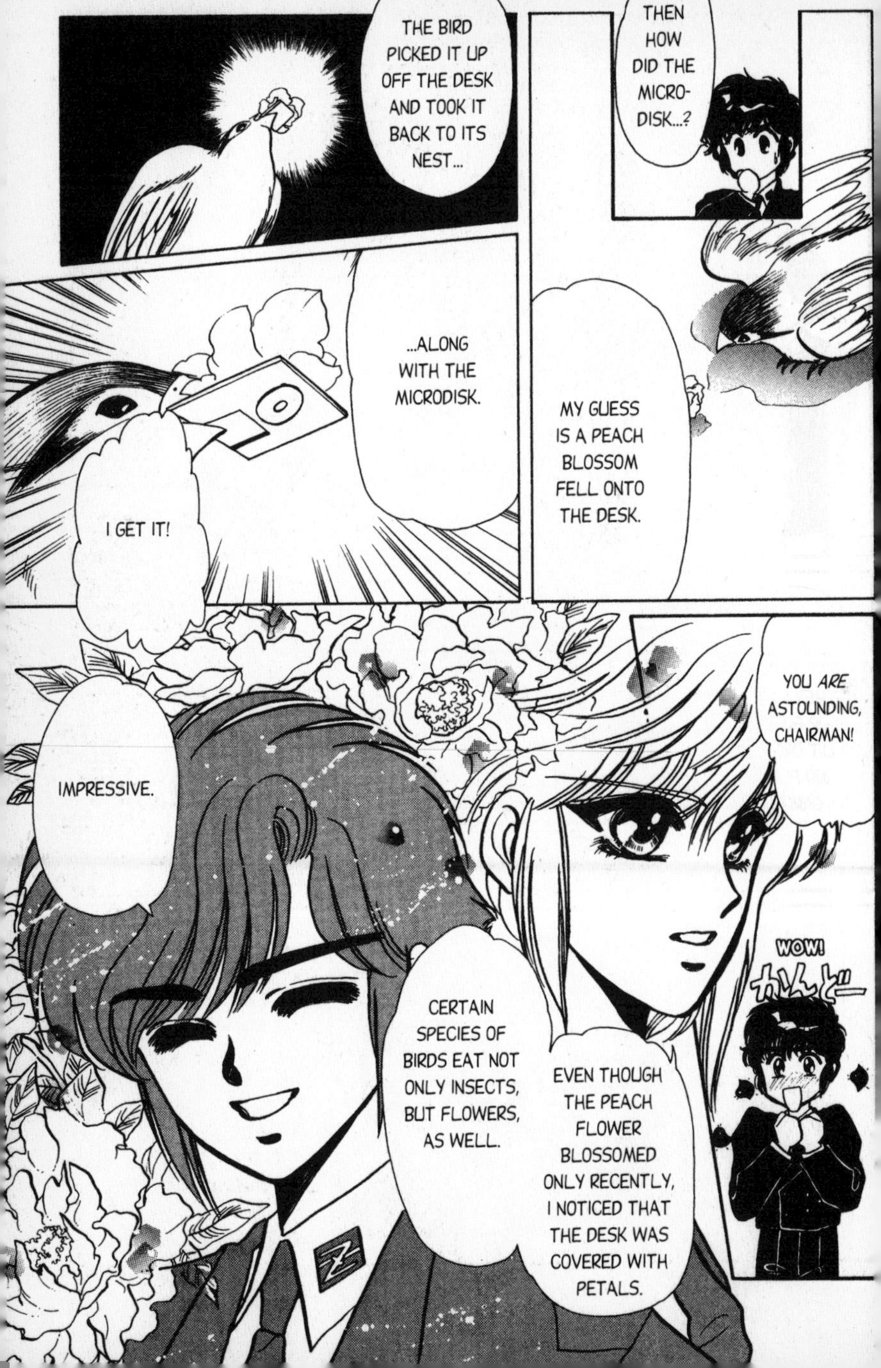
THEN HOW DID THE MICRO-DISK...?
MY GUESS IS A PEACH BLOSSOM FELL ONTO THE DESK.
THE BIRD PICKED IT UP OFF THE DESK AND TOOK IT BACK TO ITS NEST...
...ALONG WITH THE MICRODISK.
I GET IT!
EVEN THOUGH THE PEACH FLOWER BLOSSOMED ONLY RECENTLY, I NOTICED THAT THE DESK WAS COVERED WITH PETALS.
CERTAIN SPECIES OF BIRDS EAT NOT ONLY INSECTS, BUT FLOWERS, AS WELL.
YOU *ARE* ASTOUNDING, CHAIRMAN!
WOW!
かんどー
IMPRESSIVE.

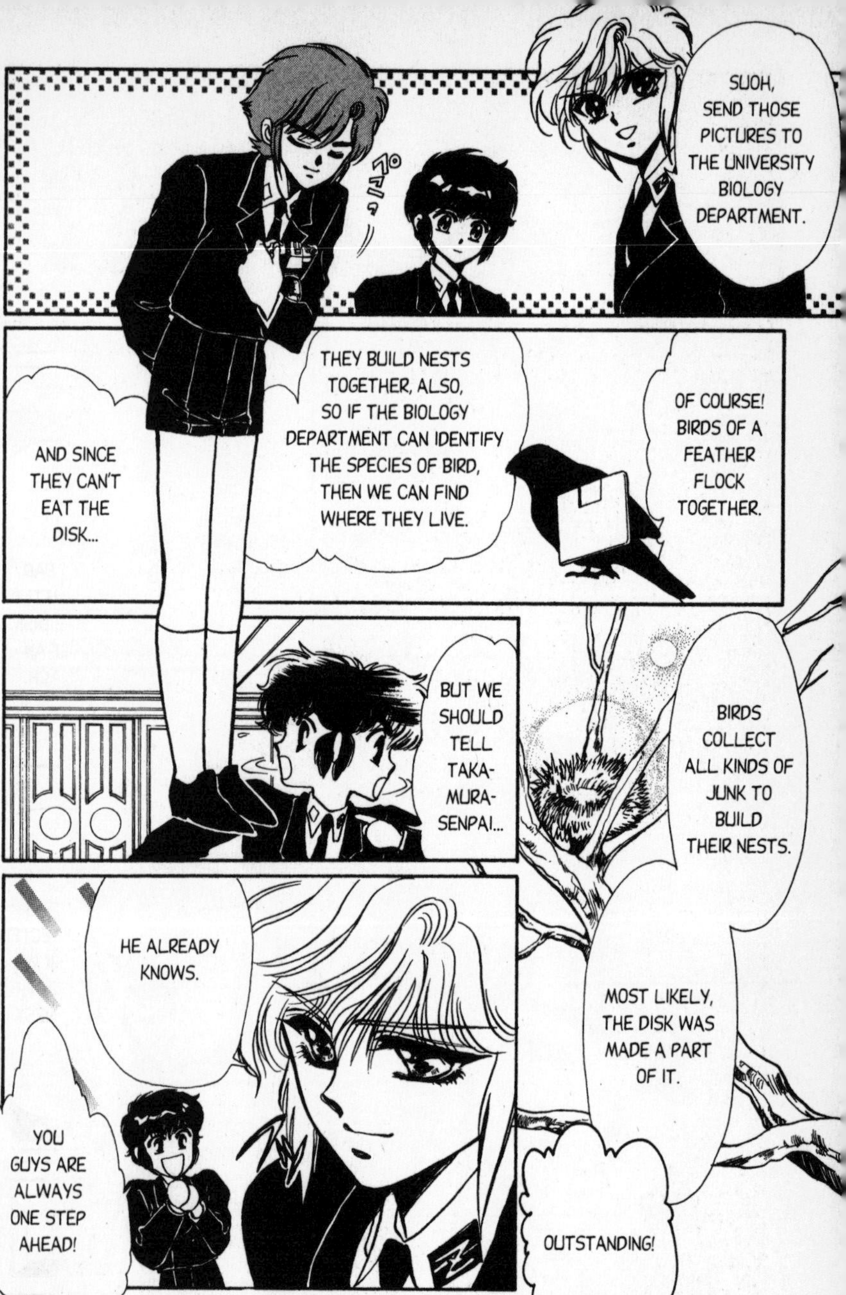
SUOH, SEND THOSE PICTURES TO THE UNIVERSITY BIOLOGY DEPARTMENT.
OF COURSE! BIRDS OF A FEATHER FLOCK TOGETHER.
THEY BUILD NESTS TOGETHER, ALSO, SO IF THE BIOLOGY DEPARTMENT CAN IDENTIFY THE SPECIES OF BIRD, THEN WE CAN FIND WHERE THEY LIVE.
AND SINCE THEY CAN'T EAT THE DISK...
BIRDS COLLECT ALL KINDS OF JUNK TO BUILD THEIR NESTS.
MOST LIKELY, THE DISK WAS MADE A PART OF IT.
OUTSTANDING!
BUT WE SHOULD TELL TAKA-MURA-SENPAI...
HE ALREADY KNOWS.
YOU GUYS ARE ALWAYS ONE STEP AHEAD!

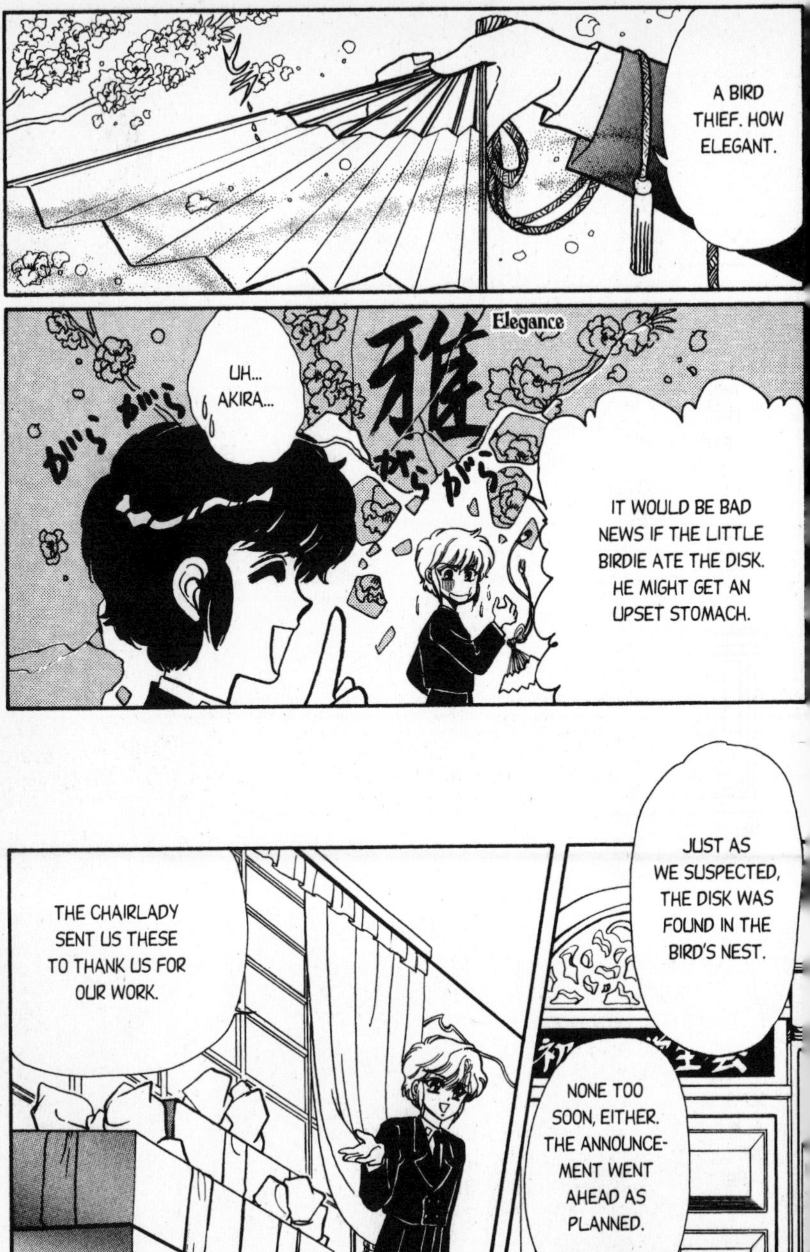
A BIRD THIEF. HOW ELEGANT.
IT WOULD BE BAD NEWS IF THE LITTLE BIRDIE ATE THE DISK. HE MIGHT GET AN UPSET STOMACH.
雅
Elegance
がらがら
UH... AKIRA...
がらがら
JUST AS WE SUSPECTED, THE DISK WAS FOUND IN THE BIRD'S NEST.
NONE TOO SOON, EITHER. THE ANNOUNCEMENT WENT AHEAD AS PLANNED.
THE CHAIRLADY SENT US THESE TO THANK US FOR OUR WORK.

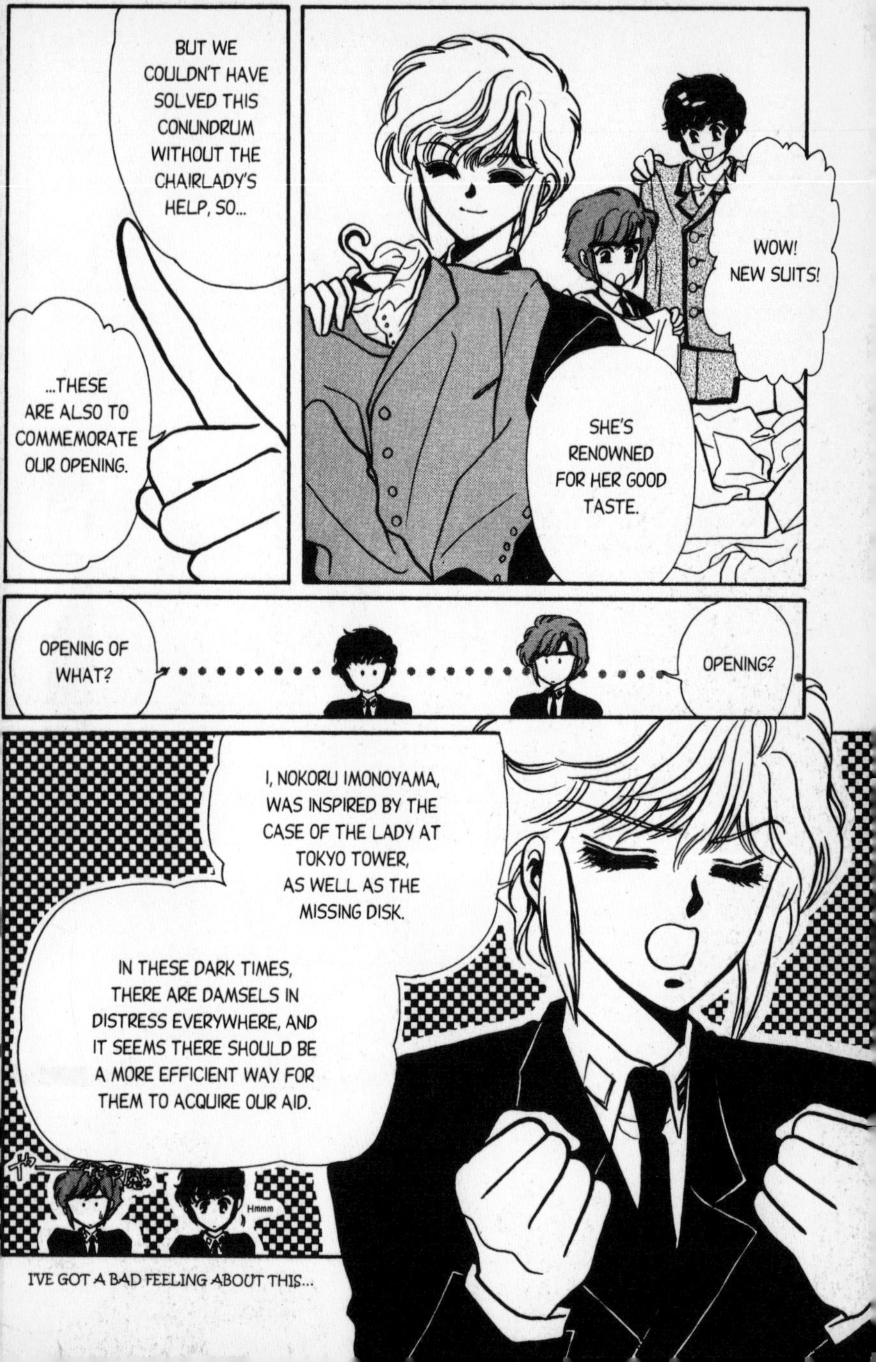
WOW! NEW SUITS!
SHE'S RENOWNED FOR HER GOOD TASTE.
BUT WE COULDN'T HAVE SOLVED THIS CONUNDRUM WITHOUT THE CHAIRLADY'S HELP, SO...
...THESE ARE ALSO TO COMMEMORATE OUR OPENING.
OPENING?
OPENING OF WHAT?
I, NOKORU IMONOYAMA, WAS INSPIRED BY THE CASE OF THE LADY AT TOKYO TOWER, AS WELL AS THE MISSING DISK.
IN THESE DARK TIMES, THERE ARE DAMSELS IN DISTRESS EVERYWHERE, AND IT SEEMS THERE SHOULD BE A MORE EFFICIENT WAY FOR THEM TO ACQUIRE OUR AID.
Hmmm
I'VE GOT A BAD FEELING ABOUT THIS...

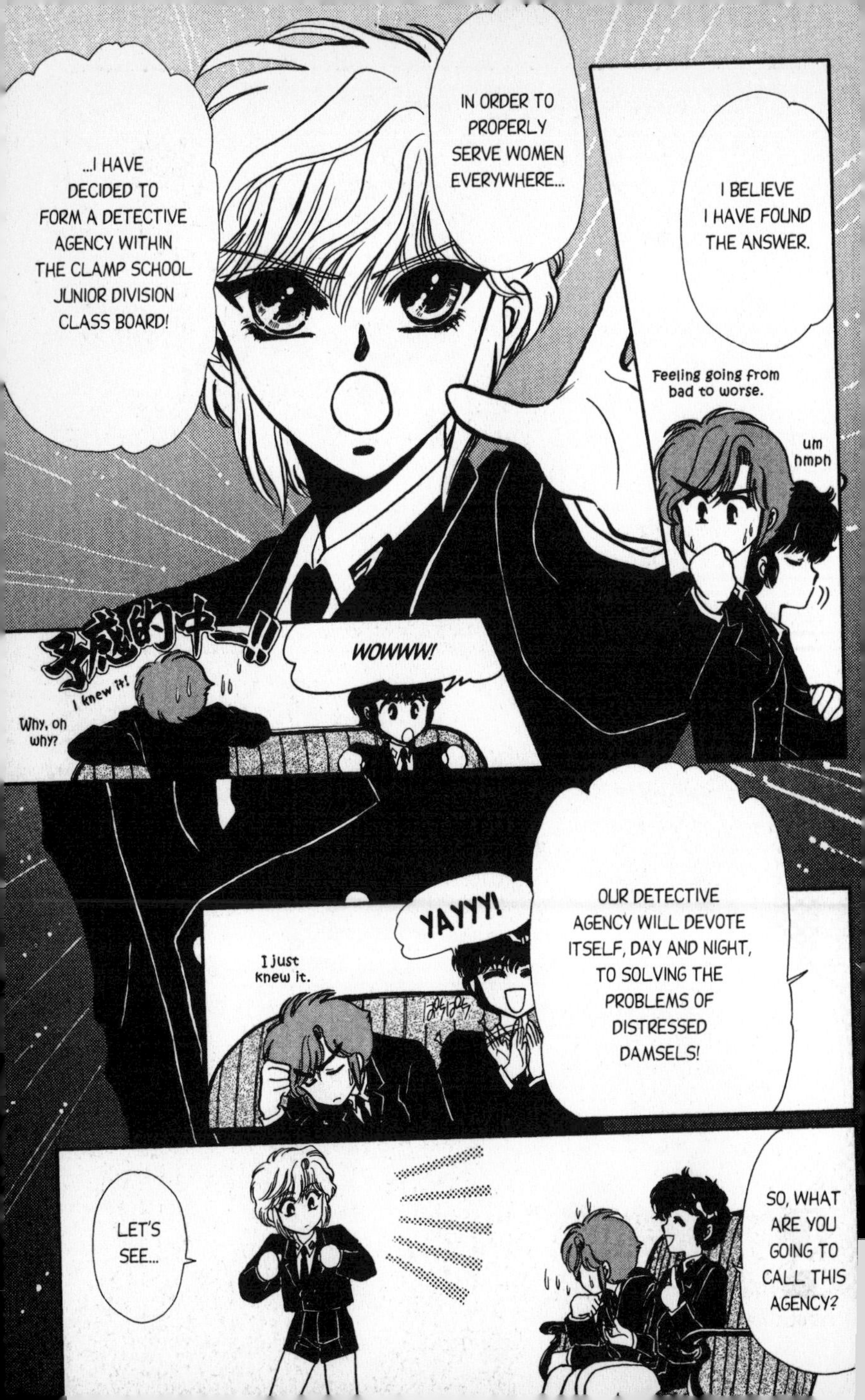
I BELIEVE I HAVE FOUND THE ANSWER.
Feeling going from bad to worse.
um hmph
IN ORDER TO PROPERLY SERVE WOMEN EVERYWHERE...
...I HAVE DECIDED TO FORM A DETECTIVE AGENCY WITHIN THE CLAMP SCHOOL JUNIOR DIVISION CLASS BOARD!
WOWWW!
予感的中ー!!
I knew it!
Why, oh why?
OUR DETECTIVE AGENCY WILL DEVOTE ITSELF, DAY AND NIGHT, TO SOLVING THE PROBLEMS OF DISTRESSED DAMSELS!
YAYYY!
I just knew it.
SO, WHAT ARE YOU GOING TO CALL THIS AGENCY?
LET'S SEE...

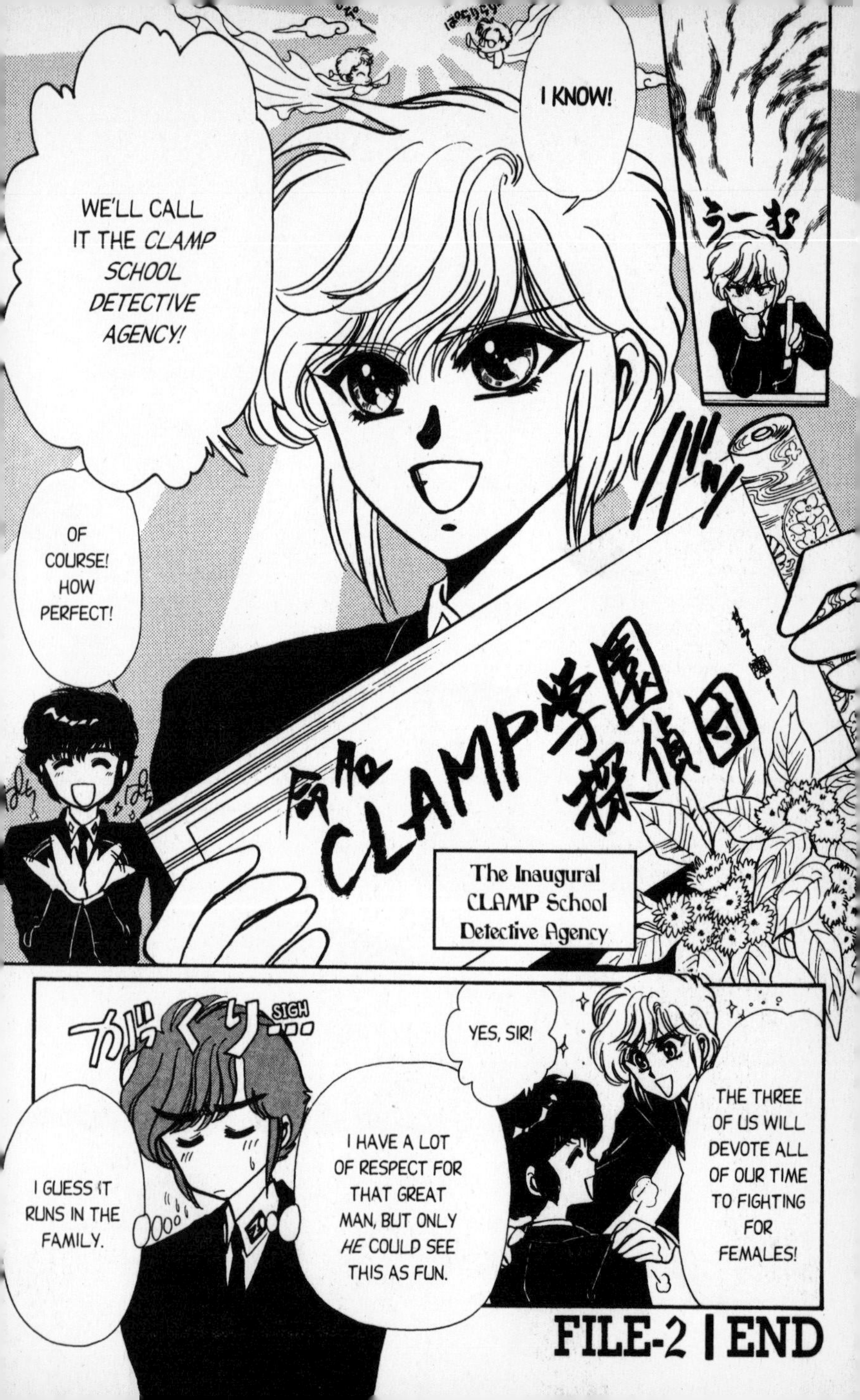
うーむ
I KNOW!
WE'LL CALL IT THE *CLAMP SCHOOL DETECTIVE AGENCY!*
OF COURSE! HOW PERFECT!
CLAMP学園探偵団
The Inaugural CLAMP School Detective Agency
THE THREE OF US WILL DEVOTE ALL OF OUR TIME TO FIGHTING FOR FEMALES!
YES, SIR!
I HAVE A LOT OF RESPECT FOR THAT GREAT MAN, BUT ONLY *HE* COULD SEE THIS AS FUN.
がっくり SIGH
I GUESS IT RUNS IN THE FAMILY.
FILE-2 | END

CLAMP学園
FILE-3 探偵団

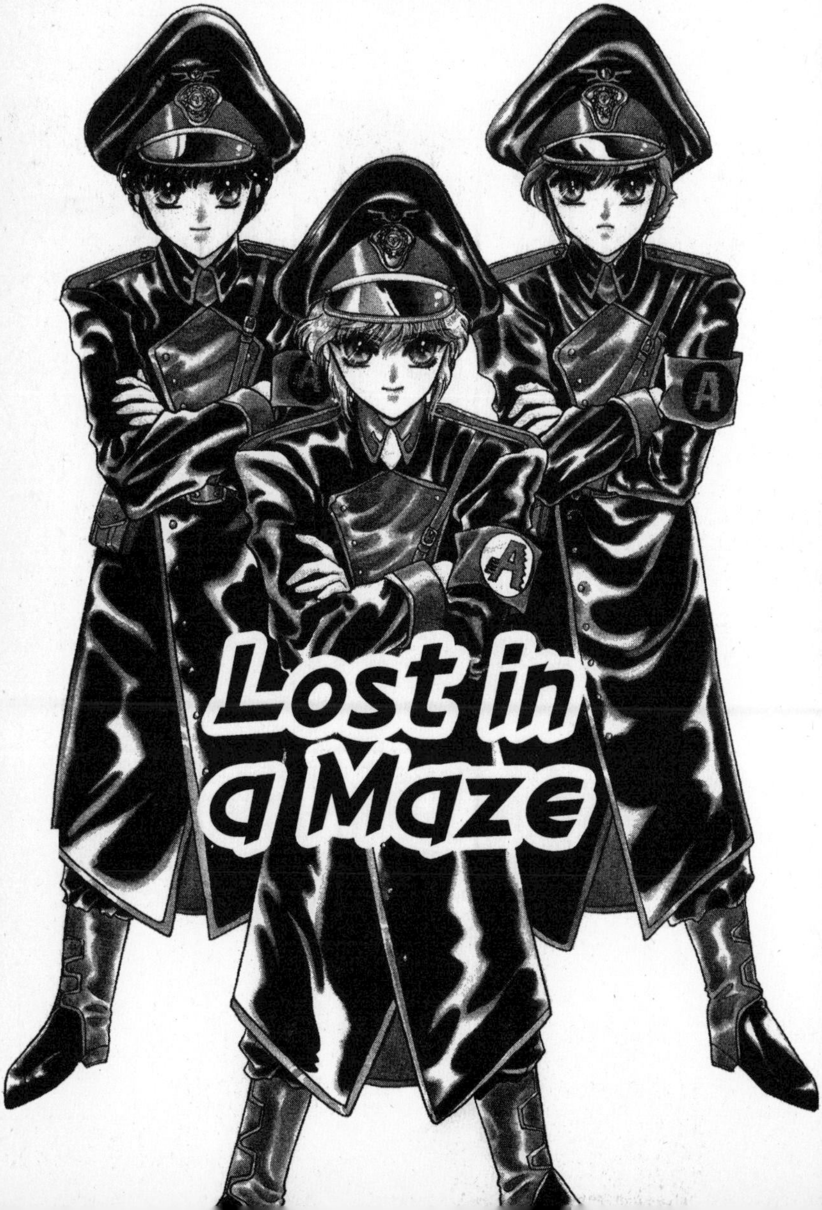
Lost in
a Maze

CLAMP学園
探偵団

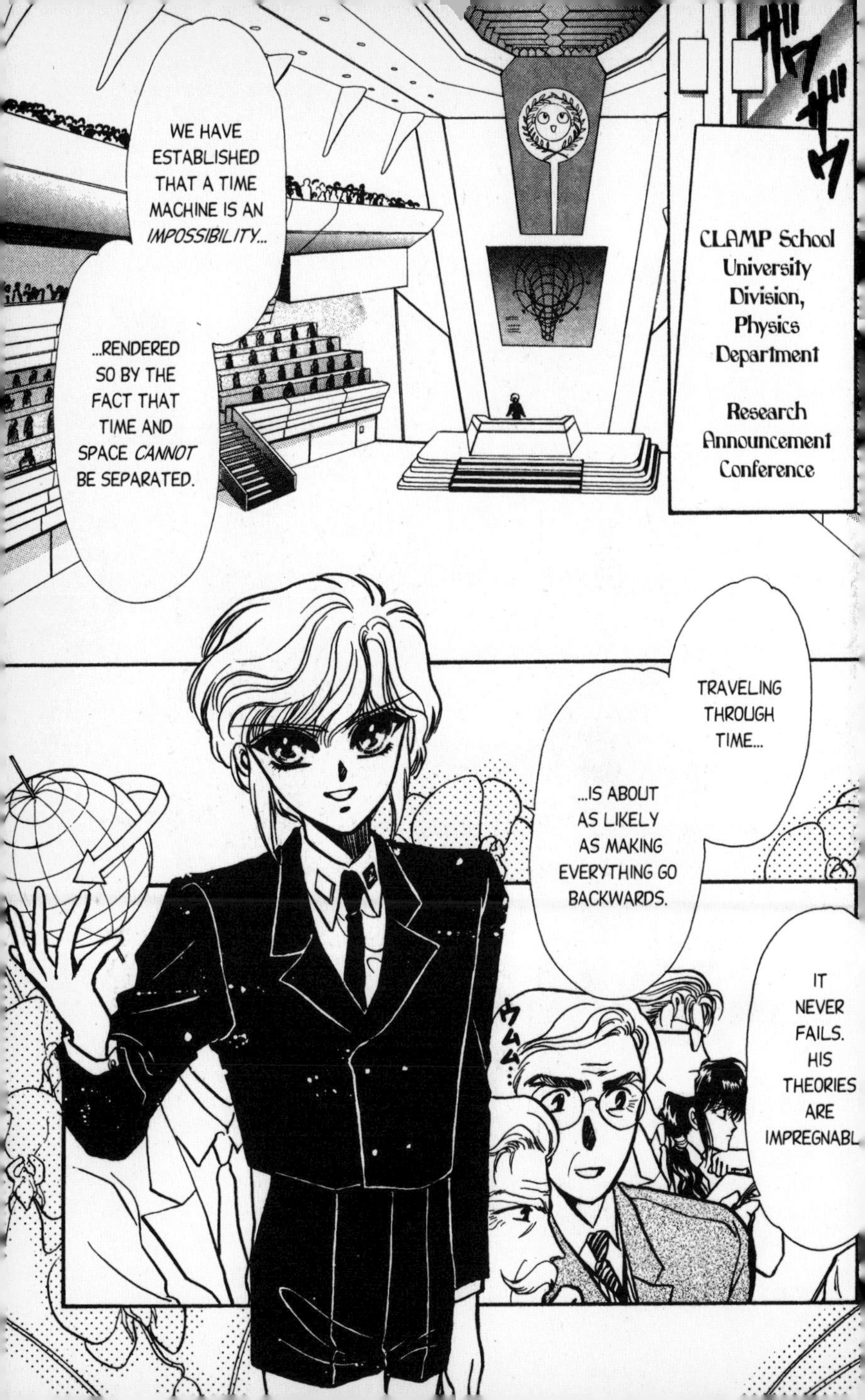
ザワ ザワ
CLAMP School University Division, Physics Department
Research Announcement Conference
WE HAVE ESTABLISHED THAT A TIME MACHINE IS AN *IMPOSSIBILITY*...
...RENDERED SO BY THE FACT THAT TIME AND SPACE *CANNOT* BE SEPARATED.
TRAVELING THROUGH TIME...
...IS ABOUT AS LIKELY AS MAKING EVERYTHING GO BACKWARDS.
IT NEVER FAILS. HIS THEORIES ARE IMPREGNABL
ウムム…

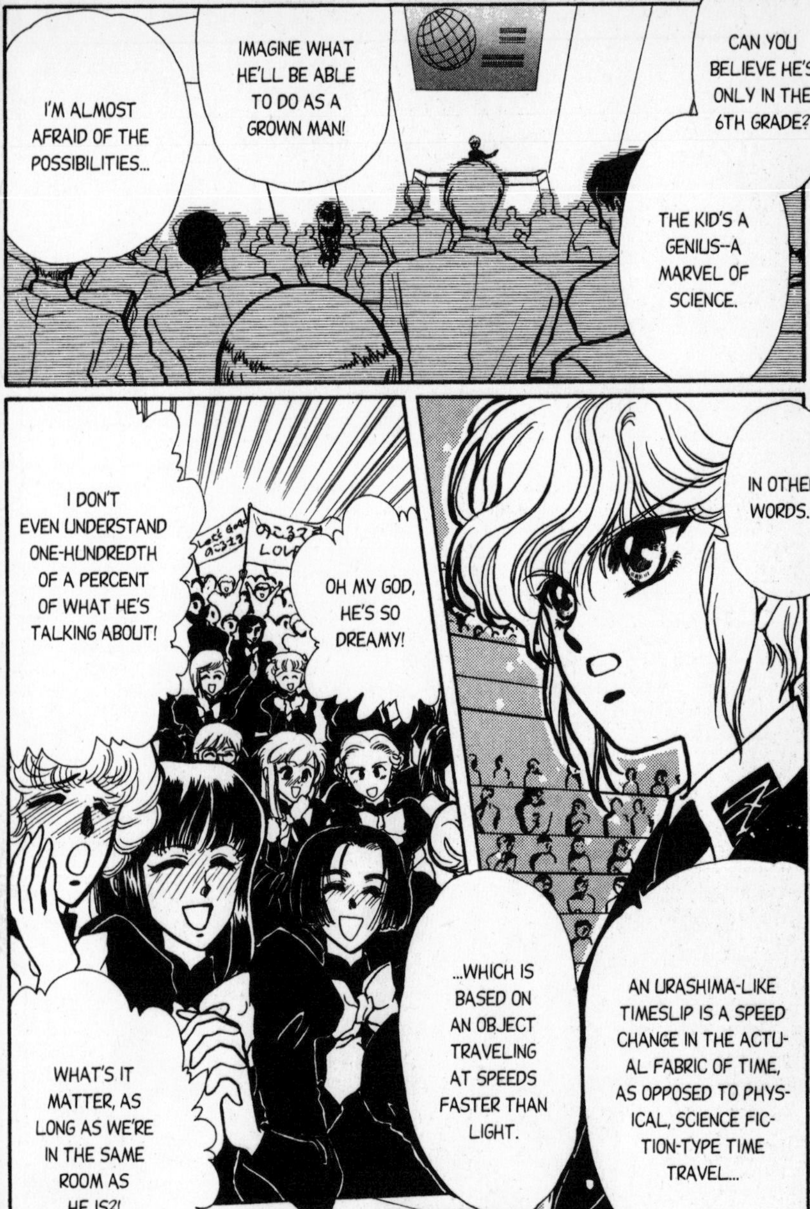
CAN YOU BELIEVE HE'S ONLY IN THE 6TH GRADE?
THE KID'S A GENIUS--A MARVEL OF SCIENCE.
IMAGINE WHAT HE'LL BE ABLE TO DO AS A GROWN MAN!
I'M ALMOST AFRAID OF THE POSSIBILITIES...
IN OTHER WORDS...
AN URASHIMA-LIKE TIMESLIP IS A SPEED CHANGE IN THE ACTUAL FABRIC OF TIME, AS OPPOSED TO PHYSICAL, SCIENCE FICTION-TYPE TIME TRAVEL...
...WHICH IS BASED ON AN OBJECT TRAVELING AT SPEEDS FASTER THAN LIGHT.
OH MY GOD, HE'S SO DREAMY!
I DON'T EVEN UNDERSTAND ONE-HUNDREDTH OF A PERCENT OF WHAT HE'S TALKING ABOUT!
WHAT'S IT MATTER, AS LONG AS WE'RE IN THE SAME ROOM AS HE IS?!

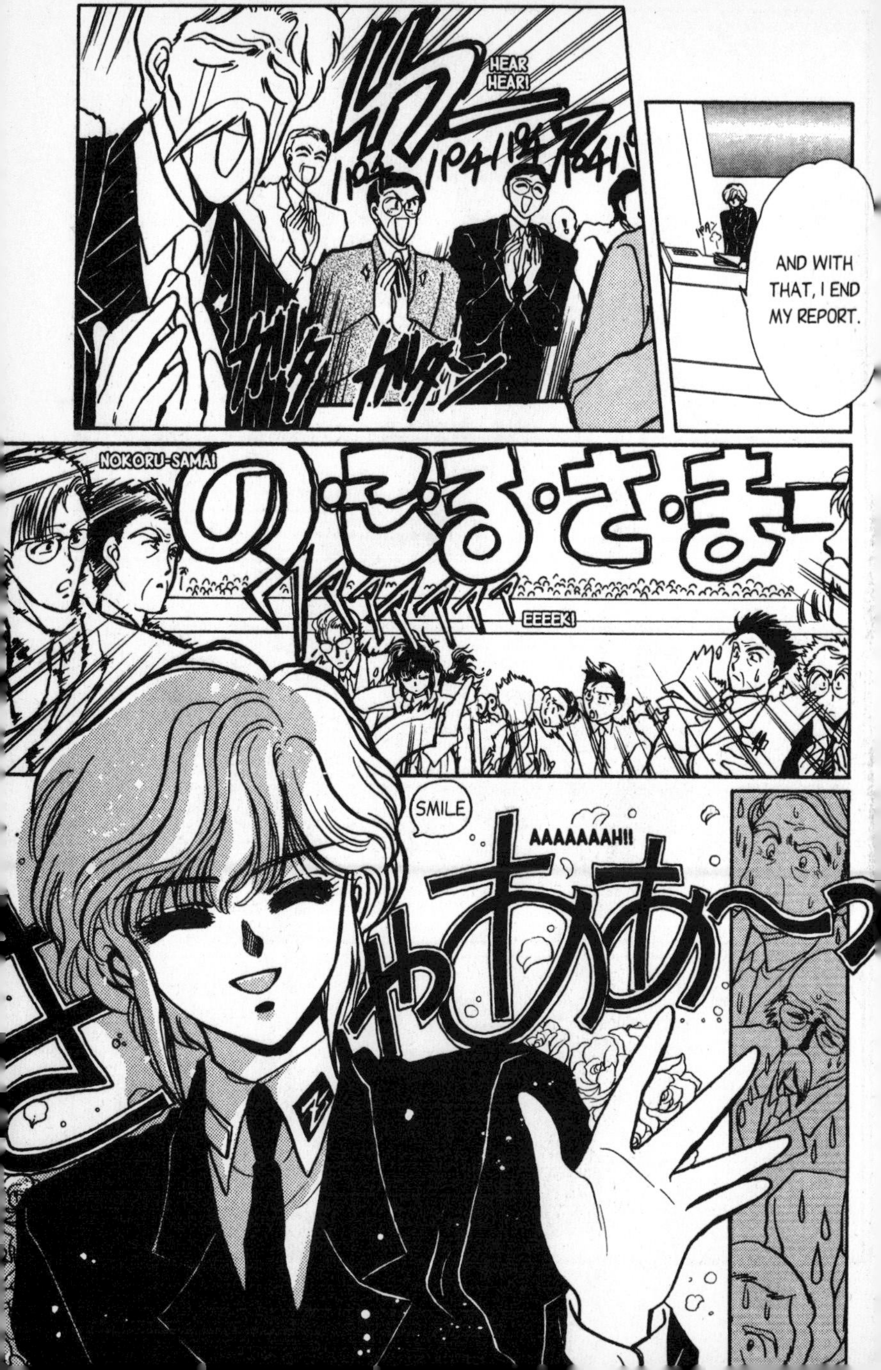
AND WITH THAT, I END MY REPORT.
HEAR HEAR!
NOKORU-SAMA!
のこるさまー
EEEEK!
SMILE
AAAAAAAH!!

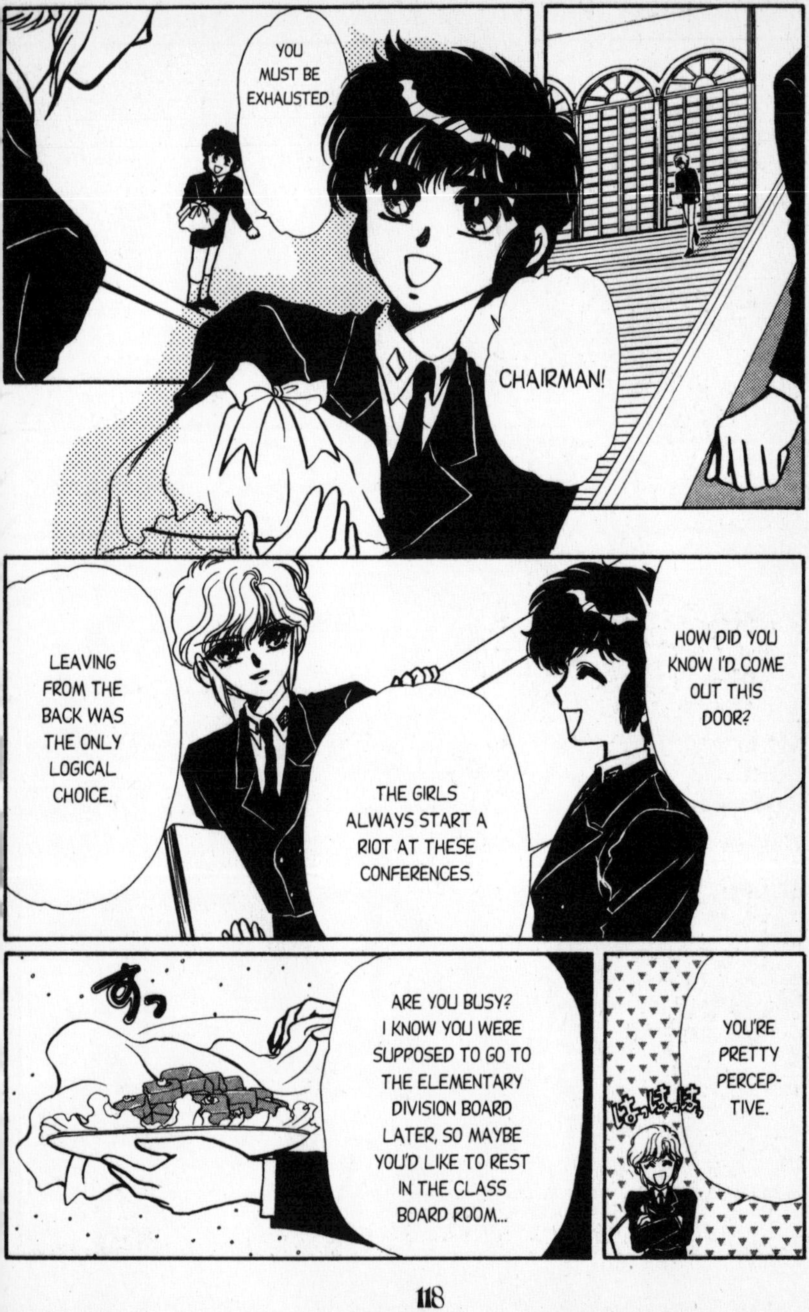
CHAIRMAN!
YOU MUST BE EXHAUSTED.
HOW DID YOU KNOW I'D COME OUT THIS DOOR?
THE GIRLS ALWAYS START A RIOT AT THESE CONFERENCES.
LEAVING FROM THE BACK WAS THE ONLY LOGICAL CHOICE.
YOU'RE PRETTY PERCEP-TIVE.
はっはっは
すっ
ARE YOU BUSY? I KNOW YOU WERE SUPPOSED TO GO TO THE ELEMENTARY DIVISION BOARD LATER, SO MAYBE YOU'D LIKE TO REST IN THE CLASS BOARD ROOM...

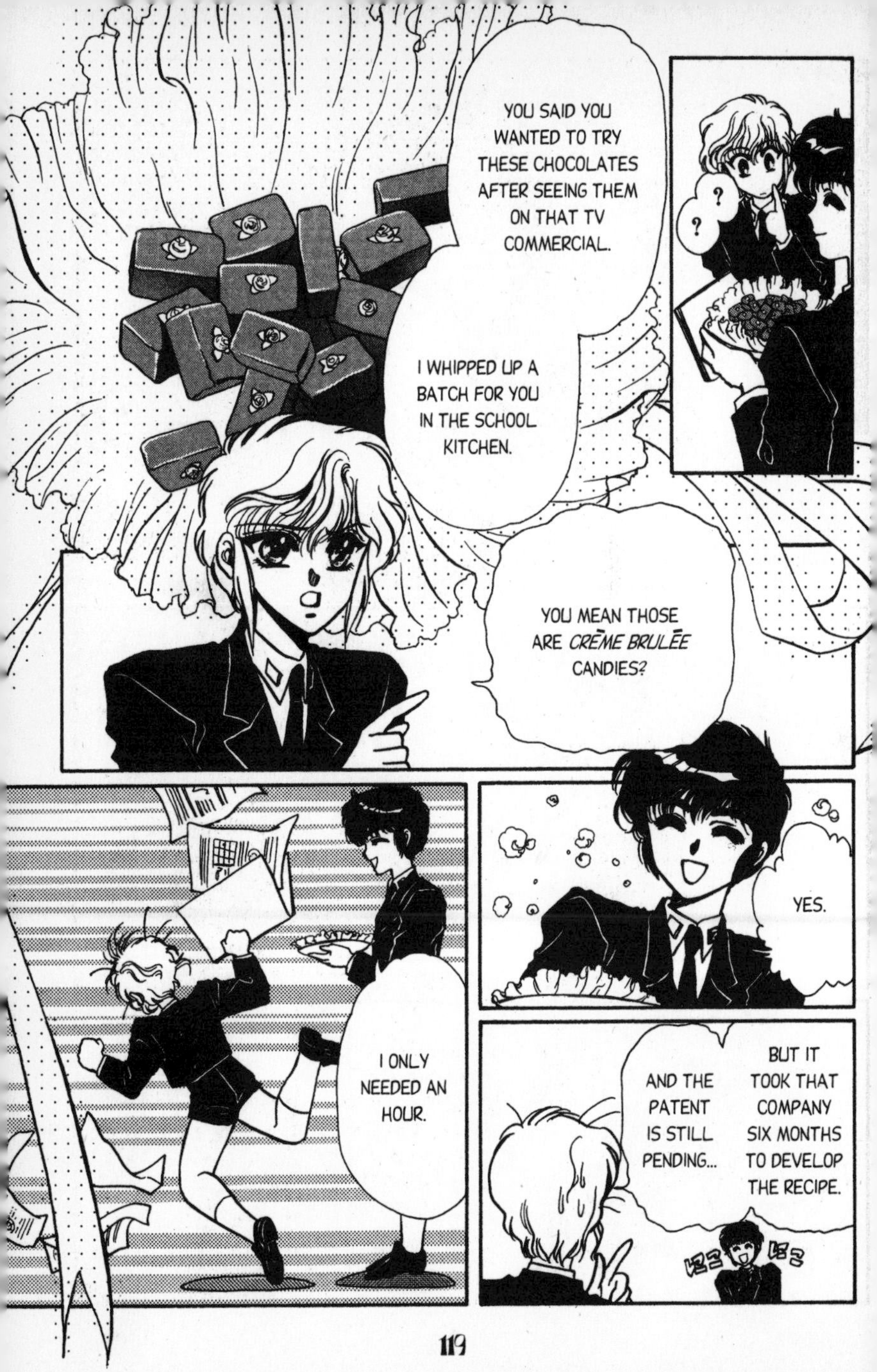
? ?
YOU SAID YOU WANTED TO TRY THESE CHOCOLATES AFTER SEEING THEM ON THAT TV COMMERCIAL.
I WHIPPED UP A BATCH FOR YOU IN THE SCHOOL KITCHEN.
YOU MEAN THOSE ARE *CRÈME BRULÉE* CANDIES?
YES.
BUT IT TOOK THAT COMPANY SIX MONTHS TO DEVELOP THE RECIPE.
AND THE PATENT IS STILL PENDING...
I ONLY NEEDED AN HOUR.

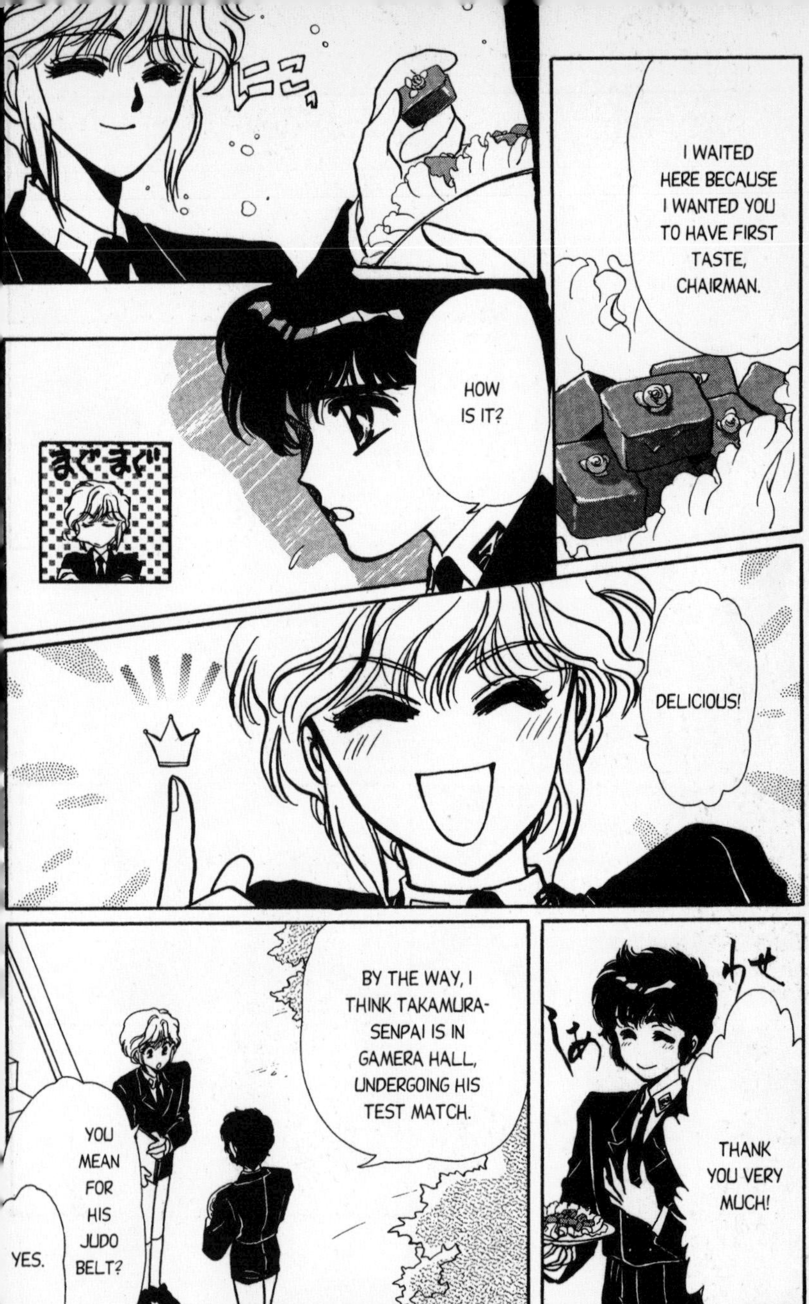
I WAITED HERE BECAUSE I WANTED YOU TO HAVE FIRST TASTE, CHAIRMAN.
にこっ
HOW IS IT?
まぐまぐ
DELICIOUS!
THANK YOU VERY MUCH!
BY THE WAY, I THINK TAKAMURA-SENPAI IS IN GAMERA HALL, UNDERGOING HIS TEST MATCH.
YOU MEAN FOR HIS JUDO BELT?
YES.

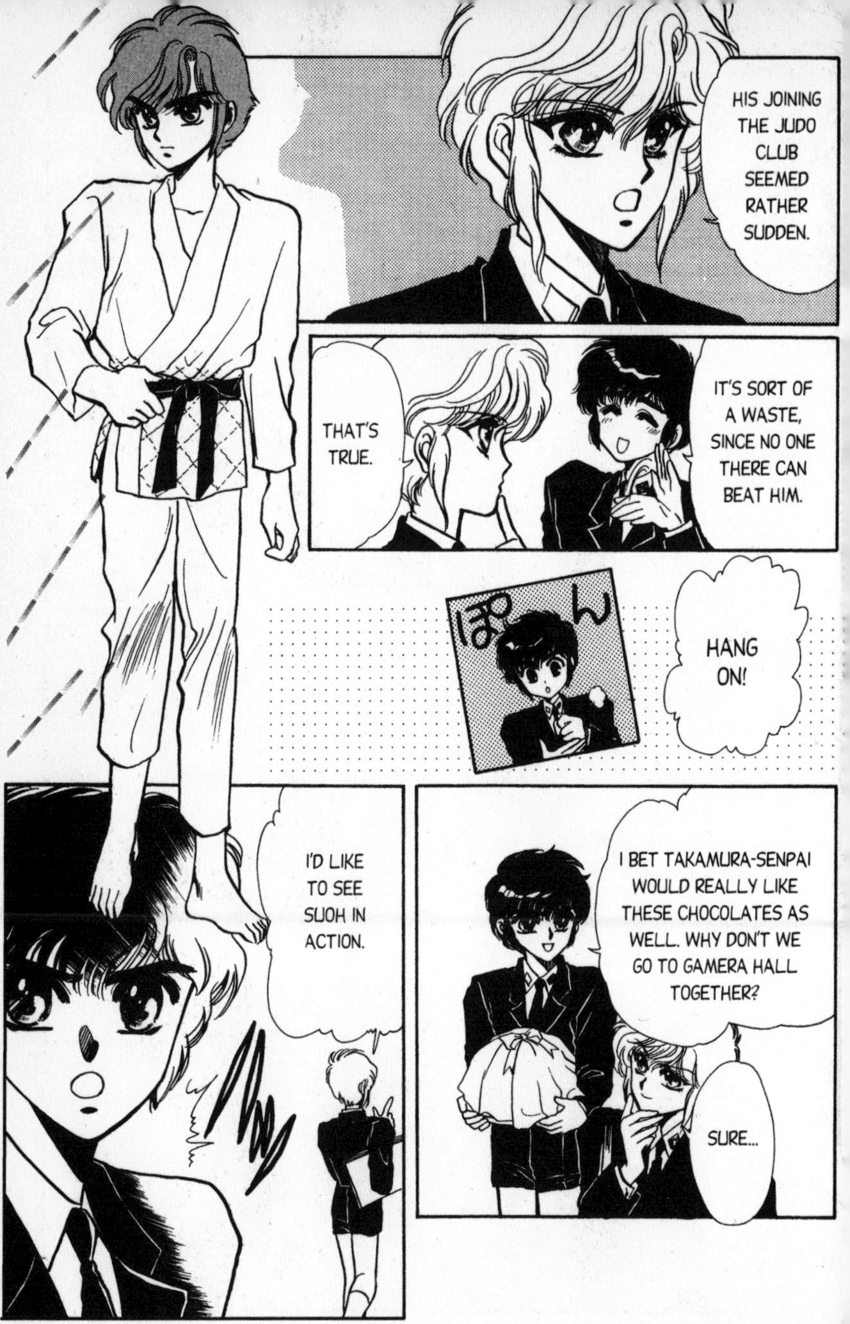
HIS JOINING THE JUDO CLUB SEEMED RATHER SUDDEN.
IT'S SORT OF A WASTE, SINCE NO ONE THERE CAN BEAT HIM.
THAT'S TRUE.
HANG ON!
ぽん
I BET TAKAMURA-SENPAI WOULD REALLY LIKE THESE CHOCOLATES AS WELL. WHY DON'T WE GO TO GAMERA HALL TOGETHER?
SURE...
I'D LIKE TO SEE SUOH IN ACTION.

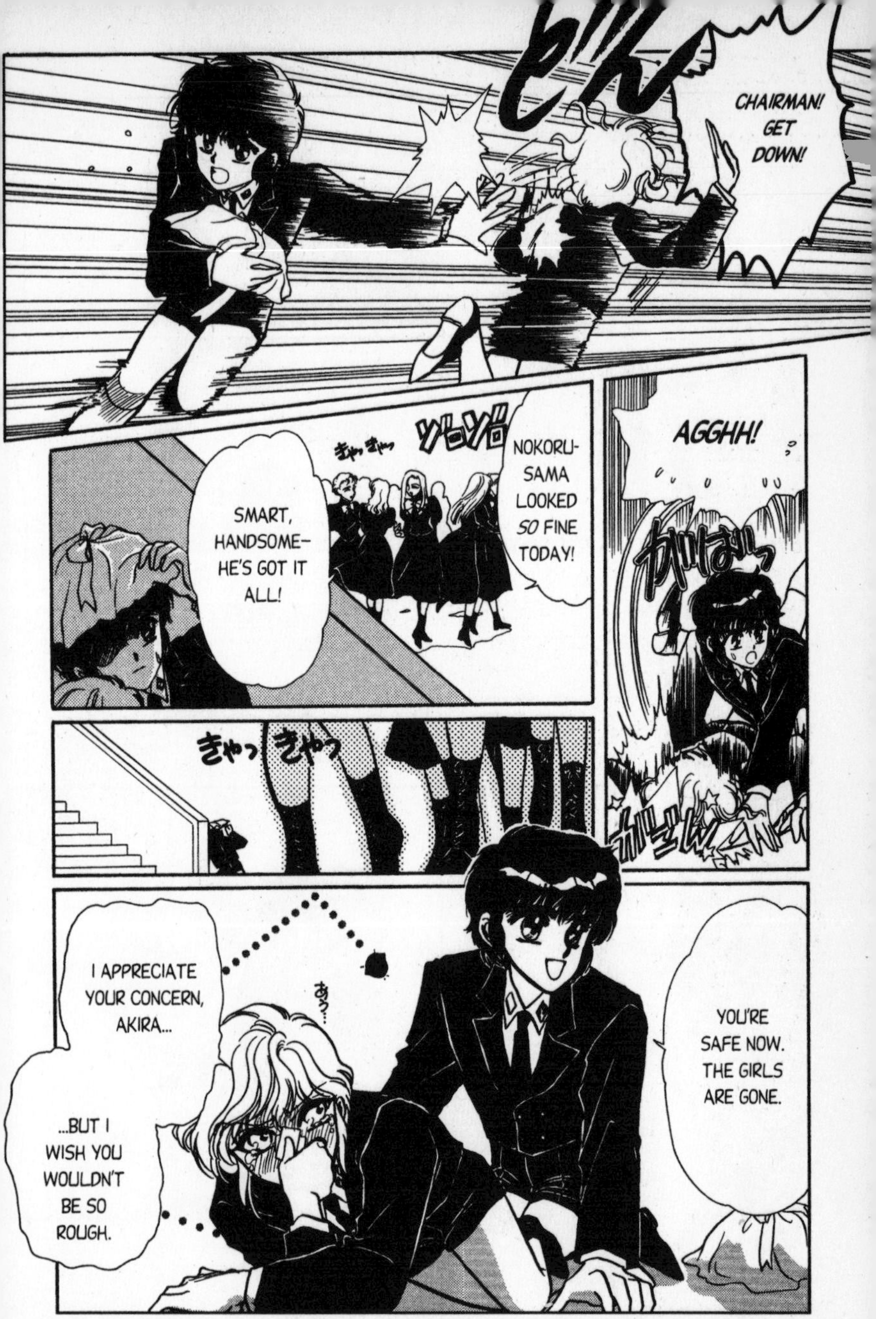
CHAIRMAN! GET DOWN!
AGGHH!
NOKORU-SAMA LOOKED SO FINE TODAY!
SMART, HANDSOME—HE'S GOT IT ALL!
きゃっ きゃっ
YOU'RE SAFE NOW. THE GIRLS ARE GONE.
I APPRECIATE YOUR CONCERN, AKIRA...
...BUT I WISH YOU WOULDN'T BE SO ROUGH.

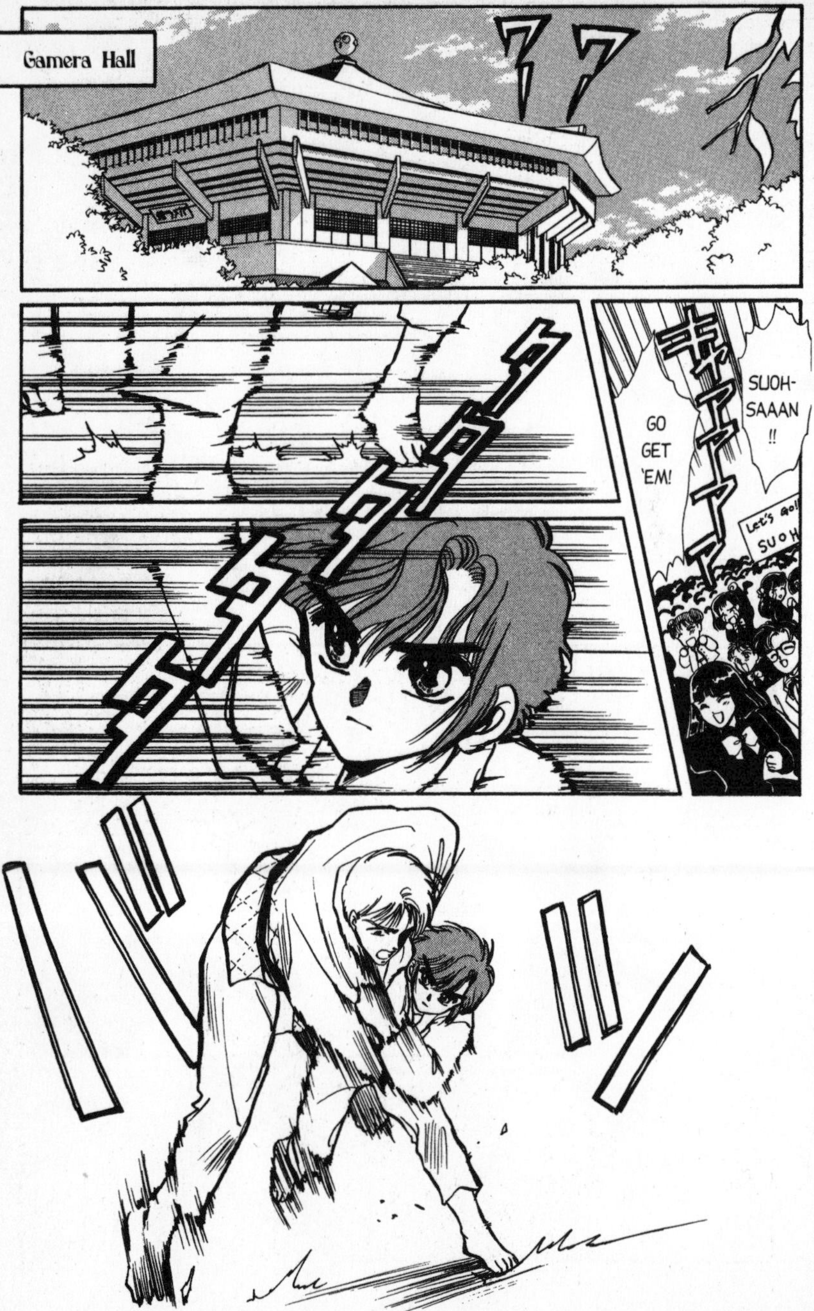

Gamera Hall
SUOH-SAAAN !!
GO GET 'EM!
Let's Go! SUOH

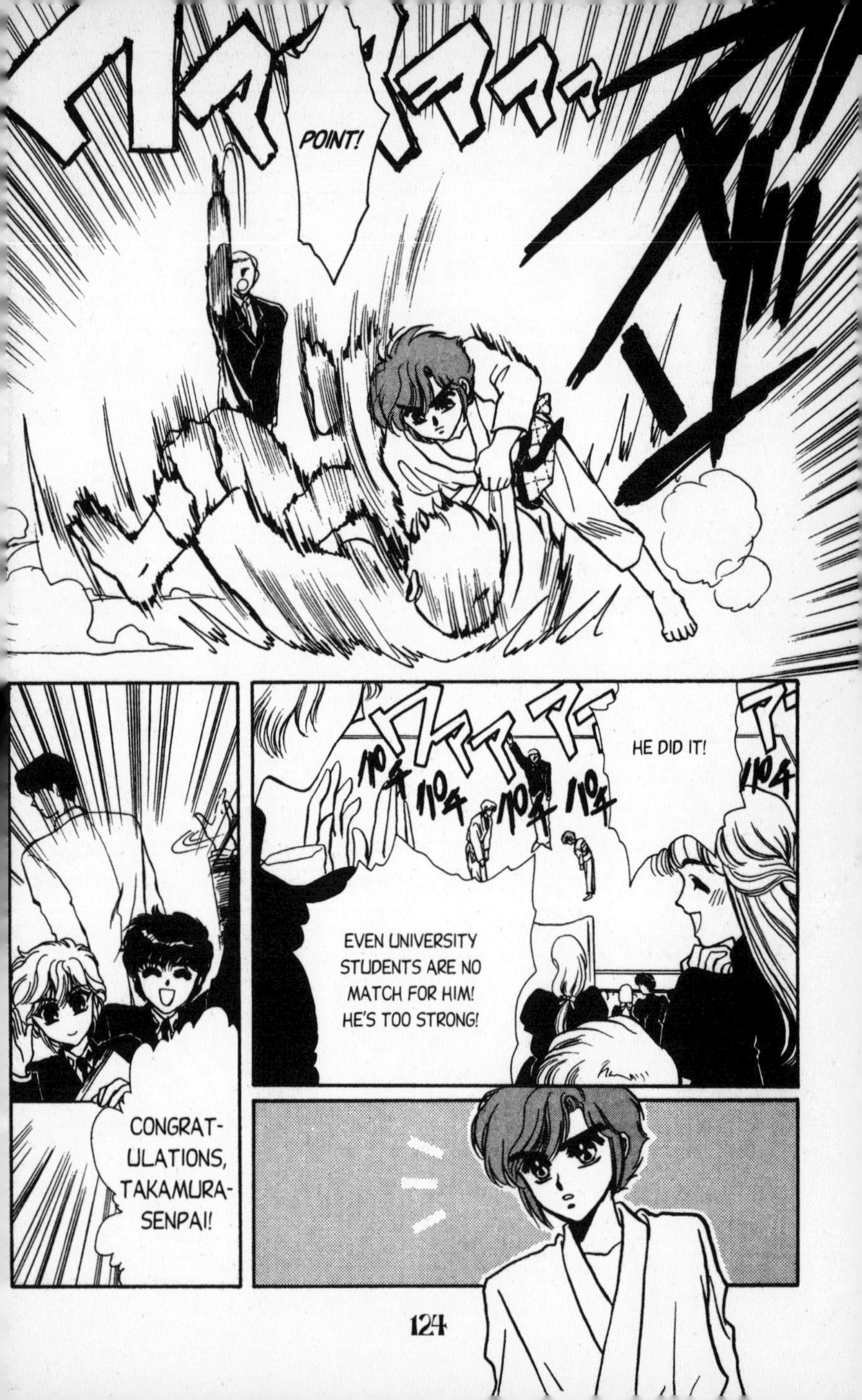
POINT!
HE DID IT!
EVEN UNIVERSITY STUDENTS ARE NO MATCH FOR HIM! HE'S TOO STRONG!
CONGRAT-ULATIONS, TAKAMURA-SENPAI!

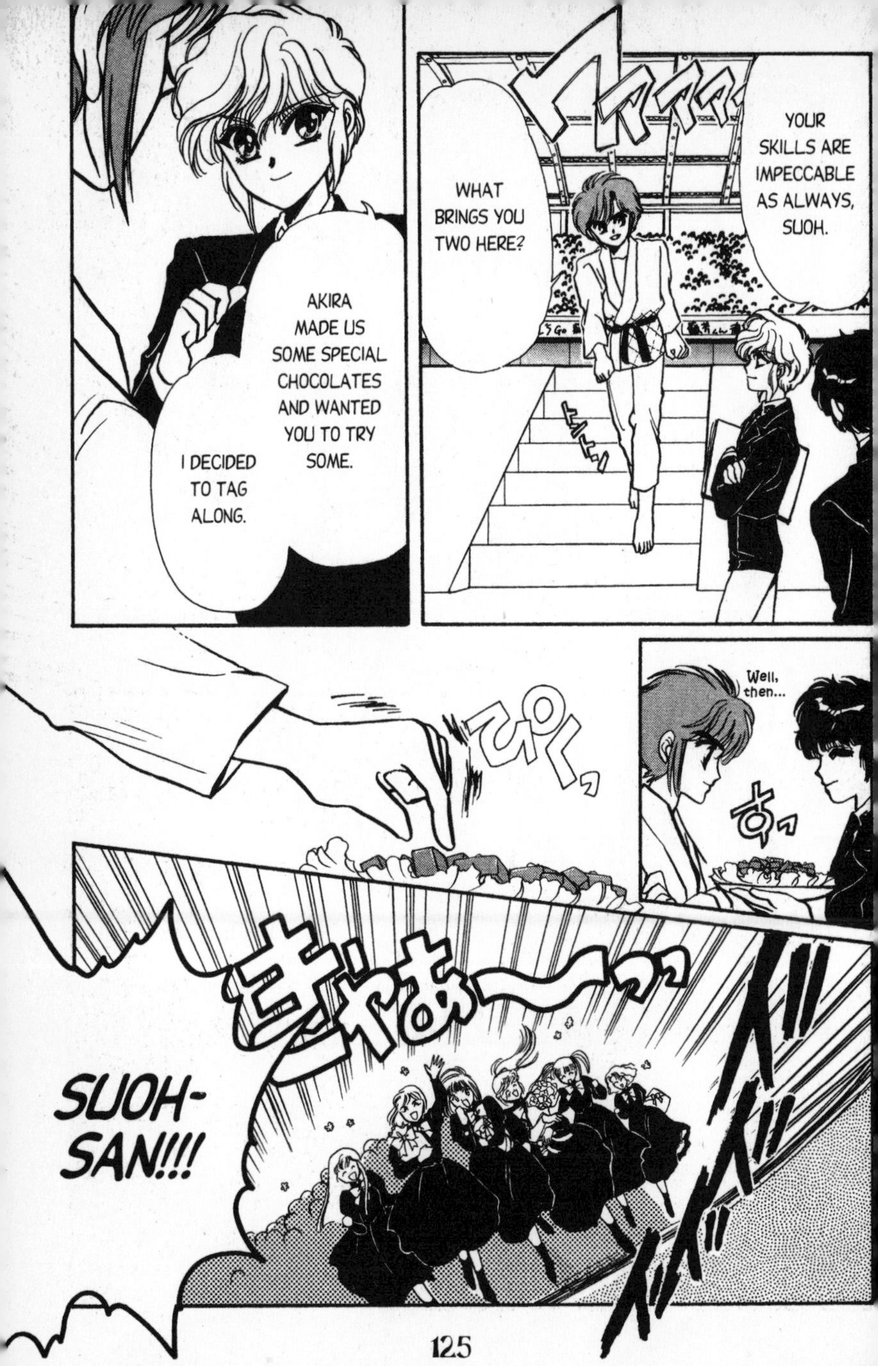
YOUR SKILLS ARE IMPECCABLE AS ALWAYS, SUOH.
WHAT BRINGS YOU TWO HERE?
AKIRA MADE US SOME SPECIAL CHOCOLATES AND WANTED YOU TO TRY SOME.
I DECIDED TO TAG ALONG.
Well, then...
SUOH-SAN!!!

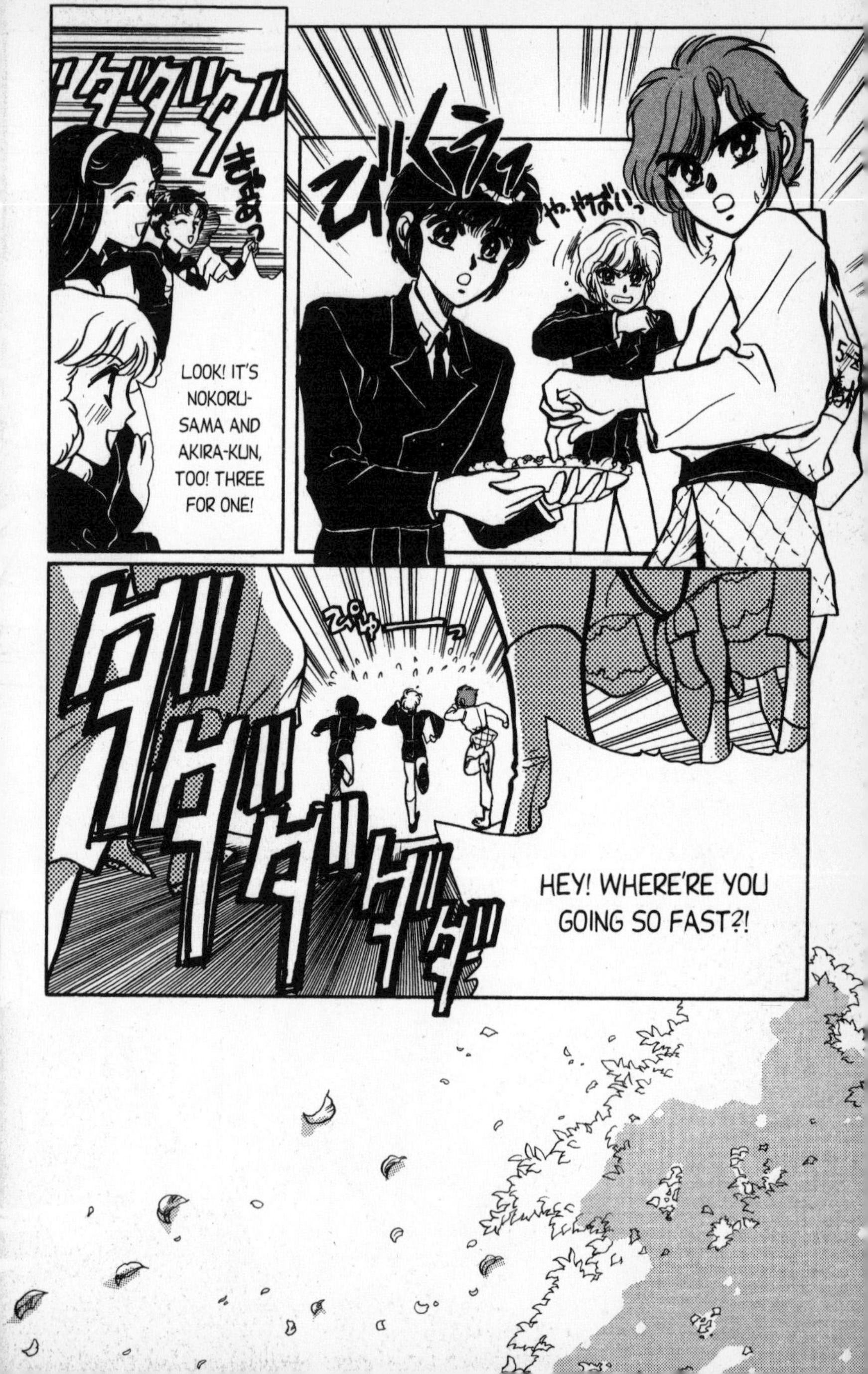
や、やばいっ
LOOK! IT'S NOKORU-SAMA AND AKIRA-KUN, TOO! THREE FOR ONE!
HEY! WHERE'RE YOU GOING SO FAST?!

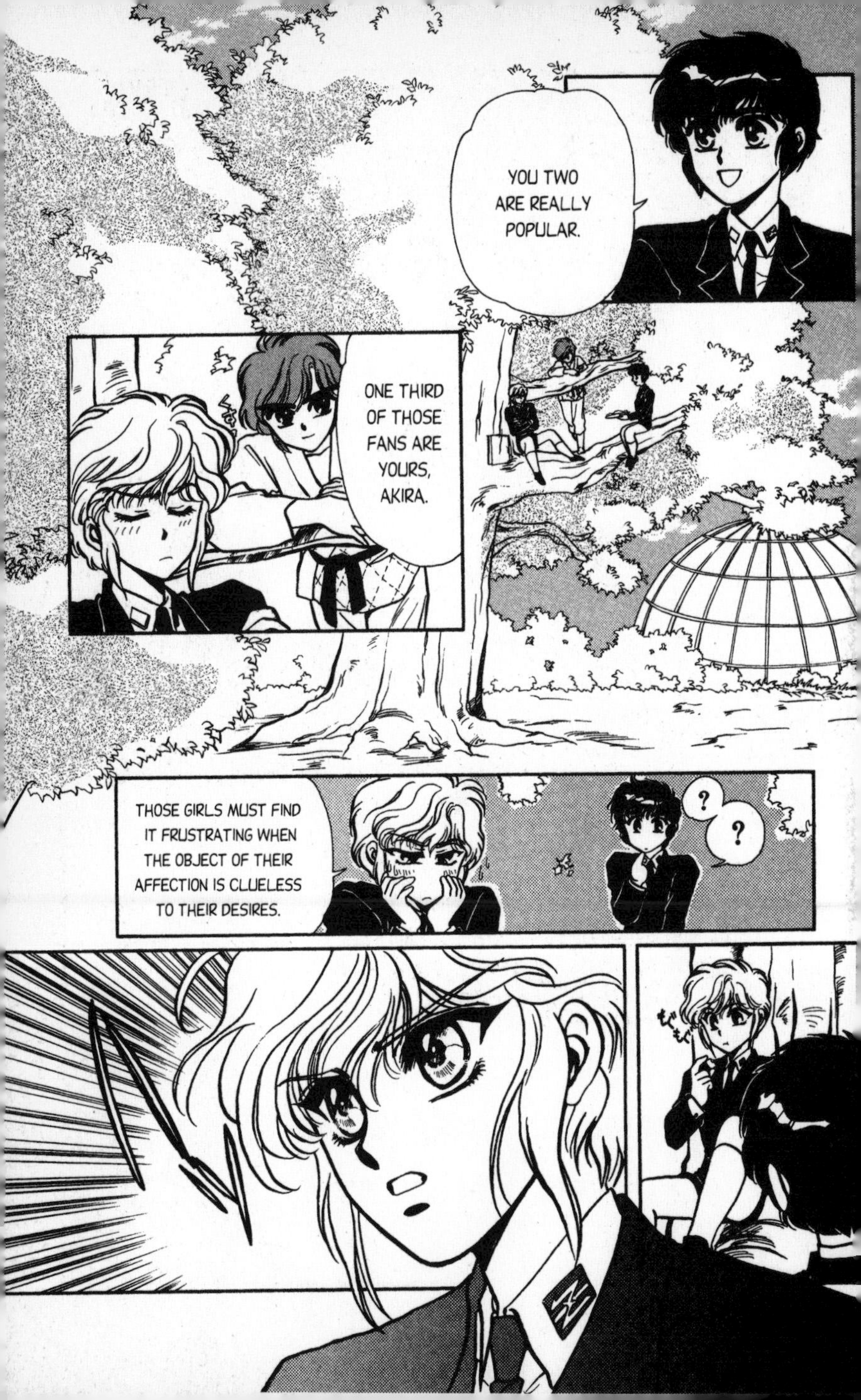
YOU TWO ARE REALLY POPULAR.
ONE THIRD OF THOSE FANS ARE YOURS, AKIRA.
? ?
THOSE GIRLS MUST FIND IT FRUSTRATING WHEN THE OBJECT OF THEIR AFFECTION IS CLUELESS TO THEIR DESIRES.

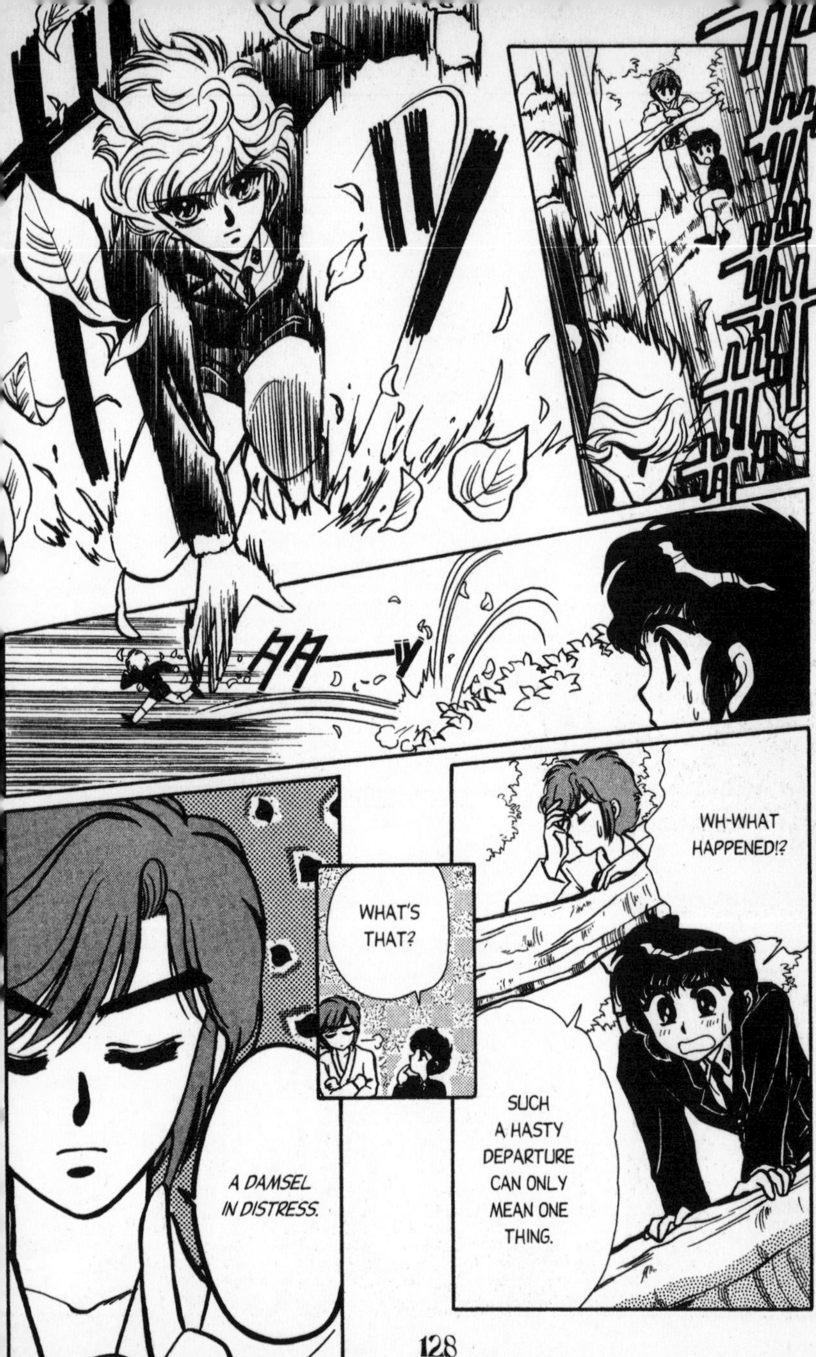
タタ——ッ
WH-WHAT HAPPENED!?
SUCH A HASTY DEPARTURE CAN ONLY MEAN ONE THING.
WHAT'S THAT?
A DAMSEL IN DISTRESS.

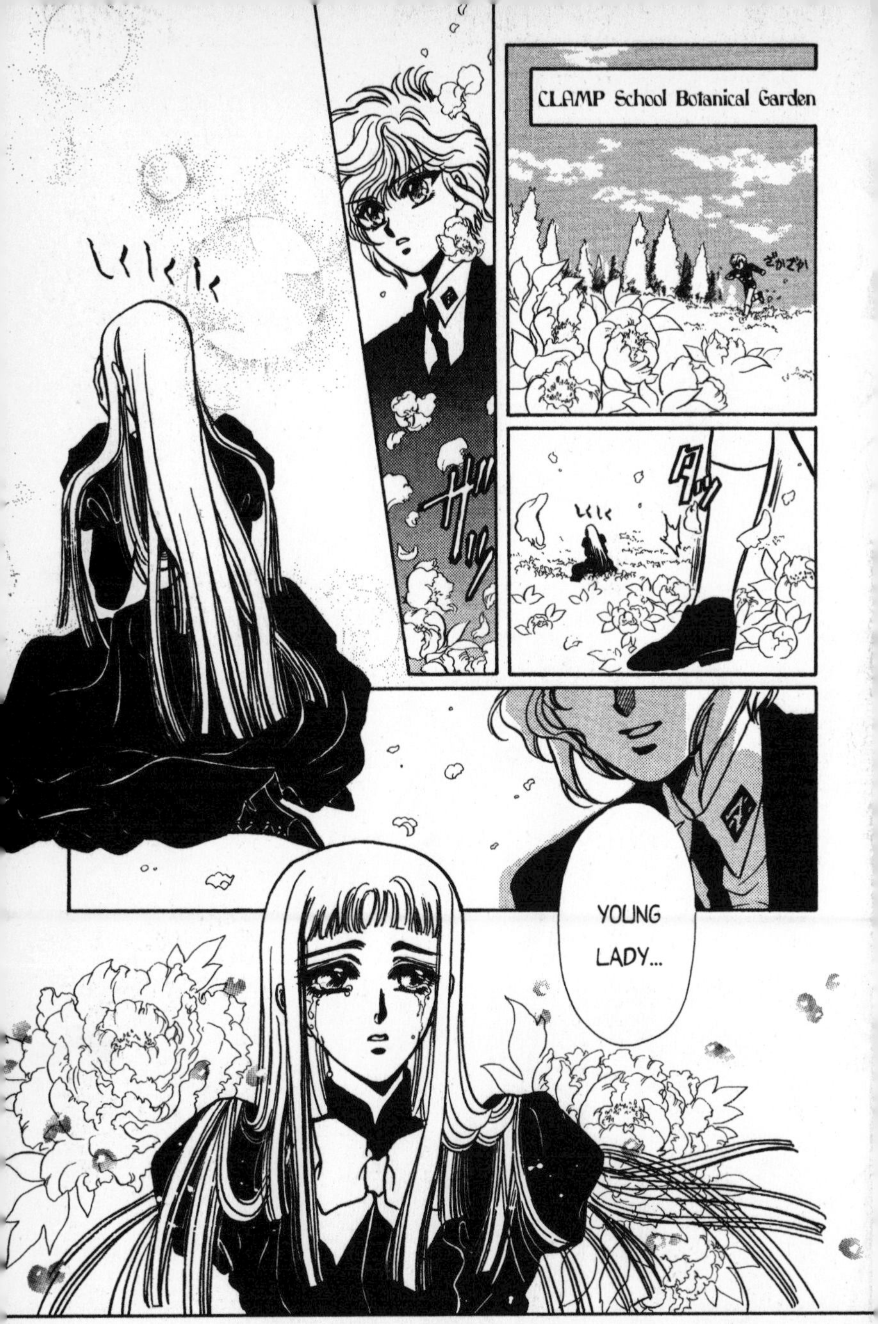
CLAMP School Botanical Garden
しくしく
YOUNG LADY...

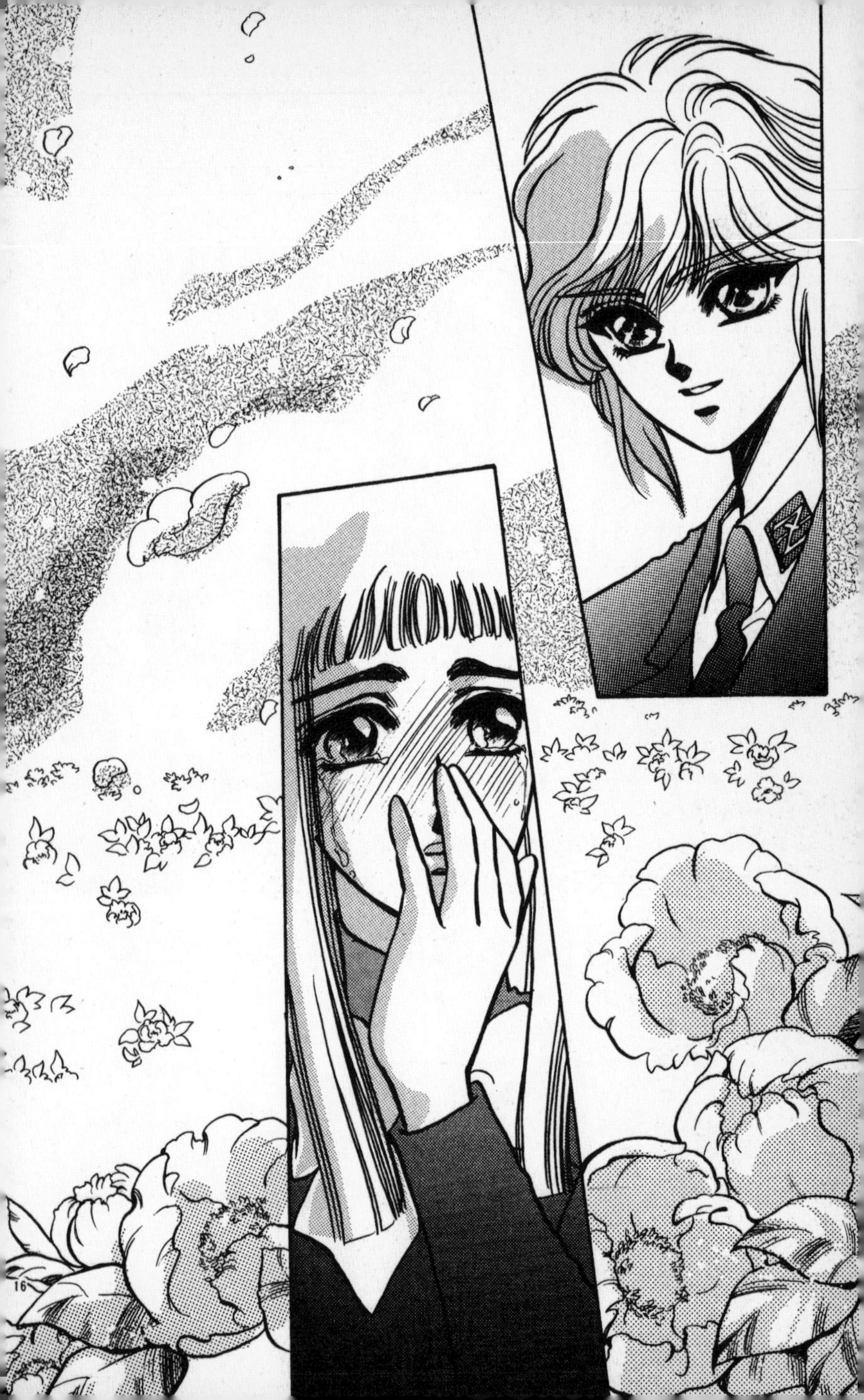

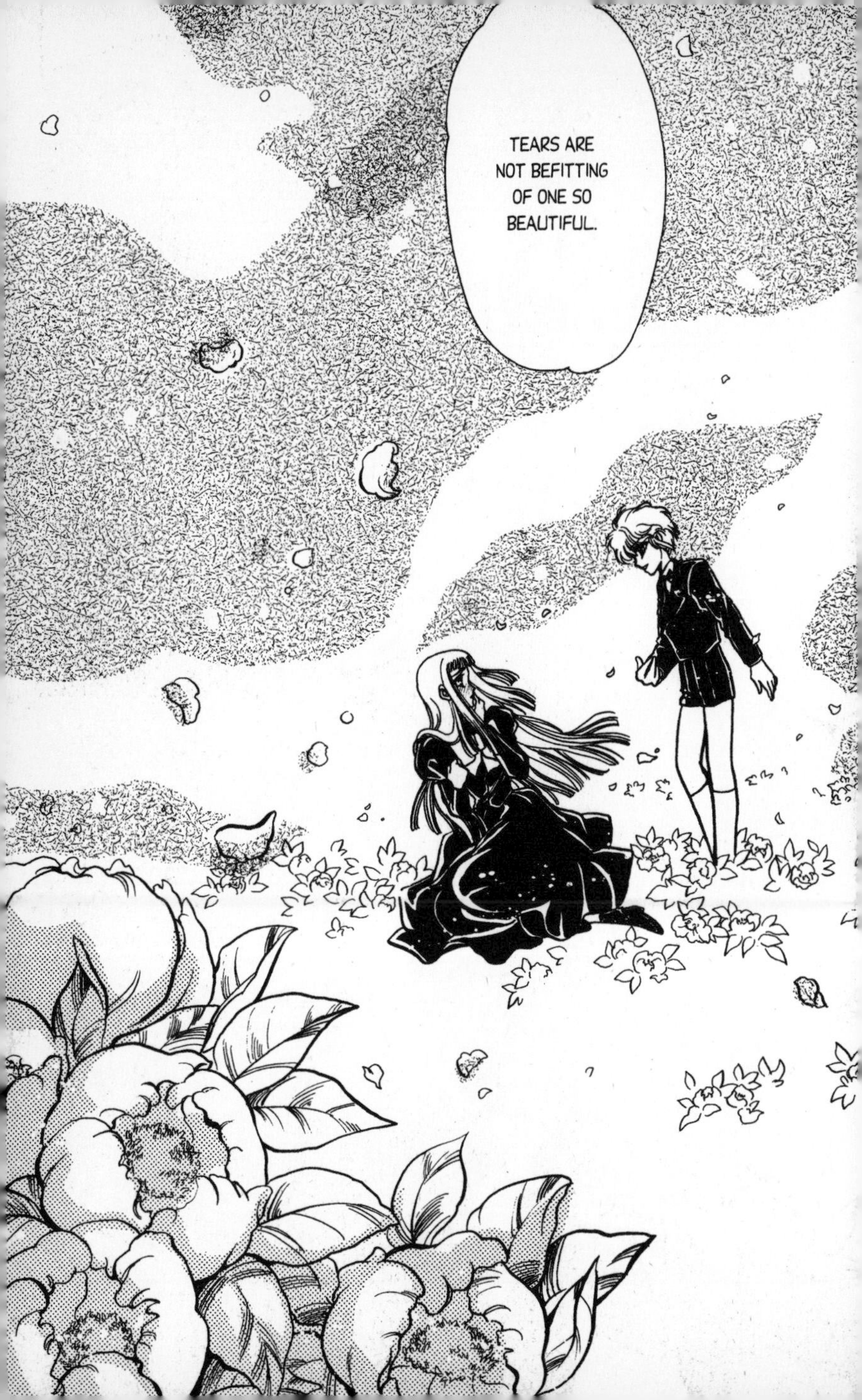
TEARS ARE NOT BEFITTING OF ONE SO BEAUTIFUL.

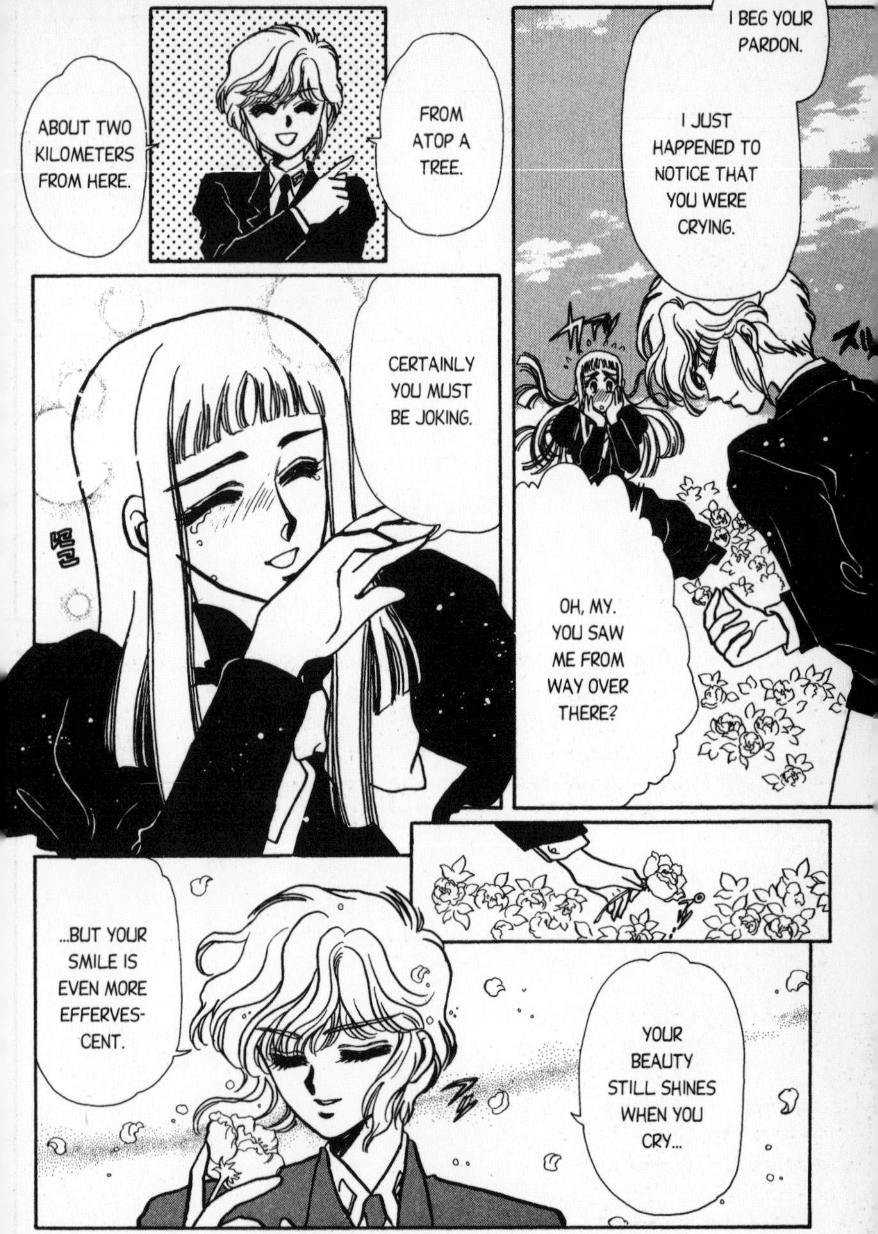
I BEG YOUR PARDON.
I JUST HAPPENED TO NOTICE THAT YOU WERE CRYING.
OH, MY. YOU SAW ME FROM WAY OVER THERE?
FROM ATOP A TREE.
ABOUT TWO KILOMETERS FROM HERE.
CERTAINLY YOU MUST BE JOKING.
YOUR BEAUTY STILL SHINES WHEN YOU CRY...
...BUT YOUR SMILE IS EVEN MORE EFFERVES-CENT.

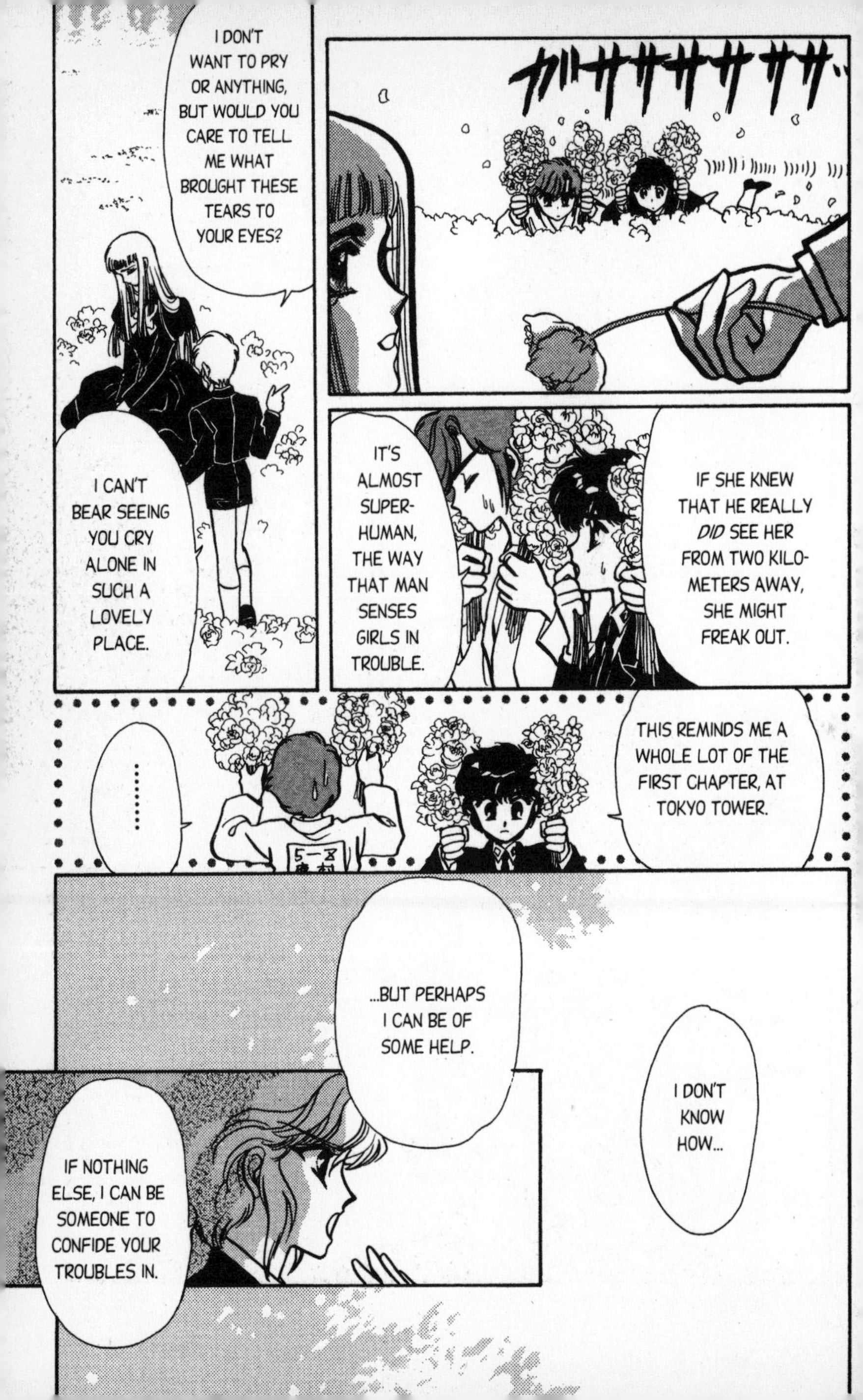
ガサササササ…
IF SHE KNEW THAT HE REALLY *DID* SEE HER FROM TWO KILOMETERS AWAY, SHE MIGHT FREAK OUT.
IT'S ALMOST SUPER-HUMAN, THE WAY THAT MAN SENSES GIRLS IN TROUBLE.
I DON'T WANT TO PRY OR ANYTHING, BUT WOULD YOU CARE TO TELL ME WHAT BROUGHT THESE TEARS TO YOUR EYES?
I CAN'T BEAR SEEING YOU CRY ALONE IN SUCH A LOVELY PLACE.
THIS REMINDS ME A WHOLE LOT OF THE FIRST CHAPTER, AT TOKYO TOWER.
……
I DON'T KNOW HOW...
...BUT PERHAPS I CAN BE OF SOME HELP.
IF NOTHING ELSE, I CAN BE SOMEONE TO CONFIDE YOUR TROUBLES IN.

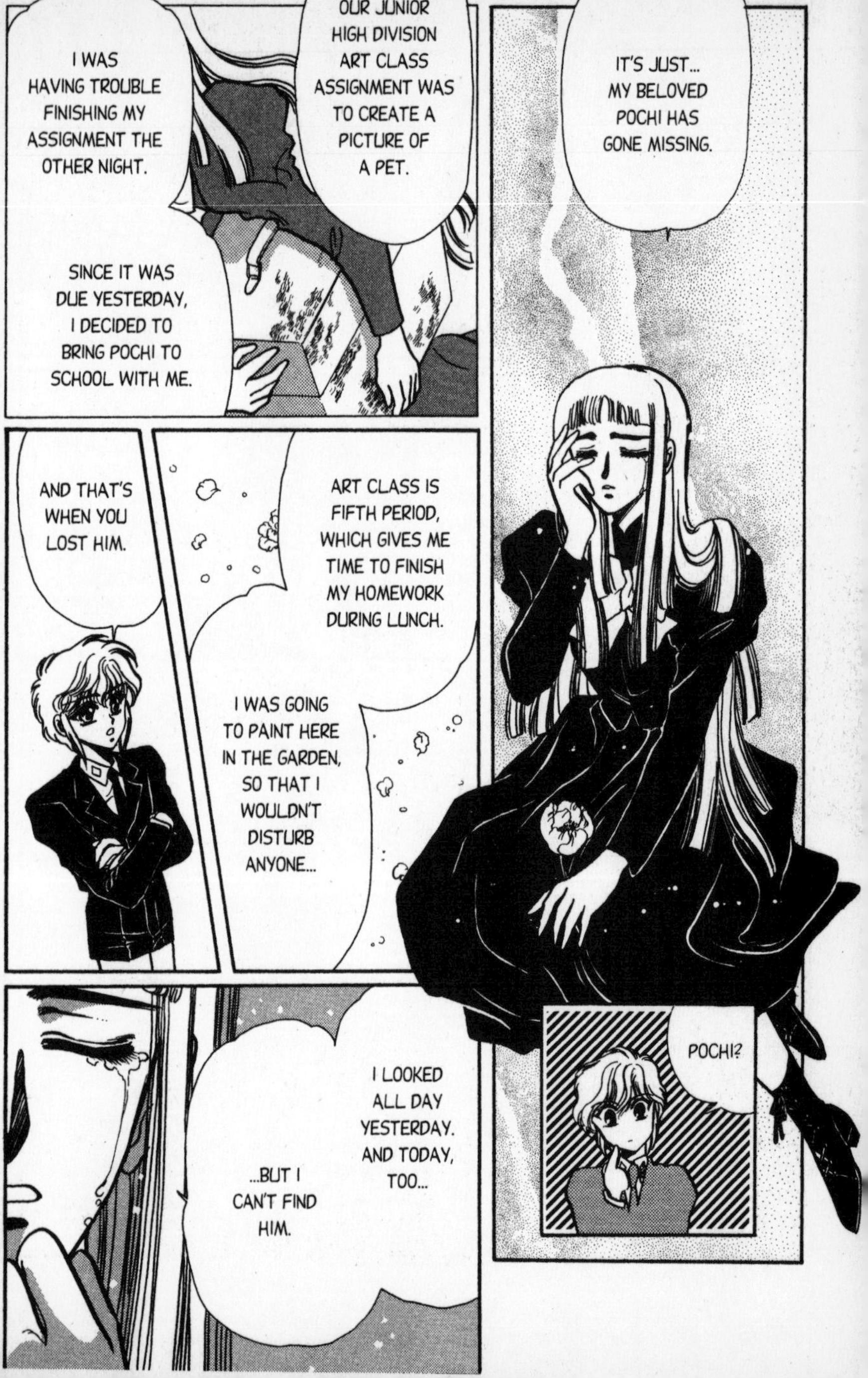
IT'S JUST... MY BELOVED POCHI HAS GONE MISSING.
POCHI?
OUR JUNIOR HIGH DIVISION ART CLASS ASSIGNMENT WAS TO CREATE A PICTURE OF A PET.
I WAS HAVING TROUBLE FINISHING MY ASSIGNMENT THE OTHER NIGHT.
SINCE IT WAS DUE YESTERDAY, I DECIDED TO BRING POCHI TO SCHOOL WITH ME.
ART CLASS IS FIFTH PERIOD, WHICH GIVES ME TIME TO FINISH MY HOMEWORK DURING LUNCH.
I WAS GOING TO PAINT HERE IN THE GARDEN, SO THAT I WOULDN'T DISTURB ANYONE...
AND THAT'S WHEN YOU LOST HIM.
I LOOKED ALL DAY YESTERDAY. AND TODAY, TOO...
...BUT I CAN'T FIND HIM.

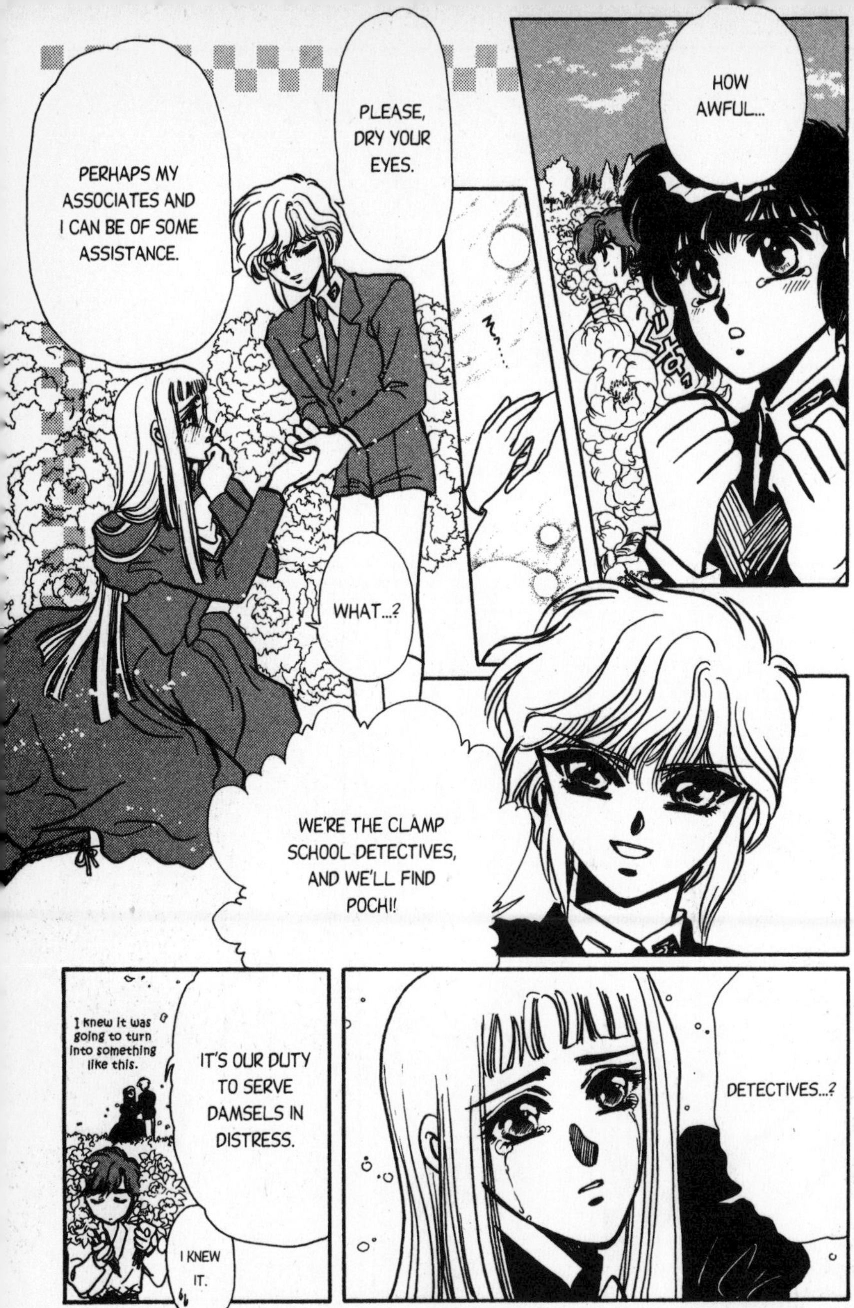
HOW AWFUL...
PLEASE, DRY YOUR EYES.
PERHAPS MY ASSOCIATES AND I CAN BE OF SOME ASSISTANCE.
WHAT...?
WE'RE THE CLAMP SCHOOL DETECTIVES, AND WE'LL FIND POCHI!
DETECTIVES...?
IT'S OUR DUTY TO SERVE DAMSELS IN DISTRESS.
I knew it was going to turn into something like this.
I KNEW IT.

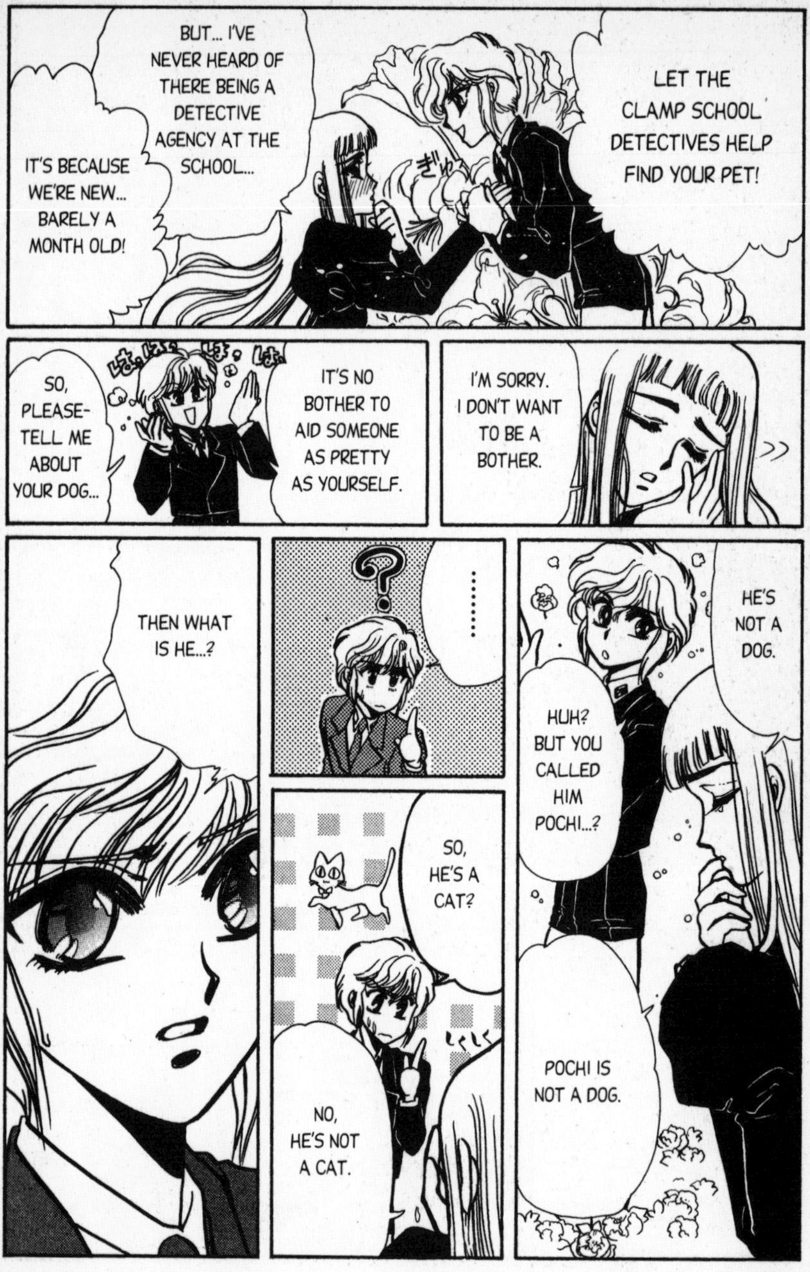
LET THE CLAMP SCHOOL DETECTIVES HELP FIND YOUR PET!
BUT... I'VE NEVER HEARD OF THERE BEING A DETECTIVE AGENCY AT THE SCHOOL...
ぎゅ
IT'S BECAUSE WE'RE NEW... BARELY A MONTH OLD!
I'M SORRY. I DON'T WANT TO BE A BOTHER.
IT'S NO BOTHER TO AID SOMEONE AS PRETTY AS YOURSELF.
SO, PLEASE-TELL ME ABOUT YOUR DOG...
HE'S NOT A DOG.
HUH? BUT YOU CALLED HIM POCHI...?
POCHI IS NOT A DOG.
......
SO, HE'S A CAT?
NO, HE'S NOT A CAT.
THEN WHAT IS HE...?

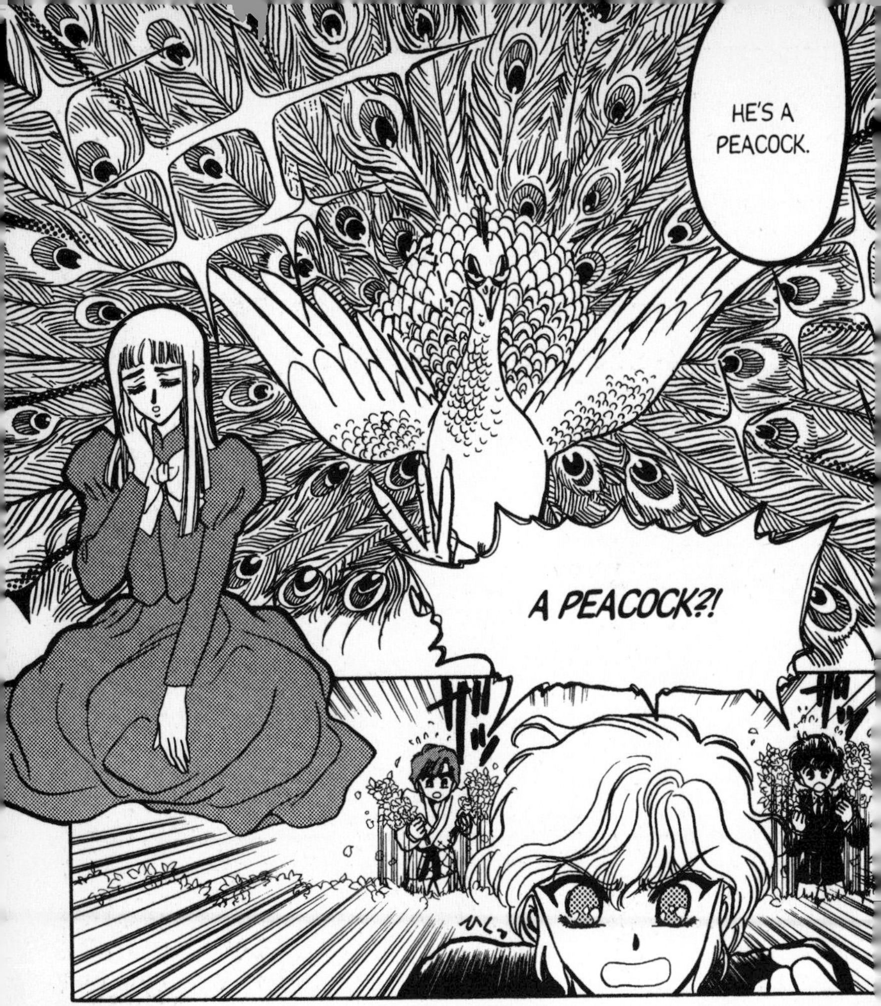
HE'S A PEACOCK.
A PEACOCK?!
ひしっ

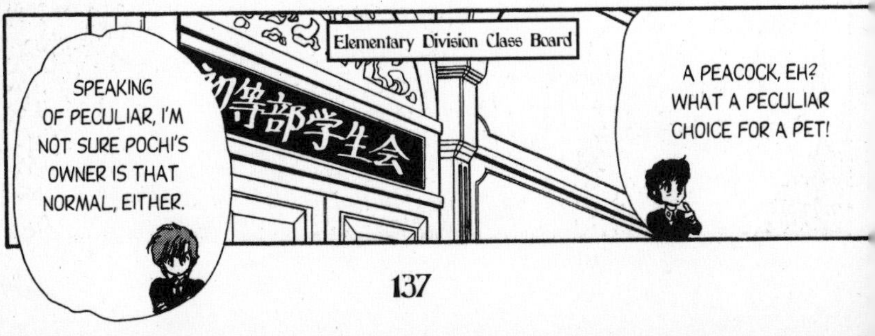
Elementary Division Class Board
初等部学生会
A PEACOCK, EH? WHAT A PECULIAR CHOICE FOR A PET!
SPEAKING OF PECULIAR, I'M NOT SURE POCHI'S OWNER IS THAT NORMAL, EITHER.

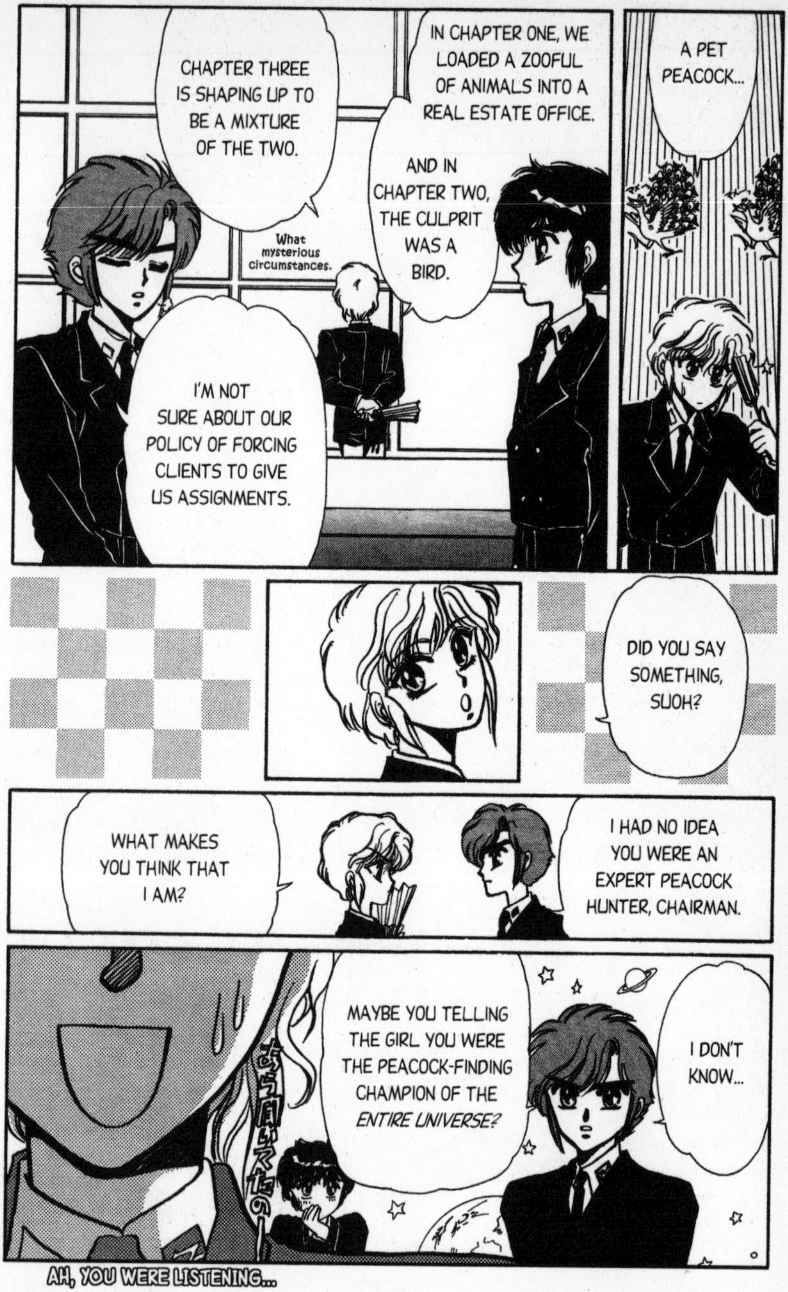
A PET PEACOCK...
IN CHAPTER ONE, WE LOADED A ZOOFUL OF ANIMALS INTO A REAL ESTATE OFFICE.
AND IN CHAPTER TWO, THE CULPRIT WAS A BIRD.
CHAPTER THREE IS SHAPING UP TO BE A MIXTURE OF THE TWO.
What mysterious circumstances.
I'M NOT SURE ABOUT OUR POLICY OF FORCING CLIENTS TO GIVE US ASSIGNMENTS.
DID YOU SAY SOMETHING, SUOH?
I HAD NO IDEA YOU WERE AN EXPERT PEACOCK HUNTER, CHAIRMAN.
WHAT MAKES YOU THINK THAT I AM?
I DON'T KNOW...
MAYBE YOU TELLING THE GIRL YOU WERE THE PEACOCK-FINDING CHAMPION OF THE *ENTIRE UNIVERSE?*
AH, YOU WERE LISTENING...

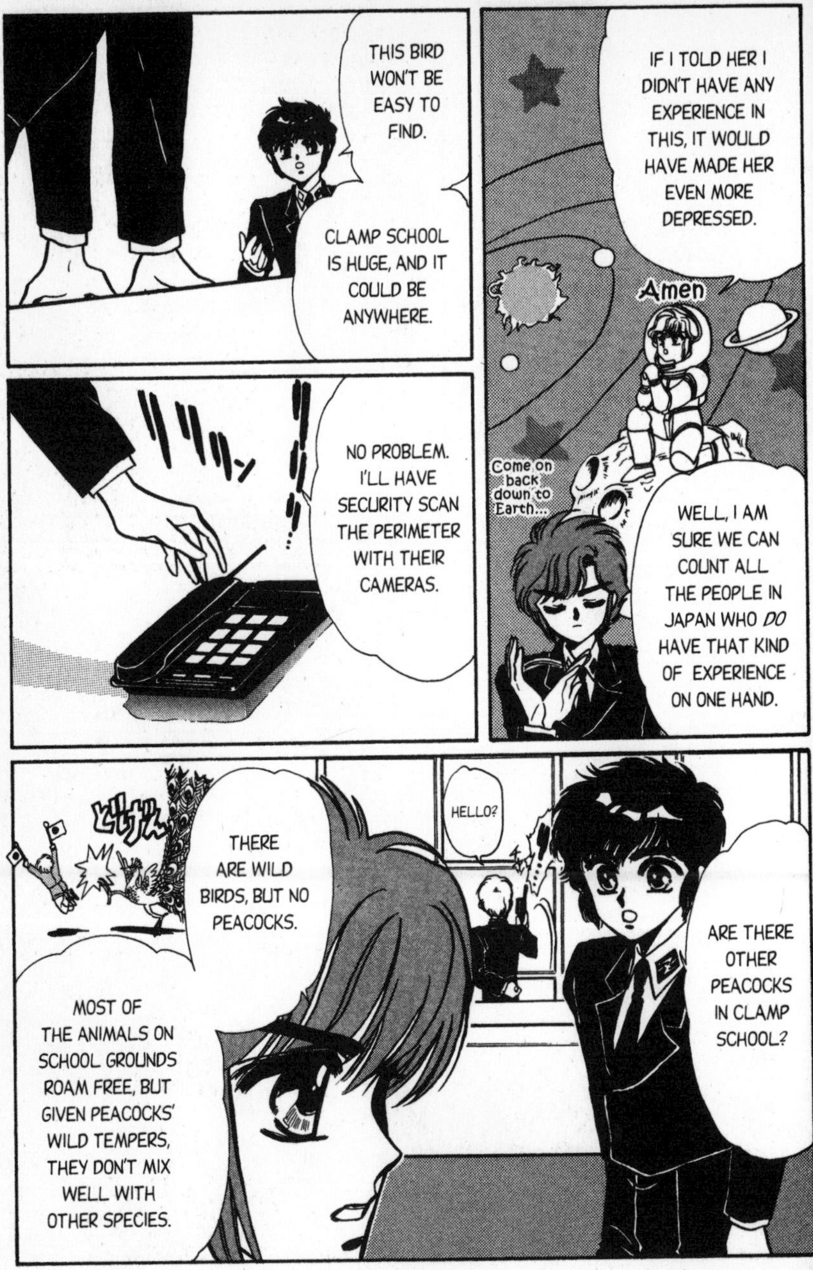
IF I TOLD HER I DIDN'T HAVE ANY EXPERIENCE IN THIS, IT WOULD HAVE MADE HER EVEN MORE DEPRESSED.
Amen
Come on back down to Earth...
WELL, I AM SURE WE CAN COUNT ALL THE PEOPLE IN JAPAN WHO *DO* HAVE THAT KIND OF EXPERIENCE ON ONE HAND.
THIS BIRD WON'T BE EASY TO FIND.
CLAMP SCHOOL IS HUGE, AND IT COULD BE ANYWHERE.
NO PROBLEM. I'LL HAVE SECURITY SCAN THE PERIMETER WITH THEIR CAMERAS.
ARE THERE OTHER PEACOCKS IN CLAMP SCHOOL?
HELLO?
THERE ARE WILD BIRDS, BUT NO PEACOCKS.
MOST OF THE ANIMALS ON SCHOOL GROUNDS ROAM FREE, BUT GIVEN PEACOCKS' WILD TEMPERS, THEY DON'T MIX WELL WITH OTHER SPECIES.

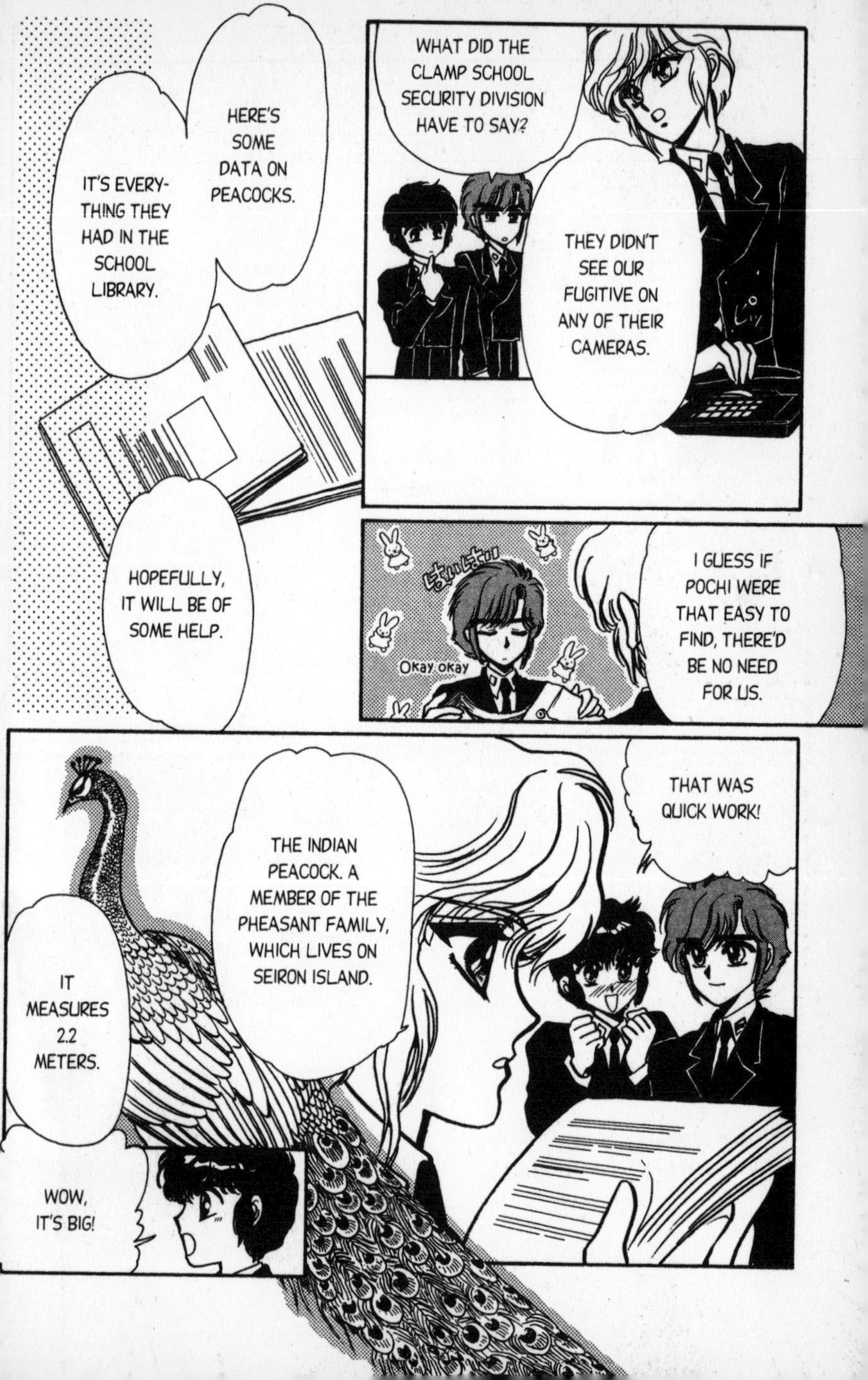
WHAT DID THE CLAMP SCHOOL SECURITY DIVISION HAVE TO SAY?
THEY DIDN'T SEE OUR FUGITIVE ON ANY OF THEIR CAMERAS.
I GUESS IF POCHI WERE THAT EASY TO FIND, THERE'D BE NO NEED FOR US.
Okay okay
HERE'S SOME DATA ON PEACOCKS.
IT'S EVERYTHING THEY HAD IN THE SCHOOL LIBRARY.
HOPEFULLY, IT WILL BE OF SOME HELP.
THAT WAS QUICK WORK!
THE INDIAN PEACOCK. A MEMBER OF THE PHEASANT FAMILY, WHICH LIVES ON SEIRON ISLAND.
IT MEASURES 2.2 METERS.
WOW, IT'S BIG!

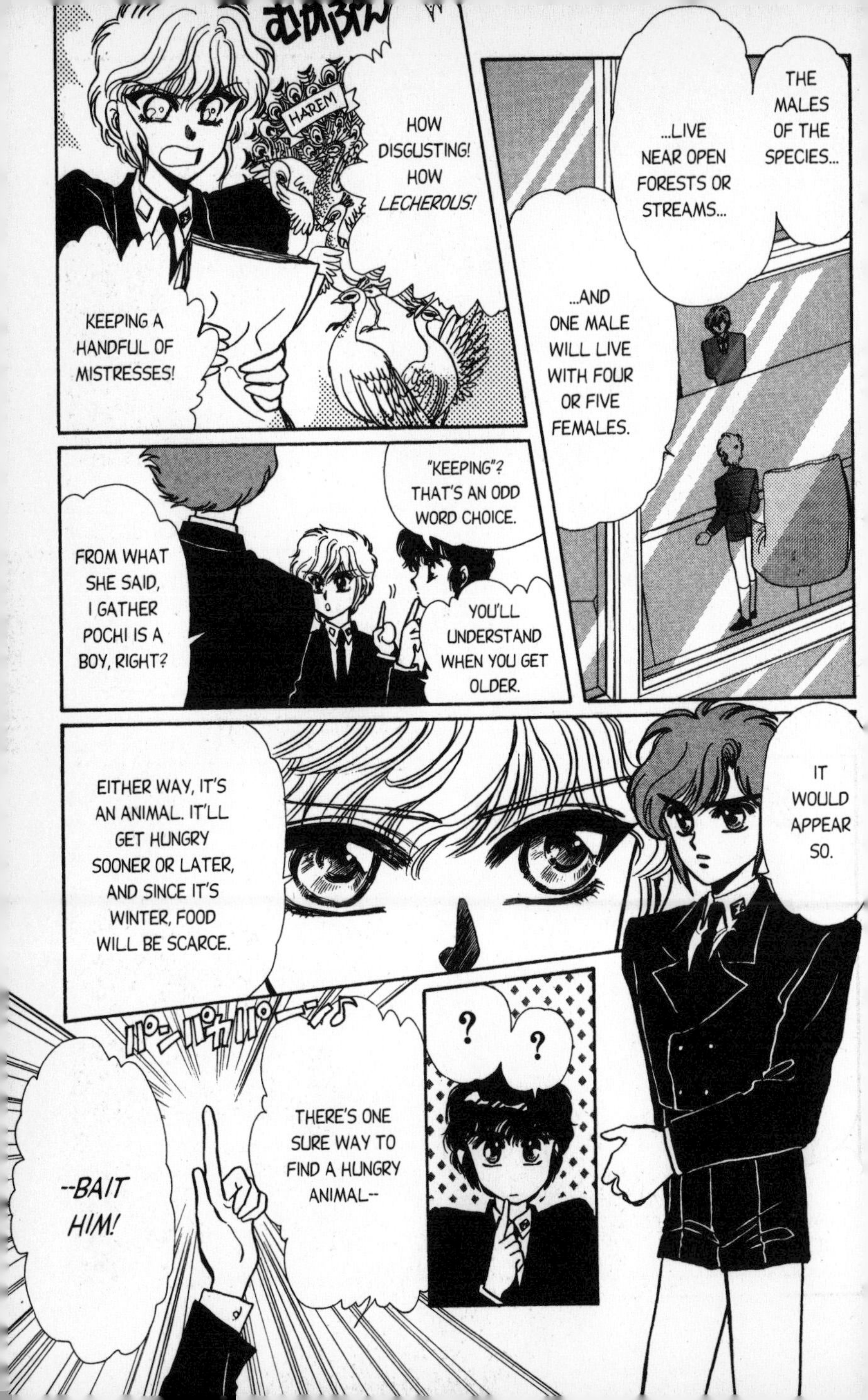
THE MALES OF THE SPECIES...
...LIVE NEAR OPEN FORESTS OR STREAMS...
...AND ONE MALE WILL LIVE WITH FOUR OR FIVE FEMALES.
むかぷん
HAREM
HOW DISGUSTING! HOW *LECHEROUS!*
KEEPING A HANDFUL OF MISTRESSES!
"KEEPING"? THAT'S AN ODD WORD CHOICE.
YOU'LL UNDERSTAND WHEN YOU GET OLDER.
FROM WHAT SHE SAID, I GATHER POCHI IS A BOY, RIGHT?
IT WOULD APPEAR SO.
EITHER WAY, IT'S AN ANIMAL. IT'LL GET HUNGRY SOONER OR LATER, AND SINCE IT'S WINTER, FOOD WILL BE SCARCE.
? ?
パンパカパーン♪
THERE'S ONE SURE WAY TO FIND A HUNGRY ANIMAL--
--BAIT HIM!

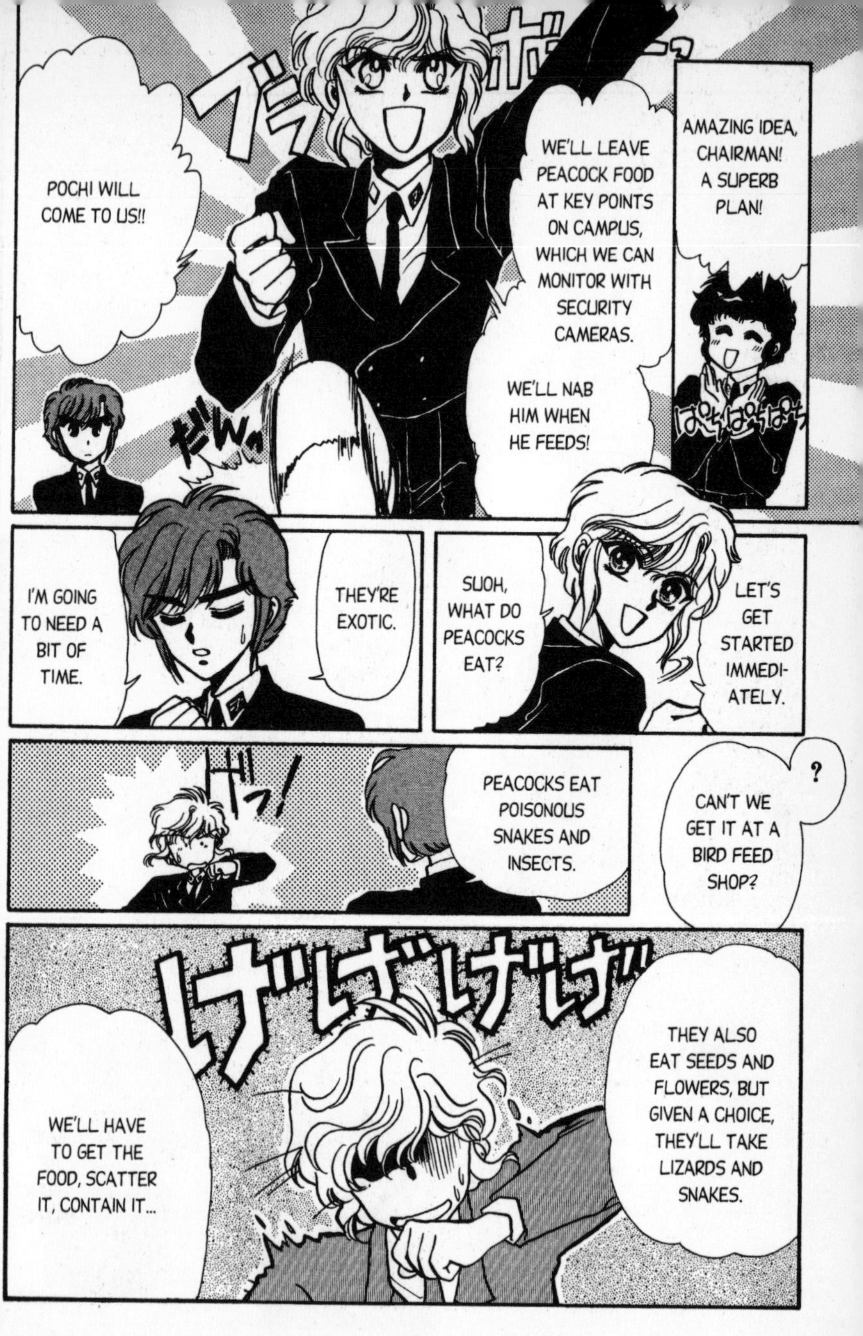
WE'LL LEAVE PEACOCK FOOD AT KEY POINTS ON CAMPUS, WHICH WE CAN MONITOR WITH SECURITY CAMERAS.
WE'LL NAB HIM WHEN HE FEEDS!
POCHI WILL COME TO US!!
AMAZING IDEA, CHAIRMAN! A SUPERB PLAN!
LET'S GET STARTED IMMEDI-ATELY.
SUOH, WHAT DO PEACOCKS EAT?
THEY'RE EXOTIC.
I'M GOING TO NEED A BIT OF TIME.
?
CAN'T WE GET IT AT A BIRD FEED SHOP?
PEACOCKS EAT POISONOUS SNAKES AND INSECTS.
THEY ALSO EAT SEEDS AND FLOWERS, BUT GIVEN A CHOICE, THEY'LL TAKE LIZARDS AND SNAKES.
WE'LL HAVE TO GET THE FOOD, SCATTER IT, CONTAIN IT...

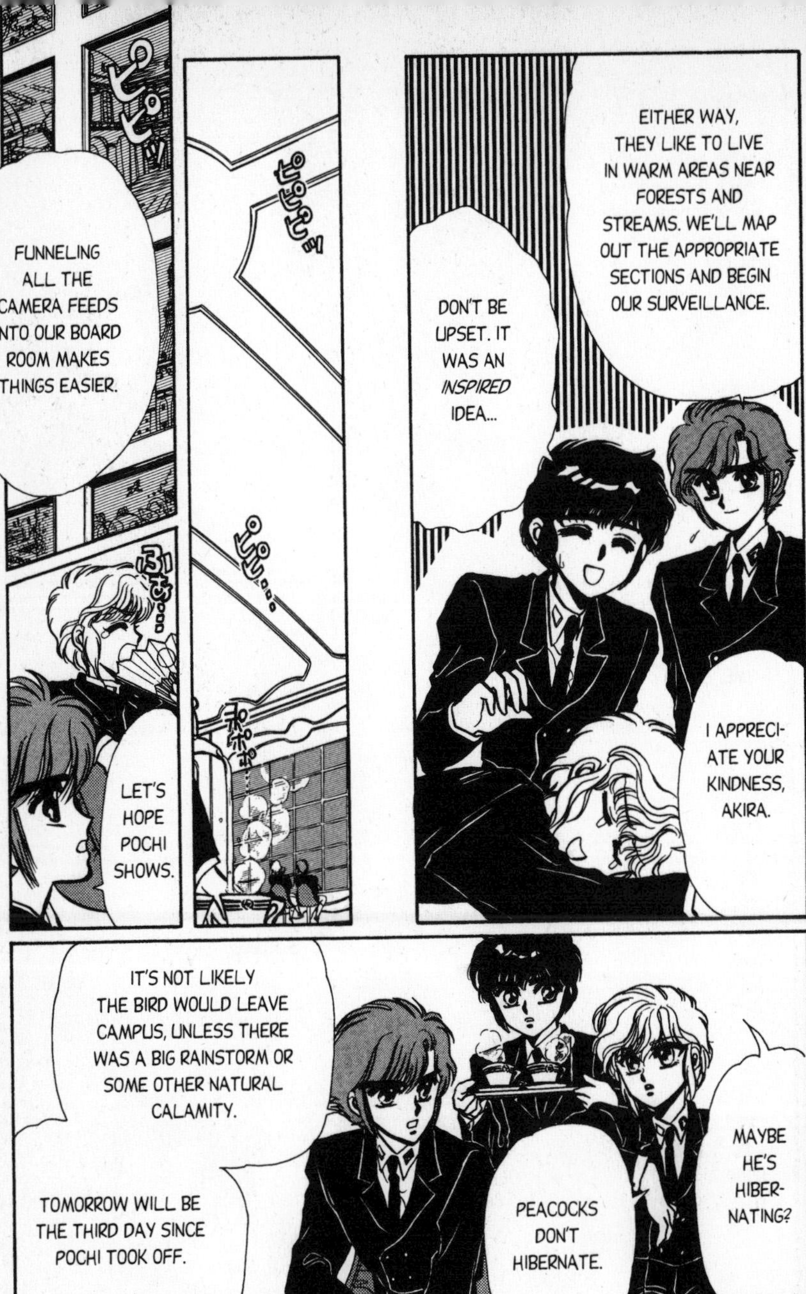
EITHER WAY, THEY LIKE TO LIVE IN WARM AREAS NEAR FORESTS AND STREAMS. WE'LL MAP OUT THE APPROPRIATE SECTIONS AND BEGIN OUR SURVEILLANCE.
DON'T BE UPSET. IT WAS AN *INSPIRED* IDEA...
I APPRECIATE YOUR KINDNESS, AKIRA.
ピピピッ
ピピ…
ピピッ
FUNNELING ALL THE CAMERA FEEDS INTO OUR BOARD ROOM MAKES THINGS EASIER.
LET'S HOPE POCHI SHOWS.
IT'S NOT LIKELY THE BIRD WOULD LEAVE CAMPUS, UNLESS THERE WAS A BIG RAINSTORM OR SOME OTHER NATURAL CALAMITY.
TOMORROW WILL BE THE THIRD DAY SINCE POCHI TOOK OFF.
MAYBE HE'S HIBERNATING?
PEACOCKS DON'T HIBERNATE.

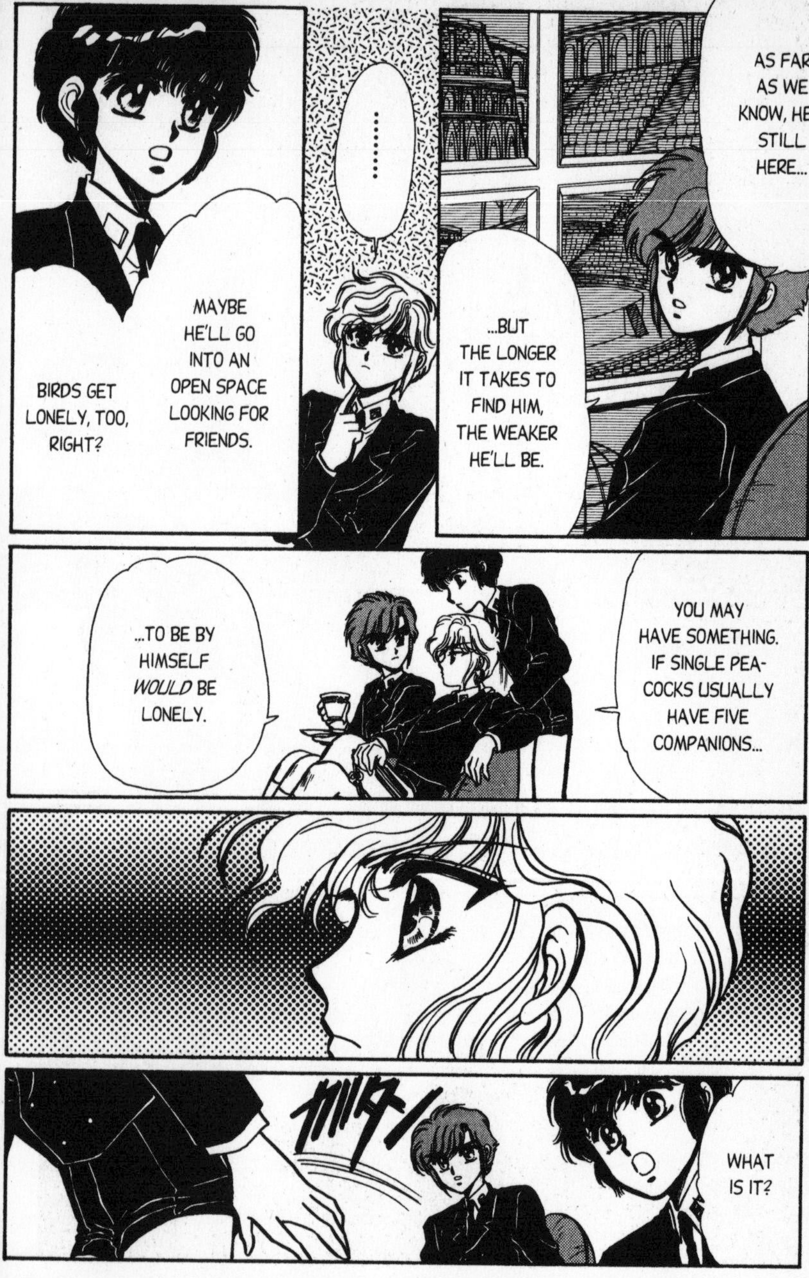
AS FAR AS WE KNOW, HE'S STILL HERE...
...BUT THE LONGER IT TAKES TO FIND HIM, THE WEAKER HE'LL BE.
......
MAYBE HE'LL GO INTO AN OPEN SPACE LOOKING FOR FRIENDS.
BIRDS GET LONELY, TOO, RIGHT?
YOU MAY HAVE SOMETHING. IF SINGLE PEA-COCKS USUALLY HAVE FIVE COMPANIONS...
...TO BE BY HIMSELF *WOULD* BE LONELY.
ガタン
WHAT IS IT?

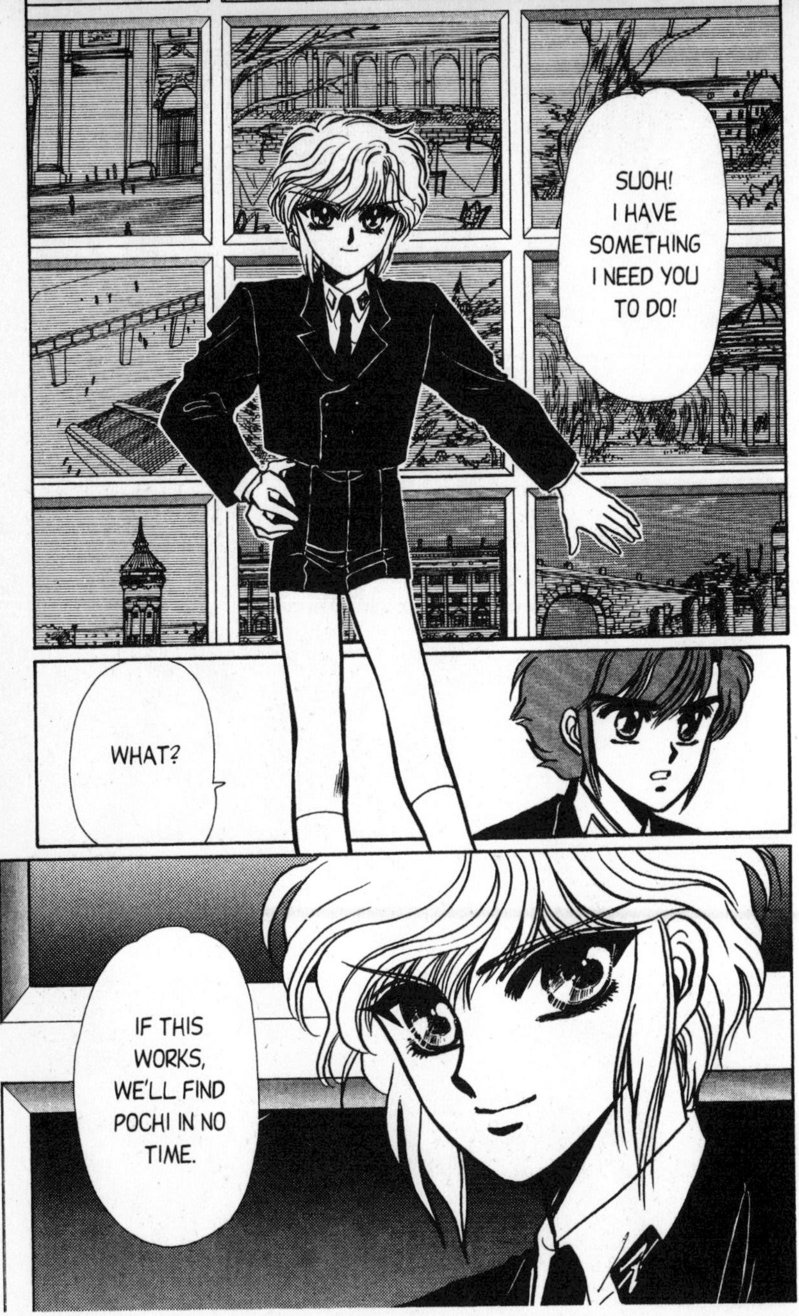
SUOH! I HAVE SOMETHING I NEED YOU TO DO!
WHAT?
IF THIS WORKS, WE'LL FIND POCHI IN NO TIME.

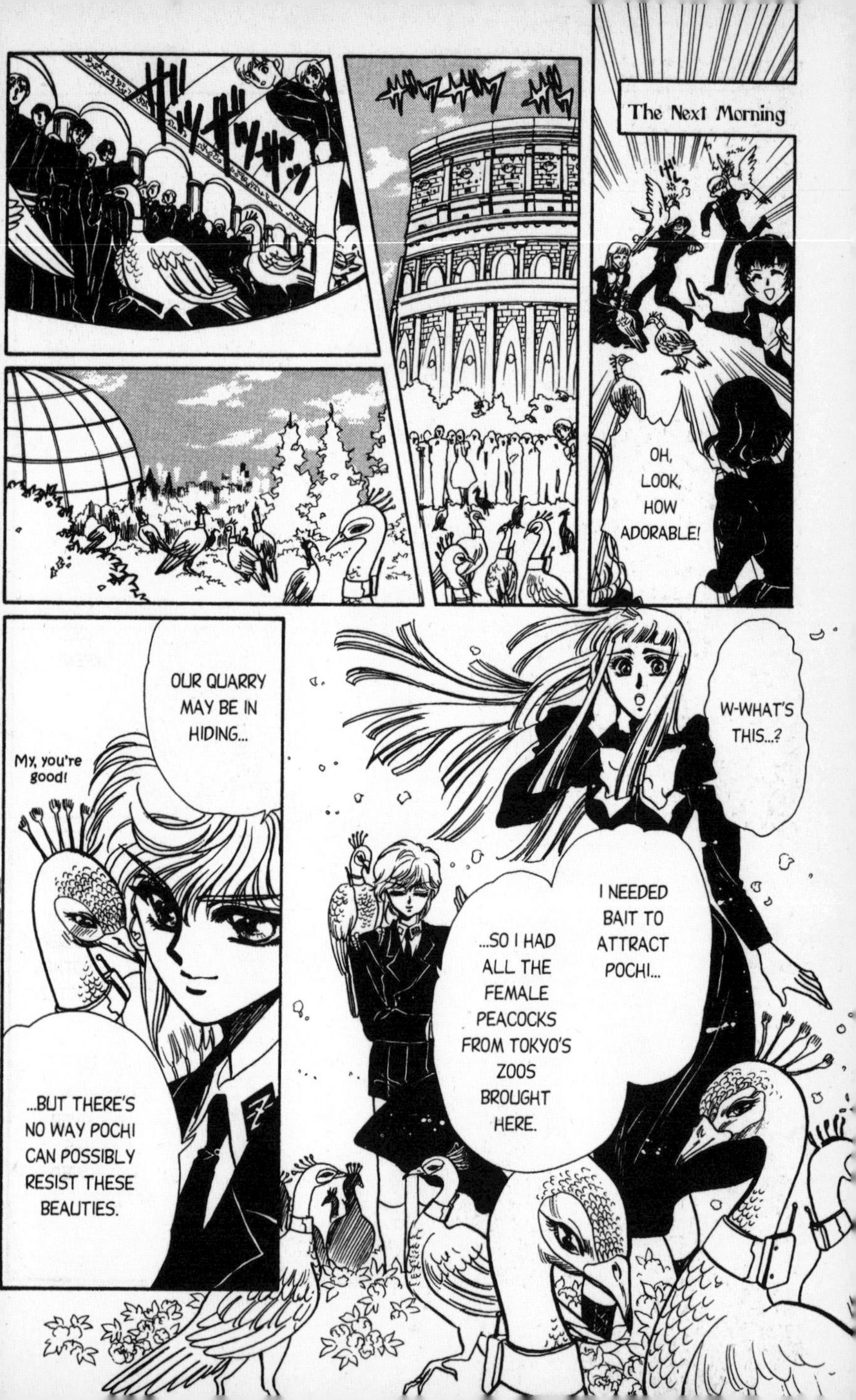
The Next Morning
OH, LOOK, HOW ADORABLE!
W-WHAT'S THIS...?
I NEEDED BAIT TO ATTRACT POCHI...
...SO I HAD ALL THE FEMALE PEACOCKS FROM TOKYO'S ZOOS BROUGHT HERE.
OUR QUARRY MAY BE IN HIDING...
My, you're good!
...BUT THERE'S NO WAY POCHI CAN POSSIBLY RESIST THESE BEAUTIES.

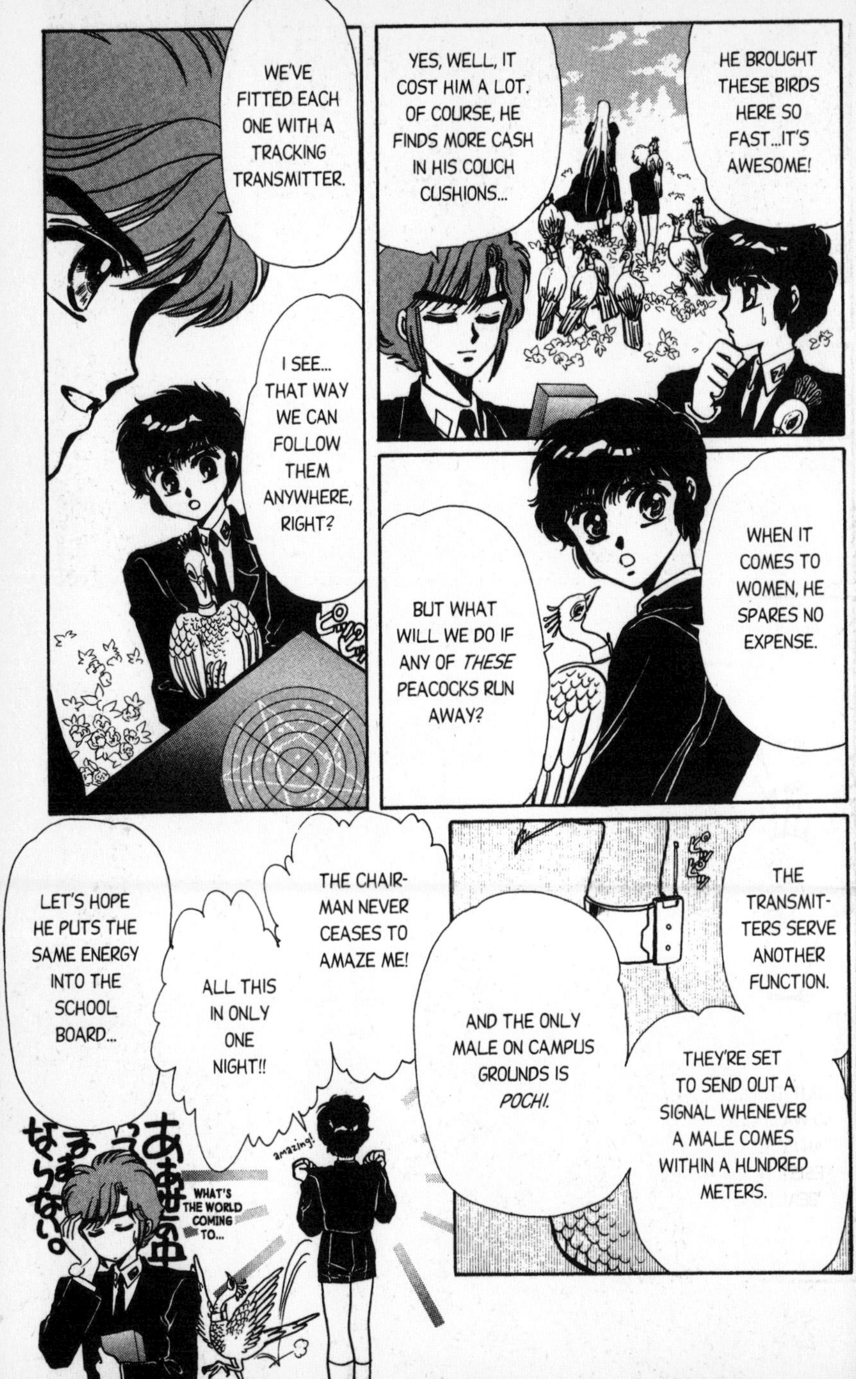
HE BROUGHT THESE BIRDS HERE SO FAST...IT'S AWESOME!
YES, WELL, IT COST HIM A LOT. OF COURSE, HE FINDS MORE CASH IN HIS COUCH CUSHIONS...
WHEN IT COMES TO WOMEN, HE SPARES NO EXPENSE.
BUT WHAT WILL WE DO IF ANY OF *THESE* PEACOCKS RUN AWAY?
WE'VE FITTED EACH ONE WITH A TRACKING TRANSMITTER.
I SEE... THAT WAY WE CAN FOLLOW THEM ANYWHERE, RIGHT?
THE TRANSMITTERS SERVE ANOTHER FUNCTION.
THEY'RE SET TO SEND OUT A SIGNAL WHENEVER A MALE COMES WITHIN A HUNDRED METERS.
AND THE ONLY MALE ON CAMPUS GROUNDS IS *POCHI*.
THE CHAIRMAN NEVER CEASES TO AMAZE ME!
ALL THIS IN ONLY ONE NIGHT!!
amazing!
LET'S HOPE HE PUTS THE SAME ENERGY INTO THE SCHOOL BOARD...
WHAT'S THE WORLD COMING TO...

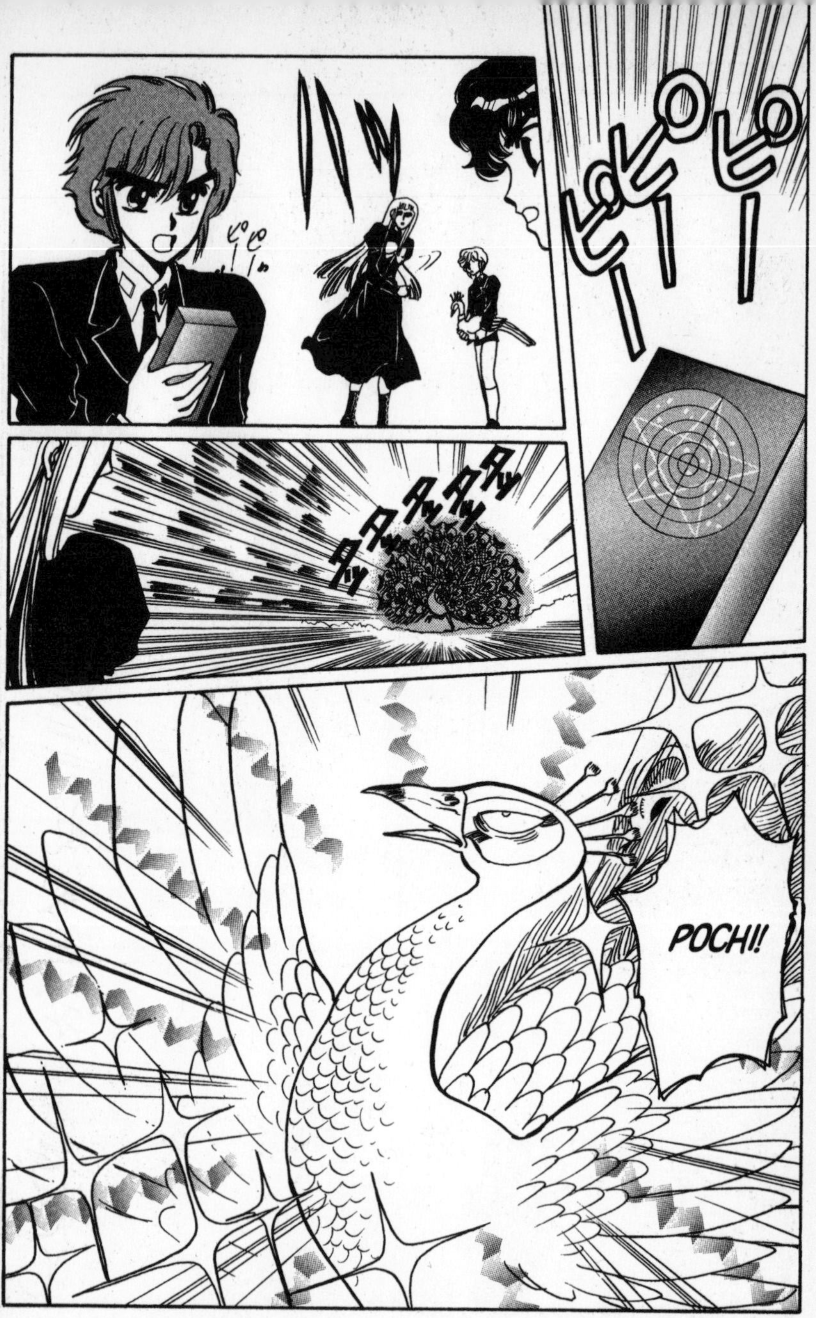
ピーピー
ピピ
タッタッタッタッタッ
POCHI!

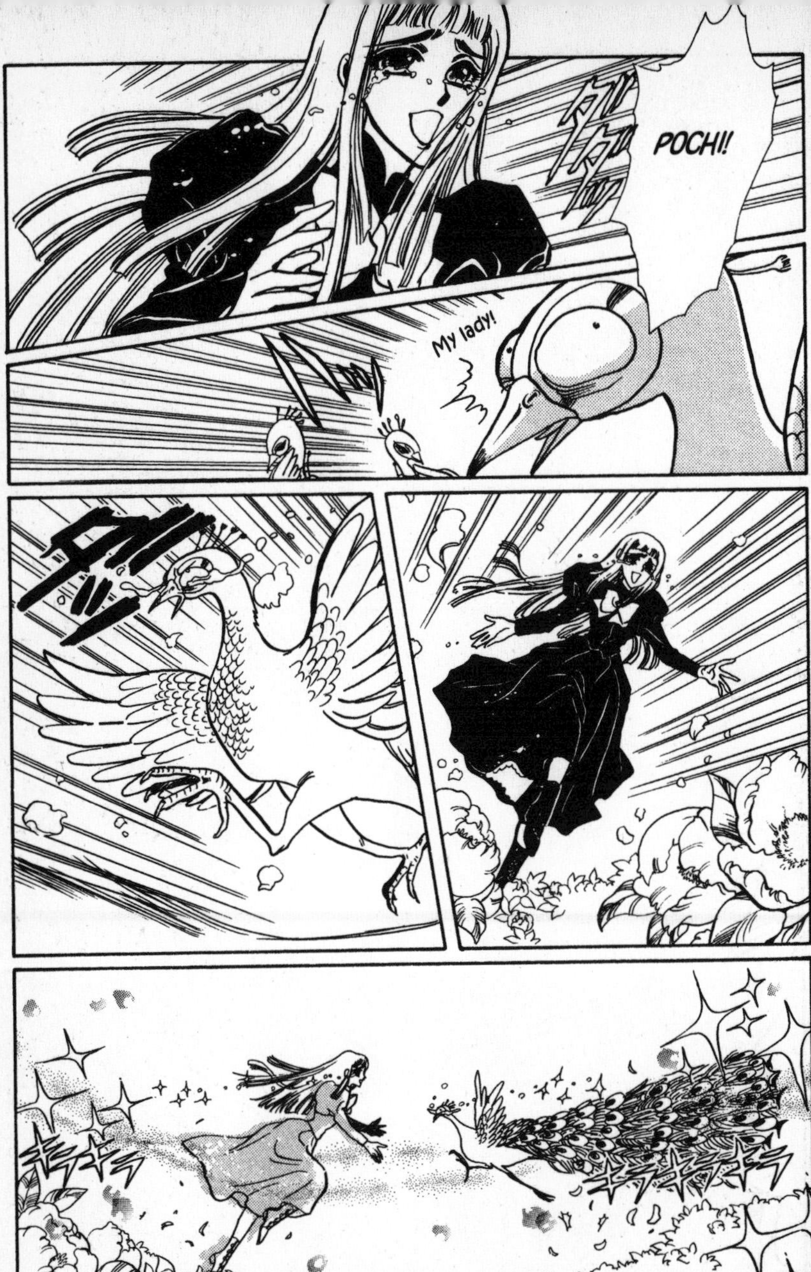
POCHI!
My lady!

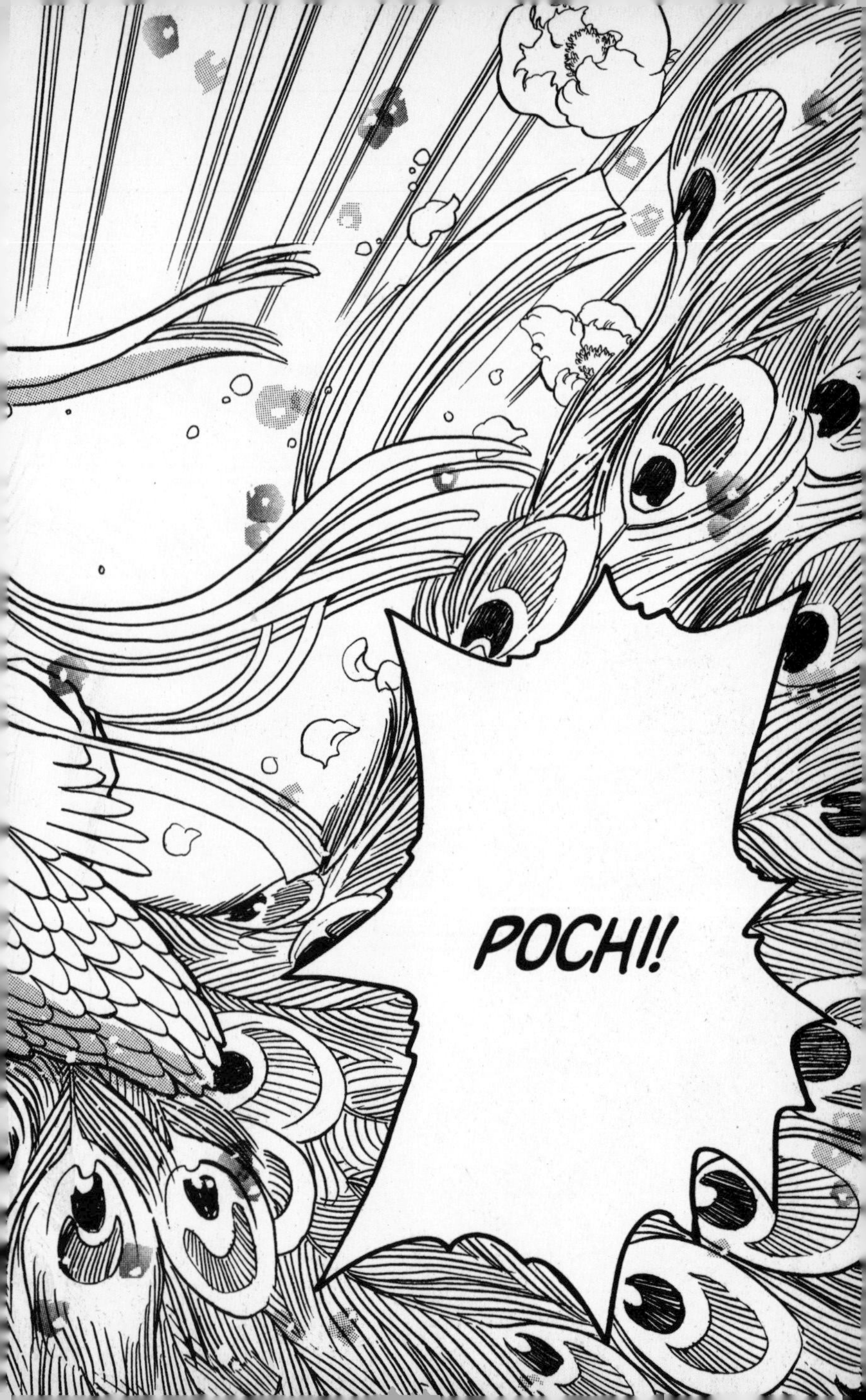
POCHI!

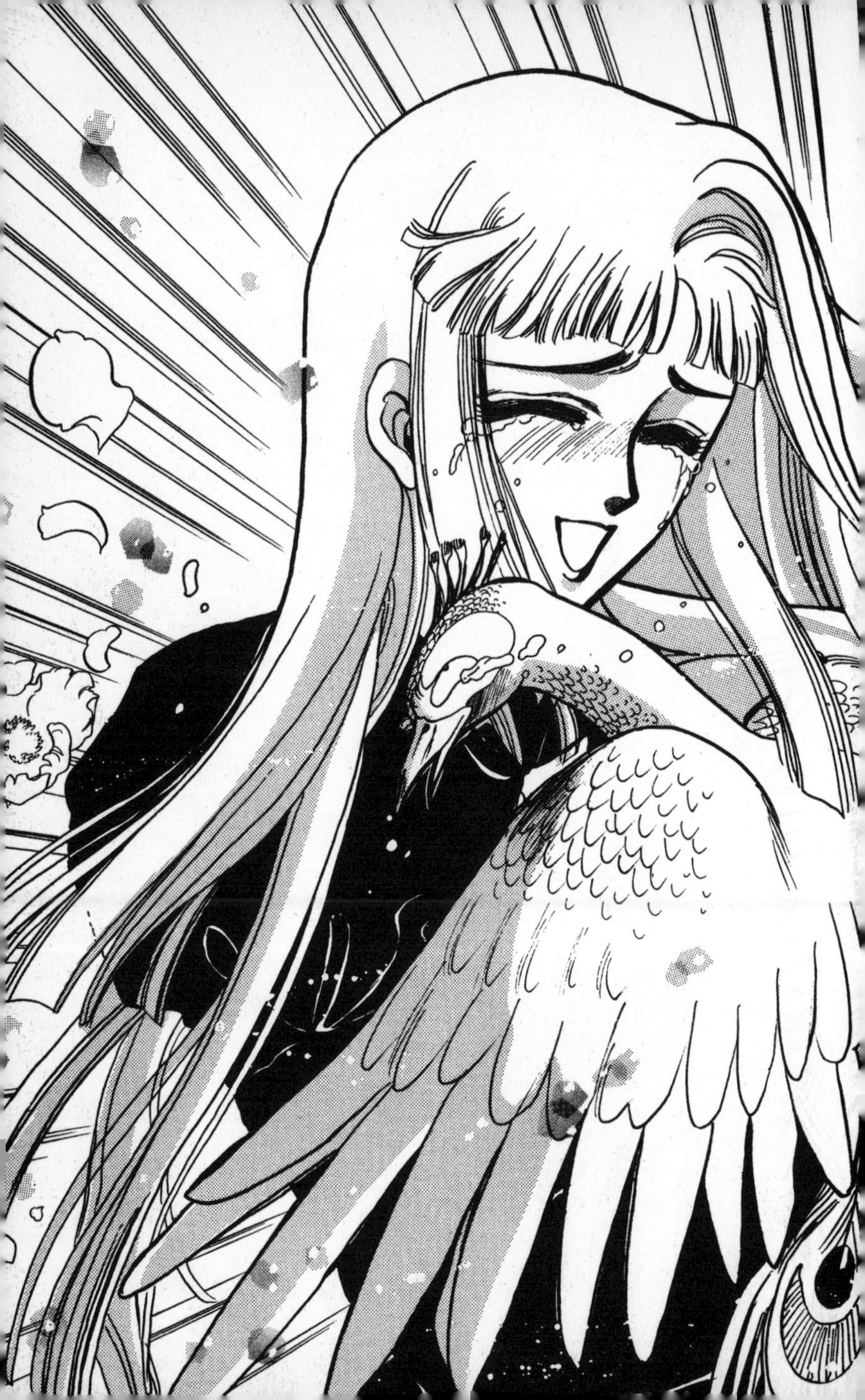

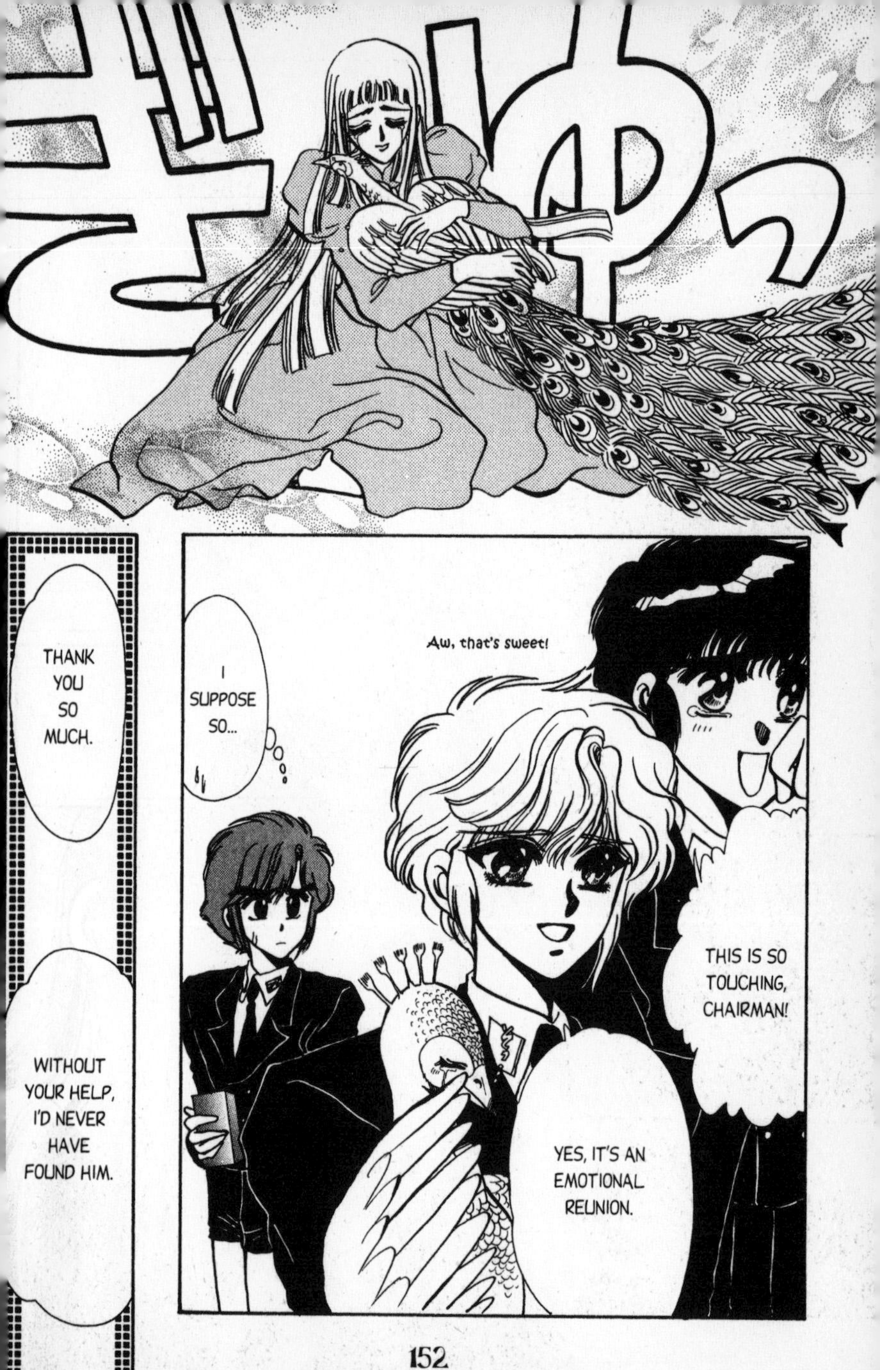
ぎゅっ
Aw, that's sweet!
THIS IS SO TOUCHING, CHAIRMAN!
I SUPPOSE SO...
YES, IT'S AN EMOTIONAL REUNION.
THANK YOU SO MUCH.
WITHOUT YOUR HELP, I'D NEVER HAVE FOUND HIM.

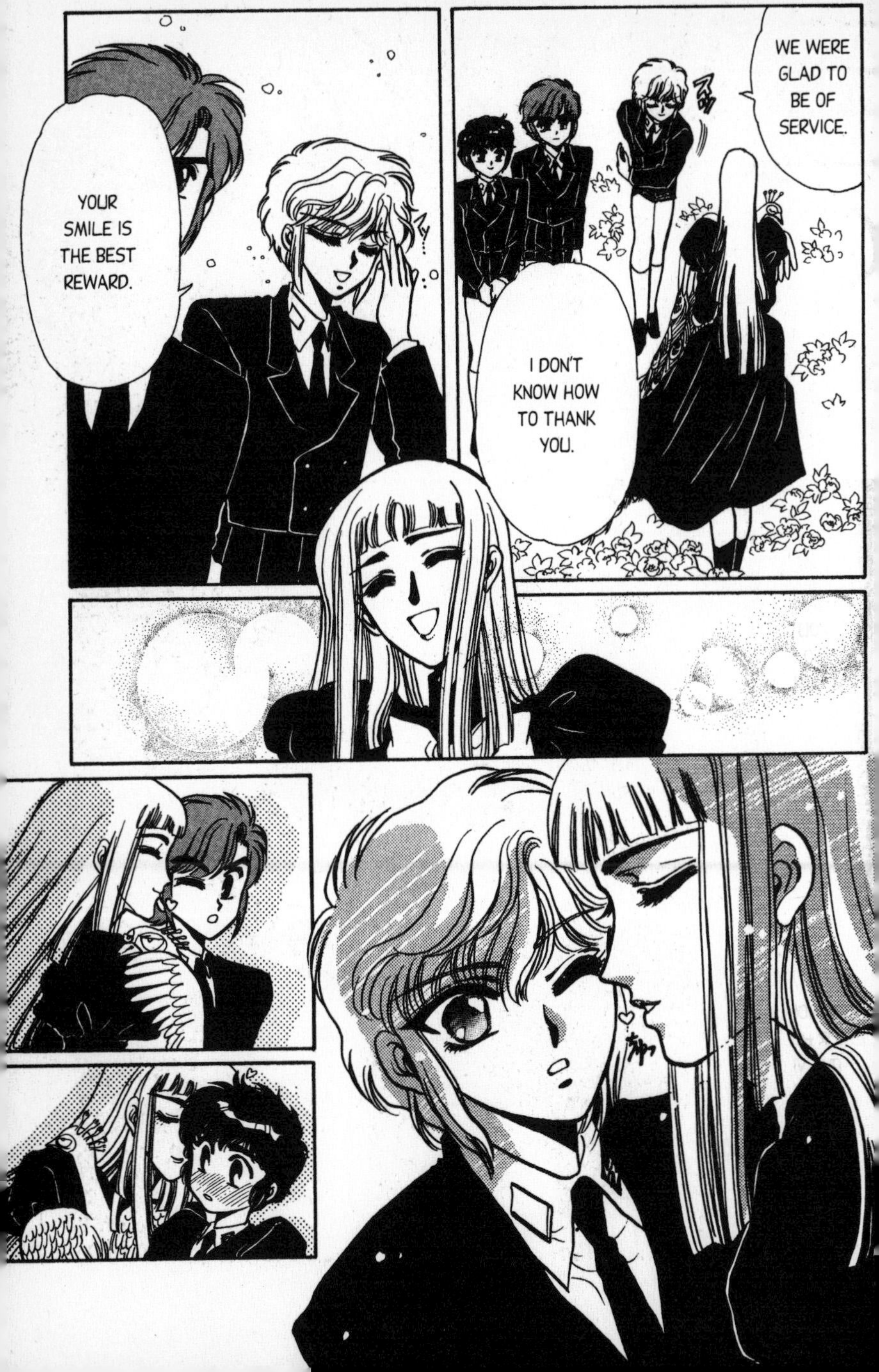
WE WERE GLAD TO BE OF SERVICE.
I DON'T KNOW HOW TO THANK YOU.
YOUR SMILE IS THE BEST REWARD.

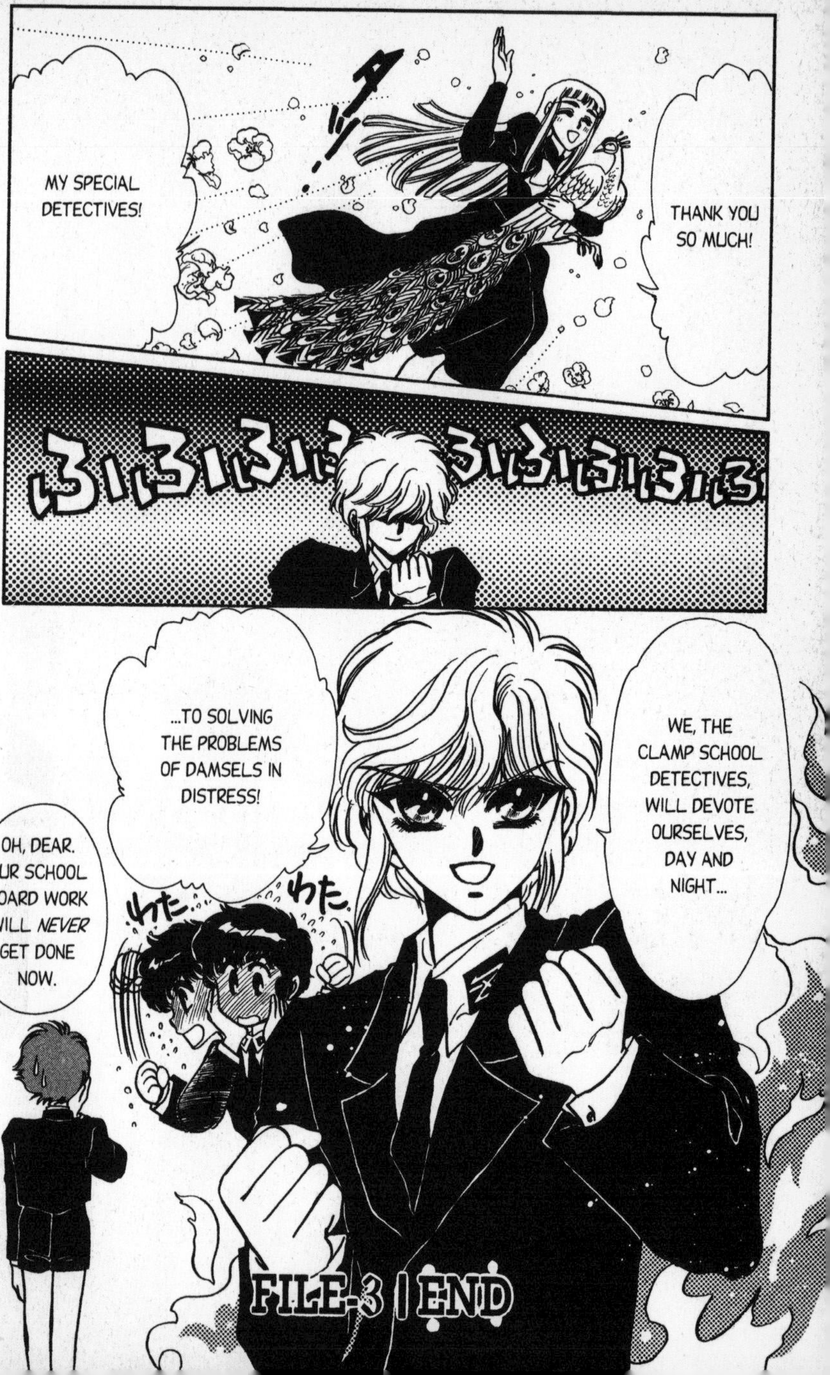
THANK YOU SO MUCH!
タッ
MY SPECIAL DETECTIVES!
WE, THE CLAMP SCHOOL DETECTIVES, WILL DEVOTE OURSELVES, DAY AND NIGHT...
...TO SOLVING THE PROBLEMS OF DAMSELS IN DISTRESS!
わた
わた
OH, DEAR. OUR SCHOOL BOARD WORK WILL *NEVER* GET DONE NOW.
FILE-3 | END

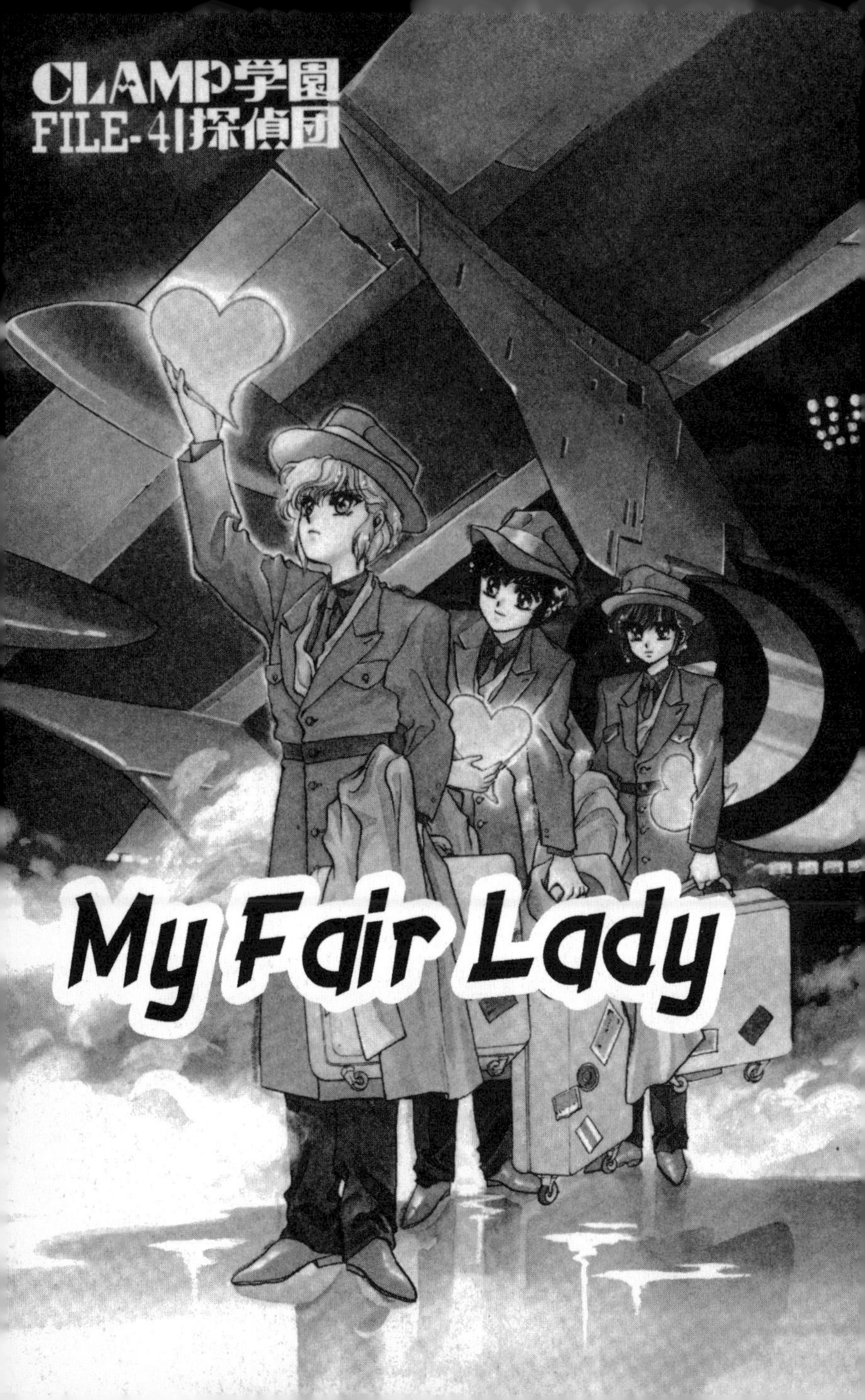
CLAMP学園
FILE-4 探偵団
My Fair Lady

CLAMP学園
探偵団

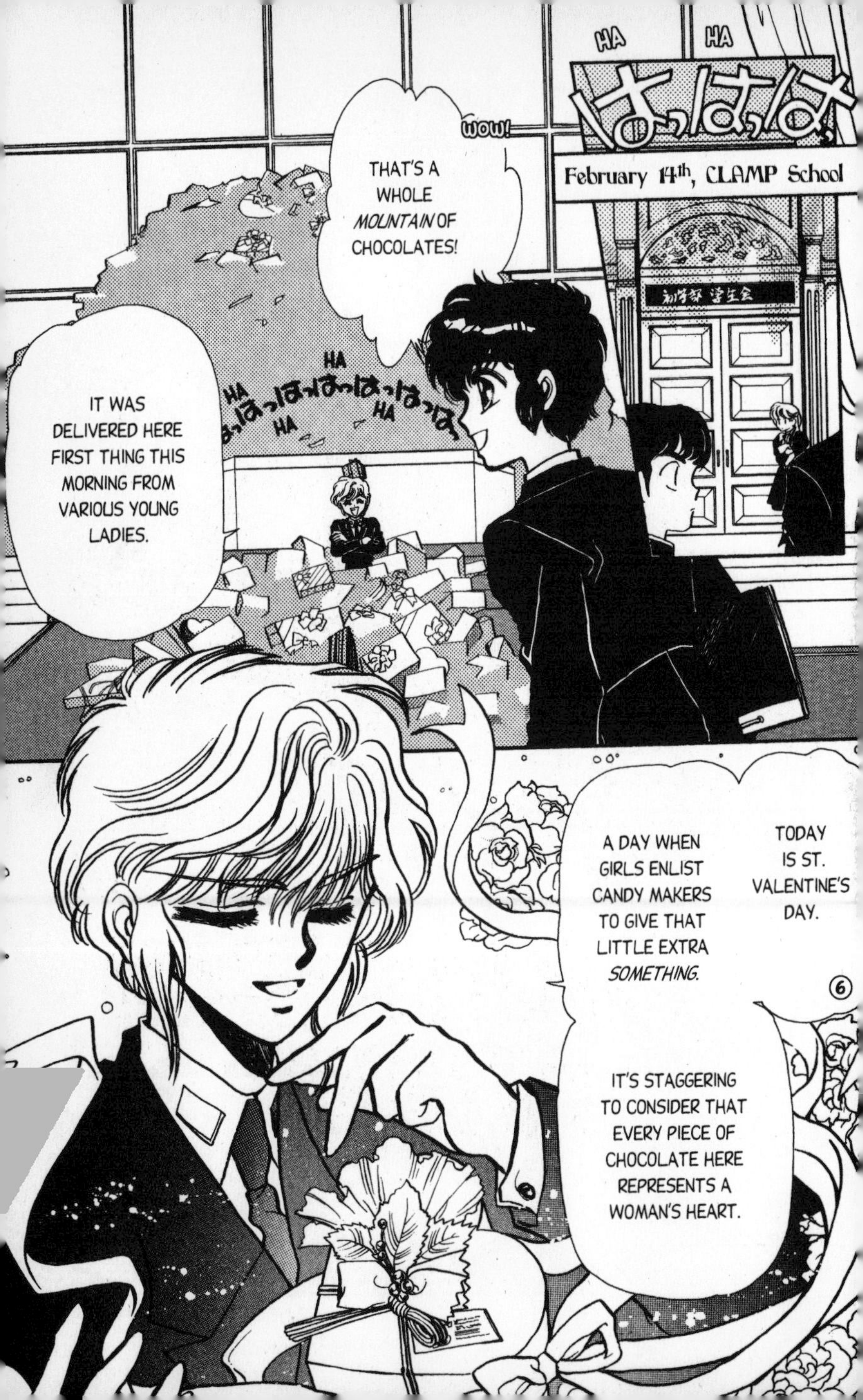
HA HA
はっはっは
February 14th, CLAMP School
WOW!
THAT'S A WHOLE MOUNTAIN OF CHOCOLATES!
HA HA HA はっはっはっはっはっはっは
IT WAS DELIVERED HERE FIRST THING THIS MORNING FROM VARIOUS YOUNG LADIES.
TODAY IS ST. VALENTINE'S DAY.
A DAY WHEN GIRLS ENLIST CANDY MAKERS TO GIVE THAT LITTLE EXTRA *SOMETHING.*
6
IT'S STAGGERING TO CONSIDER THAT EVERY PIECE OF CHOCOLATE HERE REPRESENTS A WOMAN'S HEART.

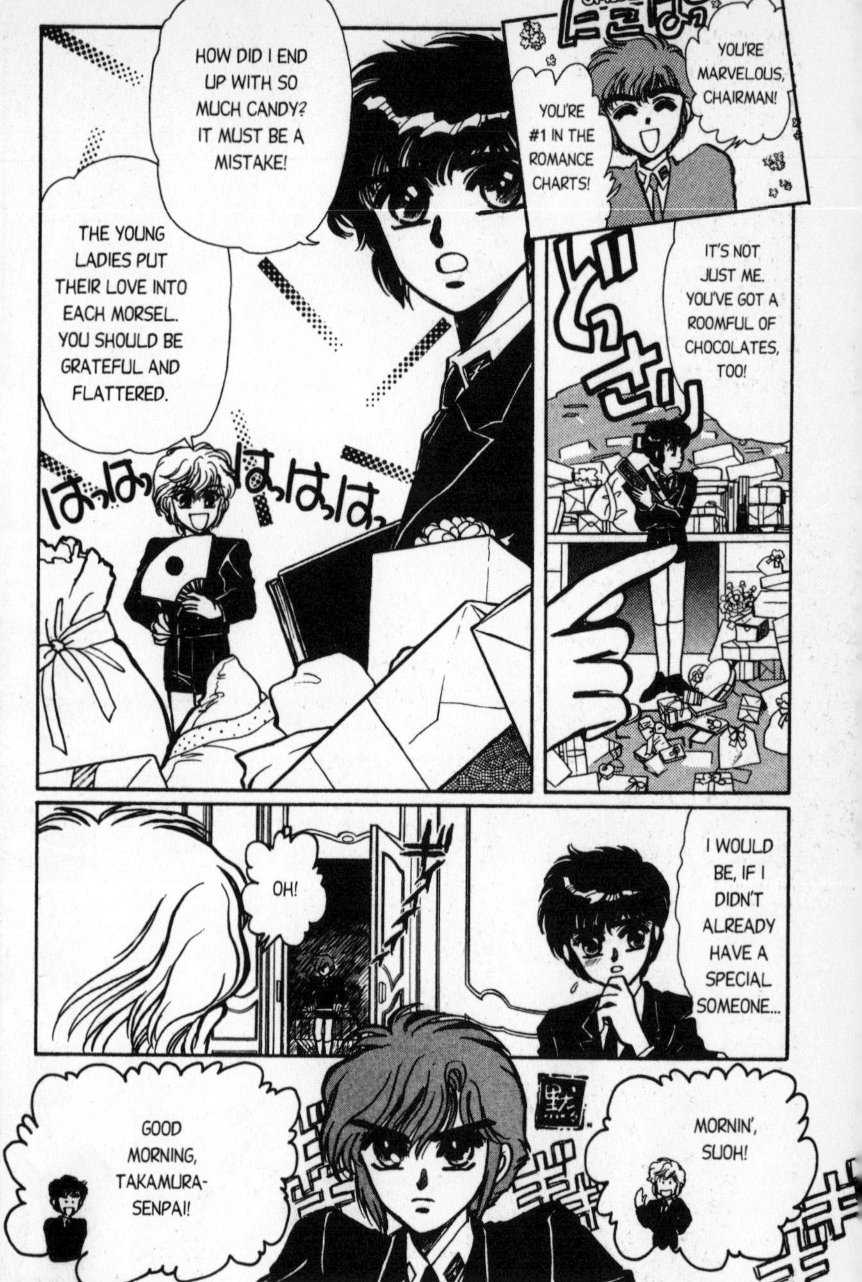
SMILE
にこぱっ
YOU'RE MARVELOUS, CHAIRMAN!
YOU'RE #1 IN THE ROMANCE CHARTS!
どっさり
IT'S NOT JUST ME. YOU'VE GOT A ROOMFUL OF CHOCOLATES, TOO!
HOW DID I END UP WITH SO MUCH CANDY? IT MUST BE A MISTAKE!
THE YOUNG LADIES PUT THEIR LOVE INTO EACH MORSEL. YOU SHOULD BE GRATEFUL AND FLATTERED.
はっはっはっはっはっ
I WOULD BE, IF I DIDN'T ALREADY HAVE A SPECIAL SOMEONE...
OH!
MORNIN', SUOH!
黙*
GOOD MORNING, TAKAMURA-SENPAI!

*The Kanji Character meaning "to become silent."

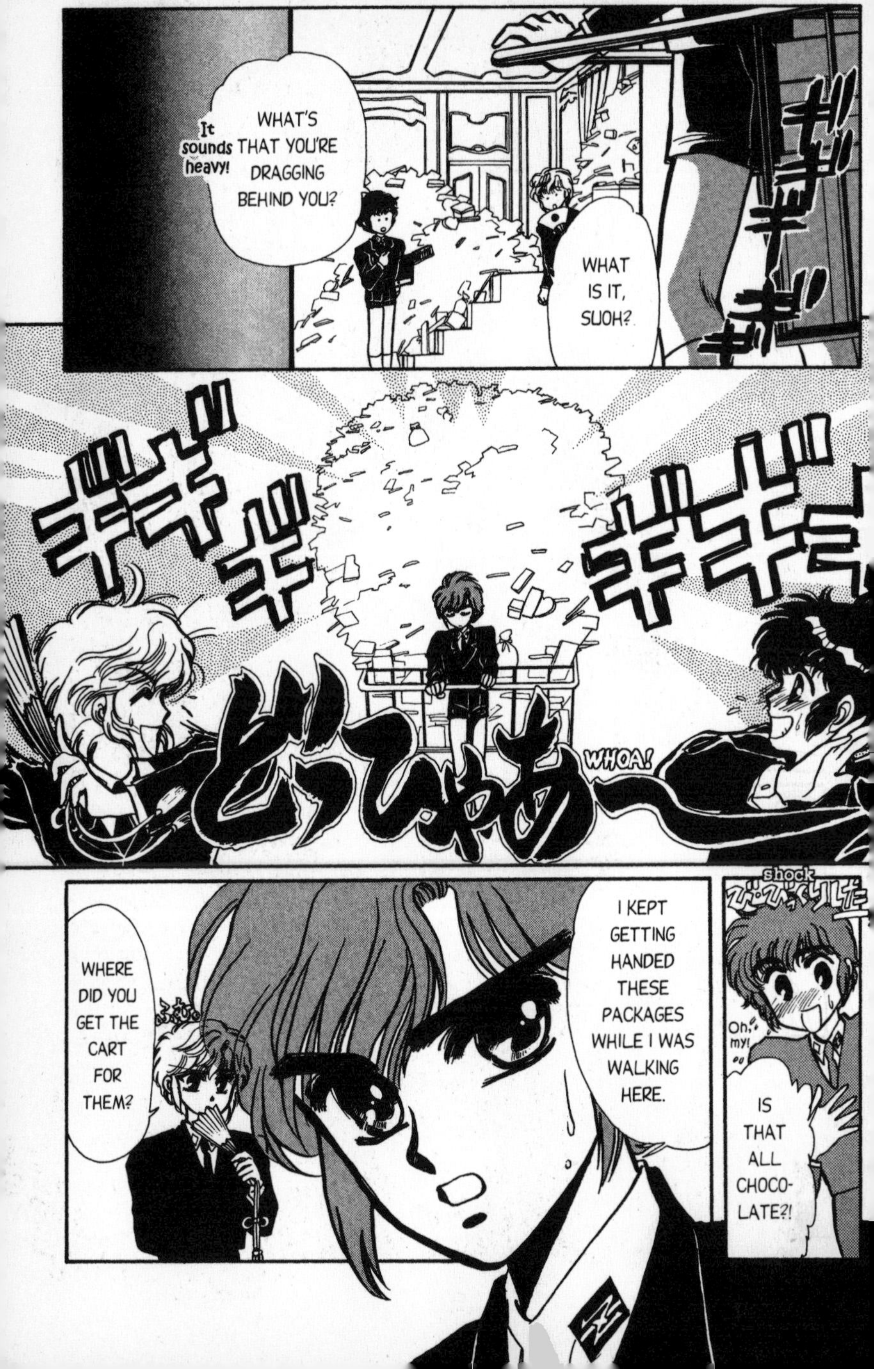

WHAT IS IT, SUOH?
WHAT'S THAT YOU'RE DRAGGING BEHIND YOU?
It sounds heavy!
WHOA!
shock
Oh, my!
IS THAT ALL CHOCO-LATE?!
I KEPT GETTING HANDED THESE PACKAGES WHILE I WAS WALKING HERE.
WHERE DID YOU GET THE CART FOR THEM?

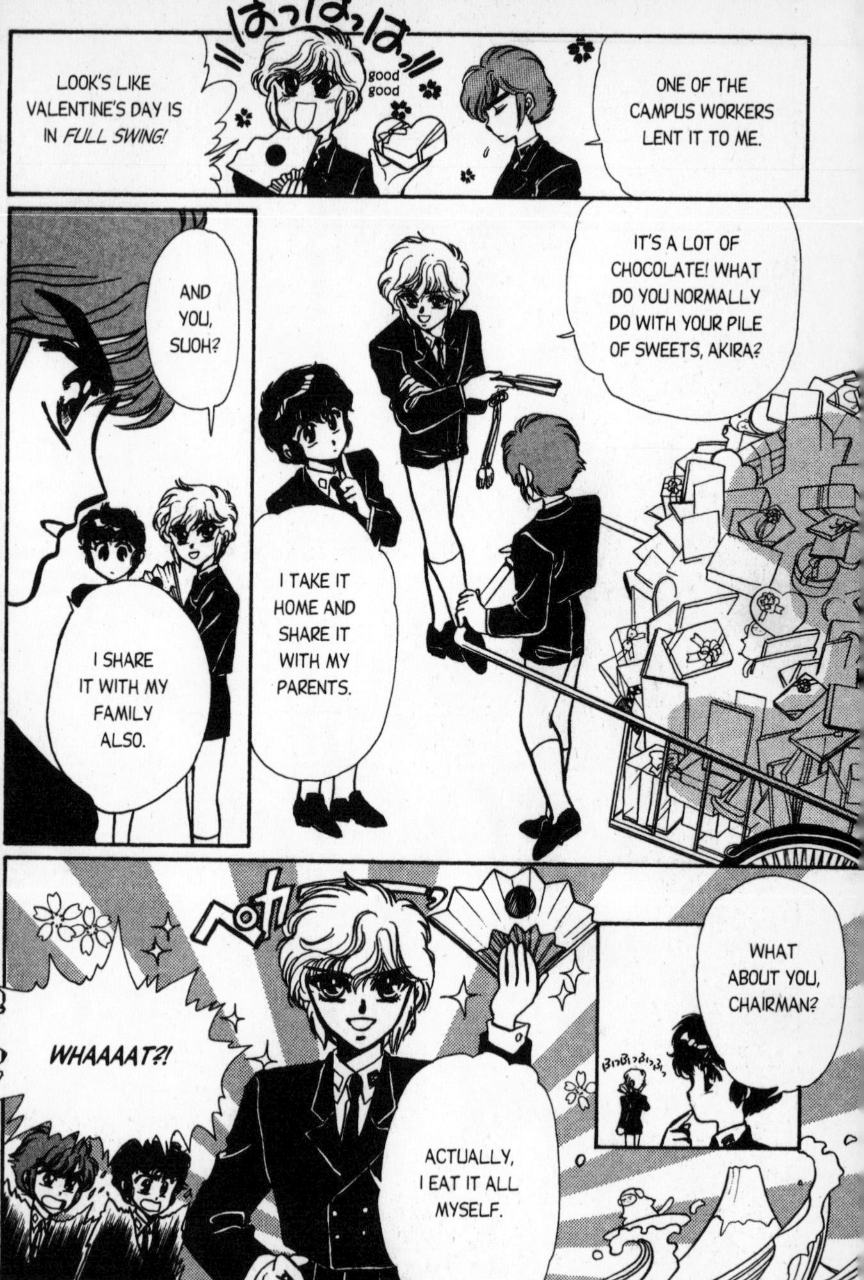
ONE OF THE CAMPUS WORKERS LENT IT TO ME.
はっはっはっ
good good
LOOK'S LIKE VALENTINE'S DAY IS IN *FULL SWING!*
IT'S A LOT OF CHOCOLATE! WHAT DO YOU NORMALLY DO WITH YOUR PILE OF SWEETS, AKIRA?
I TAKE IT HOME AND SHARE IT WITH MY PARENTS.
AND YOU, SUOH?
I SHARE IT WITH MY FAMILY ALSO.
WHAT ABOUT YOU, CHAIRMAN?
ACTUALLY, I EAT IT ALL MYSELF.
WHAAAAT?!

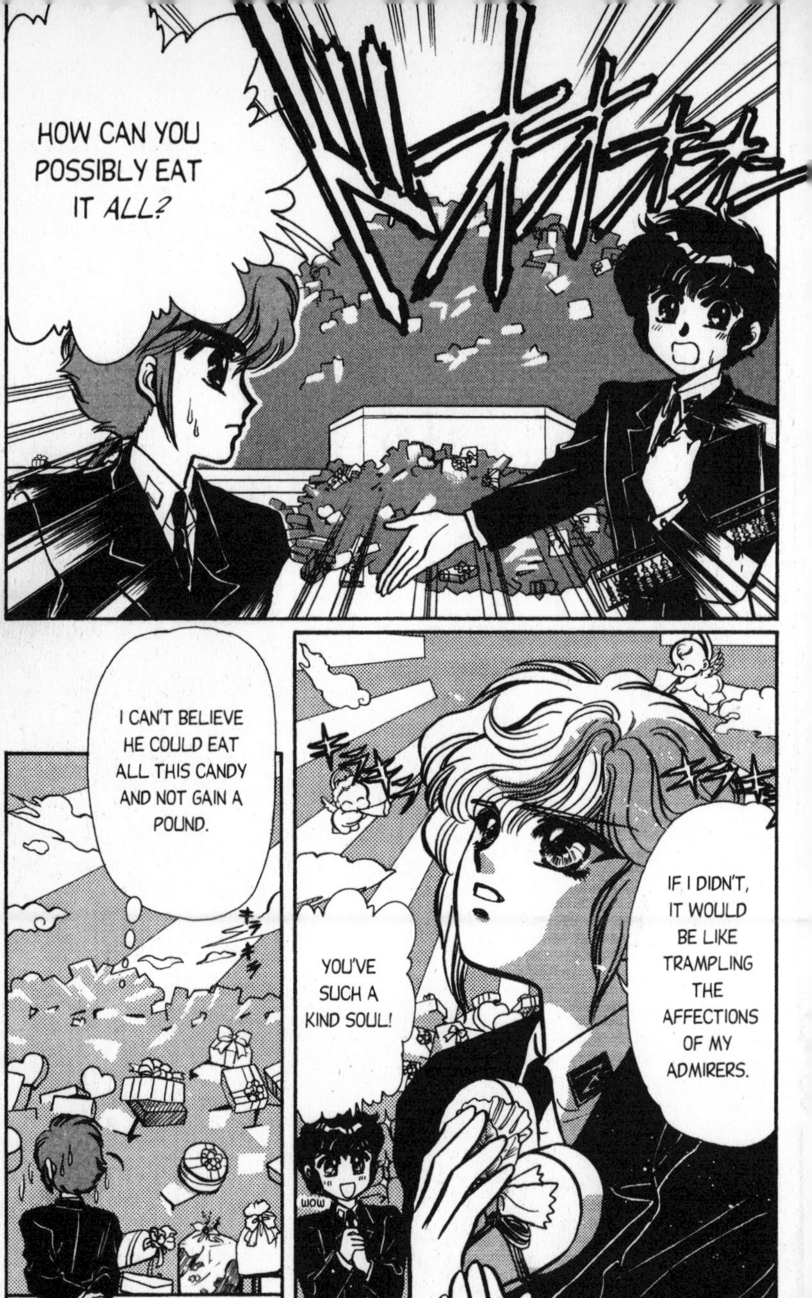
HOW CAN YOU POSSIBLY EAT IT ALL?
IF I DIDN'T, IT WOULD BE LIKE TRAMPLING THE AFFECTIONS OF MY ADMIRERS.
YOU'VE SUCH A KIND SOUL!
WOW
I CAN'T BELIEVE HE COULD EAT ALL THIS CANDY AND NOT GAIN A POUND.

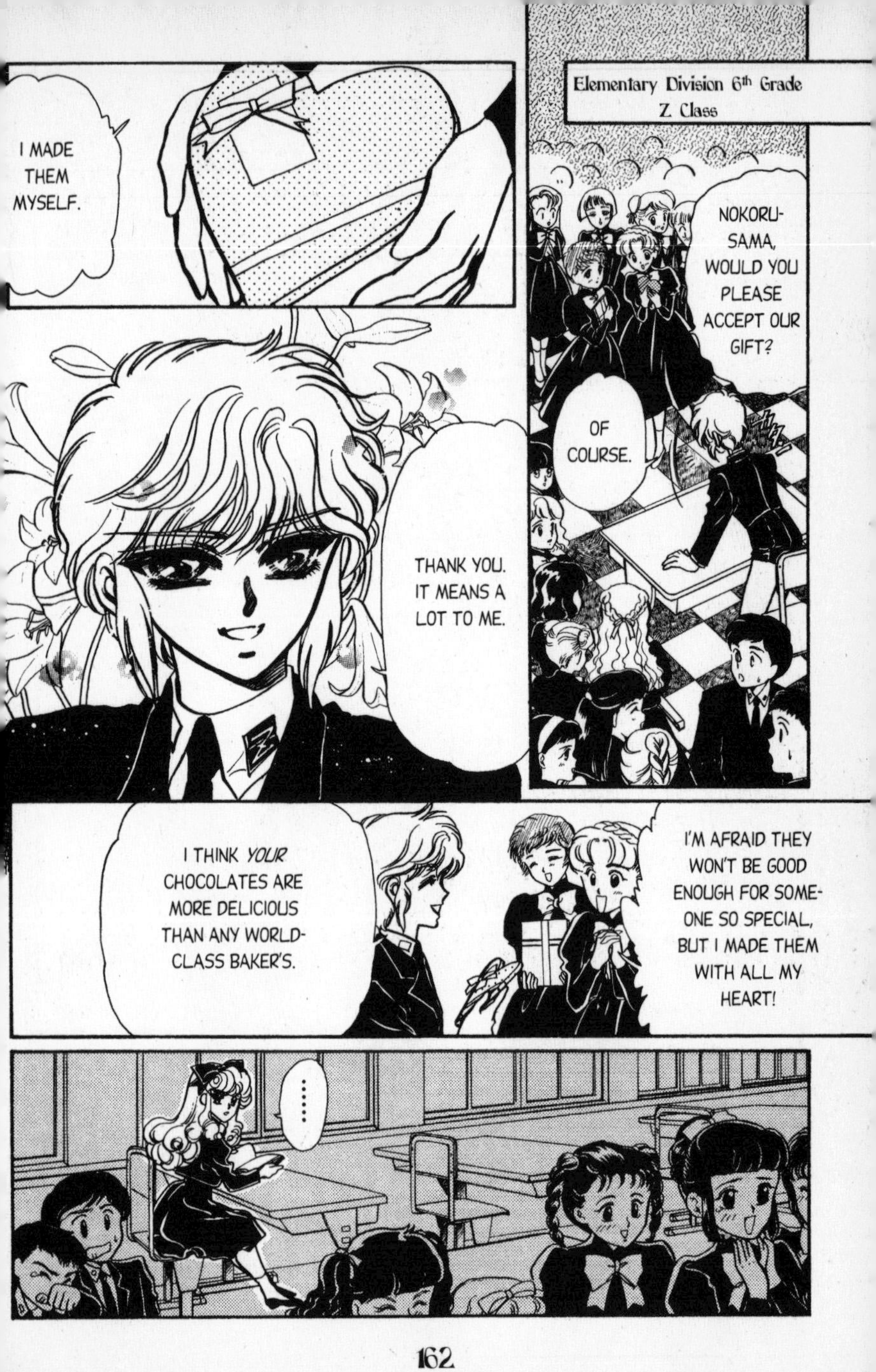
Elementary Division 6th Grade
Z Class
NOKORU-SAMA, WOULD YOU PLEASE ACCEPT OUR GIFT?
OF COURSE.
I MADE THEM MYSELF.
THANK YOU. IT MEANS A LOT TO ME.
I'M AFRAID THEY WON'T BE GOOD ENOUGH FOR SOME-ONE SO SPECIAL, BUT I MADE THEM WITH ALL MY HEART!
I THINK *YOUR* CHOCOLATES ARE MORE DELICIOUS THAN ANY WORLD-CLASS BAKER'S.
......

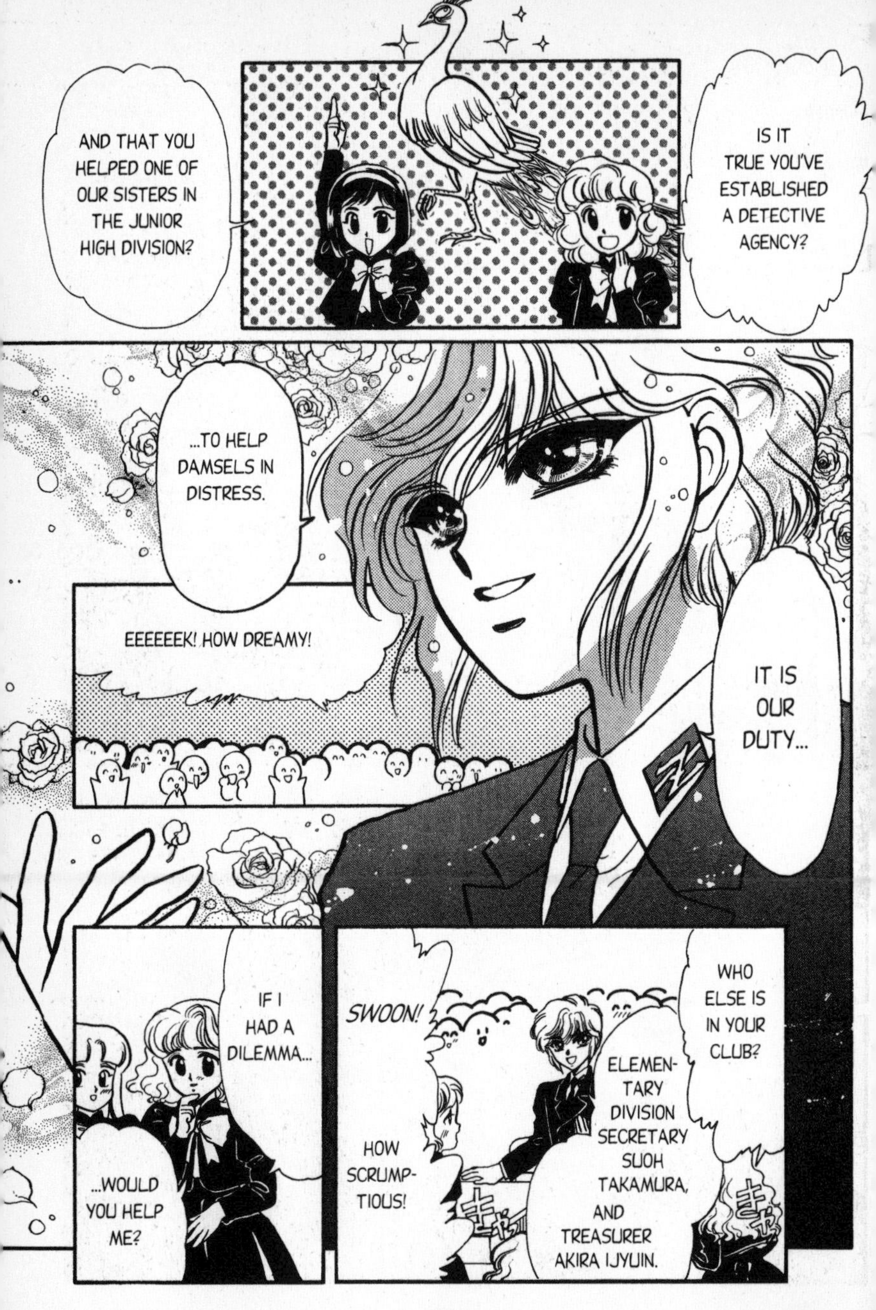
IS IT TRUE YOU'VE ESTABLISHED A DETECTIVE AGENCY?
AND THAT YOU HELPED ONE OF OUR SISTERS IN THE JUNIOR HIGH DIVISION?
IT IS OUR DUTY...
...TO HELP DAMSELS IN DISTRESS.
EEEEEEK! HOW DREAMY!
WHO ELSE IS IN YOUR CLUB?
ELEMENTARY DIVISION SECRETARY SUOH TAKAMURA, AND TREASURER AKIRA IJYUIN.
SWOON!
HOW SCRUMPTIOUS!
IF I HAD A DILEMMA...
...WOULD YOU HELP ME?

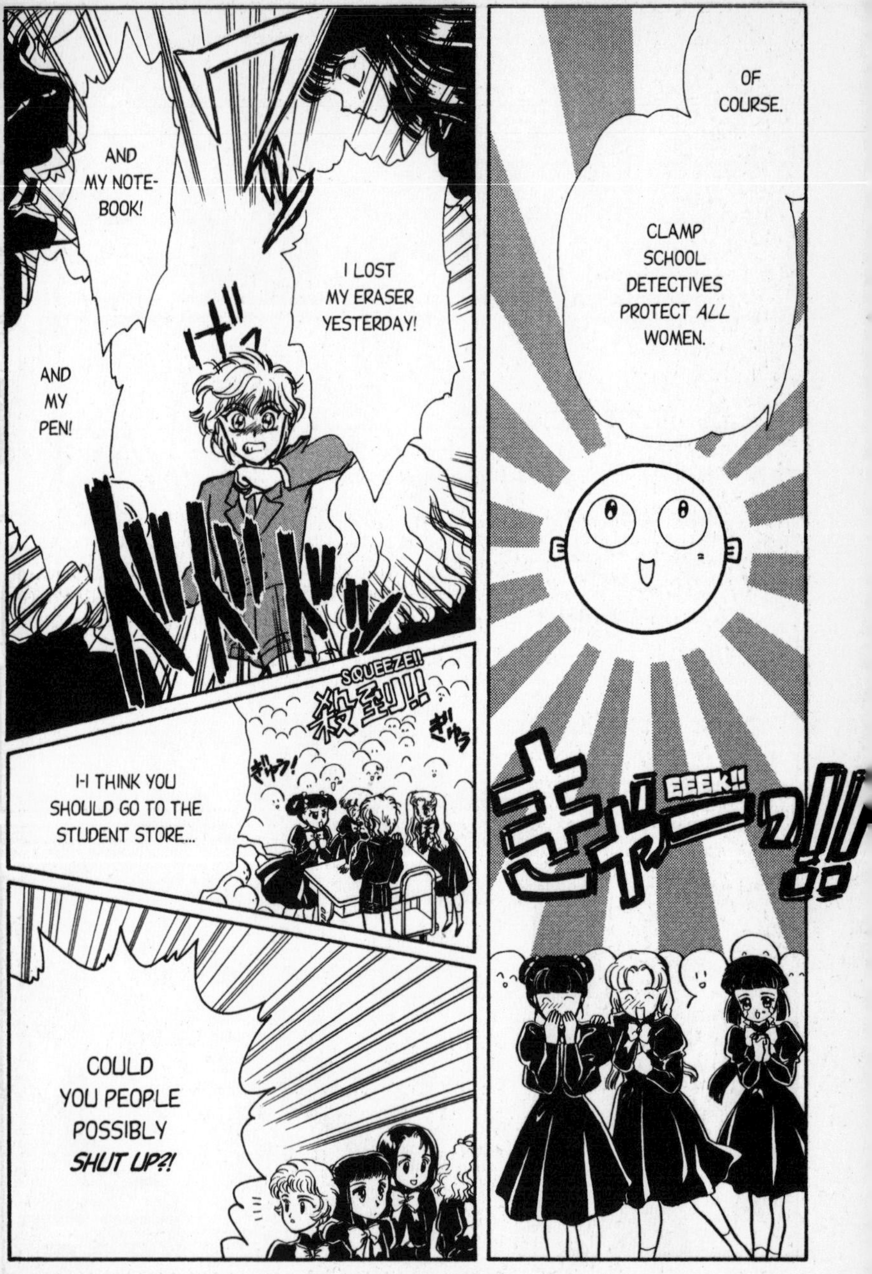
OF COURSE.
CLAMP SCHOOL DETECTIVES PROTECT ALL WOMEN.
EEEK!!
きゃーっ!!
I LOST MY ERASER YESTERDAY!
AND MY NOTE-BOOK!
AND MY PEN!
SQUEEZE!!
殺到!!
I-I THINK YOU SHOULD GO TO THE STUDENT STORE...
COULD YOU PEOPLE POSSIBLY *SHUT UP?!*

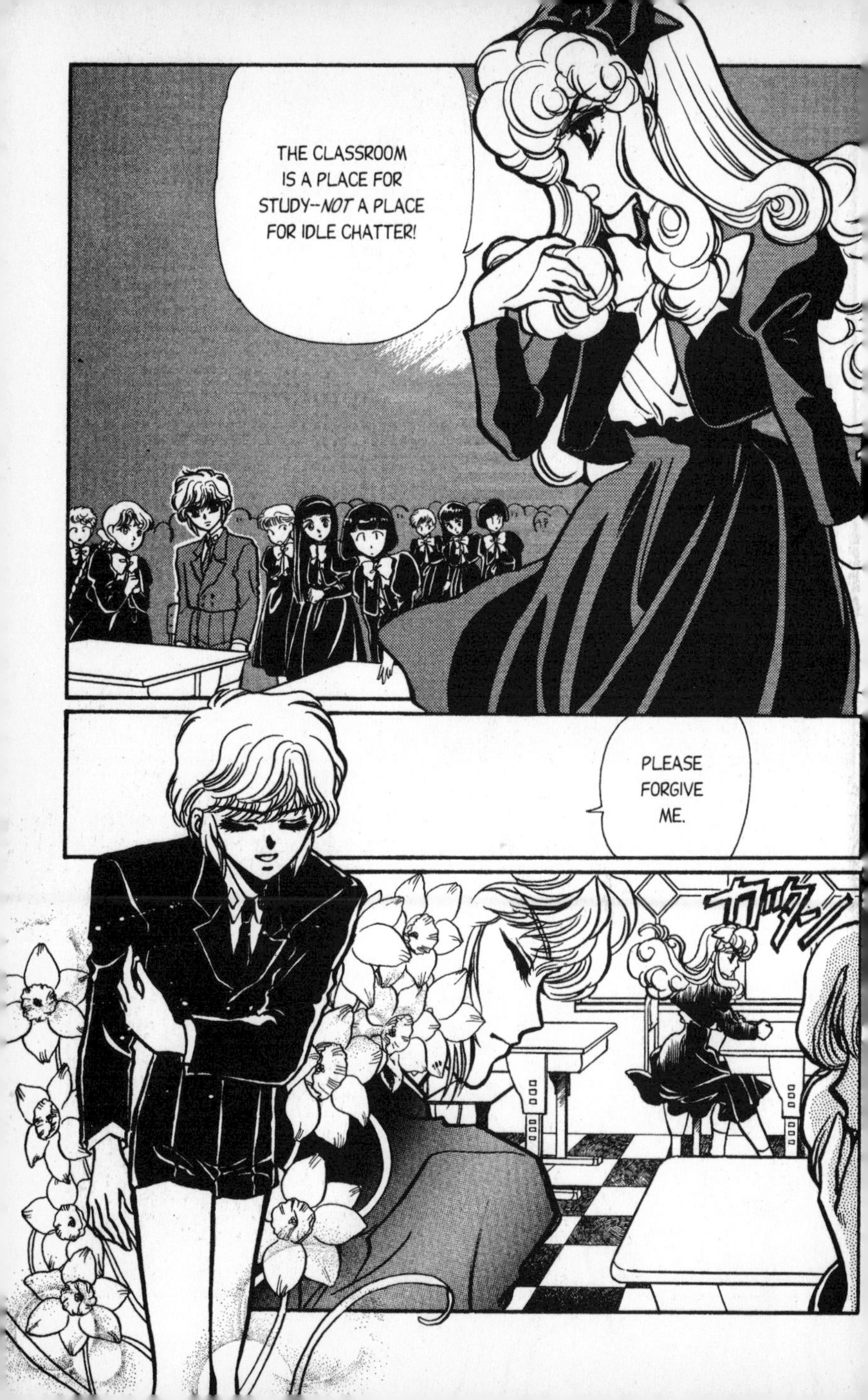
THE CLASSROOM IS A PLACE FOR STUDY--*NOT* A PLACE FOR IDLE CHATTER!
PLEASE FORGIVE ME.

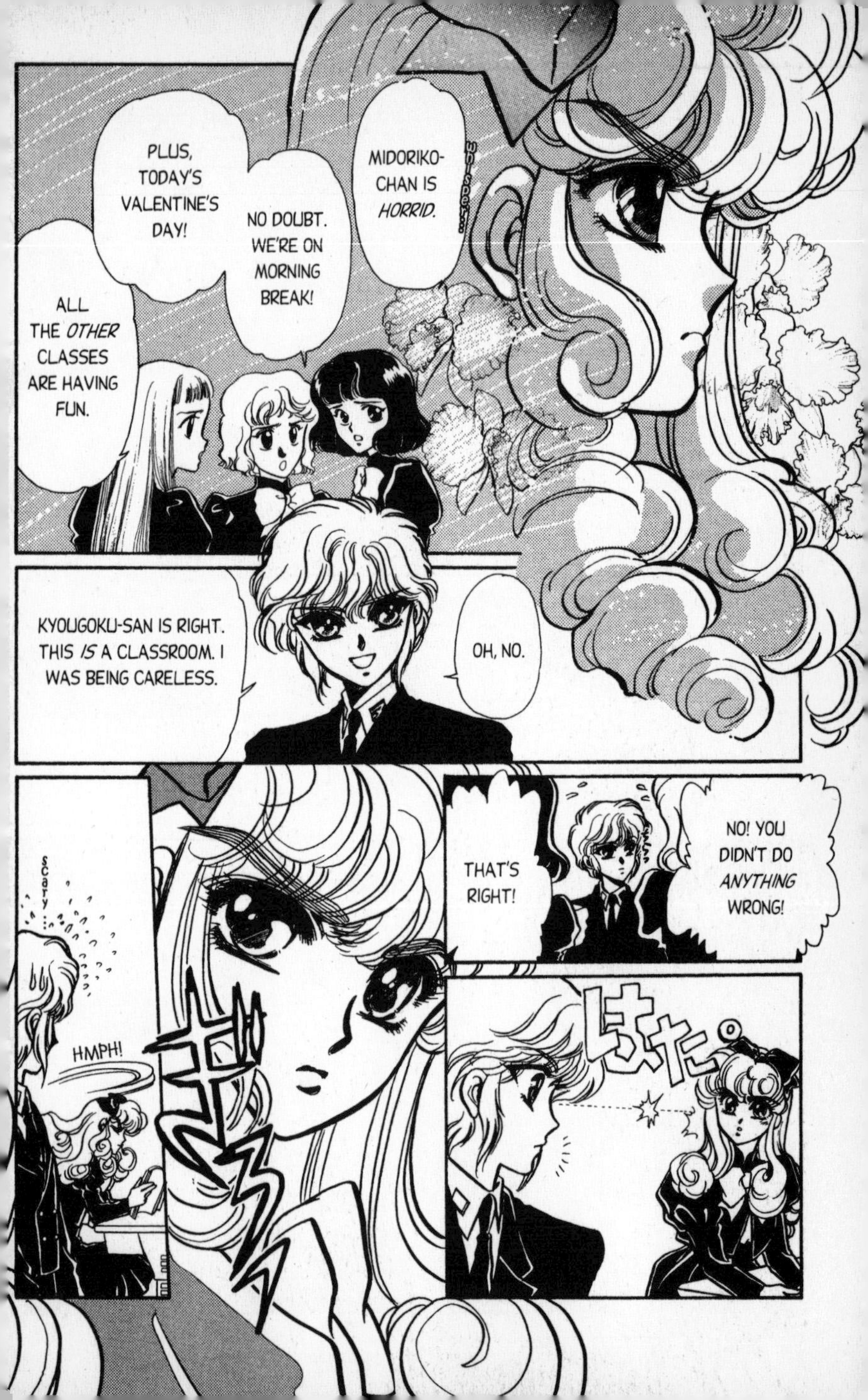
whisper...
MIDORIKO-CHAN IS *HORRID.*
NO DOUBT. WE'RE ON MORNING BREAK!
PLUS, TODAY'S VALENTINE'S DAY!
ALL THE *OTHER* CLASSES ARE HAVING FUN.
OH, NO.
KYOUGOKU-SAN IS RIGHT. THIS *IS* A CLASSROOM. I WAS BEING CARELESS.
NO! YOU DIDN'T DO *ANYTHING* WRONG!
THAT'S RIGHT!
scary...
HMPH!

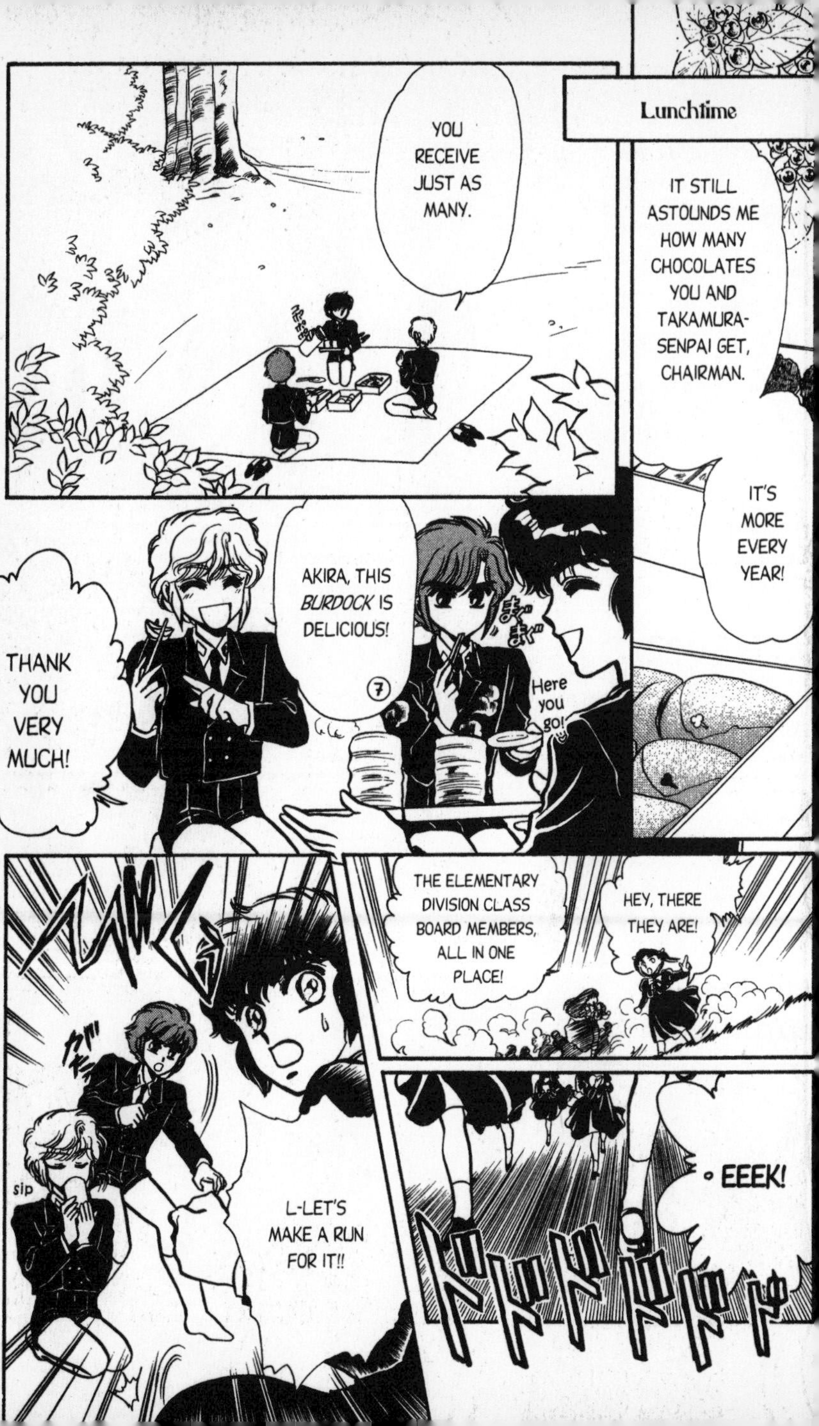
Lunchtime
IT STILL ASTOUNDS ME HOW MANY CHOCOLATES YOU AND TAKAMURA-SENPAI GET, CHAIRMAN.
IT'S MORE EVERY YEAR!
YOU RECEIVE JUST AS MANY.
Here you go!
AKIRA, THIS *BURDOCK* IS DELICIOUS!
THANK YOU VERY MUCH!
HEY, THERE THEY ARE!
THE ELEMENTARY DIVISION CLASS BOARD MEMBERS, ALL IN ONE PLACE!
EEEK!
L-LET'S MAKE A RUN FOR IT!!
sip

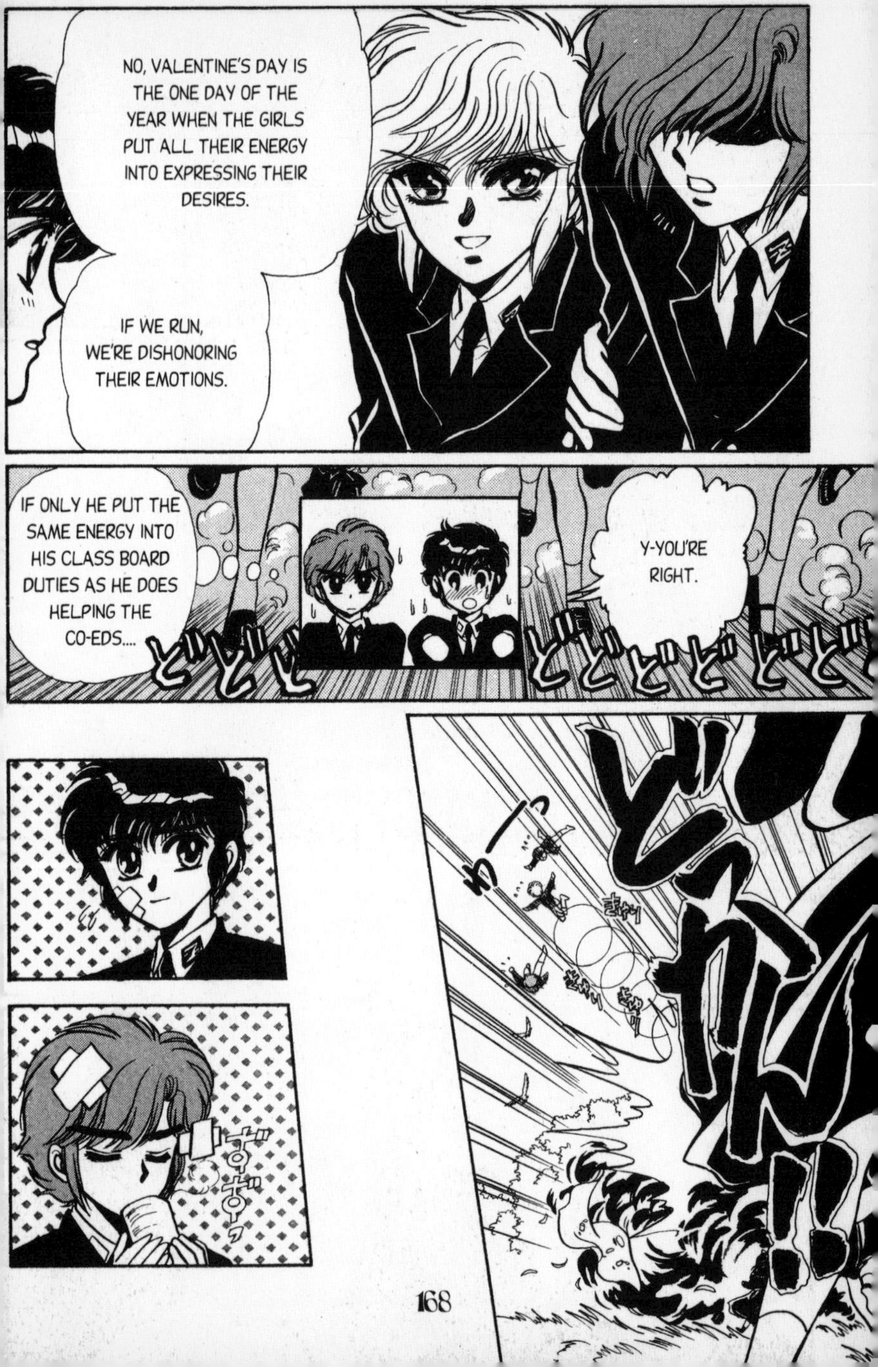
NO, VALENTINE'S DAY IS THE ONE DAY OF THE YEAR WHEN THE GIRLS PUT ALL THEIR ENERGY INTO EXPRESSING THEIR DESIRES.
IF WE RUN, WE'RE DISHONORING THEIR EMOTIONS.
Y-YOU'RE RIGHT.
どどどどどど
IF ONLY HE PUT THE SAME ENERGY INTO HIS CLASS BOARD DUTIES AS HE DOES HELPING THE CO-EDS....
どどど

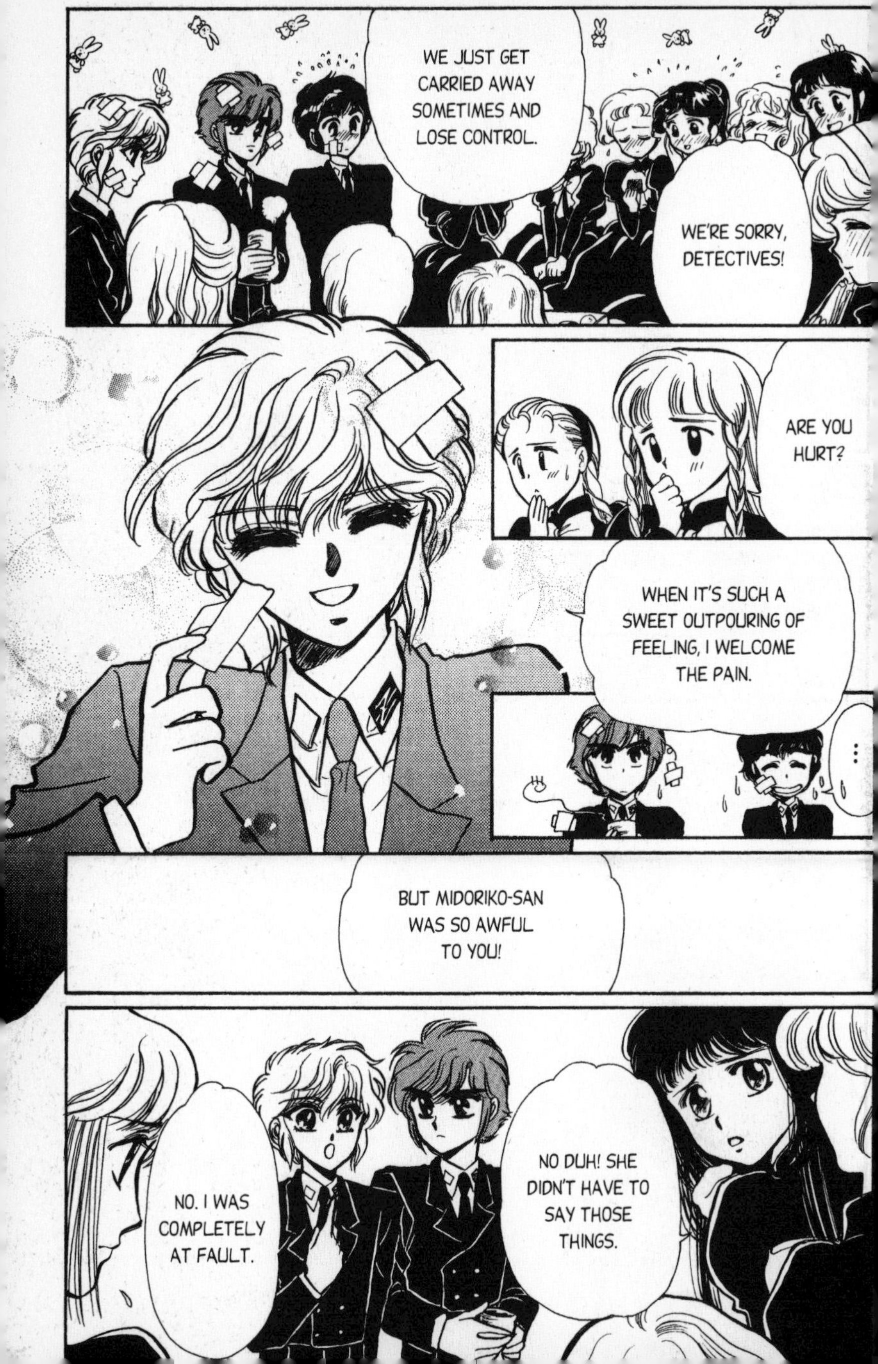
WE JUST GET CARRIED AWAY SOMETIMES AND LOSE CONTROL.
WE'RE SORRY, DETECTIVES!
ARE YOU HURT?
WHEN IT'S SUCH A SWEET OUTPOURING OF FEELING, I WELCOME THE PAIN.
...
BUT MIDORIKO-SAN WAS SO AWFUL TO YOU!
NO DUH! SHE DIDN'T HAVE TO SAY THOSE THINGS.
NO. I WAS COMPLETELY AT FAULT.

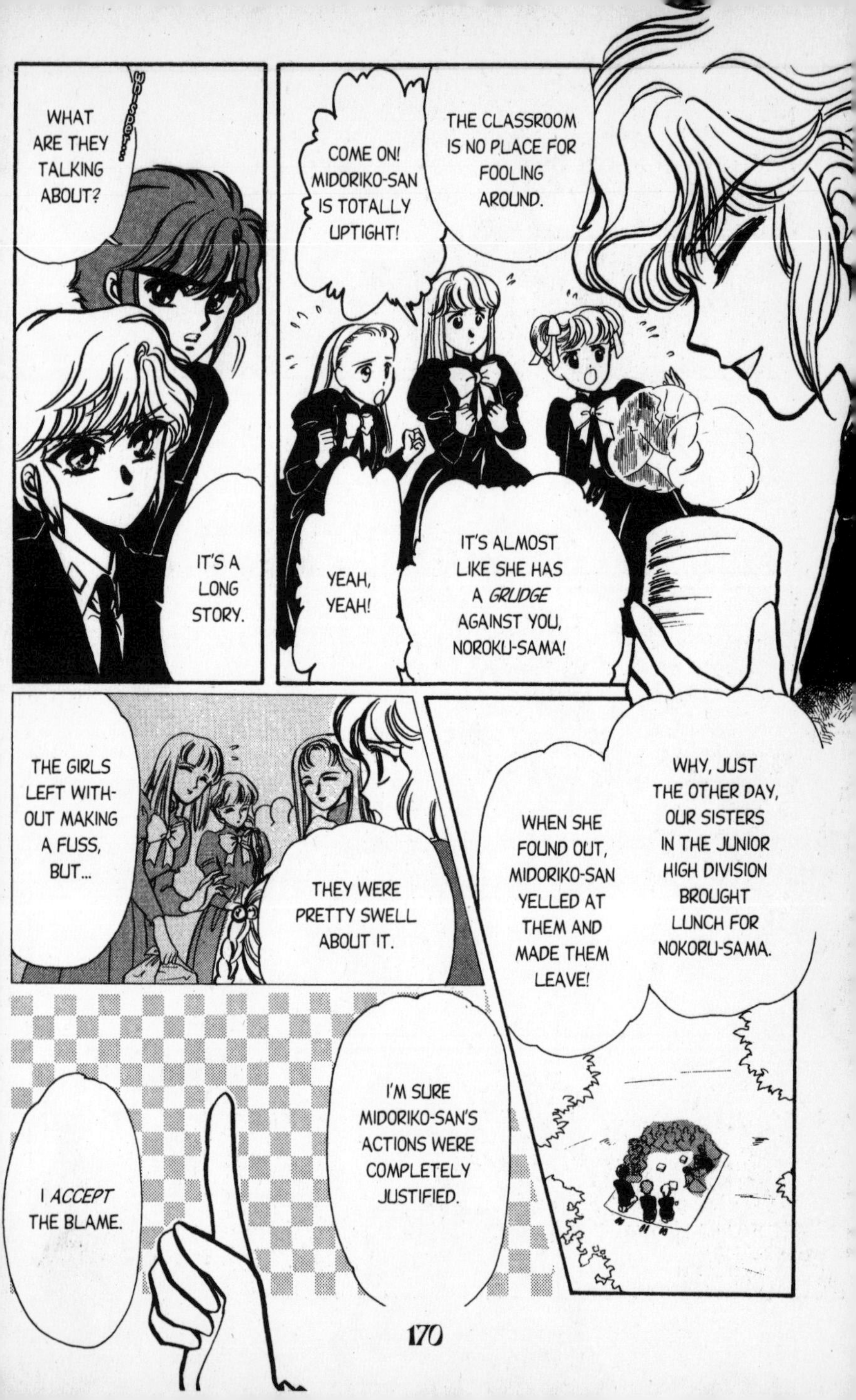
THE CLASSROOM IS NO PLACE FOR FOOLING AROUND.
COME ON! MIDORIKO-SAN IS TOTALLY UPTIGHT!
IT'S ALMOST LIKE SHE HAS A *GRUDGE* AGAINST YOU, NOROKU-SAMA!
YEAH, YEAH!
whisper...
WHAT ARE THEY TALKING ABOUT?
IT'S A LONG STORY.
WHY, JUST THE OTHER DAY, OUR SISTERS IN THE JUNIOR HIGH DIVISION BROUGHT LUNCH FOR NOKORU-SAMA.
WHEN SHE FOUND OUT, MIDORIKO-SAN YELLED AT THEM AND MADE THEM LEAVE!
THE GIRLS LEFT WITH-OUT MAKING A FUSS, BUT...
THEY WERE PRETTY SWELL ABOUT IT.
I'M SURE MIDORIKO-SAN'S ACTIONS WERE COMPLETELY JUSTIFIED.
I *ACCEPT* THE BLAME.

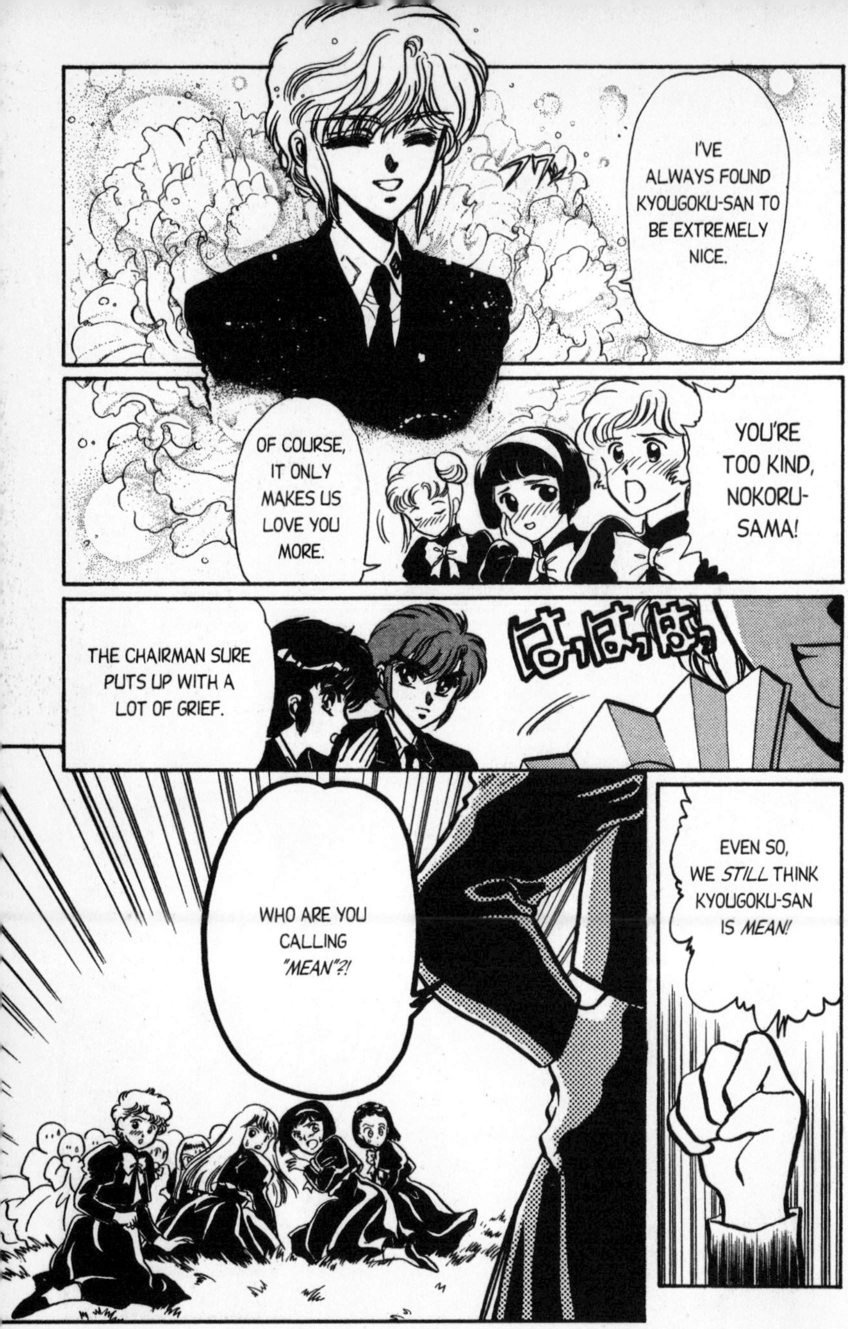
I'VE ALWAYS FOUND KYOUGOKU-SAN TO BE EXTREMELY NICE.
YOU'RE TOO KIND, NOKORU-SAMA!
OF COURSE, IT ONLY MAKES US LOVE YOU MORE.
はっはっはっ
THE CHAIRMAN SURE PUTS UP WITH A LOT OF GRIEF.
EVEN SO, WE *STILL* THINK KYOUGOKU-SAN IS *MEAN!*
WHO ARE YOU CALLING *"MEAN"?!*

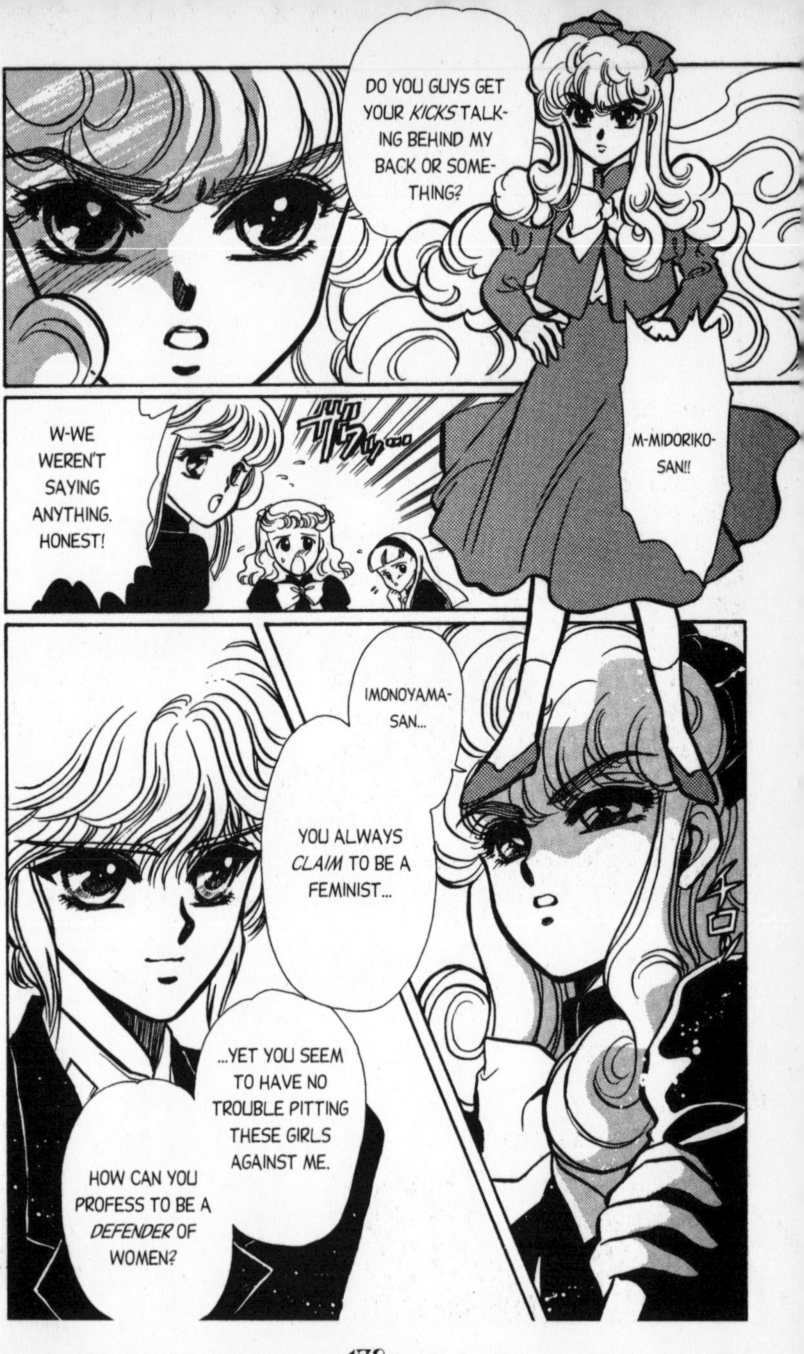

DO YOU GUYS GET YOUR *KICKS* TALKING BEHIND MY BACK OR SOMETHING?
M-MIDORIKO-SAN!!
W-WE WEREN'T SAYING ANYTHING. HONEST!
IMONOYAMA-SAN...
YOU ALWAYS *CLAIM* TO BE A FEMINIST...
...YET YOU SEEM TO HAVE NO TROUBLE PITTING THESE GIRLS AGAINST ME.
HOW CAN YOU PROFESS TO BE A *DEFENDER* OF WOMEN?

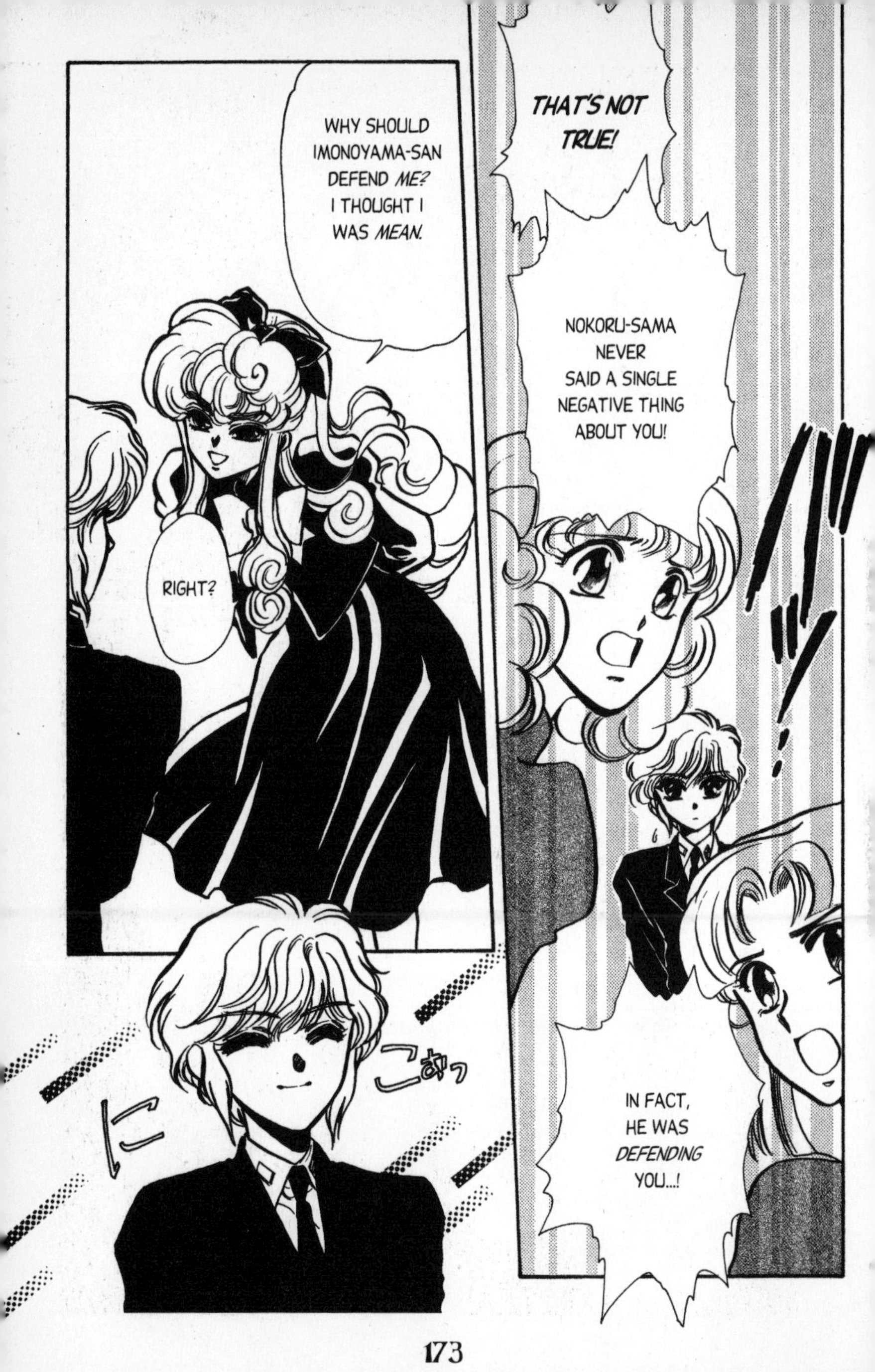
THAT'S NOT TRUE!
NOKORU-SAMA NEVER SAID A SINGLE NEGATIVE THING ABOUT YOU!
IN FACT, HE WAS *DEFENDING* YOU...!
WHY SHOULD IMONOYAMA-SAN DEFEND *ME?* I THOUGHT I WAS *MEAN.*
RIGHT?
にこ

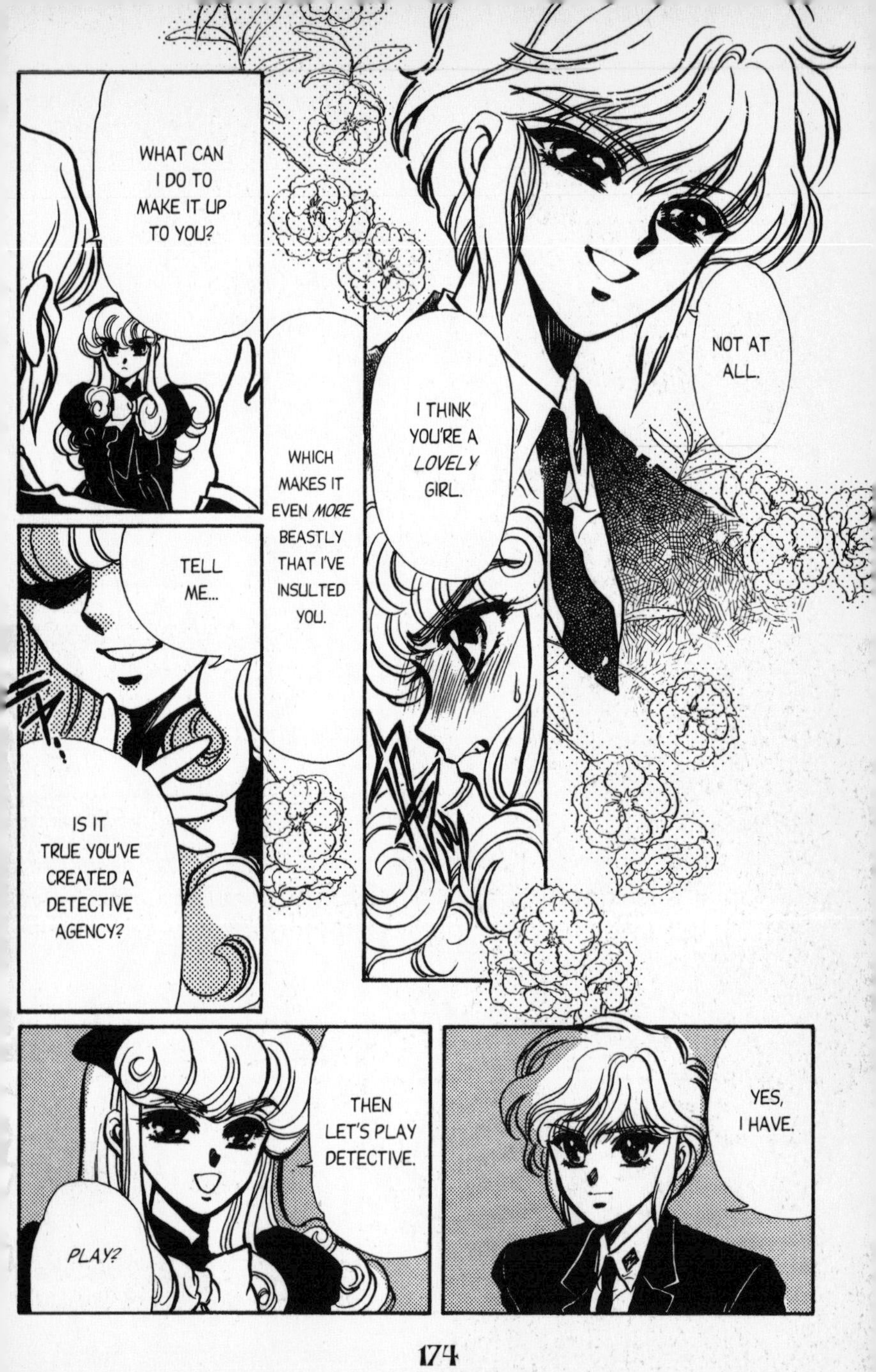
NOT AT ALL.
I THINK YOU'RE A *LOVELY* GIRL.
WHICH MAKES IT EVEN *MORE* BEASTLY THAT I'VE INSULTED YOU.
WHAT CAN I DO TO MAKE IT UP TO YOU?
TELL ME...
IS IT TRUE YOU'VE CREATED A DETECTIVE AGENCY?
YES, I HAVE.
THEN LET'S PLAY DETECTIVE.
PLAY?

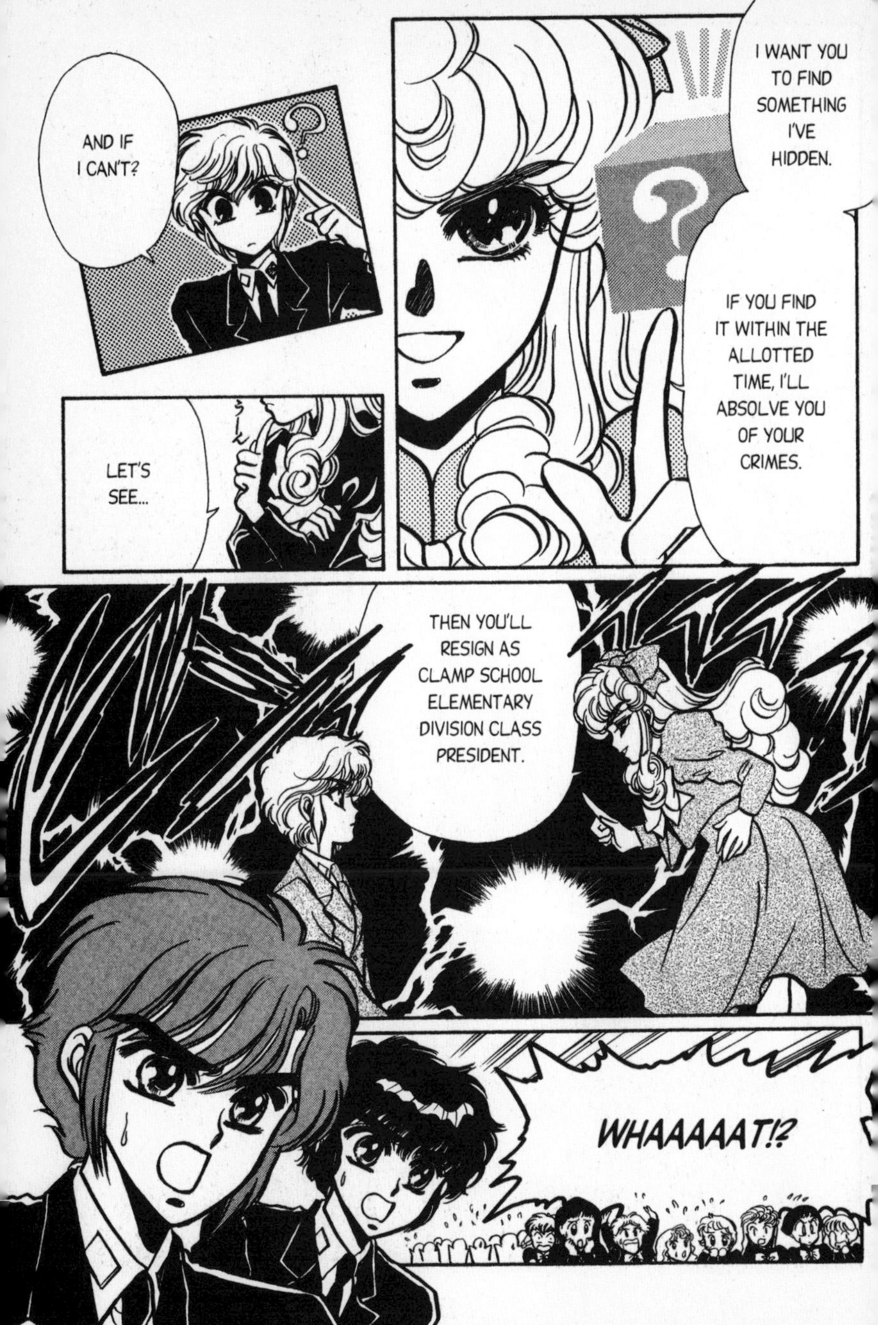
I WANT YOU TO FIND SOMETHING I'VE HIDDEN.
IF YOU FIND IT WITHIN THE ALLOTTED TIME, I'LL ABSOLVE YOU OF YOUR CRIMES.
AND IF I CAN'T?
LET'S SEE...
THEN YOU'LL RESIGN AS CLAMP SCHOOL ELEMENTARY DIVISION CLASS PRESIDENT.
WHAAAAAT!?

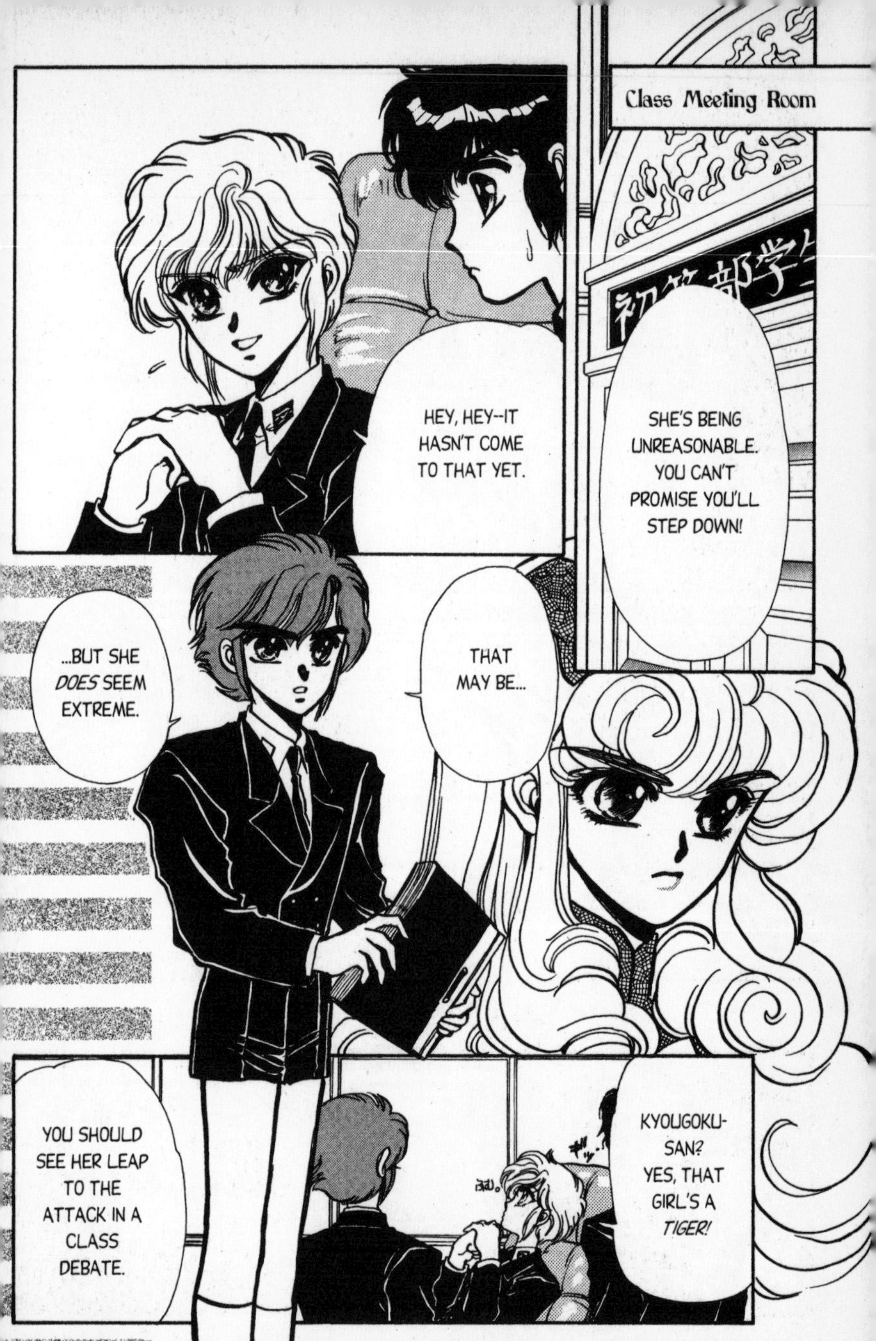

Class Meeting Room
初等部学
SHE'S BEING UNREASONABLE. YOU CAN'T PROMISE YOU'LL STEP DOWN!
HEY, HEY--IT HASN'T COME TO THAT YET.
THAT MAY BE...
...BUT SHE *DOES* SEEM EXTREME.
KYOUGOKU-SAN? YES, THAT GIRL'S A *TIGER!*
YOU SHOULD SEE HER LEAP TO THE ATTACK IN A CLASS DEBATE.

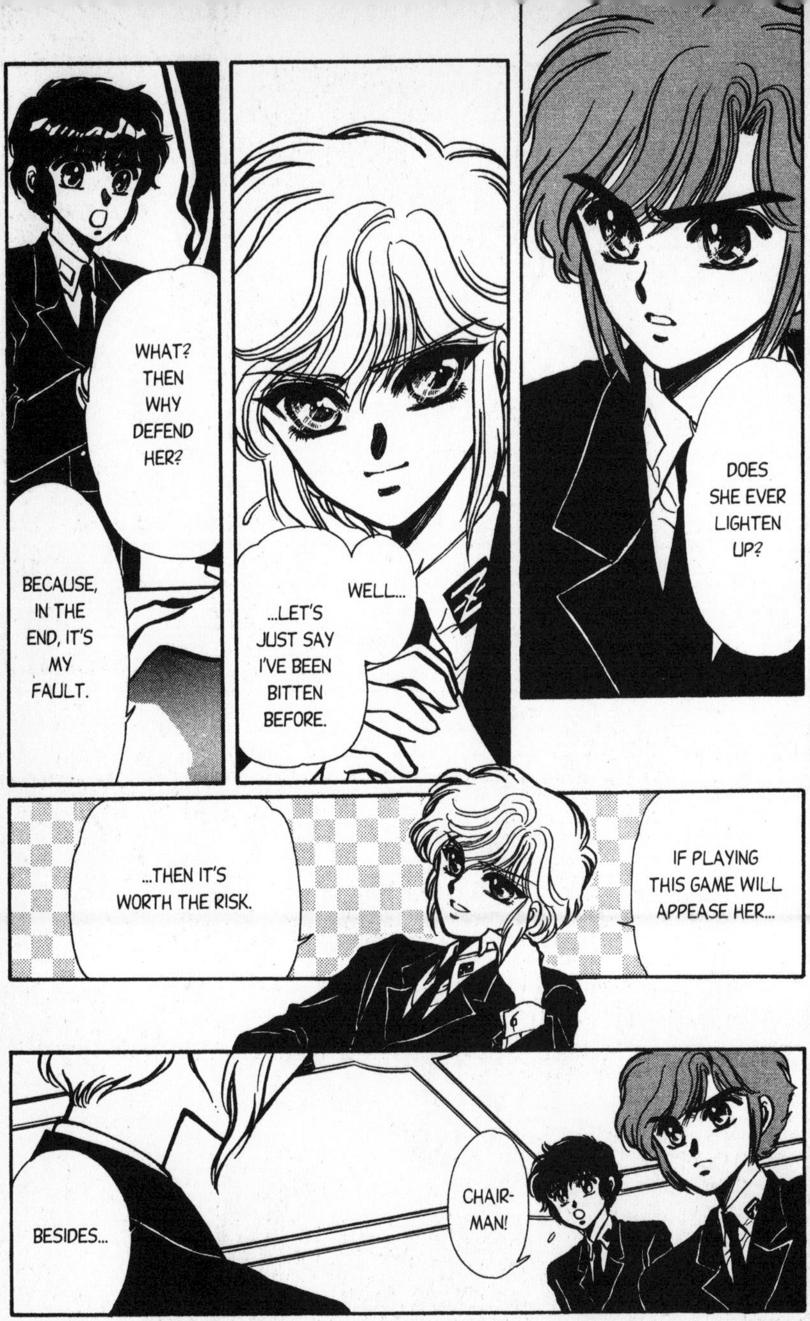
DOES SHE EVER LIGHTEN UP?
WELL...
...LET'S JUST SAY I'VE BEEN BITTEN BEFORE.
WHAT? THEN WHY DEFEND HER?
BECAUSE, IN THE END, IT'S MY FAULT.
IF PLAYING THIS GAME WILL APPEASE HER...
...THEN IT'S WORTH THE RISK.
CHAIR-MAN!
BESIDES...

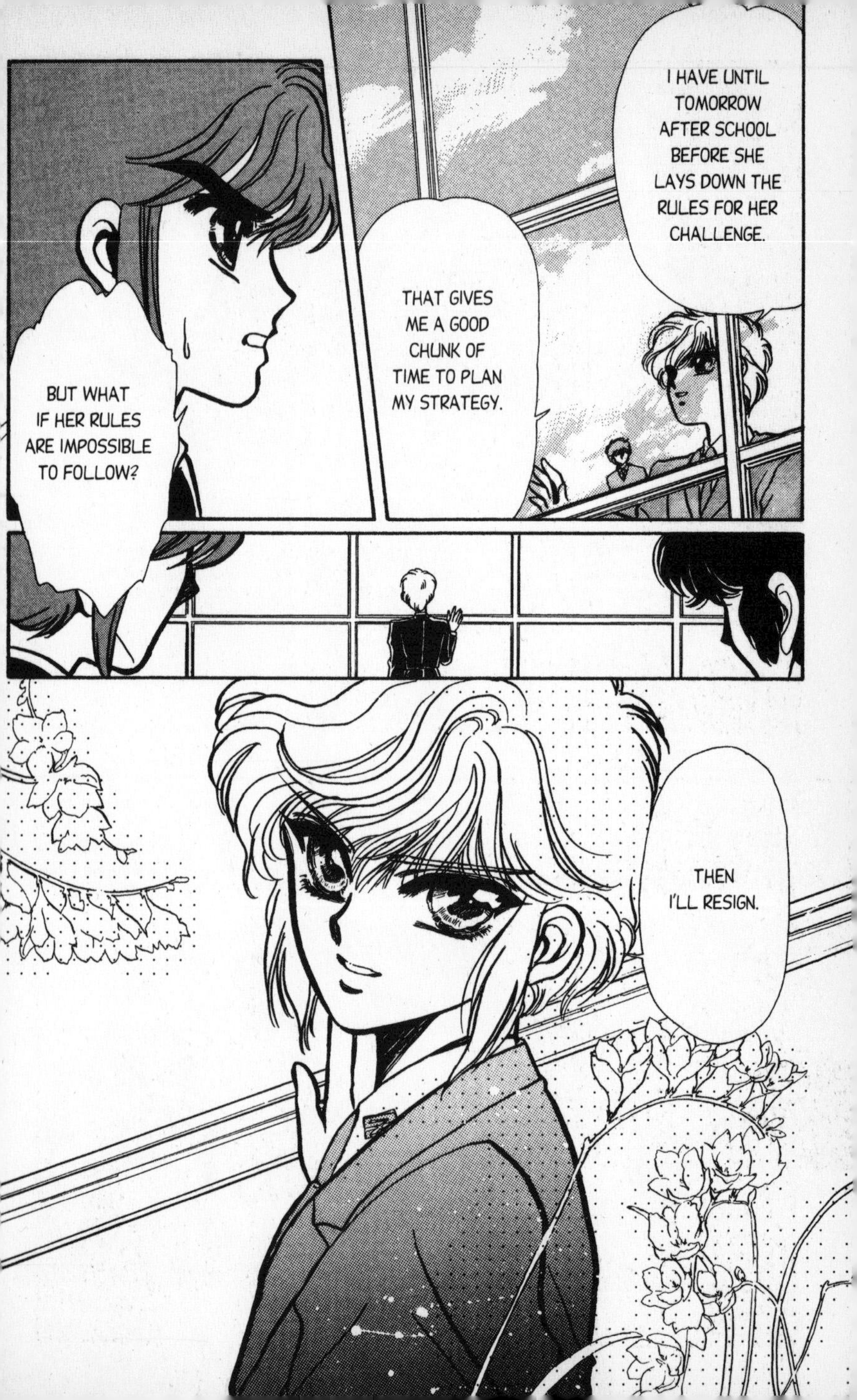
I HAVE UNTIL TOMORROW AFTER SCHOOL BEFORE SHE LAYS DOWN THE RULES FOR HER CHALLENGE.
THAT GIVES ME A GOOD CHUNK OF TIME TO PLAN MY STRATEGY.
BUT WHAT IF HER RULES ARE IMPOSSIBLE TO FOLLOW?
THEN I'LL RESIGN.

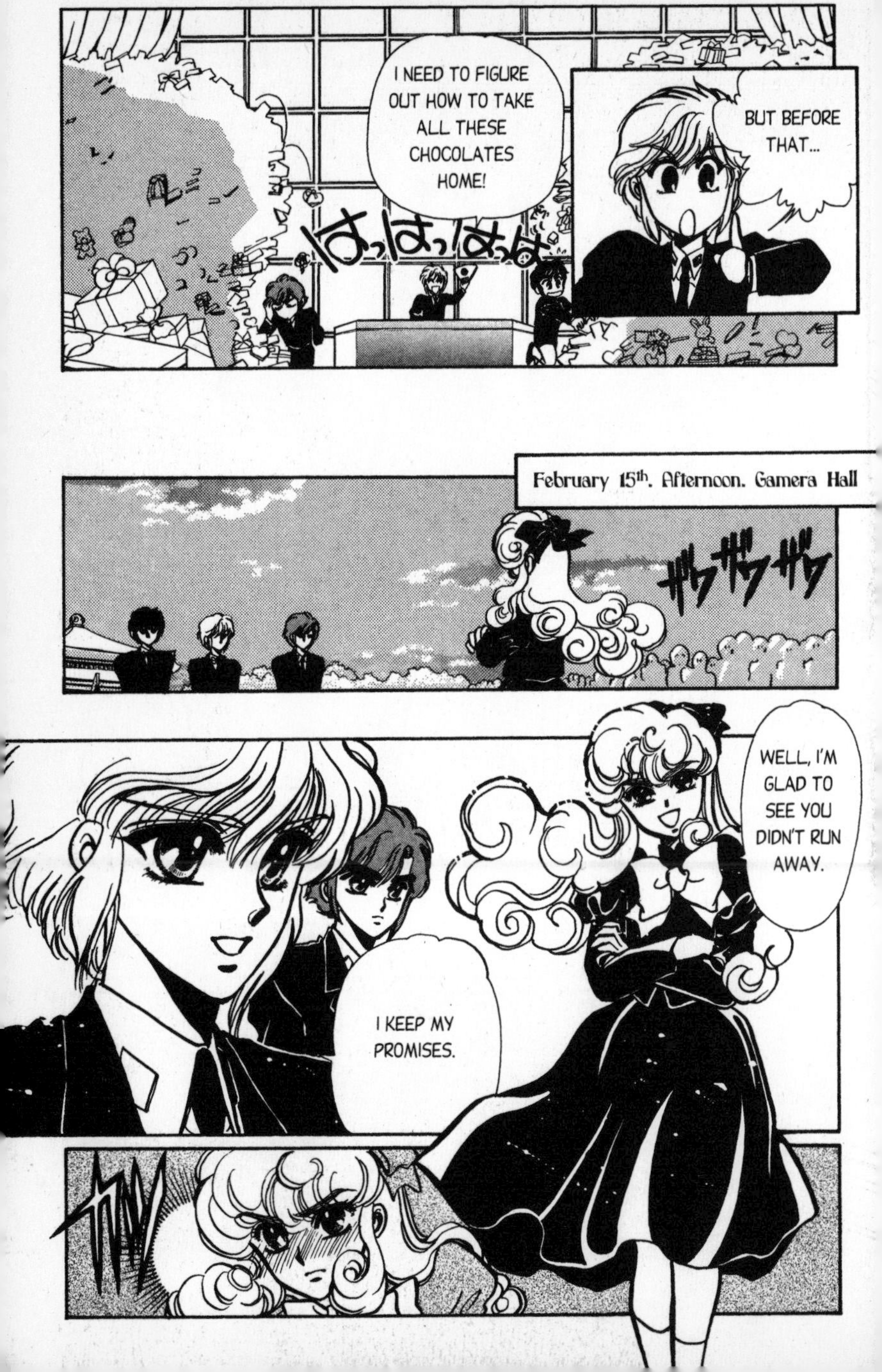
I NEED TO FIGURE OUT HOW TO TAKE ALL THESE CHOCOLATES HOME!
はっはっはっは
BUT BEFORE THAT...
February 15th. Afternoon. Gamera Hall
ザワザワザワ
WELL, I'M GLAD TO SEE YOU DIDN'T RUN AWAY.
I KEEP MY PROMISES.

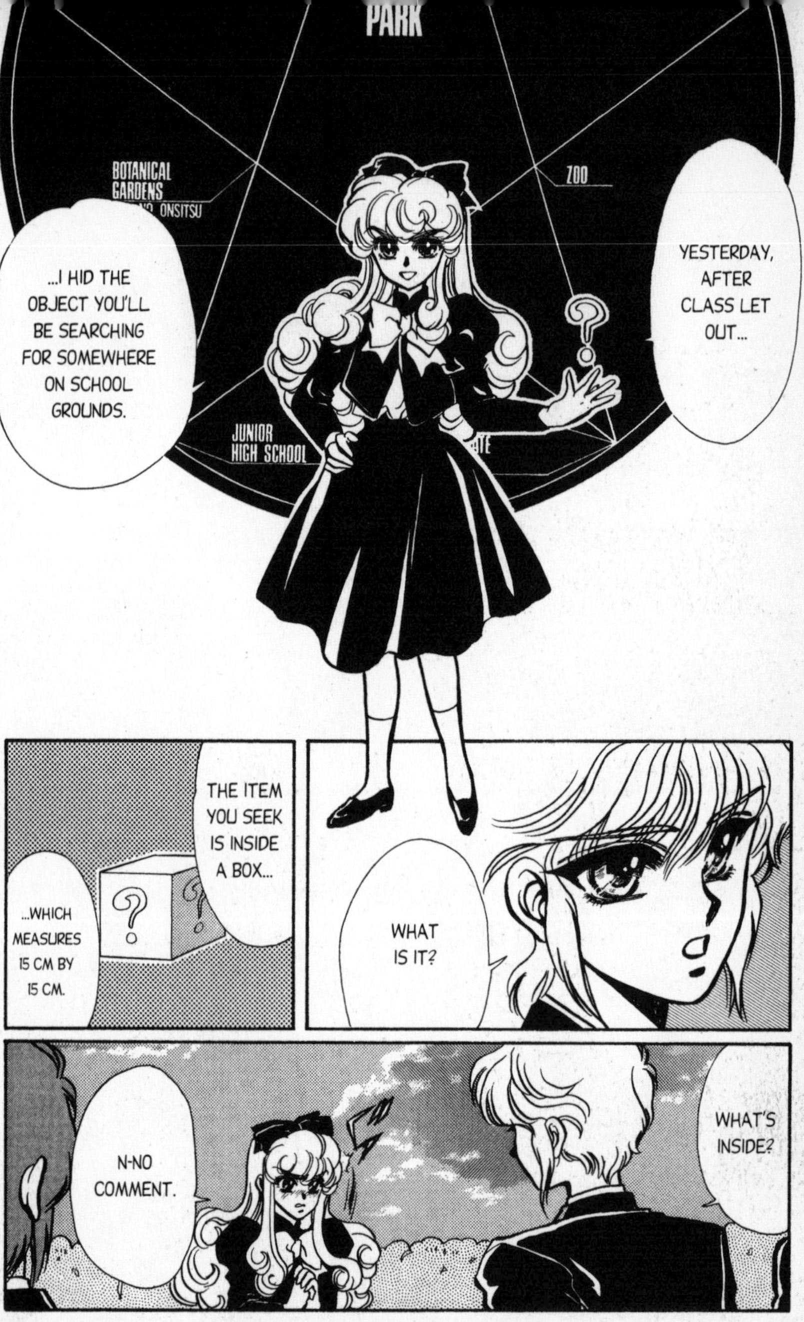
PARK
ZOO
BOTANICAL GARDENS
ONSITSU
YESTERDAY, AFTER CLASS LET OUT...
...I HID THE OBJECT YOU'LL BE SEARCHING FOR SOMEWHERE ON SCHOOL GROUNDS.
JUNIOR HIGH SCHOOL
WHAT IS IT?
THE ITEM YOU SEEK IS INSIDE A BOX...
...WHICH MEASURES 15 CM BY 15 CM.
WHAT'S INSIDE?
N-NO COMMENT.

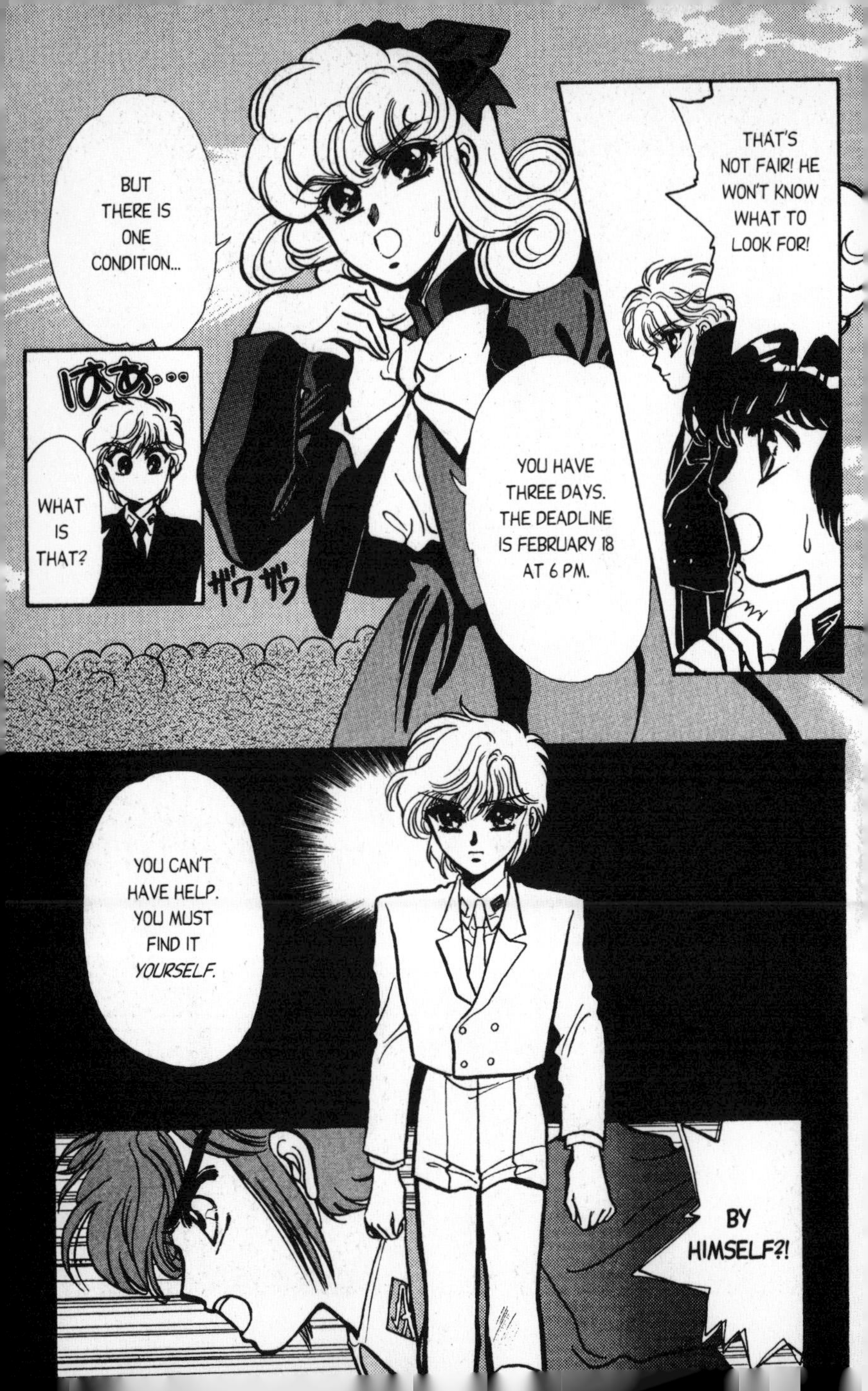
BUT THERE IS ONE CONDITION...
はあ…
WHAT IS THAT?
ザワザワ
YOU HAVE THREE DAYS. THE DEADLINE IS FEBRUARY 18 AT 6 PM.
THAT'S NOT FAIR! HE WON'T KNOW WHAT TO LOOK FOR!
YOU CAN'T HAVE HELP. YOU MUST FIND IT *YOURSELF*.
BY HIMSELF?!

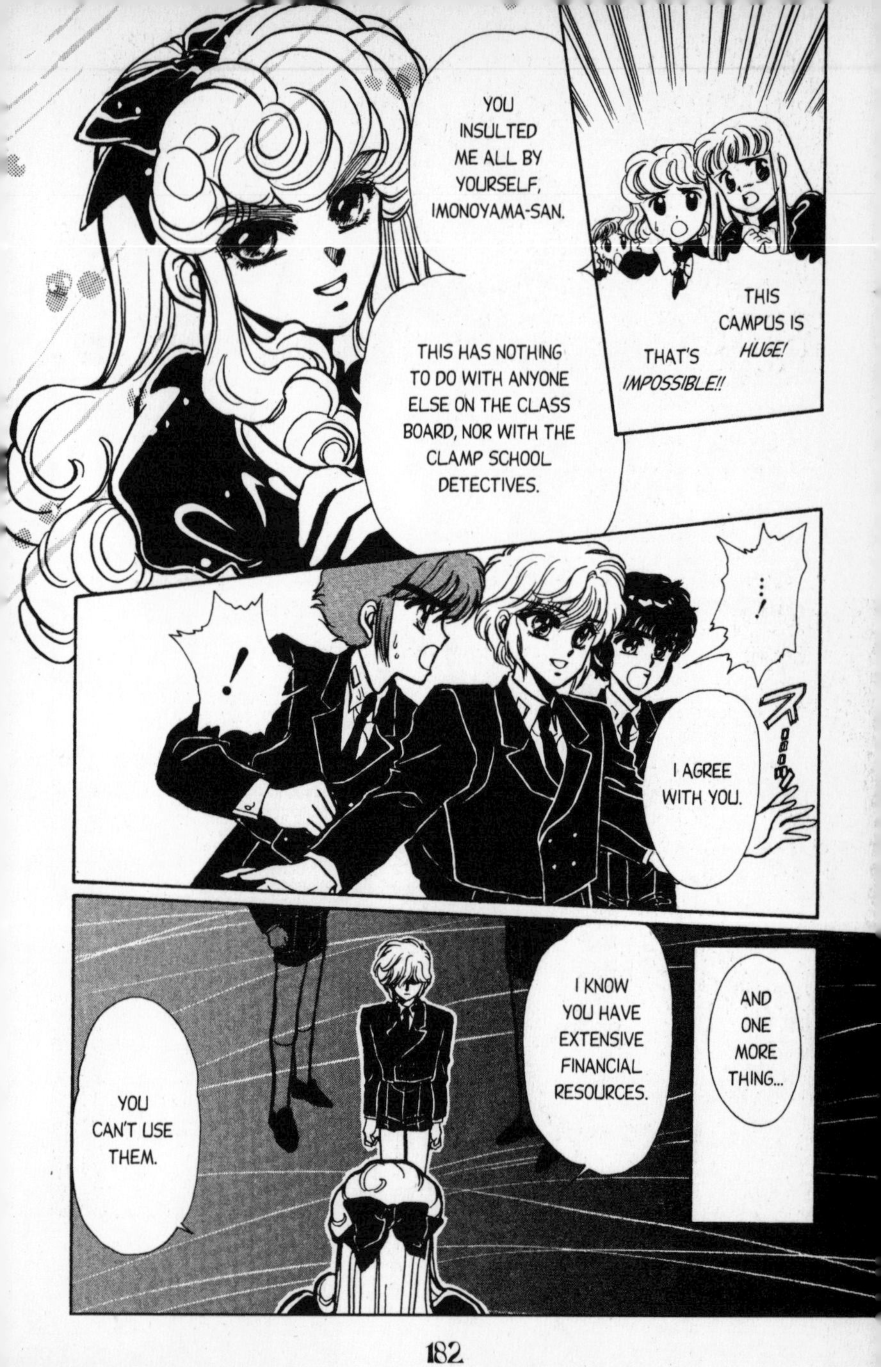
THIS CAMPUS IS *HUGE!*
THAT'S *IMPOSSIBLE!!*
YOU INSULTED ME ALL BY YOURSELF, IMONOYAMA-SAN.
THIS HAS NOTHING TO DO WITH ANYONE ELSE ON THE CLASS BOARD, NOR WITH THE CLAMP SCHOOL DETECTIVES.
...!
I AGREE WITH YOU.
!
AND ONE MORE THING...
I KNOW YOU HAVE EXTENSIVE FINANCIAL RESOURCES.
YOU CAN'T USE THEM.

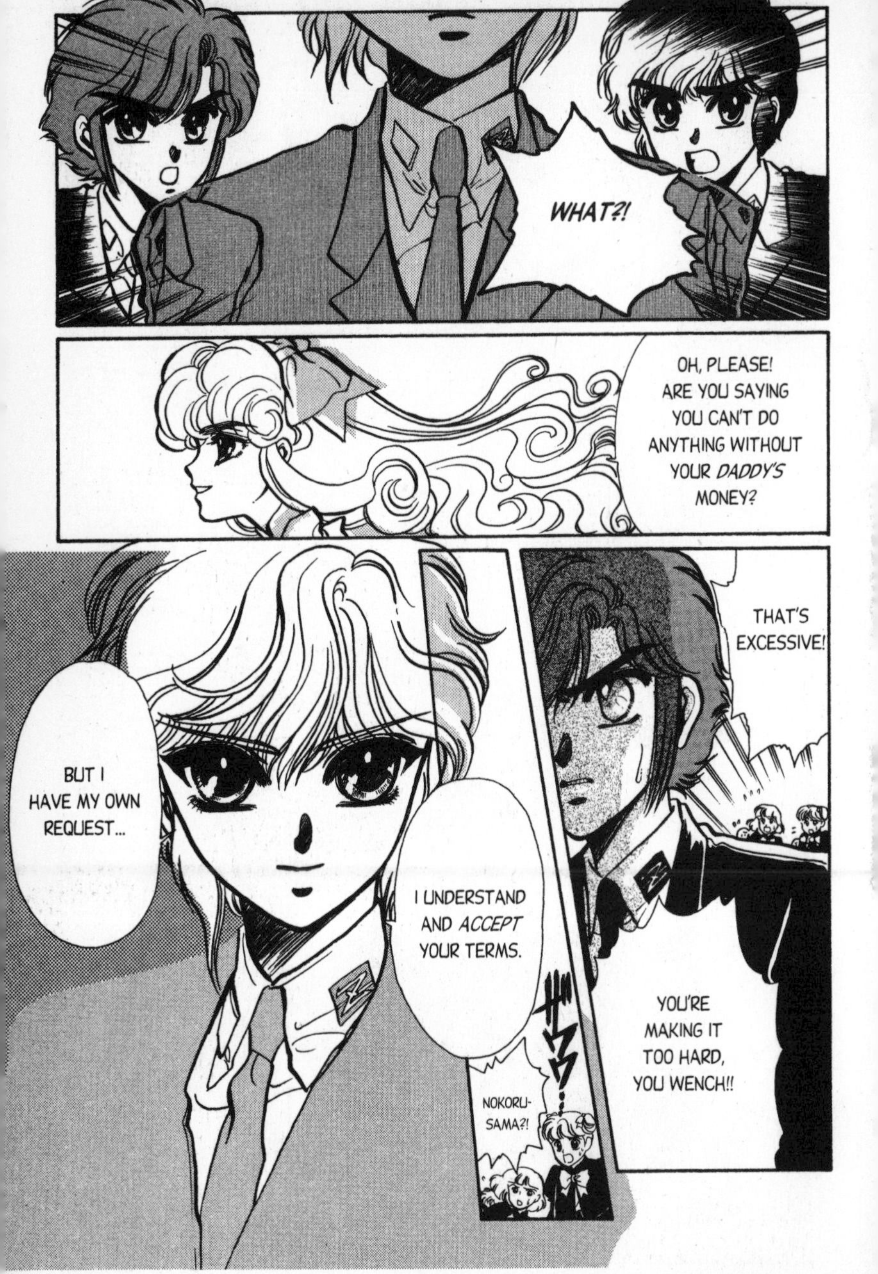
WHAT?!
OH, PLEASE! ARE YOU SAYING YOU CAN'T DO ANYTHING WITHOUT YOUR *DADDY'S* MONEY?
THAT'S EXCESSIVE!
YOU'RE MAKING IT TOO HARD, YOU WENCH!!
NOKORU-SAMA?!
I UNDERSTAND AND *ACCEPT* YOUR TERMS.
BUT I HAVE MY OWN REQUEST...

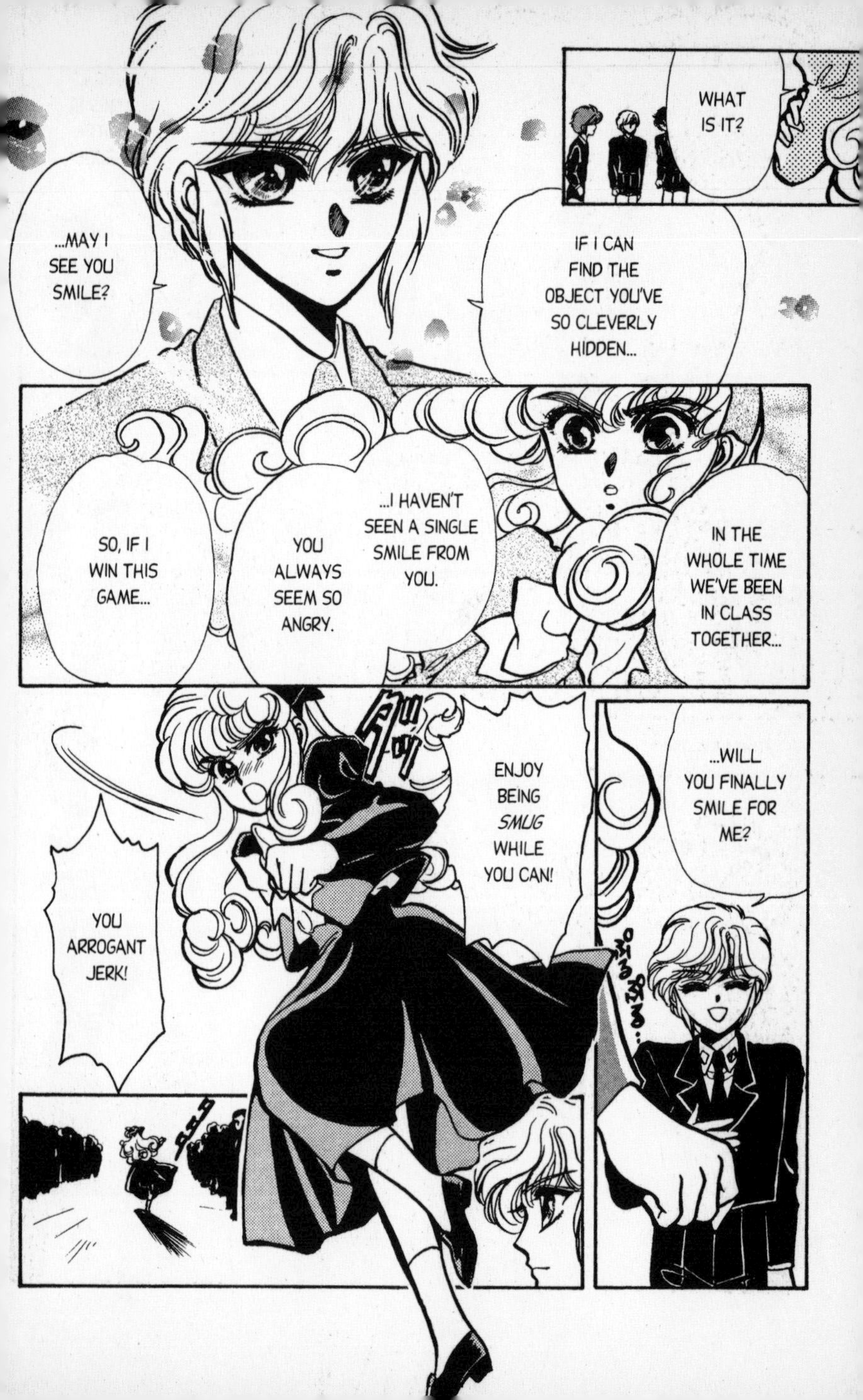
WHAT IS IT?
IF I CAN FIND THE OBJECT YOU'VE SO CLEVERLY HIDDEN...
...MAY I SEE YOU SMILE?
IN THE WHOLE TIME WE'VE BEEN IN CLASS TOGETHER...
...I HAVEN'T SEEN A SINGLE SMILE FROM YOU.
YOU ALWAYS SEEM SO ANGRY.
SO, IF I WIN THIS GAME...
...WILL YOU FINALLY SMILE FOR ME?
ENJOY BEING *SMUG* WHILE YOU CAN!
YOU ARROGANT JERK!

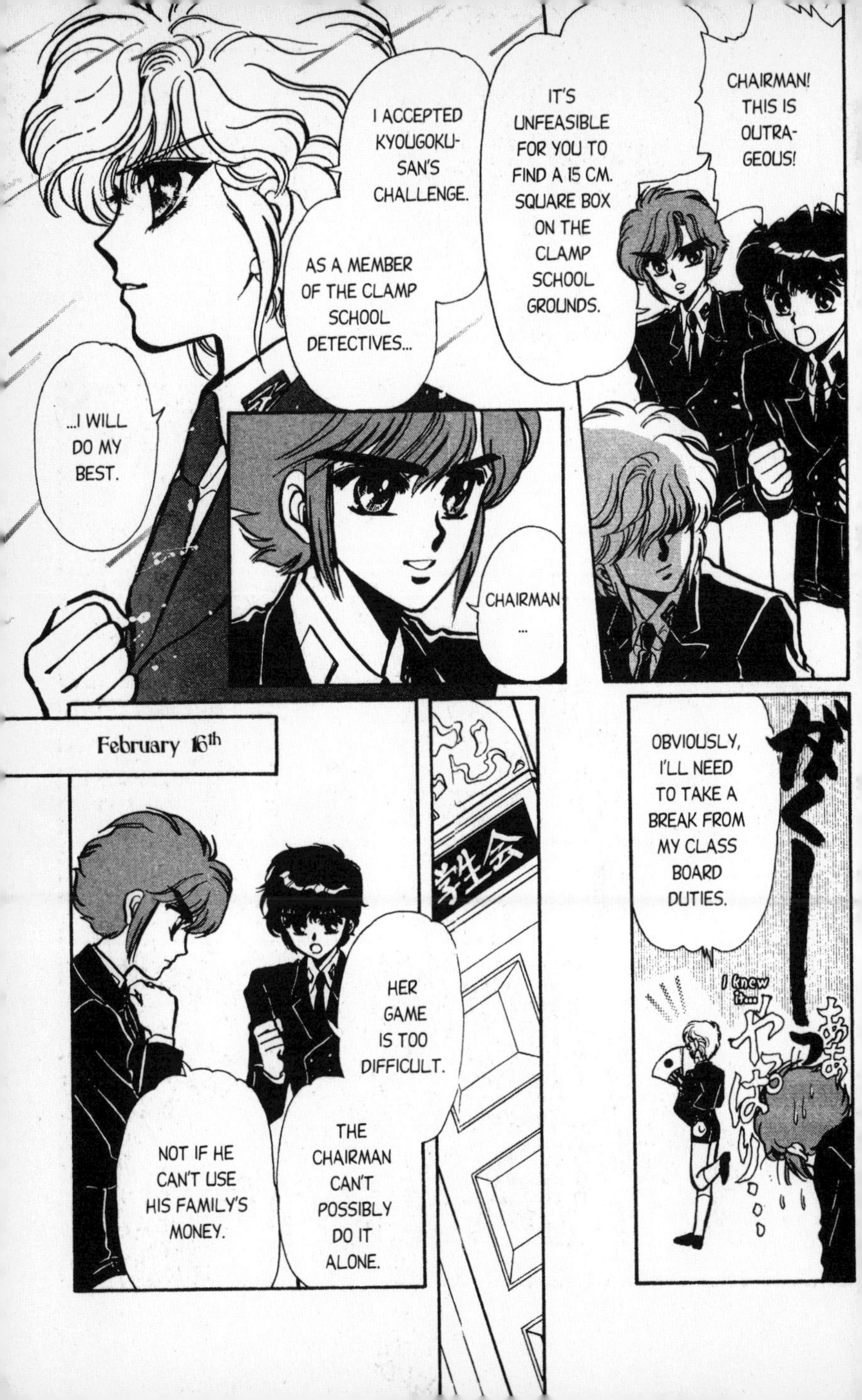
CHAIRMAN! THIS IS OUTRAGEOUS!
IT'S UNFEASIBLE FOR YOU TO FIND A 15 CM. SQUARE BOX ON THE CLAMP SCHOOL GROUNDS.
I ACCEPTED KYOUGOKU-SAN'S CHALLENGE.
AS A MEMBER OF THE CLAMP SCHOOL DETECTIVES...
...I WILL DO MY BEST.
CHAIRMAN ...
OBVIOUSLY, I'LL NEED TO TAKE A BREAK FROM MY CLASS BOARD DUTIES.
がくー
I knew it...
やっぱり
February 16th
学生会
HER GAME IS TOO DIFFICULT.
THE CHAIRMAN CAN'T POSSIBLY DO IT ALONE.
NOT IF HE CAN'T USE HIS FAMILY'S MONEY.

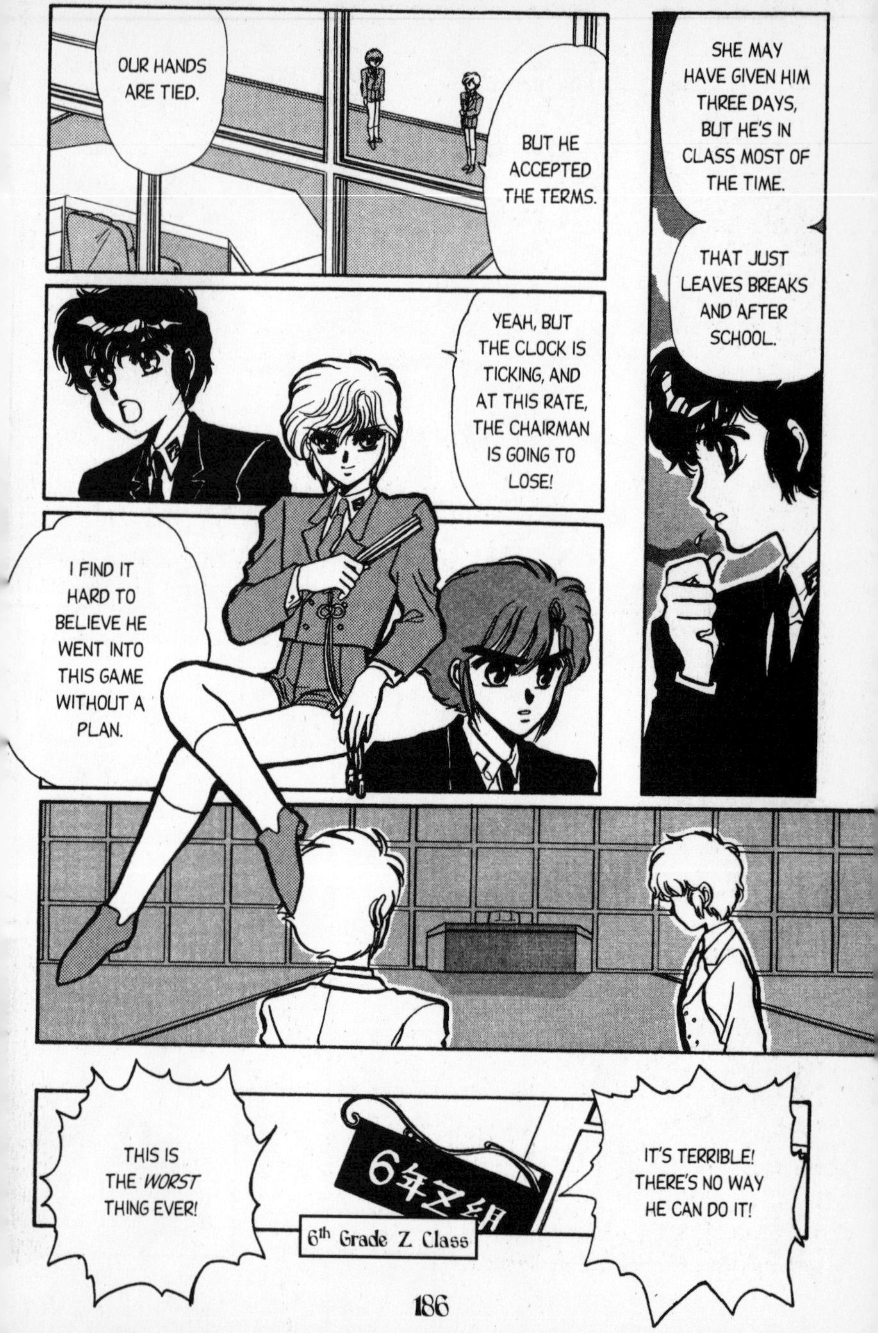
SHE MAY HAVE GIVEN HIM THREE DAYS, BUT HE'S IN CLASS MOST OF THE TIME.
THAT JUST LEAVES BREAKS AND AFTER SCHOOL.
BUT HE ACCEPTED THE TERMS.
OUR HANDS ARE TIED.
YEAH, BUT THE CLOCK IS TICKING, AND AT THIS RATE, THE CHAIRMAN IS GOING TO LOSE!
I FIND IT HARD TO BELIEVE HE WENT INTO THIS GAME WITHOUT A PLAN.
IT'S TERRIBLE! THERE'S NO WAY HE CAN DO IT!
THIS IS THE *WORST* THING EVER!
6年Z組
6th Grade Z Class

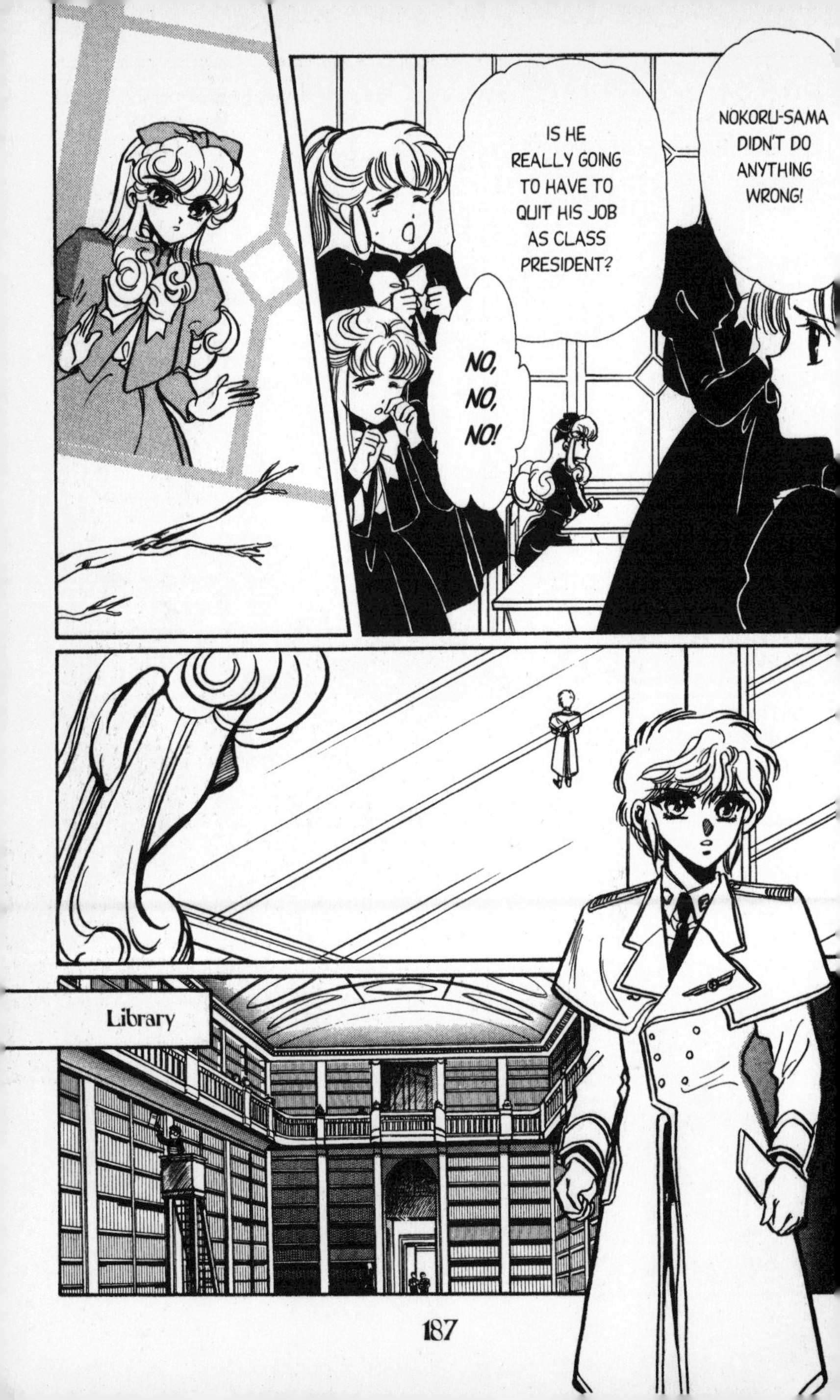
NOKORU-SAMA DIDN'T DO ANYTHING WRONG!
IS HE REALLY GOING TO HAVE TO QUIT HIS JOB AS CLASS PRESIDENT?
NO, NO, NO!
Library

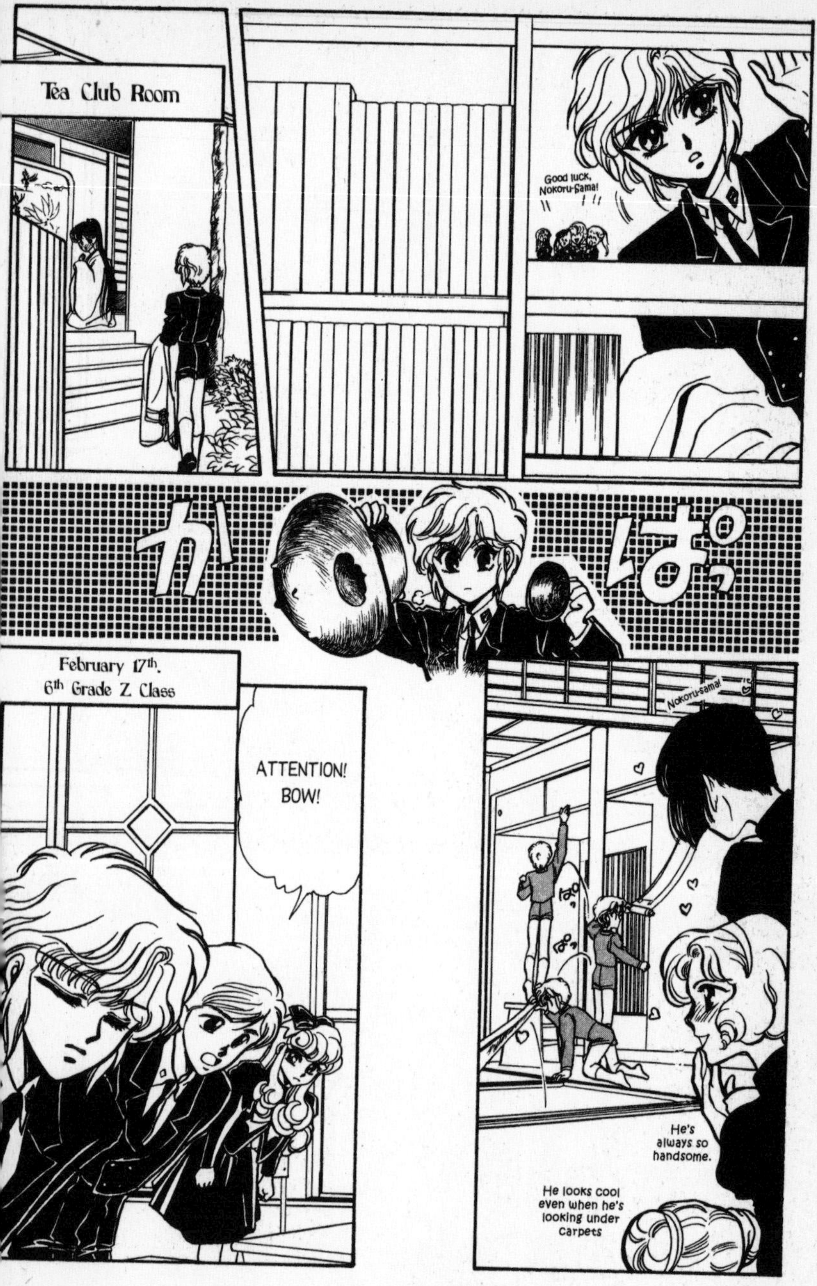
Good luck, Nokoru-Sama! !!!
Tea Club Room
かぱっ
Nokoru-sama!
He's always so handsome.
He looks cool even when he's looking under carpets
February 17th, 6th Grade Z Class
ATTENTION! BOW!

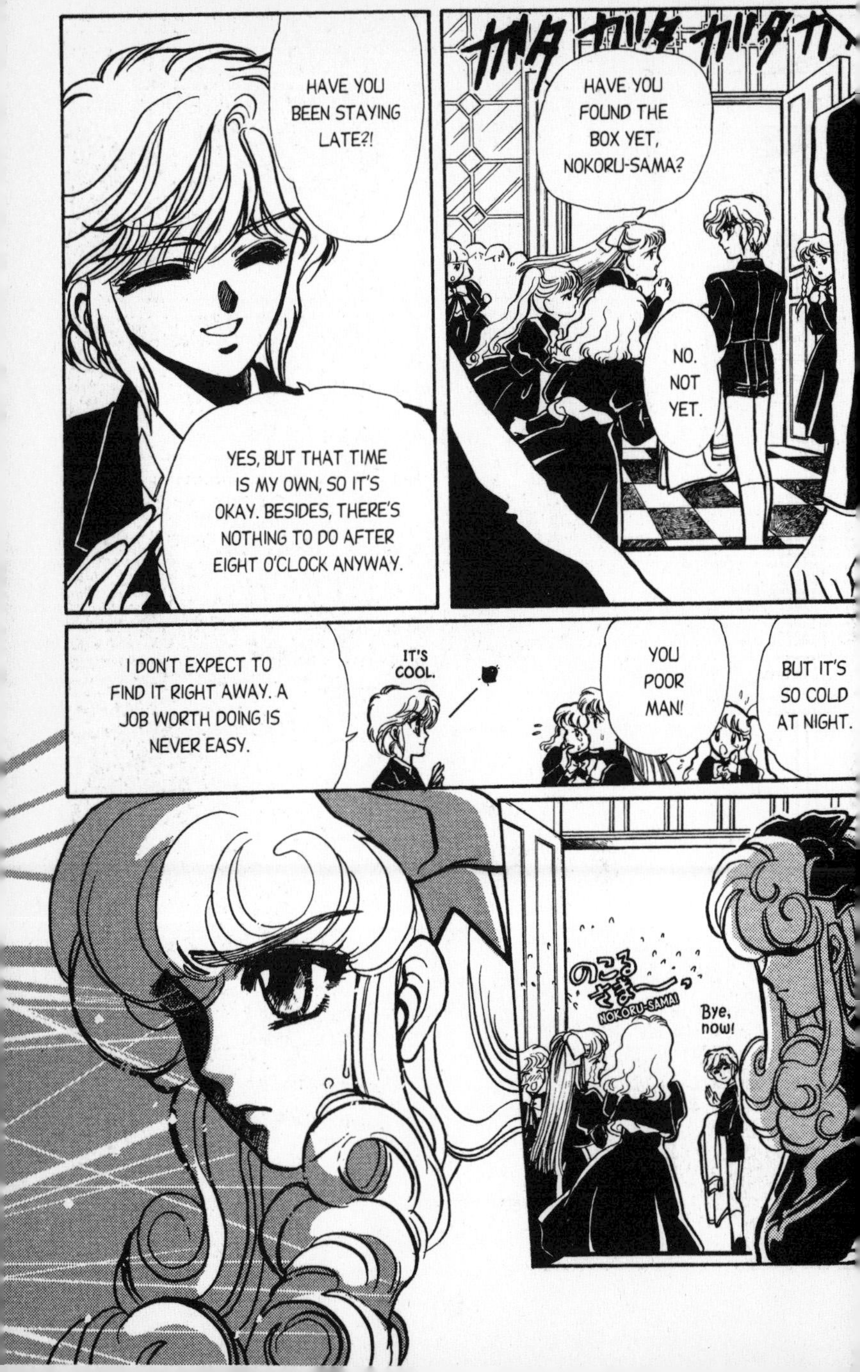

カタ カタ カタ カ
HAVE YOU FOUND THE BOX YET, NOKORU-SAMA?
NO. NOT YET.
HAVE YOU BEEN STAYING LATE?!
YES, BUT THAT TIME IS MY OWN, SO IT'S OKAY. BESIDES, THERE'S NOTHING TO DO AFTER EIGHT O'CLOCK ANYWAY.
BUT IT'S SO COLD AT NIGHT.
YOU POOR MAN!
IT'S COOL.
I DON'T EXPECT TO FIND IT RIGHT AWAY. A JOB WORTH DOING IS NEVER EASY.
のこるさま〜
NOKORU-SAMA!
Bye, now!

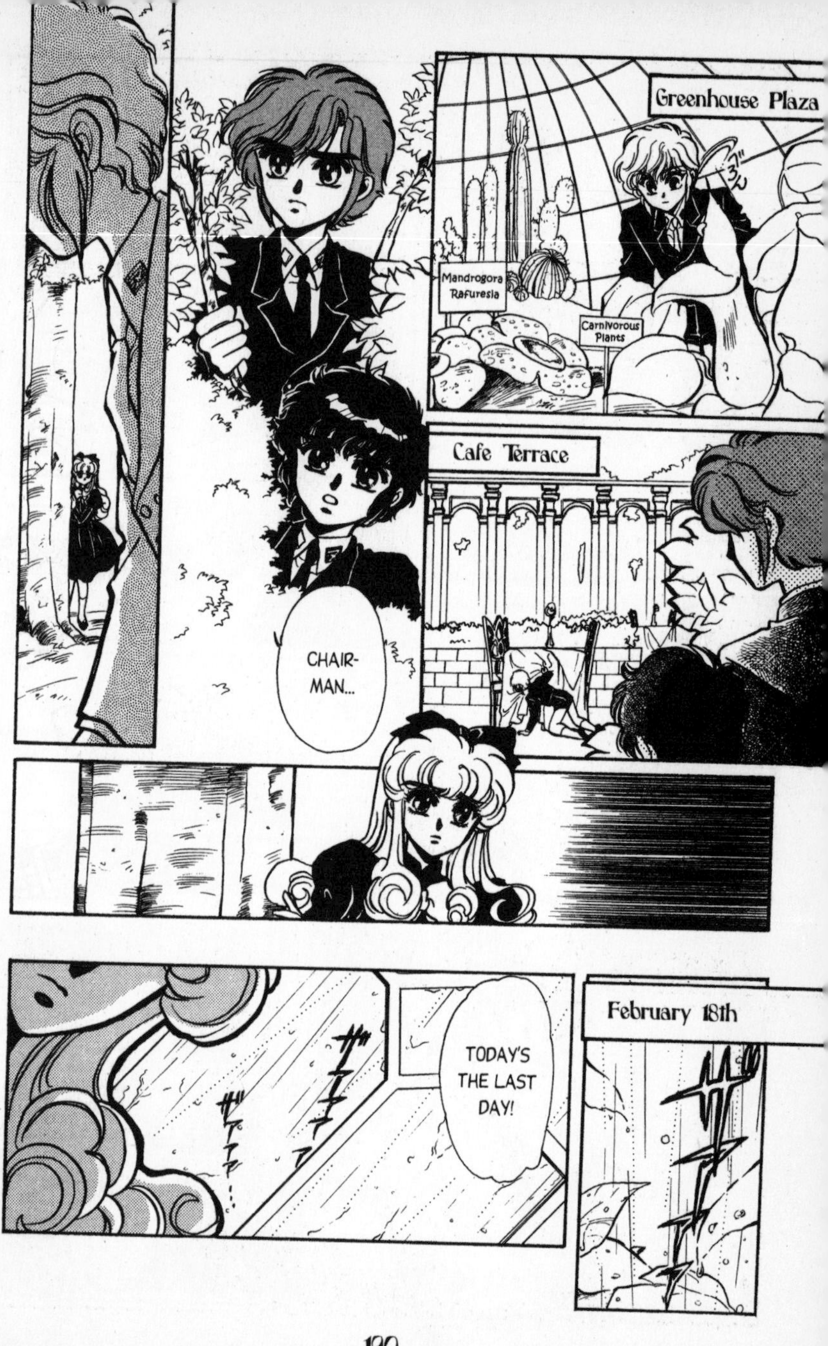
Greenhouse Plaza
Mandrogora Rafuresia
Carnivorous Plants
Cafe Terrace
CHAIR-MAN...
February 18th
TODAY'S THE LAST DAY!

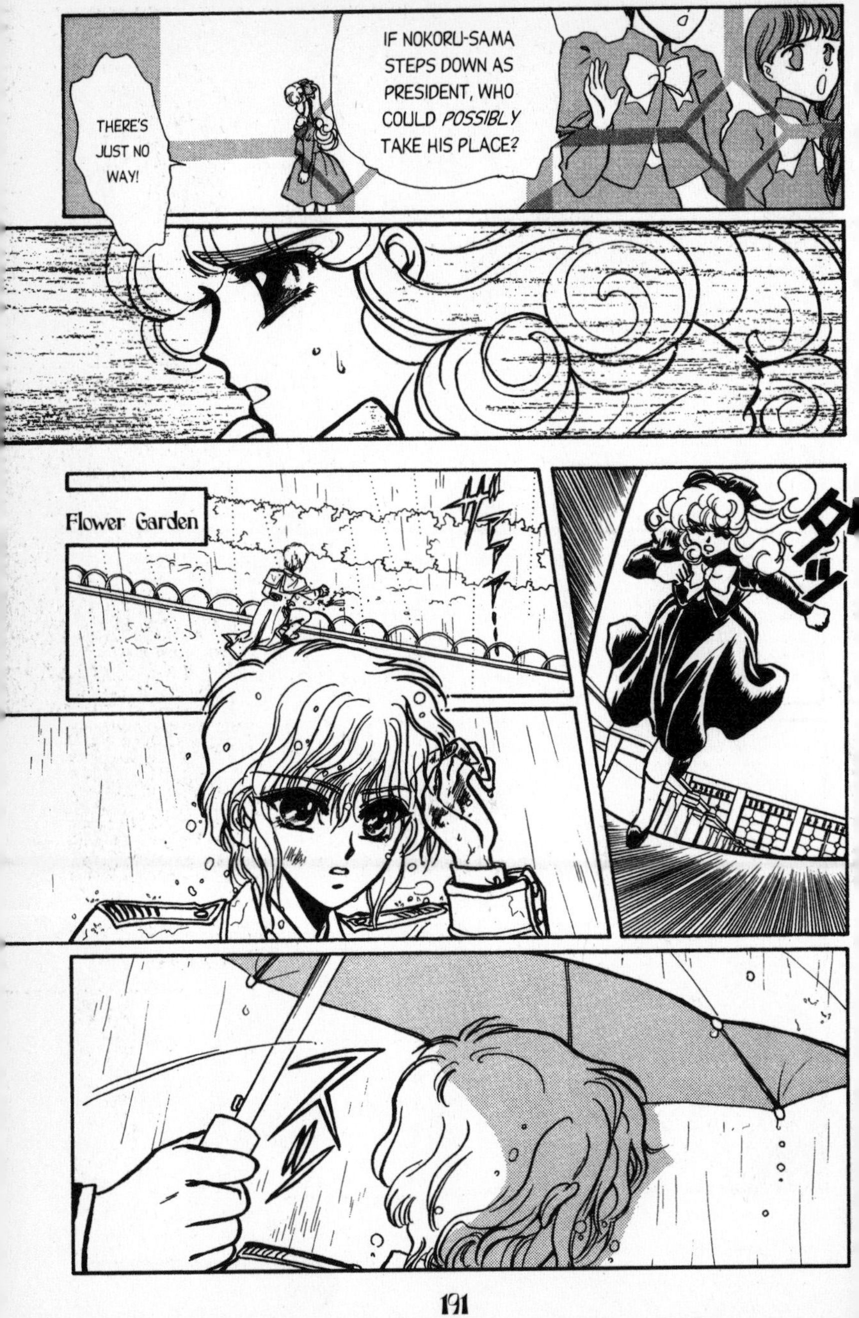
IF NOKORU-SAMA STEPS DOWN AS PRESIDENT, WHO COULD *POSSIBLY* TAKE HIS PLACE?
THERE'S JUST NO WAY!
Flower Garden

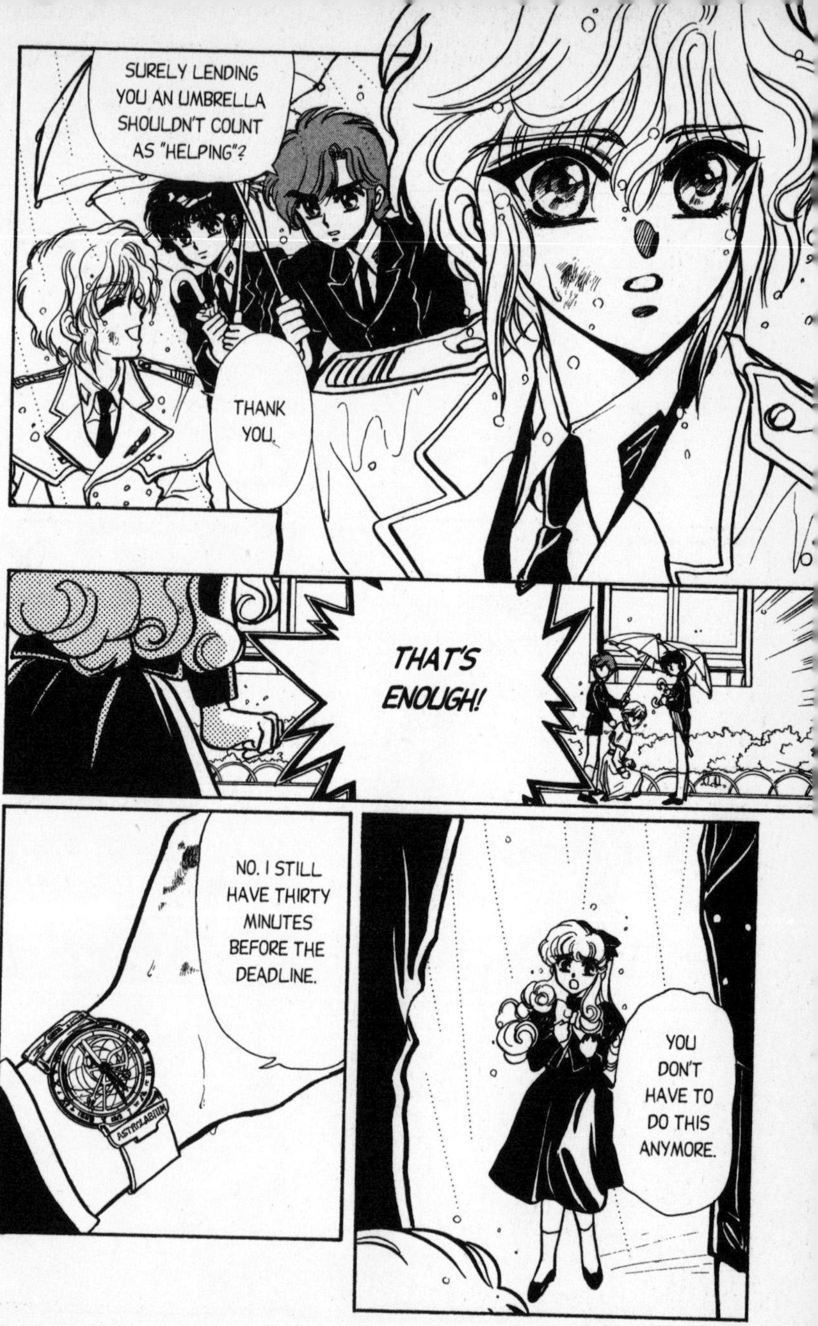
SURELY LENDING YOU AN UMBRELLA SHOULDN'T COUNT AS "HELPING"?
THANK YOU.
THAT'S ENOUGH!
YOU DON'T HAVE TO DO THIS ANYMORE.
NO. I STILL HAVE THIRTY MINUTES BEFORE THE DEADLINE.
ASTROLABIUM

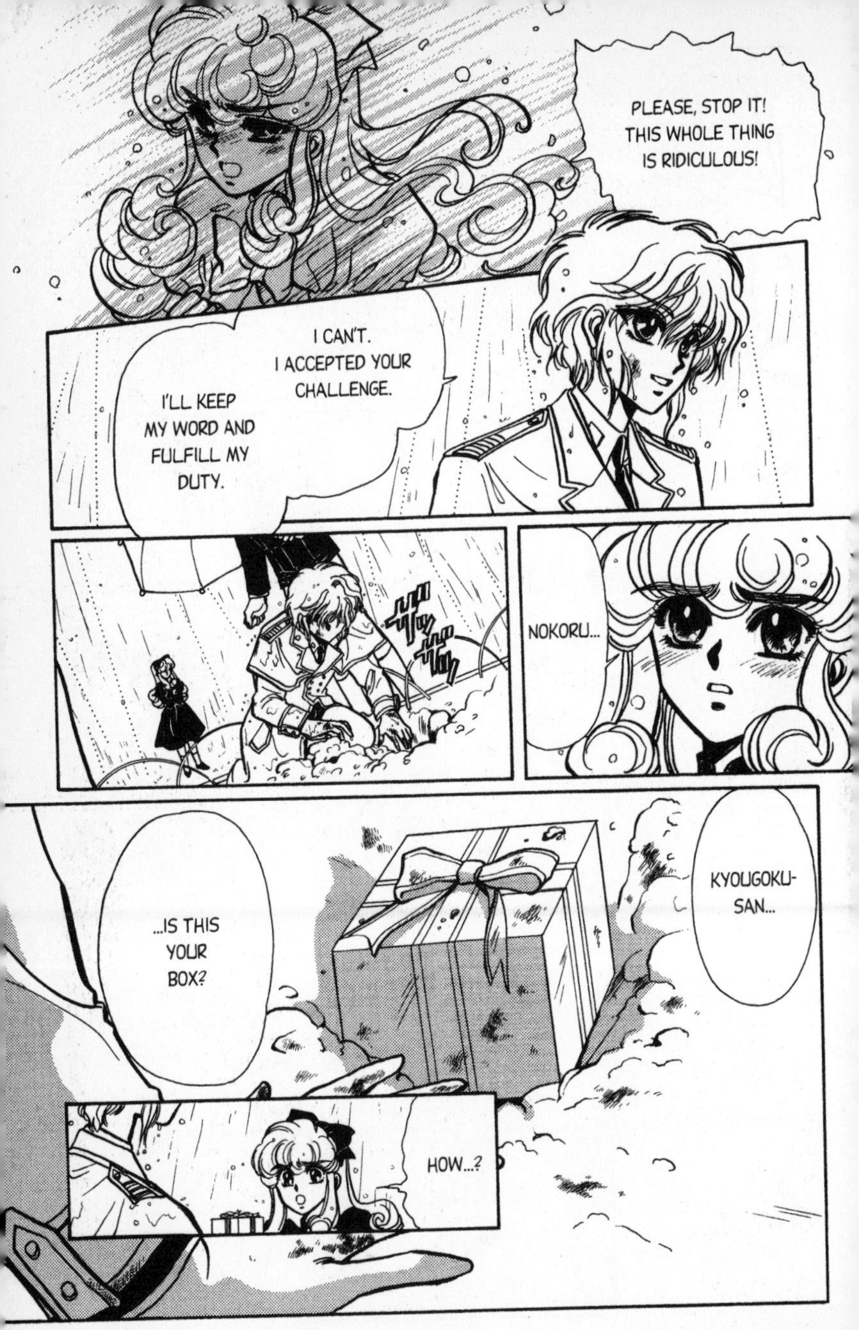
PLEASE, STOP IT! THIS WHOLE THING IS RIDICULOUS!
I CAN'T. I ACCEPTED YOUR CHALLENGE.
I'LL KEEP MY WORD AND FULFILL MY DUTY.
NOKORU...
KYOUGOKU-SAN...
...IS THIS YOUR BOX?
HOW...?

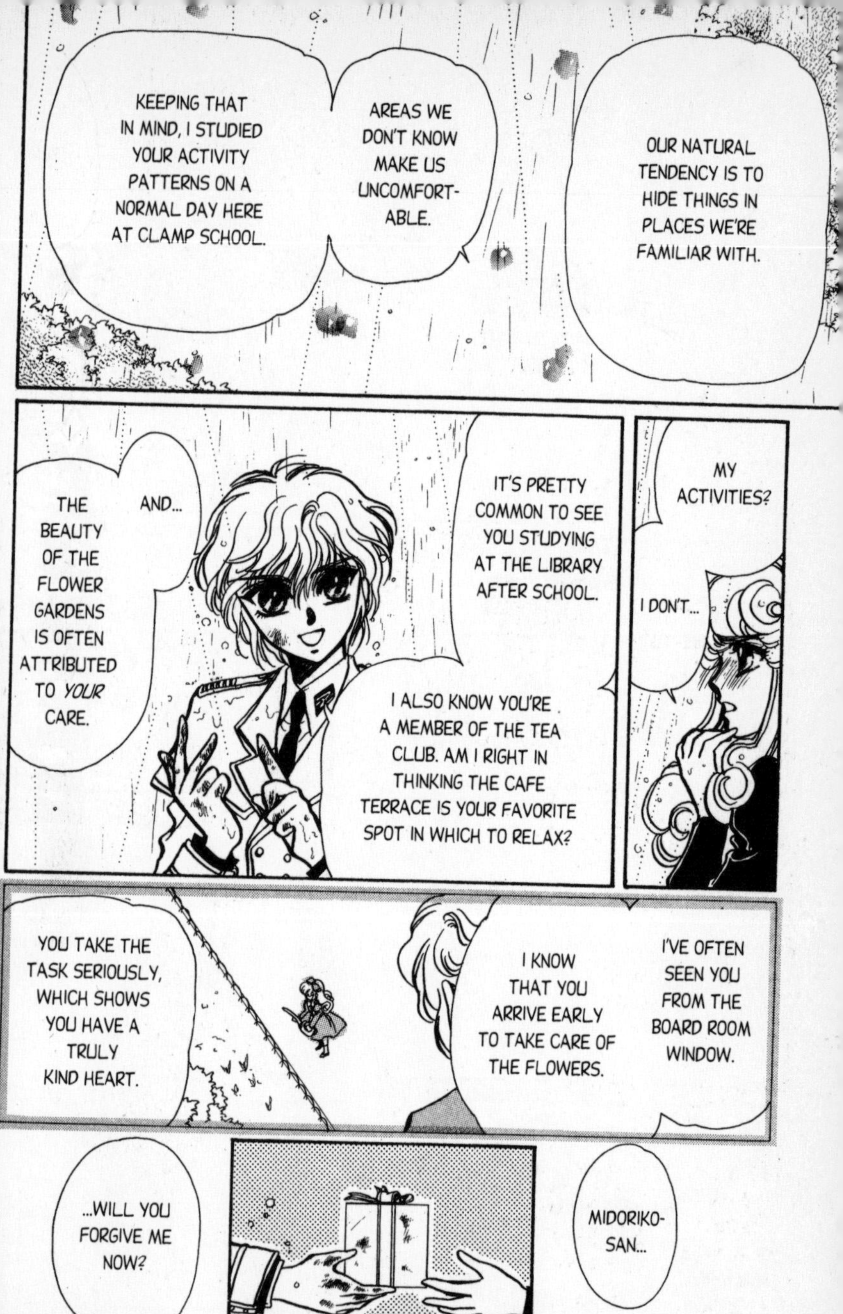
OUR NATURAL TENDENCY IS TO HIDE THINGS IN PLACES WE'RE FAMILIAR WITH.
AREAS WE DON'T KNOW MAKE US UNCOMFORT-ABLE.
KEEPING THAT IN MIND, I STUDIED YOUR ACTIVITY PATTERNS ON A NORMAL DAY HERE AT CLAMP SCHOOL.
MY ACTIVITIES?
I DON'T...
IT'S PRETTY COMMON TO SEE YOU STUDYING AT THE LIBRARY AFTER SCHOOL.
I ALSO KNOW YOU'RE A MEMBER OF THE TEA CLUB. AM I RIGHT IN THINKING THE CAFE TERRACE IS YOUR FAVORITE SPOT IN WHICH TO RELAX?
AND...
THE BEAUTY OF THE FLOWER GARDENS IS OFTEN ATTRIBUTED TO *YOUR* CARE.
I'VE OFTEN SEEN YOU FROM THE BOARD ROOM WINDOW.
I KNOW THAT YOU ARRIVE EARLY TO TAKE CARE OF THE FLOWERS.
YOU TAKE THE TASK SERIOUSLY, WHICH SHOWS YOU HAVE A TRULY KIND HEART.
MIDORIKO-SAN...
...WILL YOU FORGIVE ME NOW?

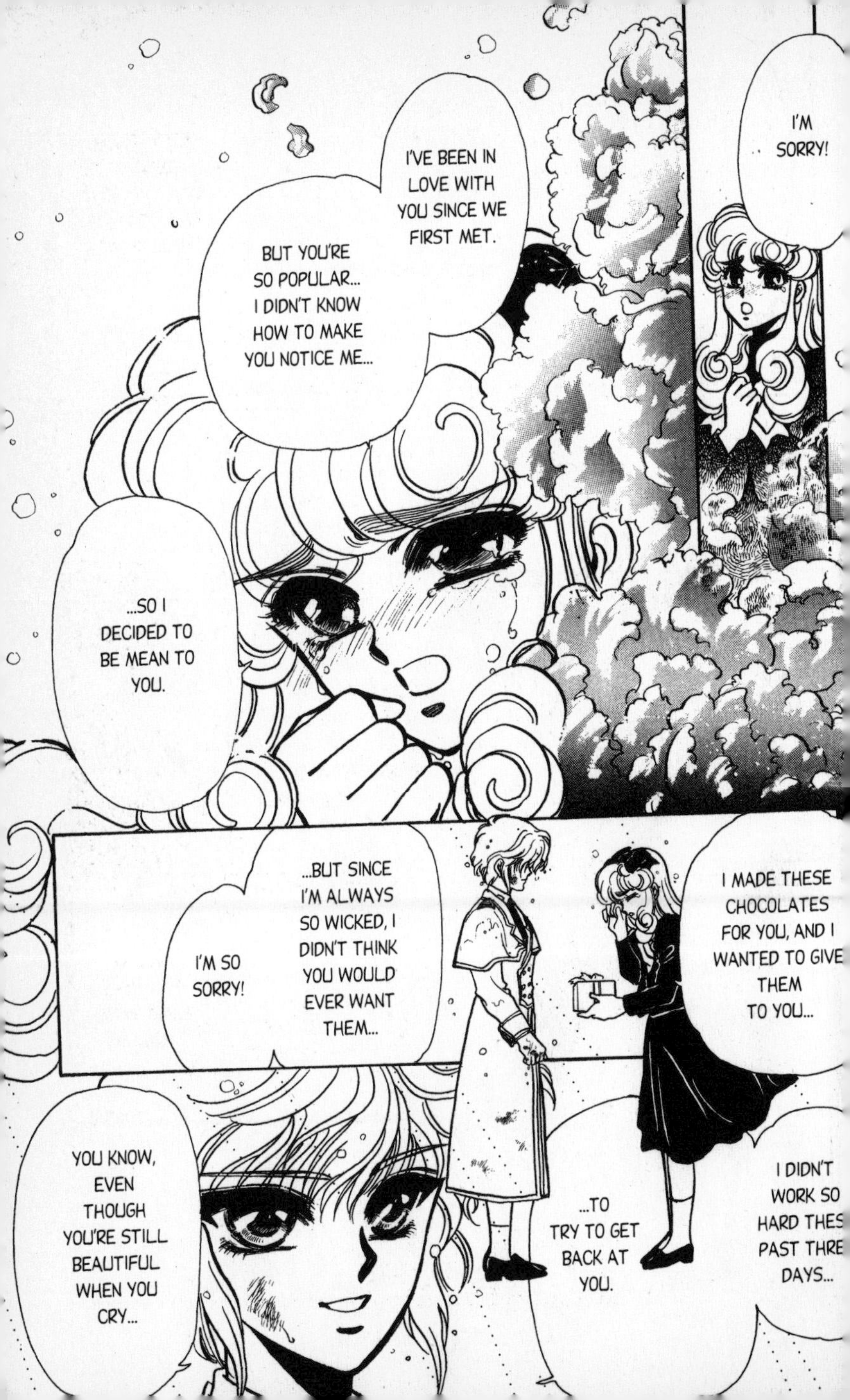
I'M SORRY!
I'VE BEEN IN LOVE WITH YOU SINCE WE FIRST MET.
BUT YOU'RE SO POPULAR... I DIDN'T KNOW HOW TO MAKE YOU NOTICE ME...
...SO I DECIDED TO BE MEAN TO YOU.
I MADE THESE CHOCOLATES FOR YOU, AND I WANTED TO GIVE THEM TO YOU...
...BUT SINCE I'M ALWAYS SO WICKED, I DIDN'T THINK YOU WOULD EVER WANT THEM...
I'M SO SORRY!
I DIDN'T WORK SO HARD THES PAST THRE DAYS...
...TO TRY TO GET BACK AT YOU.
YOU KNOW, EVEN THOUGH YOU'RE STILL BEAUTIFUL WHEN YOU CRY...

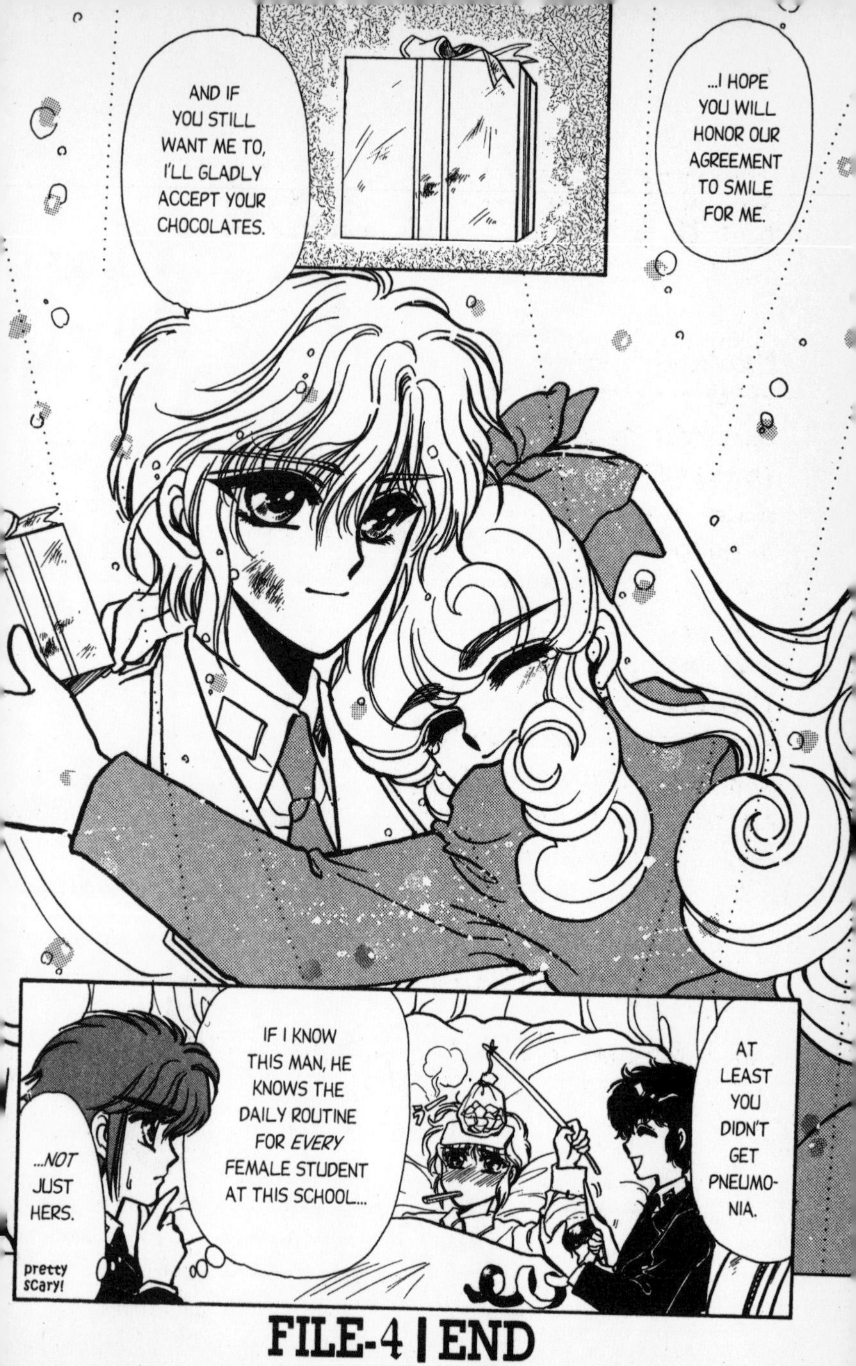
...I HOPE YOU WILL HONOR OUR AGREEMENT TO SMILE FOR ME.
AND IF YOU STILL WANT ME TO, I'LL GLADLY ACCEPT YOUR CHOCOLATES.
AT LEAST YOU DIDN'T GET PNEUMO-NIA.
IF I KNOW THIS MAN, HE KNOWS THE DAILY ROUTINE FOR *EVERY* FEMALE STUDENT AT THIS SCHOOL...
...*NOT* JUST HERS.
pretty scary!

FILE-4 | END

STAFF LIST

Planning & Production: CLAMP

Story/script: Nanase Ohkawa
Character Design/Illustration: Mokona Apapa
Illustration Director: Mick Nekoi
Illustration Assistant Director: Satsuki Igarashi

Cover Illustration: Mokona Apapa
Back Cover Comic: Mick Nekoi
Colors: Mokona Apapa
CLAMP Times comic: Mick Nekoi
Cover Design: Nanase Ohkawa
Design Assistant: Satsuki Igarashi
Special Thanks: Mr. Seichiro Aoki
               Mr. Keichi Segawa
               Mr. Sachiko Higuchi
               Mr. Ichiro Nishihide

Very Special Thanks to ALL READERS

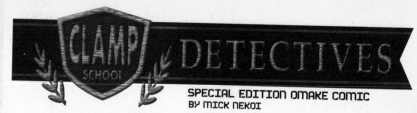

CLAMP SCHOOL DETECTIVES

SPECIAL EDITION OMAKE COMIC
BY MICK NEKOI

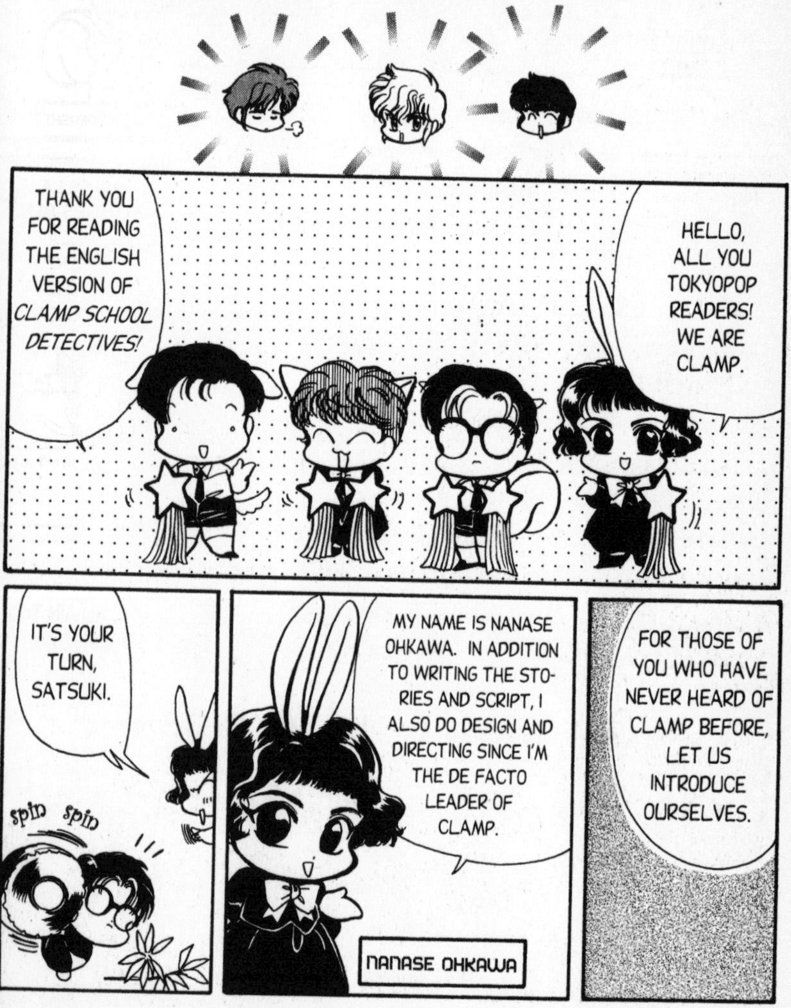
HELLO, ALL YOU TOKYOPOP READERS! WE ARE CLAMP.
THANK YOU FOR READING THE ENGLISH VERSION OF *CLAMP SCHOOL DETECTIVES!*
FOR THOSE OF YOU WHO HAVE NEVER HEARD OF CLAMP BEFORE, LET US INTRODUCE OURSELVES.
MY NAME IS NANASE OHKAWA. IN ADDITION TO WRITING THE STO-RIES AND SCRIPT, I ALSO DO DESIGN AND DIRECTING SINCE I'M THE DE FACTO LEADER OF CLAMP.
NANASE OHKAWA
IT'S YOUR TURN, SATSUKI.
spin spin

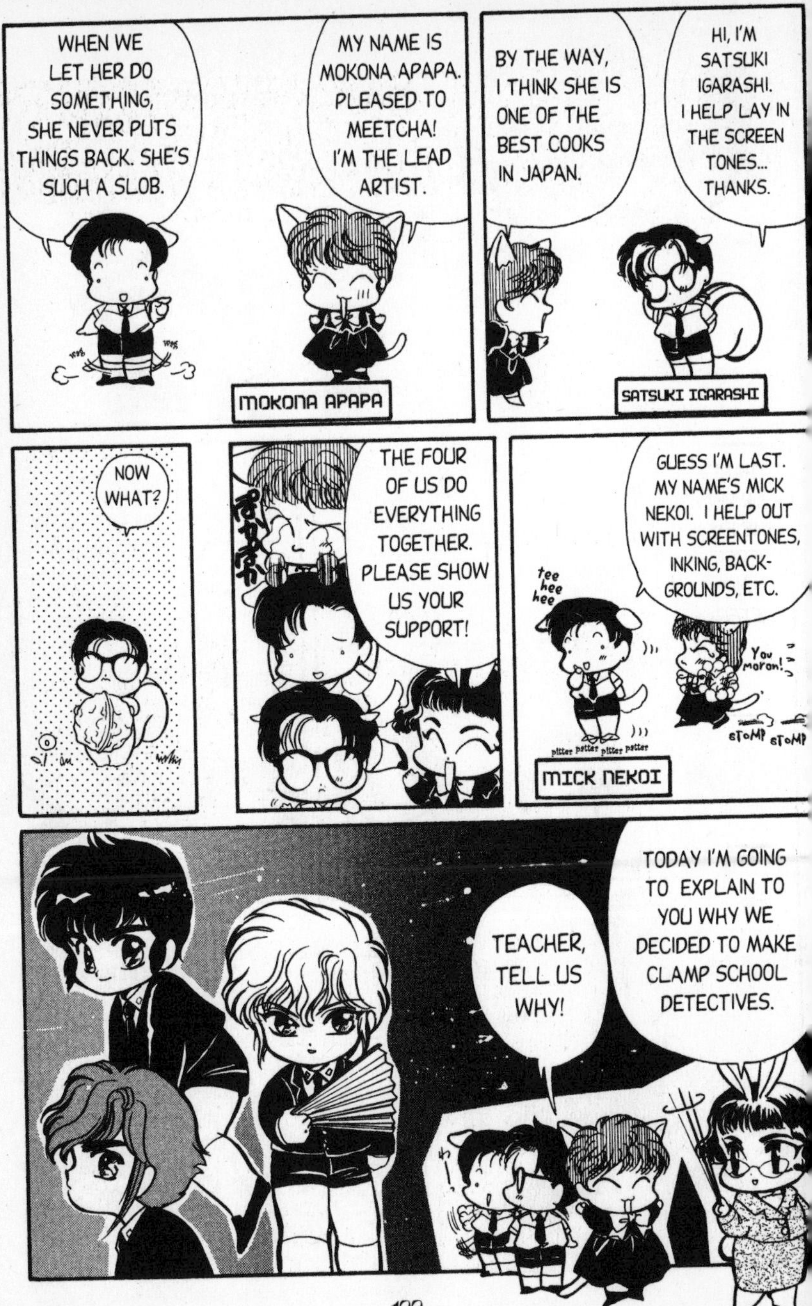
HI, I'M SATSUKI IGARASHI. I HELP LAY IN THE SCREEN TONES... THANKS.
BY THE WAY, I THINK SHE IS ONE OF THE BEST COOKS IN JAPAN.
SATSUKI IGARASHI
MY NAME IS MOKONA APAPA. PLEASED TO MEETCHA! I'M THE LEAD ARTIST.
WHEN WE LET HER DO SOMETHING, SHE NEVER PUTS THINGS BACK. SHE'S SUCH A SLOB.
MOKONA APAPA
GUESS I'M LAST. MY NAME'S MICK NEKOI. I HELP OUT WITH SCREENTONES, INKING, BACK-GROUNDS, ETC.
tee hee hee
You moron!
STOMP STOMP
pitter patter pitter patter
MICK NEKOI
THE FOUR OF US DO EVERYTHING TOGETHER. PLEASE SHOW US YOUR SUPPORT!
NOW WHAT?
TODAY I'M GOING TO EXPLAIN TO YOU WHY WE DECIDED TO MAKE CLAMP SCHOOL DETECTIVES.
TEACHER, TELL US WHY!

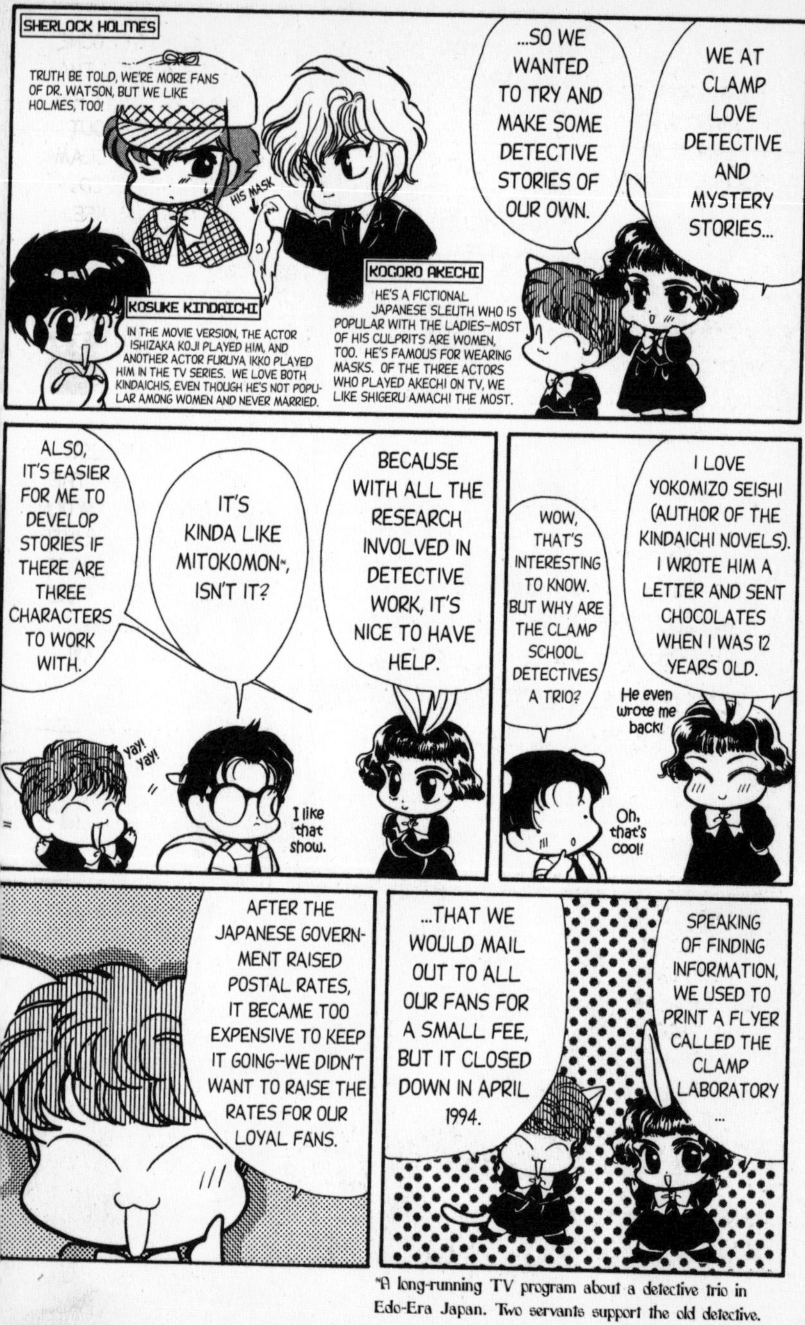
WE AT CLAMP LOVE DETECTIVE AND MYSTERY STORIES...
...SO WE WANTED TO TRY AND MAKE SOME DETECTIVE STORIES OF OUR OWN.
SHERLOCK HOLMES
TRUTH BE TOLD, WE'RE MORE FANS OF DR. WATSON, BUT WE LIKE HOLMES, TOO!
HIS MASK
KOGORO AKECHI
HE'S A FICTIONAL JAPANESE SLEUTH WHO IS POPULAR WITH THE LADIES--MOST OF HIS CULPRITS ARE WOMEN, TOO. HE'S FAMOUS FOR WEARING MASKS. OF THE THREE ACTORS WHO PLAYED AKECHI ON TV, WE LIKE SHIGERU AMACHI THE MOST.
KOSUKE KINDAICHI
IN THE MOVIE VERSION, THE ACTOR ISHIZAKA KOJI PLAYED HIM, AND ANOTHER ACTOR FURUYA IKKO PLAYED HIM IN THE TV SERIES. WE LOVE BOTH KINDAICHIS, EVEN THOUGH HE'S NOT POPULAR AMONG WOMEN AND NEVER MARRIED.
I LOVE YOKOMIZO SEISHI (AUTHOR OF THE KINDAICHI NOVELS). I WROTE HIM A LETTER AND SENT CHOCOLATES WHEN I WAS 12 YEARS OLD.
He even wrote me back!
WOW, THAT'S INTERESTING TO KNOW. BUT WHY ARE THE CLAMP SCHOOL DETECTIVES A TRIO?
Oh, that's cool!
BECAUSE WITH ALL THE RESEARCH INVOLVED IN DETECTIVE WORK, IT'S NICE TO HAVE HELP.
IT'S KINDA LIKE MITOKOMON*, ISN'T IT?
ALSO, IT'S EASIER FOR ME TO DEVELOP STORIES IF THERE ARE THREE CHARACTERS TO WORK WITH.
I like that show.
Yay! yay!
SPEAKING OF FINDING INFORMATION, WE USED TO PRINT A FLYER CALLED THE CLAMP LABORATORY ...
...THAT WE WOULD MAIL OUT TO ALL OUR FANS FOR A SMALL FEE, BUT IT CLOSED DOWN IN APRIL 1994.
AFTER THE JAPANESE GOVERNMENT RAISED POSTAL RATES, IT BECAME TOO EXPENSIVE TO KEEP IT GOING--WE DIDN'T WANT TO RAISE THE RATES FOR OUR LOYAL FANS.

*A long-running TV program about a detective trio in Edo-Era Japan. Two servants support the old detective.

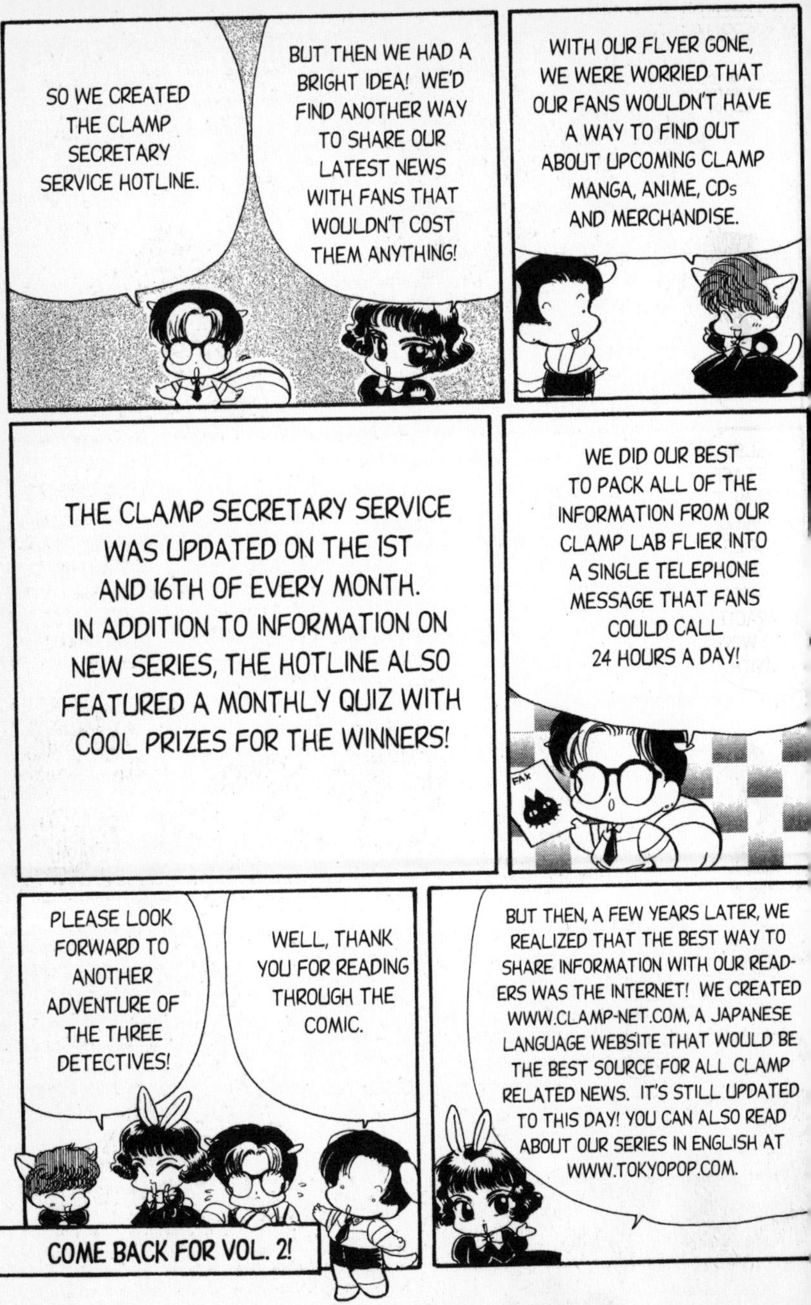
WITH OUR FLYER GONE, WE WERE WORRIED THAT OUR FANS WOULDN'T HAVE A WAY TO FIND OUT ABOUT UPCOMING CLAMP MANGA, ANIME, CDs AND MERCHANDISE.
BUT THEN WE HAD A BRIGHT IDEA! WE'D FIND ANOTHER WAY TO SHARE OUR LATEST NEWS WITH FANS THAT WOULDN'T COST THEM ANYTHING!
SO WE CREATED THE CLAMP SECRETARY SERVICE HOTLINE.
WE DID OUR BEST TO PACK ALL OF THE INFORMATION FROM OUR CLAMP LAB FLIER INTO A SINGLE TELEPHONE MESSAGE THAT FANS COULD CALL 24 HOURS A DAY!
FAX
THE CLAMP SECRETARY SERVICE WAS UPDATED ON THE 1ST AND 16TH OF EVERY MONTH. IN ADDITION TO INFORMATION ON NEW SERIES, THE HOTLINE ALSO FEATURED A MONTHLY QUIZ WITH COOL PRIZES FOR THE WINNERS!
BUT THEN, A FEW YEARS LATER, WE REALIZED THAT THE BEST WAY TO SHARE INFORMATION WITH OUR READERS WAS THE INTERNET! WE CREATED WWW.CLAMP-NET.COM, A JAPANESE LANGUAGE WEBSITE THAT WOULD BE THE BEST SOURCE FOR ALL CLAMP RELATED NEWS. IT'S STILL UPDATED TO THIS DAY! YOU CAN ALSO READ ABOUT OUR SERIES IN ENGLISH AT WWW.TOKYOPOP.COM.
WELL, THANK YOU FOR READING THROUGH THE COMIC.
PLEASE LOOK FORWARD TO ANOTHER ADVENTURE OF THE THREE DETECTIVES!
COME BACK FOR VOL. 2!

Appendix·

1 – "Showa Year 33" (pg 11)
In Japan, years are traditionally based on rule of an emperor. The *Showa* era was the name for the years of Emperor Hirohito's reign and lasted from 1926-1989. When Suoh says that Tokyo Tower was built in Showa Year 33, this is a formal way of saying that the tower was built on the 33rd year of Hirohito's rule, or 1958.

2.1 – *Syoutengai* (pg 22)
A shopping arcade; a street dedicated to shops.

2.2 – *Zaibatsu* (pg 22)
The term for the great family-controlled Banking/Industrial combines that dominated Japan's economy in the 20th century. Following World War II, many great zaibatsu networked together to form *keiretsu*, helping Japan to become the world economic power that it is today. The top zaibatsu are Mitsui, Mitsubishi, Dai Ichi Kangyo, Sumitomo, Sanwa, and Fuyo. To say that the Imonoyama zaibatsu's wealth exceeds the annual budget of all Japan is a stretch, but not by much. In the early 20th century, over one third of all Japan's wealth and almost all of its industry was in the hands of the zaibatsu.

3 – Japanese Festivals (pg 31)
Tanabata Star Festival—According to legend, a Weaver and a Shepherd were betrothed, but when their love prevented them from doing their duties, the two were turned into stars and placed on opposite sides of the Milky Way. July 7th is the one day they're said to be able to cross the heavens to meet each other.

Cherry Blossom Festival—The Cherry blossom is the national flower of Japan, and it is an important part of Japanese art, culture, and history. To celebrate the arrival of spring and the blooming of the Cherry Blossoms, this festival is held beneath the cherry trees in many cities in Japan.

Autumn Culture Festival—A celebration of Japanese culture and history put on by schools in the fall. It's kind of like the "Back to School Day" events at many American schools.

Athletic Festival—An intramural field day event, celebrating many sports and inviting friendly competition from neighboring schools.

4 – *Oku* (pg 47)
1 Oku = 100,000,000, so 10 Oku = 1 Billion yen. This equals roughly 10 million dollars.

5 – Adult-Child relations (pg 91)
It is highly unusual that the chairlady, being in the same family as Nokoru and his superior, would address him with the respectful "-san." This shows just how formal the Imonoyama family really is.

6 – Valentine's Day (pg 157)
In Japan, Valentine's Day is a day when girls give chocolates to boys that they like. One month later is White Day (March 14), the day when guys return the girls' favor and give special chocolates to the girls.

7 – Burdock (pg 167)
A plant with a long, skinny root that is used in Japanese cuisine. The root can be pickled or peeled and scalded before being prepared in other ways. Young roots can also be eaten raw.

CLAMP SCHOOL DETECTIVES

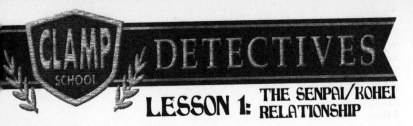

LESSON 1: THE SENPAI/KOHEI RELATIONSHIP

As you can see in *CLAMP School Detectives*, the Japanese language is very relational. Depending on who you're speaking to, different forms of communication are used based on your relationship with that person. These distinctions stem from the Five Constant Relationships of Confucianism, which are as follows: parent and child; older sibling and younger sibling; husband and wife; older friend and younger friend; and ruler and subject.

The Chinese philosophy of Confucianism came to Japan many centuries ago and greatly influenced the way society was structured. The higher a person's status, the more polite and complicated the speech patterns. (There is even an appropriate form to speak to the Japanese emperor, although most Japanese people would not know how to use it!) You can see this very polished and stylized high-class pattern reflected in Nokoru's speech.

The most important relationships in *CLAMP School Detectives* belong to the category known as *senpai/kohei*, which means older friend/younger friend. In the West, this relationship is often referred to as mentor and student, but that is only a small part of this group. The senpai/kohei relationship can apply to friends, colleagues, classmates, as well as students and teachers. The distinction in this relationship is that one party is older, and therefore considered wiser, than the other.

This is best illustrated in the relationship that Akira has with Suoh and Nokoru. He speaks very politely and addresses Suoh with the appropriate suffix–senpai. He also shows a lack of assertiveness and a desire for guidance from the other two because of his young age. It might seem like Akira is just insecure, but there is a centuries old tradition behind his politeness. This isn't a negative trait, because in time he will learn, grow older and become the senpai to a new generation of students.

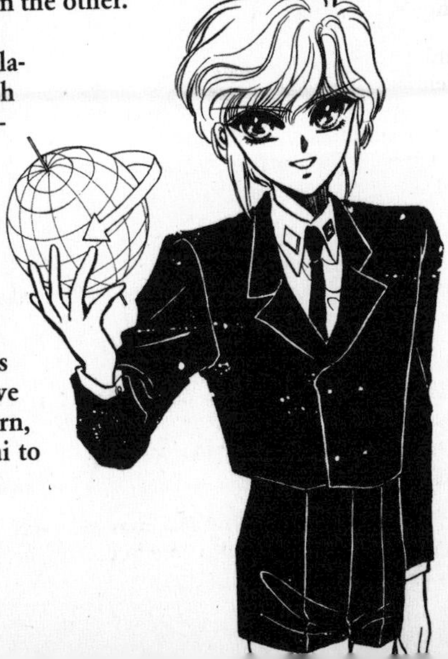

Arriving June 2003 for your reading pleasure.

Apparitions, celebrations and gastronomic sensations! Nokoru, Suoh and Akira are back with a vengeance in the second volume of CLAMP School Detectives.

Look for these other CLAMP School series from TOKYOPOP®!

DUKLYON: CLAMP School Defenders: Bigger crimes call for slightly bigger crime fighters.
Volume 1 Available September 2003

Man of Many Faces : The solo escapades of CLAMP School treasurer Akira Iijyuin, aka the notorious thief 20 Faces!
Volume 1 Available May 2003.

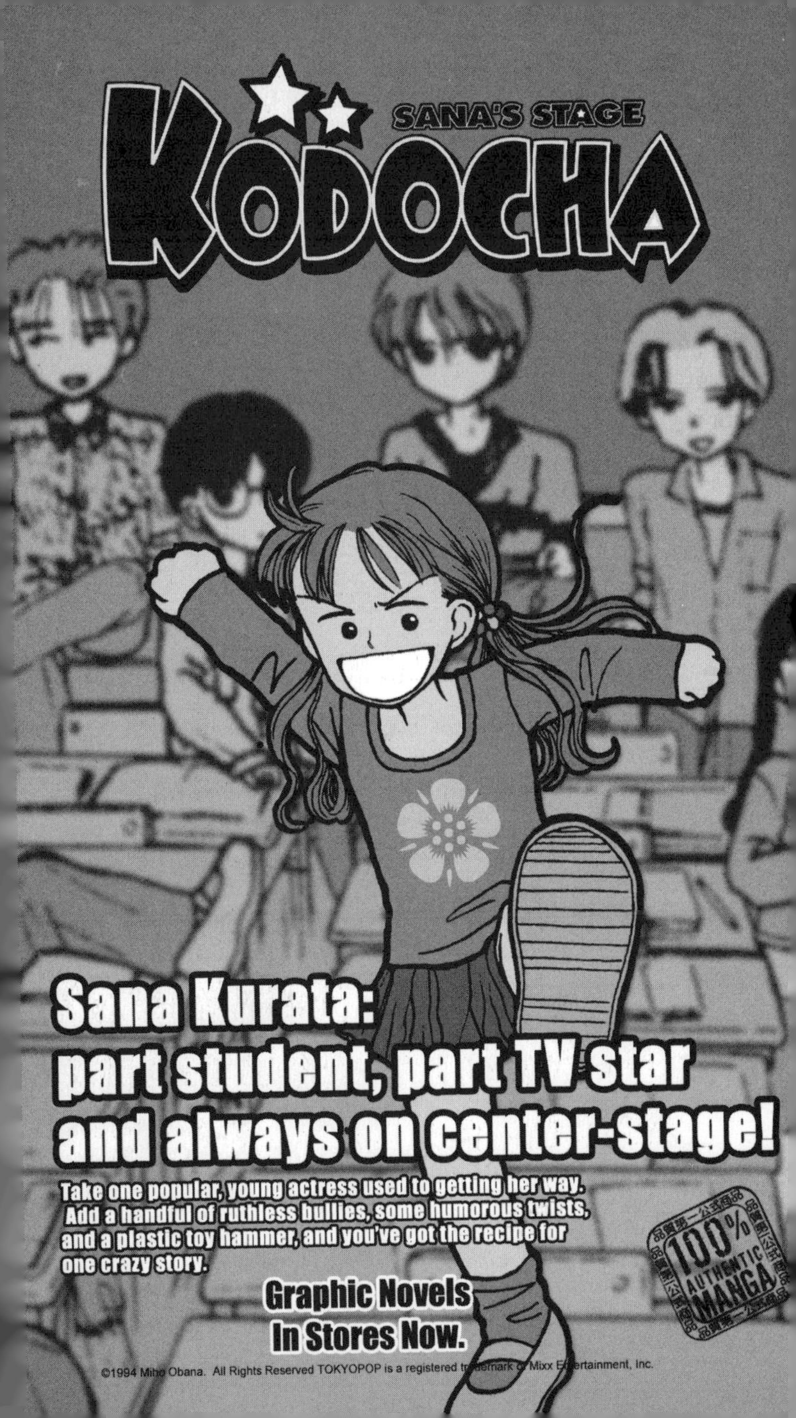
KODOCHA
SANA'S STAGE
Sana Kurata:
part student, part TV star
and always on center-stage!
Take one popular, young actress used to getting her way.
Add a handful of ruthless bullies, some humorous twists,
and a plastic toy hammer, and you've got the recipe for
one crazy story.
Graphic Novels
In Stores Now.
100% AUTHENTIC MANGA
©1994 Miho Obana. All Rights Reserved TOKYOPOP is a registered trademark of Mixx Entertainment, Inc.

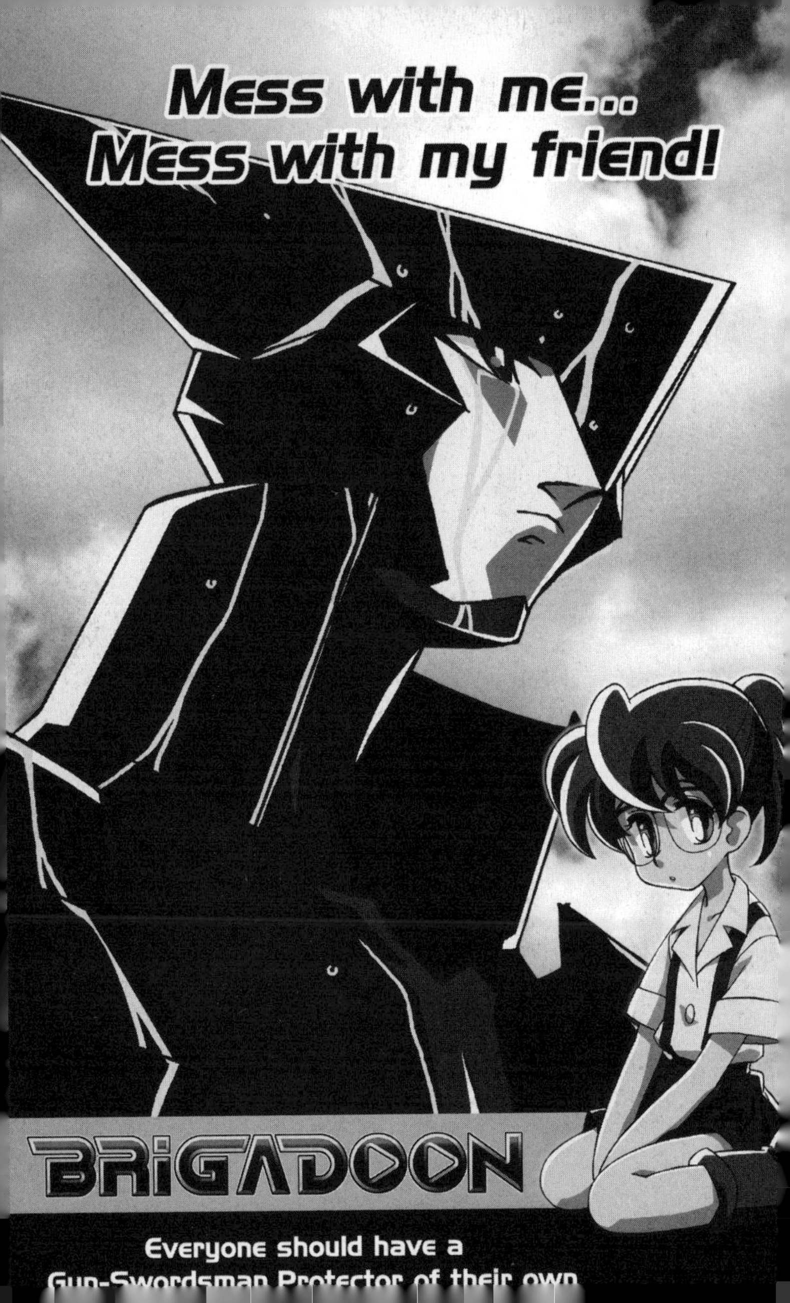

Mess with me...
Mess with my friend!
BRIGADOON
Everyone should have a
Gun-Swordsman Protector of their own

STOP!

This is the back of the book.
You wouldn't want to spoil a great ending!

This book is printed "manga-style," in the authentic Japanese right-to-left format. Since none of the artwork has been flipped or altered, readers get to experience the story just as the creator intended. You've been asking for it, so TOKYOPOP® delivered: authentic, hot-off-the-press, and far more fun!

DIRECTIONS

If this is your first time reading manga-style, here's a quick guide to help you understand how it works.

It's easy... just start in the top right panel and follow the numbers. Have fun, and look for more 100% authentic manga from TOKYOPOP®!